Principles of Retirement Planning

7th Edition

At press time, this edition contains the most complete and accurate information currently available. Owing to the nature of license examinations, however, information may have been added recently to the actual test that does not appear in this edition. Please contact the publisher to verify that you have the most current edition.

This publication is designed to provide accurate and authoritative information in regard to the subject matter covered. It is sold with the understanding that the publisher is not engaged in rendering legal, accounting, or other professional services. If legal advice or other expert assistance is required, the services of a competent professional should be sought.

PRINCIPLES OF RETIREMENT PLANNING, 7TH EDITION
©2018 Kaplan, Inc. All rights reserved.

The text of this publication, or any part thereof, may not be reproduced in any manner whatsoever without written permission from the publisher.

Published in December 2018 by Kaplan Financial Education.
Revised August 2021.

Printed in the United States of America.

10 9 8 7 6 5 4 3 2

ISBN: 978-1-4754-8648-3

Contents

1

Introduction to Retirement Planning

With all the attention given to retirement planning, it would seem remarkable for any financial professional not to be aware of consumer interest in the subject. Hardly a week goes by without a media story covering one or more of the financial challenges of retirement, underscoring the need for retirement planning. The oft-cited approaching retirement of the baby boomers, now facing the need for serious saving, continues to feed the growing interest in savings and investments.

The range of issues that fall under the banner of retirement planning is broad, making this an area in which virtually every financial practitioner can participate. Securities, life insurance, interest-bearing accounts, annuities, and long-term care (LTC) insurance each play a role in the ever-growing retirement planning market.

Not only has the interest in retirement planning increased, so, too, has its complexity. At the risk of over-simplifying the past (certainly, retirement has always posed financial challenges of one sort or another), retirement planning today demands a higher level of attention than ever before. Today, with little sense of job security and doubts about Social Security's future, most American workers must accept the responsibility for securing their own financially sound retirement. This requires making savings and investment decisions that are increasingly diverse and complex.

During retirement, there are new challenges. Living longer means a lot of things, including the need for more money on which to live. Retirement means living about one-third of your adult life on the money and benefits you accrued in the first two-thirds. It means an increasing chance of suffering a medical or mental infirmity requiring long-term nursing care. ■

ILLUSTRATION 1

Facts About Retirement

Financial professionals who doubt the importance of retirement planning should consider the following developments.

- In 1935, when Social Security was created, the average worker's life expectancy at birth was less than age 65—Social Security's definition of normal retirement age. But although Americans continue to think of age 65 as the benchmark for a normal retirement, life expectancy of 65-year-olds is about 20 years. We're adding more and more time to our golden years, but at what cost? Plenty, as we'll soon see.

- The Social Security Administration actively promotes the idea that a financially sound retirement stands on three legs: pensions, personal savings, and Social Security. Weakness in any one leg usually means financial insecurity. Of the three legs, only personal savings is directly under the individual's control.

- Social Security provides only about 40% of the average retiree's preretirement income level. For higher income earners, the Social Security replacement rate is closer to 25%.

- In 1995, those aged 65 numbered approximately two million. In 2025, the population of 65-year-olds is expected to be over four million.

- With increasing longevity also comes a heightened risk of long-term nursing care needs. People may be living longer, but that doesn't mean they're all playing tennis at age 90. The annual cost of a nursing home stay can be as much as $85,000 or more, and Medicare covers very little (if any) of that.

- The increasing proliferation and complexity of qualified retirement plans (and the tax penalties that await their misuse) have created a need for knowledgeable financial practitioners who can advise consumers on making the right decisions for their needs.

- Increasingly, the need for retirement planning advice is reaching those who aren't even expecting it. More and more Americans are finding themselves with lump-sum distributions from their retirement plans upon leaving their company (whether planned or unplanned). The wrong decision here can cost hundreds or even thousands of dollars in unnecessary taxes and penalties. On the other hand, the right advice can help secure a financially sound retirement.

UNIT OBJECTIVES

To be effective, retirement planning must begin years before retirement—ideally, upon entry to the adult workforce—and continue throughout. As consumers become aware of these realities, many become increasingly apprehensive about current or potential financial problems. This, in turn, creates an opportunity for retirement planners.

On completion of this unit, you should be able to:

- list the financial needs faced by most retirees;

- identify the chief sources of retirement resources and explain their value and shortcomings; and

- explain the role of a financial planner in assessing a client's expected retirement needs and evaluating existing resources.

THE IMPORTANCE OF RETIREMENT PLANNING

Key Point   Retirees need substantial savings to pay living expenses for a long period of retirement.

Key Point   Social Security and employer-sponsored retirement plans may not be enough.

Thanks to medical technology and better health care, people are living much longer after retirement. People reaching age 65 can, on average, expect to live into their 80s. In fact, the 73 million baby boomers (Americans born between 1946 and 1964) are now retiring and constitute one-quarter of the population. About 10,000 baby boomers apply for Social Security every day. Without cash inflows from savings and adequate retirement planning, these retirees should be as concerned about living "too long" and outliving their financial resources as they are about dying too soon.

Some people begin to plan for their retirement as soon as they begin their first job, but most people wait until their 40s or 50s. They may feel that saving for retirement will be easier after the children have left home and expenditures decrease. By waiting, they may reach their peak earning power and be able to set more aside. Unfortunately, such an approach allows fewer years for the money saved to earn interest or accumulate returns until it is needed for retirement.

Maintaining the Preretirement Standard of Living

Retirement planning is no longer a luxury reserved for the wealthy or an optional indulgence for the disciplined investor. The following issues combine to make retirement planning essential for every American.

- Even with an employer-sponsored retirement plan and Social Security benefits, workers and their spouses may not have adequate funds to maintain their preretirement standard of living during retirement. Changes in tax rates, interest rates, and inflation rates will affect spending power.

- Employer-sponsored retirement plans rarely provide 100% of the income needed for retirement. Most employer-sponsored retirement plans typically replace only a fraction of an employee's salary. Even retiring executives with special arrangements, such as deferred compensation plans, may face shortfalls.

- Although medical care for older Americans may be improving, many people older than age 65 still have to deal with poor health during their retirement years. Poor health means increased medical bills for services, medicine, and equipment. An extended hospital stay or round-the-clock nursing care can quickly deplete a lifetime of savings.

- Contrary to common opinion, the cost of living does not automatically decline in retirement. While retirees might no longer feel the need to buy clothes for the office, that hardly means their need for cash diminishes. What do they hope to do to fill the time previously spent on the job? Travel? Activities? Whatever it is, it will probably represent a new expense. If the level of income drops in retirement, previously routine living expenses, such as rent, utilities, and food, may consume all available dollars, leaving nothing for luxuries such as travel and entertainment.

- People who count heavily on Social Security benefits for retirement income and financial security are sure to face disappointment. Social Security was founded solely to provide a safety net that would assure workers of the minimum amount needed to survive. It was never intended to secure a financially comfortable retirement. In fact, the higher an individual's pay, the less the individual will receive proportionately in Social Security retirement benefits. Furthermore, the pending financial strain from the retiring baby boomers calls into question Social Security's ability to fulfill even its basic promises, leading to a growing number of overhaul proposals that are certain to place even greater decision-making responsibilities on individuals.

■   Inflation is a very real problem. With a retirement of 20 years or more, even a moderate rate of inflation will have a significant effect on the value of retirement income. Rising prices mean that retirees living on a fixed income will have to struggle to replace their decreased purchasing power.

Taking Serious Action

The increasing awareness of the need to prepare for retirement has created a large and growing market for members of the financial services field. Life insurance agents and brokers, securities representatives, accountants, and banking personnel each have unique opportunities for sales and service. Accumulating money is at the heart of preretirement planning (as opposed to conserving it, which is the goal of post-retirement planning), and the life insurance, securities, and banking fields each offer products that can fit just about any savings plan.

ILLUSTRATION 2

The Value of Starting Early

The time value of money rewards those who start saving early. Consider the following:
Investors A and B are both 30-years-old and plan to retire in 35 years. Both have access to an investment that will yield a consistent annual return of 10%. A contributes $2,000 annually to this investment for the first 10 years and then stops making contributions. B waits 10 years and then begins investing $2,000 into the same investment for the remaining 25 years to retirement. Who comes out ahead? Through the power of compound interest, at age 65:
■   A (total contribution: $20,000) will have an account of almost $418,000; and
■   B (total contribution: $50,000) will have only about half that amount, $240,000.
What you don't have in time must be made up with money.

How important is it to save money for retirement? Consider this: a study by the Social Security Administration revealed that almost half—46%—of a retiree's income would have to come from personal savings and investments if the goal is to maintain a level standard of living. Pensions and Social Security provide about 54% of the average retiree's income. With the growing length of retirement, it is apparent that the amount of money needed to ensure a comfortable retirement is far greater than what most people have accumulated. Here, the retirement planner's role is to motivate people to take serious action and guide them in following the best strategy.

Practitioners who help their clients achieve financially secure post-retirement years do not leave them at the gates of retirement but accompany them during these years to make sure their savings are protected. Only then can the financial planner feel that he has helped a client achieve true financial security in retirement. In post-retirement planning, the practitioner's role is to help clients conserve assets and take the steps necessary to guarantee financial security for their remaining years.

THE PROCESS OF RETIREMENT PLANNING

Key Point Retirement planning includes a review of existing retirement plans, life and health insurance, and other financial resources.

Key Point Retirement needs include maintaining economic independence, providing for family members, and being prepared for emergencies.

It is the retirement planner's role to assist clients in developing a financial profile, determining retirement needs, and developing strategies to meet those needs. While knowledge of the financial aspects of retirement is crucial to carrying out this role, other sides to retirement planning demand the planner's attention. Successful retirement planners know how to take the broader view of retirement planning.

ILLUSTRATION 3

Sources of Retirement Income

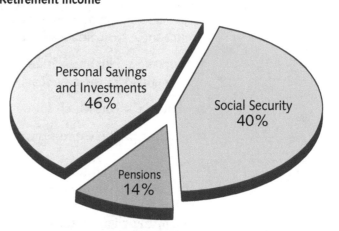

Personal Savings and Investments 46%

Social Security 40%

Pensions 14%

First, planners must realize that financial matters cannot and should not be separated from personal and emotional issues. Although the focus of the retirement planner's recommendations may be financial, the planner may also be asked to act as an advisor about the nonfinancial aspects of retirement. For example, a client who has no hobbies or interests other than work may find himself feeling useless after retirement. A financial planner who can suggest worthwhile activities, such as volunteering, may provide the greatest single enhancement to that individual's retirement. The successful retirement planner will strive to meet the client's financial, personal, and emotional needs to assure a happy, comfortable retirement.

Key Areas of Retirement Planning

Four broad areas must be addressed in retirement planning. Retirement planners may specialize in one or more areas. Each area has its own set of techniques and technicalities, but they can be summarized as follows:

- Determine the amount of income needed in retirement and how to accumulate the money needed to provide that income

- Help plot a strategy for the distribution of retirement income

- Evaluate health care and health care insurance coverages

- Formulate an estate plan for wealth distribution at death

Each of these areas will be discussed in greater detail in later units. The remainder of this unit continues the overview of the retirement planner's role and responsibilities.

Develop a Financial Profile

Retirement planners need to know what they're working with before developing a retirement strategy. The first step in the planning process, therefore, is to develop a client profile that illustrates the client's current financial situation and resources. The planner often begins by analyzing the client's three basic financial statements:

- Income statement, which shows where the client has been financially (usually over the past year)

- Balance sheet, which shows the current financial position

- Budget, which expresses where the client would like to be in the future

These financial statements give the planner an indication of the client's available financial resources.

The financial planner will ask about the type of savings and investment program the client wishes to establish. Such a program should be centered on the client's short-term and long-term objectives. It should also consider the client's feelings about important investment factors such as risk, growth, liquidity, and income. In addition, the planner must ask about the client's future plans, aspirations, and goals. Using all this information, the retirement planner will develop a financial profile—an overview of the client's current situation.

Determine Retirement Needs

The retirement planner will also ask clients to list their retirement goals. Most people's goals will include financial as well as nonfinancial objectives. Common retirement goals include the following.

- **Maintaining a comfortable standard of living.** For most clients, one of their primary goals after retirement is to maintain the same standard of living that they enjoyed during their working years. In fact, many clients see retirement as an opportunity to enhance their lifestyle through travel and entertainment. You can help them to achieve their goals by developing saving and investment strategies in both the preretirement and retirement years.

■ **Maintaining economic self-sufficiency.** Most people do not want to become a financial burden in their senior years. The prospect of becoming financially dependent on others, particularly their children, is a real concern for them. Consequently, maintaining financial independence during retirement is a key goal in the retirement process. Most people regard the following three tasks as essential for economic self-sufficiency after their retirement:

— Obtaining coverage for health care costs not covered by Medicare

— Investing money in such a way as to minimize potential losses

— Making sure that retirement income keeps pace with inflation

ILLUSTRATION 4

Current Trends in Retirement Planning

Current trends and realities in retirement planning point to one conclusion: an individual's future financial security depends on what the individual does now. Those who understand the need to plan and start saving now will be able to look forward to a comfortable retirement.

What's Happening	What It Means
■ People are living longer.	The average life expectancy for 65-year-olds is about 20 years; future generations of retirees can expect to live even longer. This means retirees will have to provide for living expenses over a longer lifetime.
■ Inflation is a fact of life.	Even at modest levels, inflation has a severe impact on fixed income. If the cost of living rose at a steady 3% a year, the spending power of a $50,000 fixed income would be reduced by over 45% in 20 years.
■ Couples are postponing having children until well into their 30s.	The major financial commitment of funding a child's education will come when the couple is in their 50s—traditionally the time devoted to saving heavily for retirement.
■ Social Security benefits may be scaled back.	The baby boom generation is retiring. This swell of retirees will is supported by a reduced workforce, requiring changes in the way Social Security benefits are funded. In anticipation of this, Congress has increased the tax on earnings and has extended the age at which a worker can receive full benefits. Normal retirement age for individuals born after 1938 will rise gradually to 67 by the year 2026.
■ Employers are cutting back on health benefits for their retirees.	Although some companies now pay part or all of a retiree's health insurance, this trend will probably not continue. Health costs increase each year—a cost that many companies are unwilling or unable to absorb. Retirees may soon have to pay a larger percentage (or perhaps all) of their retiree health insurance costs.
■ Fewer and fewer companies are offering defined benefit plans.	The defined benefit pension plan, which promises a specific monthly benefit to retiring employees and places the burden for ensuring the benefit on the employer, is being replaced by other types of plans, such as defined contribution plans. These plans do not guarantee any specific future benefits; in fact, most require that the employee assume much of the responsibility for her future payout because the employee must contribute to the plan or direct how the funds are to be invested.
■ The pace of technology and change is quickening.	As more consumers have access to information, they become better informed and more sophisticated. This creates new and greater expectations from the financial services field for service, flexibility, and performance.

Additionally, retiring businessowners often want to keep a family business under family control or effectively dispose of a closely held business with maximum gain.

■ **Providing for family members.** Retirees who bear financial responsibility for others (e.g., a spouse) usually express a concern for their financial welfare after the retiree's death. This concern is heightened if the dependent requires special medical care or assistance.

■ **Transferring wealth.** Transferring assets with minimal loss to estate and income taxation is important to clients, especially those with a higher net worth. Here, retirement planning and estate planning come together. A basic understanding of estate planning and asset transfer concepts is crucial for planners who wish to practice in this particular area.

■ **Satisfying personal nonfinancial goals.** In addition to financial goals, most clients also have several nonfinancial or personal goals. These goals may include the following:

— Selling the family home and relocating after retirement

— Maintaining health and fitness after retirement

— Learning to cope with leisure time and adapting to a nonworking lifestyle

— Planning for future lifestyle changes

Formulating and implementing a full retirement plan requires planners to address all these financial and nonfinancial goals and objectives.

Getting Clients to See the Need

Because the future is uncertain, people often regard today's problems and responsibilities as far more important than issues they'll face 10, 20, 30, or even 40 years from now. It is the retirement planner's job to impress upon clients the financial cost that is awaiting everyone who enters retirement. Most people are shocked when they first see the numbers involved; some might conclude that there's little use in even trying to save. Successful retirement planners direct their clients' attention away from these negative thoughts by leading them into adopting an "I can" attitude. They do this by showing their clients how they can achieve at least some of their goals through a realistic savings and investment plan.

Although most people understand that saving for retirement is important, they can usually find one or more reasons not to save. Some may say that their pension benefits will be enough or that they will save more when they get older. The financial planner must overcome these obstacles to successful retirement planning. Some of the most common obstacles to implementing a retirement plan include the following.

■ **Failure to save systematically.** Many people save only if and when a surplus exists after paying their monthly expenses. Unfortunately, savings is not high on their list of financial priorities—or it takes a back burner to other more immediate commitments—and happens only sporadically. Without systematic savings, a retirement plan has very little chance of succeeding.

- **Failure to establish an emergency fund.** It makes little sense to save for retirement if it might become necessary to withdraw those funds (possibly with tax penalties) to cover current financial needs. Before a retirement savings plan is implemented, an emergency fund to pay for unexpected expenses such as home or auto repairs, medical bills, or loss of employment should be set up. Most financial planners agree that the amount of the fund should be enough to cover a minimum of three (and preferably six) months of living expenses.

- **Inadequate insurance.** An easy way to make sure dependents are financially protected in the event of the client's death is through an adequate life insurance program. Without life insurance, a client's retirement savings could be consumed by the surviving beneficiaries long before they reach retirement. A life insurance program that includes permanent life insurance has the added benefit of cash values, which can be a source of retirement capital.

- **Tendency to buy now and pay later.** The tendency of many people to buy now and pay later leads to careless spending and debt, both of which make retirement planning more difficult for two reasons. First, they leave little money for saving. Second, they reduce the amount of future income that can be used for savings, since current debt has to be paid out of future income.

- **College costs.** For many individuals, one of the biggest financial outlays they will encounter is the cost of putting their children through college. A generation or so ago, parents faced this issue on a much smaller scale and when they were still fairly young, leaving them a number of years to address the need to save for retirement. Today, as people delay having families, college tuition bills are likely to arrive at the same time that, historically, individuals have focused on funding their retirement. For most, paying the former takes priority, because the cost of paying for college comes before they retire. Couple this with the staggering costs of college tuition today and it is easy to see how paying for a college education can easily consume most savings dollars and relegate retirement planning to the back burner.

- **Changes in employment.** Although Americans have always been more likely to change jobs than people from most other countries, the trend to move from one job to another has increased remarkably in the past decade. Corporate downsizing and a general willingness to change for a better opportunity mean that fewer workers are becoming vested in any meaningful level of company pension benefits. Terminated employees are also likely to face the challenge of dealing with lump-sum distributions of their vested pension benefits.

- **Divorce.** There are many unfortunate consequences of divorce, not the least of which is the possibility that one or both spouses could be left with little accumulation of personal assets—assets that could have been used as a source of retirement income. Many spouses are cut off completely from the pension or qualified plan assets of their ex-spouse. Also, alimony or extra child support payments may limit an individual's ability to save for her own retirement.

■ **Retirement myths.** Finally, there are many myths surrounding retirement that pose obstacles to adequate planning. For example, many people assume that their taxes will be lower once they retire. But, the effective tax rate may not change at all, and property taxes have gone up, and Social Security benefits are now subject to tax. Another myth is that Medicare will cover all necessary health care costs, including the costs of a nursing home. In fact, Medicare does not cover lengthy nursing home stays, and it does not cover custodial care at all. Finally, there is the persistent myth that Social Security benefits will replace a large portion of an individual's preretirement income. The fact is, the higher one's wages, the less Social Security will provide proportionately. For example, at retirement, individuals who have always earned the maximum taxable income can expect to receive only about 25% of that portion of their pay subject to Social Security taxes.

Retirement planners can determine which of these obstacles exist with their clients by studying the profile created for each. A successful retirement plan will address these obstacles head-on, showing how they can be overcome while at the same time building retirement capital. Retirement planners can help clients understand how insurance, investments, company benefits, Social Security benefits, and estate planning can be used and integrated to assist them in meeting all their retirement goals.

THE ROLE OF THE FINANCIAL PROFESSIONAL

Key Point   It is the job of the financial professional to help clients define financial objectives and to propose a plan to meet those objectives economically.

Retirement planning today is a multifaceted undertaking that must consider everything from the availability of employer-sponsored plans to federal regulations that control where and how money is saved. It is concerned with helping workers save for retirement and helping retirees do what they can to secure their income from the potential ravages of inflation, medical care, and long-term care. It involves helping individuals plan and implement an income strategy during retirement that will ensure that retirement funds last through the clients' lifetimes. These diverse needs require financial professionals to have both the knowledge of retirement planning topics as well as the ability to apply this knowledge to each client's unique situation.

From a retirement planner's standpoint, the basic purpose of retirement planning is to help clients identify their goals and develop strategies to meet them, which requires a great deal of skill and sensitivity. The client must be comfortable enough with the situation to answer personal questions that often reveal the need for products and assistance you can provide. To formulate a retirement plan, a retirement planner might begin by asking prospects the following questions.

- What do you have now?

- What do you want to have in the future?

- How do you currently plan to get from what you have to what you want?

The answers to questions like these guide planners in determining the most appropriate financial strategy for each client.

Helping Clients Identify Financial Objectives

We all have our individual financial wants and fears. Most Americans have a mortgage to cover, bills to pay, and children to raise and educate, as well as a general desire to continually improve the quality of their lives. Many people today feel they lack the disposable income, discipline, or commitment to save for retirement—yet when asked, they state a desire to maintain their standard of living as they pass into retirement. Some clients face technical challenges: what to do with a lump-sum pension distribution at age 51, for example, or how to take full advantage of the tax-deferral opportunities present with certain retirement savings programs. Among their more personal concerns, clients may express the need to take care of a dependent parent, spouse, or child before and during retirement.

Top-level retirement planners are able to identify and empathize with their clients' financial and personal objectives, attitudes, and preferences. To do this, they listen intently to the clients' comments and responses to questions. Once identified, the information gleaned from the interview process is used to guide planners in assembling plans geared to individual needs. In this respect, retirement planning is more an art than a science. It employs scientific principles (e.g., the time value of money), as technical as retirement planning may be, it is also a field that requires a sense of creativity on the part of the practitioner.

The Financial Services Arena

No matter which industry or industries you represent in financial services—insurance, securities, or banking—you know the vital role you play in your community. Each field offers products that are specifically designed to help in the retirement planning process. In fact, the invisible lines that once divided these three fields are steadily eroding; today it is common for insurance agents to sell security products (e.g., variable insurance contracts and mutual funds), securities representatives to sell life insurance and annuities, and banks to offer both life insurance and security products through a subsidiary.

Regardless of the industry they represent, financial practitioners are in a strong position to offer retirement planning guidance and assistance. Most practitioners are experienced communicators who know how to get their clients to open up and speak frankly about their financial needs and goals. They also know how to motivate people to break the inertia that keeps many from taking action. Finally, the cross-industry product marketing mentioned here makes it possible for most financial practitioners to offer just about any type of financial product to a client.

ILLUSTRATION 5

Future Income Needed to Maintain $50,000 Annual Income in Current Dollars (Based on 4% Annual Inflation)

The need for retirement planning can be demonstrated by the erosion of buying power that results due to inflation. As illustrated in the table, a 65-year-old retired person with an income of $50,000 who lives 15 years into retirement will need more than $90,000 just to stay even with inflation. Proper planning can help ensure that the needed income will be available throughout retirement.

Year of Retirement	Retiree's Age	Future Annual Income Needed
1	65	$50,000
2	66	$52,000
3	67	$54,080
4	68	$56,243
5	69	$58,493
6	70	$60,833
7	71	$63,266
8	72	$65,797
9	73	$68,428
10	74	$71,166
11	75	$74,012
12	76	$76,973
13	77	$80,052
14	78	$83,254
15	79	$90,047

Create a Plan for Today's Needs

Your primary role as a financial practitioner is to identify your clients' personal, financial, and business needs and whenever possible, to satisfy those needs with the right investment, life insurance, annuity, and health insurance products. Most commonly, your clients will need funds to protect their families in the event of a death, disability, or other financial contingency. Your clients may also ask your assistance in choosing investments, protecting their business, and funding their retirement.

Your goal will be to meet your clients' financial needs by recommending products that will:

■ strengthen a client's financial worth;

■ accumulate income for investment and retirement;

■ protect business interests;

■ provide for final expenses and dependents' support; and

■ provide for an effective estate transfer.

ILLUSTRATION 6

Consumer Expectations and Retirement Realities

For those who work in the retirement planning market, one of the biggest hurdles is overcoming consumer apathy and dispelling common misconceptions about the realities of retirement and where the money will come from. For example:

Consumer Expectations	Retirement Realities
Pre-retirees express concern about the level of financial support they will receive from Social Security and employer pension plans.	Yet these same individuals remain optimistic about their ability to maintain their standard of living during retirement.
According to surveys conducted by a large brokerage house, nearly three-quarters of those surveyed expect their standard of living to be the same during their retirement.	Yet these respondents have done little or nothing to replace the income they will lose during retirement.
Individuals increasingly agree that funding one's retirement is the individual's responsibility.	Yet people continue to point to Social Security and employer pensions as their primary sources of expected retirement income.

WRAP-UP

For the financial professional, the rewards of retirement planning entail a myriad of things: providing a valuable service to clients, selling retirement plan products, and potentially helping direct the investment of client assets. However, as a process, retirement planning goes far beyond the simple selling of a product or the investment of an asset. It is a multidimensional process that includes evaluating current conditions and long-range goals. It involves prioritizing needs, coordinating assets, and filling the financial gaps—tasks that most financial practitioners are qualified to do.

Clients may range in age from 25 to 65 and older, and their needs and objectives will be as different as their ages and lifestyles. As a result, your strategies and product recommendations must vary according to your clients' objectives. In Unit 2, we will discuss how to identify your market, determine its needs, and sell the appropriate product to meet those needs.

UNIT TEST

1. For average retirees, the retirement benefit provided by Social Security is equal to what percentage of their preretirement income level?

   A. 20%
   B. 40%
   C. 60%
   D. 80%

2. The ideal time to begin retirement planning is

   A. upon entry to the workforce
   B. when the retiree applies for Social Security benefits
   C. when financial obligations such as funding a college education have been met
   D. upon receiving a distribution from a retirement plan

3. All of these are part of the financial practitioner's role in helping a client formulate a retirement plan EXCEPT

   A. developing financial and income objectives
   B. evaluating health care needs
   C. assessing a client's current financial situation
   D. drafting a will

4. Which of these would NOT be an issue a retirement planner should expect to address?

   A. Helping the client make sure that retirement income keeps up with inflation
   B. Arranging a client's assets for orderly distribution at death
   C. Structuring a client's compensation package so that he is entitled to greater Social Security benefits
   D. Helping the client plan for future lifestyle changes

5. If an individual wants to maintain a level standard of living after retirement, what percentage of retirement income is estimated to have to come from personal savings?

   A. 15%
   B. 35%
   C. 45%
   D. 75%

ANSWERS AND RATIONALES

1. **B.** For the average retiree, the retirement benefit provided by Social Security is equal to 40% of preretirement income level. This drops off for high-income individuals.

2. **A.** The earlier an individual starts saving, the more he will have for retirement. This is the inevitable result of the time value of money.

3. **D.** A financial practitioner will help a client evaluate needs and the resources that can be used to meet those needs. The actual drafting of documents, like a will, is the job of an attorney.

4. **C.** A retirement planner will generally be unable to arrange for a client to receive greater Social Security benefits. The rates that apply to wage earners is set in the law and can be manipulated only by earning more, something beyond the capability of a financial planner.

5. **C.** Social Security and employer-sponsored retirement benefits generally will not provide much more than half a retiree's needs. The balance must come from personal savings. A typical amount would be 45%.

2

The Demographics of Retirement Planning

To be most effective, retirement planners must have a technician's knowledge and a craftsperson's skill. Technical knowledge regarding financial products and relevant tax issues is important, but it is of little value if the planner does not have the skill to use it properly in making recommendations. The ability to define and explain the various products and tax laws related to retirement is evidence of technical knowledge. Being able to match a client's particular situation with the proper financial services and products is a demonstration of that skill.

Retirement planning begins by identifying and understanding the client's financial needs, goals, and personal situation. This could be a very time-consuming task if it was necessary to start from scratch with each client, but fortunately it is possible to make certain assumptions that can guide the planning process. Every person is unique, but there are common issues facing members of various social and economic classes (market segments) that make it possible to develop general guidelines with respect to financial needs and goals.

Age is an especially significant factor in determining a person's retirement needs and goals because much of retirement planning revolves around this issue. Age and time directly influence the amount of money that can be saved before retirement, the amount of money that will be needed to live on after retirement, and even the likelihood of needing expensive long-term medical and nursing care. Therefore, one way to develop planning guidelines is to recognize the common retirement needs and goals of people within an identifiable age segment. ■

UNIT OBJECTIVES

This unit examines the major age-based segments that make up the retirement planning market. It studies the demographic profile and characteristics of each segment and looks at some of the unique issues each faces.

On completion of this unit, you should be able to:

■ describe how client perceptions of retirement needs change as retirement approaches and then arrives;

■ explain how different financial products are appropriate for retirement planning for different stages in an individual's life;

■ discuss additional retirement concerns for clients who own businesses; and

■ discuss the role of the financial services professional in working with clients to plan for retirement.

MARKET FOR RETIREMENT PLANNING

Key Point Retirees are the fastest growing segment of the population.

Key Point Competition in the retirement planning market includes insurance, securities, and banking.

The demographic profile of the U.S. population is undergoing a remarkable transformation. Changes are evident across the board, from lifestyle patterns to career expectations. Shifts in the nation's age distribution will make senior Americans the fastest growing segment of the population for at least the next several decades. Affected by this grand-scale change is the way Americans view financial products—and how financial professionals view their prospective clients.

Consumers today expect more from both financial products as well as from the people who sell them. As the invisible walls that once separated the insurance, banking, and securities industries continue to erode, consumers increasingly look to each for a broad range of financial services. In response to these changes:

■ life insurance agents and brokers now routinely sell investment-based insurance products and mutual funds;

■ securities representatives assist with their clients' life insurance, annuity, and even long-term care insurance needs; and

■ banks are setting up marketing relationships with mutual fund companies and life insurance companies, and are gaining ground in their effort to sell insurance directly.

Consumers expect retirement planners to understand and address all their financial needs, regardless of the practitioner's particular field. This, in turn, requires a broad level of technical knowledge on the planner's part as well as a solid understanding of each market segment's particular needs.

YOUNGER CONSUMERS—40 TO 50

Key Point   People begin to think about retirement at a time in their lives when providing for children and helping parents compete for their disposable income.

Key Point   Permanent life insurance, long-term investments, and qualified retirement plans are products most in demand by this age group.

Group Profile

People seem to start taking retirement seriously in their early 40s. As their careers (indeed, their lives) crest at an invisible halfway mark, they begin to see retirement more in real terms than in the abstract sense common with younger people. Clients who have reached this point in their lives are especially interested in discussing how to save for retirement.

It is easy to sense a heightened urgency to save among many young consumers entering this stage of their lives, largely the consequence of poor spending and savings habits in the past. Saving at this stage, however, is not necessarily easier. The tendency among young consumers to have delayed marriage and child-rearing means that many are facing college tuition bills just as they're becoming aware of the need to save for retirement. Increasingly, parents are finding themselves squeezed between the financial needs of their young children and their aging parents, spawning yet another social class, the "sandwich generation." The challenge before retirement planners is to help consumers address both their immediate cash and income needs and their longer-term savings goals.

Young consumers who implement a retirement savings plan in their 40s still have between 15 and 30 years to accumulate retirement capital (depending on when they want to retire). This allows time for significant savings, but only if immediate action is taken. For many members of this market segment, this will require drastic changes in their spending patterns. The challenge facing retirement planners is to help these clients see the benefits of making such changes.

ILLUSTRATION 1

The Retirement Planner's Many Roles

A retirement planner will be called upon to play many roles.

■ **Teacher**—A good retirement planner educates prospects and clients about the real potential for a retirement income shortfall. He must be able to explain clearly and simply how this unpleasant shortfall can occur. More importantly, the retirement planner must be able to communicate the process and discipline involved in successful retirement planning.

■ **Provider**—A good retirement planner provides the best in retirement planning products and services to clients. He provides reliable follow-up service and is able to adjust the existing retirement plan when a client's situation requires that it be changed.

■ **Team Captain**—A good retirement planner will coordinate with each member of the retirement planning team. In addition to the client or prospect, that team includes the client's accountant, attorney, and others. The retirement planner refers clients to other financial professionals when appropriate.

■ **Counselor and Friend**—A good retirement planner is a good listener and is aware that those awaiting retirement may have nagging concerns. These worries are usually about finances, but occasionally, they are nonfinancial.

Needs and Objectives

For the most part, young consumers share the same retirement goals as their predecessors, namely, an active and healthy retirement with no drop in their standard of living. To achieve these objectives, consumers need:

■ income that keeps pace with inflation;

■ protection from the cost of long-term medical and nursing care; and

■ a healthy lifestyle.

While retirement planners can do little more than offer their advice in the lifestyle department, they can play an important role in securing the other two needs.

Few young consumers have full confidence in Social Security's ability to meet their collective retirement income needs. Changing attitudes within the workplace about job security and loyalty are making company pensions at once more valuable and more uncertain. With Social Security and company pensions in doubt, personal savings takes on even greater importance. Most young consumers understand that they will have to rely primarily on their personal savings and investments for retirement. At work, programs that feature rapid or immediate full vesting and the opportunity for workers to kick in some of their own money (e.g., 401(k) plans) will remain popular.

Will Social Security even survive in the future? This question weighs heavily in retirement planning for young consumers. At present, for all but very high-income earners, Social Security retirement benefits constitute anywhere from 25%–40% of a worker's final average earnings. While not sufficient to secure a financially sound retirement on its own, this income certainly plays an important role in providing economic security.

There is no question that the disappearance of Social Security would have dire social and economic consequences, making its dissolution unlikely under almost any conceivable scenario. But if it is to continue, Social Security will have to undergo some changes. Although economists generally agree that long-term changes are necessary if the program is to survive, opinions differ on what form those changes should take. As the debate continues, however, one thing is certain—the publicity surrounding the challenges facing Social

Security will further elevate people's awareness of the responsibility they bear to provide for their own retirement.

Beginning in 2003, Social Security's normal retirement age began to gradually rise from age 65 to age 67. Many defined benefit pension programs are threatened as companies struggle to meet the heavy expenses of complying with the federal regulations and administrative costs of these programs. Companies that now pay all or some of their retirees' group health plan will probably decline to do so in the future. Increasingly, retirees will have to pay for their own insurance and any additional medical costs not covered by insurance. Finally, those who wait until their late 30s or early 40s to have children will have less disposable income to save for retirement. Money previously earmarked for retirement will be spent on educating their children. Clearly, young consumers face retirement challenges that call for careful planning.

Product Recommendations

With about 20 years to go before retirement, young consumers can benefit from a wide range of financial products. Though by no means complete, here is a list of select products that may cover one or more needs.

■ **Permanent life insurance.** Because many young consumers have family responsibilities, life insurance protection is important. Permanent life insurance policies, which generate a cash value, can cover two needs by providing life insurance protection during the working years and capital accumulation for retirement. Especially popular are interest-sensitive and variable life insurance policies, which provide an opportunity to realize competitive interest and investment returns on their cash values. Life insurance has important income tax benefits that enhance its value.

■ **Quality stocks and bonds.** Quality stocks and bonds that offer the potential for growth or income are often recommended for individuals who have long-term investment horizons. When growth is a primary objective, common stocks issued by growing companies may provide for substantial capital appreciation. Bonds, though not generally purchased for growth, may offer interest that can be used to supplement an individual's income.

■ **Mutual funds.** A mutual fund is an investment company through which individuals can pool their money to buy stocks, bonds, certificates of deposit, and other securities under the guidance and expertise of professional money managers. These funds allow the small investor to benefit from both diversification and professional management. Mutual funds may be used as part of a qualified retirement program (such as an IRA or 401(k) plan), or they may simply be used on an after-tax basis to accumulate wealth. Either way, mutual funds give average savers an opportunity to realize stock market returns without having to be an expert in picking stocks.

■ **Annuities.** An annuity is an insurance contract designed to provide income in the form of periodic payments (usually monthly). Optional benefit periods and guarantees make it possible to guarantee income for the annuitant's lifetime and even for the lifetime of a second, or joint, annuitant. For this reason, annuities are used primarily for retirement income purposes. A deferred annuity is an annuity that includes an accumulation phase (i.e., annuity benefit payments are deferred to a future date). During the accumulation phase (during which owners, depending on the type of contract usually may make deposits on any frequency), investment and interest gains are income tax-deferred until withdrawn—making deferred annuities a good way to save for retirement. Especially popular are variable deferred annuities which, like variable life insurance policies, give owners the opportunity to realize competitive investment returns.

■ **Qualified retirement plans.** Federal tax laws permit employers, employees, and individuals under various circumstances to participate in a number of different types of qualified retirement plans (so named because such plans qualify for favorable tax treatment). Qualified plans range from huge employer-sponsored defined benefit and defined contribution pension plans to individual retirement accounts maintained by individual consumers. They include 401(k) plans, profit-sharing plans, SEP plans, SIMPLE plans for small employers, and Keogh (or HR-10) plans for sole proprietors and owners of other unincorporated businesses. Employees of certain not-for-profit charitable organizations (e.g., schools and hospitals) may participate in 403(b) (or tax-sheltered annuity) plans. In most cases, consumers and businesses may turn to life insurance companies, securities firms, or banks for assistance with their qualified plan needs.

MATURE CONSUMERS—50 TO 65

Key Point People approaching retirement, though generally well off, need to reduce future expenses and increase future income.

Key Point People in this age group also begin to be concerned about health issues during retirement and long-term care.

Key Point Deferred annuities, health insurance, and long-term care insurance are added to the typical mix of long-term investments begun when these individuals were younger.

Preceding the young consumers are today's mature consumers—people in their early 50s to mid-60s. This generation, which is now crossing over into the mature consumer market segment, was born between 1946 and 1964. There are more than 73 million men and women who fit into this demographic bulge.

These baby boomers are said to have controlled social trends, and as they reach the age of the mature consumer, this segment controls the wealth. More than three-quarters of the nation's private wealth is held by members of this age group.

This market segment accounts for 42% of all after-tax income—which translates into one-half of the total domestic discretionary income—or around $160 billion annually. Nearly 75% of households falling into the mature category own their own homes, and a large percentage of these homeowners own their homes mortgage-free. Clearly, this market provides a remarkable opportunity for financial services professionals to offer products and services that will enhance quality of life during these mature years.

Group Profile

As with every market segment, the demographic profile of the mature consumer is based on average statistics that most likely will not match any particular consumer's profile. As always, retirement planners who service this market must understand that it represents a diverse group of people, varying widely by income, family status, occupation, and social class.

Characteristics of Americans in this age segment (50 to 65 years old) include the following:

■ People who see retirement as a decade or more away

■ Some who are winding down their careers in anticipation of retirement

■ Some who are already retired

■ A larger percentage of whom are developing health problems, although most are healthy and active

■ An increasing share are becoming widowed (i.e., death becomes a greater risk)

■ A fair share are starting a second career, perhaps even their own business

■ People who generally are in better health and are better educated about matters such as personal finances than their predecessors; health naturally becomes a growing concern with age. Studies have shown that mature buyers of goods and services are strongly influenced by quality and service, not just price

■ People who want everything, from long-term capital accumulation to an immediate source of retirement income

Needs and Objectives

Advances in health care and increased longevity are shifting the mature client's retirement planning focus from preparation for death to preparation for longer life. In addition to covering the family's income needs in the event of the retiree's death, there is now the challenge of covering the family's needs in the event the retiree lives another 20 years or more. The key needs of this group as they approach retirement are to:

■ maintain the same standard of living before and after retirement;

■ reduce financial risk and debt;

- secure adequate insurance against the cost of good medical care;

- provide for adequate long-term nursing care; and

- begin planning for the distribution of their wealth after death.

ILLUSTRATION 2

The Aging of America

During the next several decades, the United States will consist of a very large, older population. As the table indicates, the total number of people between the ages of 55 and 74 will rise dramatically in the next several years. The number of people who are age 65 and older, for example, will increase from over 72 million in 2015 to nearly 140 million by 2040. This demographic change will present tremendous opportunities for financial professionals interested in retirement planning.

Age	Projected Population in Thousands				Change 2015 to 2040
	2015	2020	2030	2040	
55–64	87,381	97,897	112,358	124,455	42%
65–74	46,873	54,804	72,092	81,238	73%
75 and older	26,162	29,089	42,053	58,541	123%

Source: Statistical Abstract of the United States, 2012

Product Recommendations

For the most part, this group is interested in the same financial products as the young consumers who follow them and then some.

- Life insurance needs are often greater (in terms of amount needed at death).

- Deferred annuities have even more relevance.

- Investment horizon remaining is enough to allow some aggressive stock or mutual fund investing.

- Mature consumers become more and more interested in long-term care insurance.

Permanent life insurance policies, deferred annuities, quality stocks and bonds, mutual funds, and qualified retirement accounts may be suitable for clients looking to accumulate capital for a financially sound retirement. Most clients will qualify for Medicare and might be interested in a Medicare supplement policy at age 65. Those in their late 50s and early 60s might start shopping for long-term care insurance, the cost of which starts rising significantly beginning around age 65.

Although the mature consumer may have the means to purchase many products to supplement personal income, with age usually comes a tendency toward conservative investing, meaning that clients will be looking for products offering safety of principal and reasonable assurance of positive returns. When servicing this market segment, retirement planners should pay close attention to the client's investment horizon; those with five years or less are generally best advised to focus on asset preservation and stability, while longer horizons can accommodate more aggressive positions. At the same time, be wary of a client's desire to convert all of his growth or accumulation assets into cash or fixed-income products. Again, there's the real possibility that the client will live 20–30 years in retirement.

Life insurance remains important; although intergenerational wealth protection may become a higher priority, replacing dependent income needs as the number one reason for acquiring and maintaining life insurance. For example, the reasons for keeping the coverage may change from protecting a child's education fund to providing resources for an aging survivor spouse.

SENIOR CONSUMERS—65 AND OLDER

Key Point Seniors' greatest concerns range from adequate health care insurance to devising a plan for passing their property to the next generation.

Key Point Product recommendations to this age group include immediate annuities, permanent life insurance, bonds, Medicare supplement insurance, blue-chip stocks or conservative stock funds and long-term care insurance.

The senior consumer group consists of approximately 70 million people who are age 65 and older. In many cases, they will have enjoyed their peak financial years just before retirement. In the early phases of retirement, seniors will be active and probably spend much of their disposable income on travel, recreation, and leisure activities. As they age, retirees often become less active and begin to face the problems that come with increasing infirmity and illness.

While every market segment displays common attributes, financial professionals would do well to understand the unique qualities of each person, even senior Americans. In fact, gerontological research shows that people follow dissimilar paths as frequently in old age as when they are young. Some will be playing golf at age 88, and others will require a walker at 68. Some will retire at 62, while others will find it impossible to quit even at age 72. They may be married, widowed, divorced, or single. Their financial profiles vary from impoverished shut-ins relying on Medicaid to affluent travelers who shuttle between north and south with the changing seasons. Most senior Americans fall somewhere between these two extremes.

Group Profile

In general, seniors have the highest net worth of any demographic age group. Characteristics of Americans in this age segment (65 and older) include the following.

- Approximately 90% of those with household incomes of more than $30,000 own their homes.

- Their mortgages are paid off, they have little or no installment debt, and often have large sums of money to invest.

- Although they want to maximize the return on their money, they are also risk-averse and lean sharply toward conservative investing.

- This group tends to reduce the number of investments they hold and are drawn to less complicated, more liquid investments. Capital preservation is a priority.

- Insured bank savings accounts and certificates of deposit and annuities are especially attractive to people at this stage of life.

Needs and Objectives

Many retirees feel that they have earned the right to a comfortable retirement after working all their lives. Some even expect that their standard of living will improve after they retire. In order to meet this expectation, retirees must find ways to invest their dollars wisely while protecting their capital. They often seek professional investment advice from their insurance or retirement planner.

Many seniors express concern about being able to maintain their current home. They may lack the funds, energy, or desire to continue living in a large house once they have retired. Children have grown and left home, a spouse may have died, or the neighborhood is no longer desirable. Relocation may therefore become an important issue during this period, along with the problems of leaving family, friends, and favorite current activities for warmer or less expensive areas.

Probably the greatest need facing seniors is the lack of adequate health care insurance. Although many retirees have some coverage, the cost for long-term care services is projected to rise as the number of elderly increases. A larger share of the costs will be borne by the retiree who may or may not have adequate insurance coverage.

Finally, seniors are concerned about creating a definite plan for the disposition of their property while they are alive or after they have died. A planner can provide a valuable service by helping a client develop an estate plan according to the client's objectives. However, the estate planning documents that support the plan—a living will, a will to transfer assets at death, a trust, etc.—should be prepared by an attorney.

Product Recommendations

At this stage in life, clients have, for the most part, shifted from capital accumulation to capital distribution (in the form of retirement income) and capital preservation (for their heirs).

- **Immediate annuities.** Immediate annuities begin paying annuity income benefits as soon as they are purchased, and are commonly recommended to clients who are looking to convert liquid assets (e.g., a lump-sum pension distribution at retirement) into a lifetime source of income.

- **Savings accounts and certificates of deposit.** Safety of principal, absence of fees (in most cases), and guaranteed interest make bank savings accounts and CDs an important way to guarantee income and preserve capital.

- **Permanent life insurance.** The cash value of permanent life insurance can be used as a planned or emergency source of retirement income. While clients are likely to maintain some life insurance for estate planning purposes, they might decide that other policies can be used to provide retirement income. Fortunately, the Internal Revenue Code makes it possible to exchange a life insurance policy for an annuity without incurring taxation on the cash value's gain, through a 1035 exchange (named after the section in the Code which addresses it).

  Second-to-die (or survivorship) life insurance, which covers two lives and pays death benefits only after both insureds die, is popular with married couples entering this age group. Such policies have important applications in estate planning, not the least of which is the fact that they make cash available to cover estate taxes at the very moment it is needed.

- **Bonds.** The primary investment objective that bonds support is income with relative safety. Therefore, high-grade quality bonds may appeal to individuals who want to supplement their retirement income or Social Security. The increased income from bonds can help individuals maintain their lifestyles.

- **Blue-chip stocks or conservative stock mutual funds.** Although this segment focuses on income distribution and capital preservation, inflation continues to be a factor with life expectancy extending to the 80s and even 90s. Some growth investments may be necessary to maintain the desired standard of living in later years.

- **Medicare supplement insurance.** Retirement often means the end of group medical insurance benefits. Medicare provides coverage, through Parts A and B, to citizens age 65 and older. Unfortunately, there are gaps in Medicare's coverage that can leave some seniors—especially those who are seriously ill—unprotected in certain areas. To fill those gaps, retirees may want to consider buying a Medicare supplement insurance policy. Since 1990, these Medigap policies have been heavily regulated to ensure that they meet minimum standards with respect to coverages.

Retirees and even those approaching retirement generally have a heightened concern about post-retirement health care benefits. Besides Medicare (covered in Unit 12) and Medicare supplement insurance, some retirees are fortunate enough to be covered under extended group medical benefits through their former employers. This is not common, though, making Medigap insurance the most practical solution to the need for greater medical care protection in retirement. To advise clients on the most appropriate coverages, a financial professional specializing in serving retirees should become familiar with the costs and features of the different Medicare supplement policies provided by insurers.

■ **Long-term care insurance.** Despite the range of services covered by Medicare and Medicare supplement policies, there remains one need that neither adequately addresses: long-term nursing care. The average annual cost of nursing home care is currently around $84,000, with the average stay for most people lasting about 2½ years. Obviously, an extended stay in a nursing home could severely affect retirement funds unless other plans have been made. For many, long-term care insurance will be the answer, providing protection against the costs of nursing home care, home health care, residential care, and other forms of long-term care services. Again, a financial professional specializing in retirement planning should become familiar with the costs, features, and benefits of LTC insurance policies.

■ **Trust services.** Trusts have a wide range of applications, but for senior consumers there are two crucial uses. The first has to do with managing funds during periods of failing health or disability. This role for a trust may also be attractive for healthy seniors who simply don't want to manage their funds, but it is almost mandatory when health begins to deteriorate. The second role of a trust is to pass assets to the next generation. Trusts can be set up to provide income for a senior's life with remaining assets to be distributed according to the trust plan, bypassing probate. The range of possibilities is almost limitless, making trust services an important benefit for members of this age group.

Other Senior Issues

Seniors who elect to sell their homes and move to smaller quarters or a warmer climate will have some financial concerns. The financial professional may be asked to comment about the pros and cons of electing the IRC Section 121 exclusion on the gain on the sale of a primary residence. Under this exclusion, taxpayers have an opportunity to exclude up to $250,000 in capital gains from the sale of their homes. For joint filers, the exclusion is $500,000. (Capital gain is basically the difference between the price paid for the house—including the cost of improvements—and the price for which it is sold.)

This is money that can be used in a variety of ways to establish financial security, perhaps through the purchase of long-term care insurance, an annuity, or both. To qualify for the full exclusion, the individual had to have lived in the home and used it as the principal residence for at least two of the five years immediately preceding the sale. (For widowed spouses, the period of ownership and use also includes the time the deceased spouse owned and used the home before death.)

For a residence owned and used for less than two years, homeowners can exclude an amount of the $250,000/$500,000 capital gain exclusion equal to the fraction of the two years that the ownership and use requirement is met. The exclusion is available to a homeowner's estate and heirs as well. Whether a Section 121 election makes sense for a particular client will depend on her relocation and estate plans. Each client's situation must be carefully analyzed.

Seniors also become increasingly concerned with estate planning issues. Estate plans and documents should be reviewed periodically, especially considering the ever-changing tax laws. Estate planning is appropriate for anyone, especially those who are nearing retirement. Estate planning is reviewed in Unit 13.

BUSINESSOWNERS

Key Point   Businessowners have additional concerns related to retirement planning.

Key Point   Small-business retirement plans may require the owner to cover employees of the business, depending on the type of plan.

When prospecting for retirement plan sales, small businesses should not be ignored. Owners are often looking to begin retirement programs that provide security as well as tax breaks that positively affect their personal financial scenarios. In fact, considering the important role employer-sponsored plans play in the world of qualified retirement programs, it would seem that businessowners would represent an especially important market for retirement planning professionals.

Here's a tip: While many employers are interested in helping their employees achieve retirement security, most are primarily interested in their own bottom line (either their own personal benefits or the benefits to the company). The ages of the principals in a business and differences in ownership interests provide useful clues as to what type of retirement program to recommend.

Group Profile

Small businesses may be organized as sole proprietorships (a business owned by one person), partnerships (a business organization owned by two or more individuals), limited liability companies (LLCs, which can be owned by one or more members), or corporations (an artificial legal entity). Sole proprietorships outnumber corporations and partnerships by a significant margin; although LLCs are becoming increasingly common. Many financial advisors prefer to concentrate on the sole proprietorship or LLC market because corporate sales generally take longer to close, and many layers of review may be required before an actual decision can be made.

Needs and Objectives

Some businessowners seek retirement arrangements that benefit themselves alone. Others seek benefits for just a few select employees; still others want to benefit all their employees. Some owners simply want to sell their interest in a business at retirement. Other owners may be motivated to minimize estate taxes, to provide cash for estate settlement costs, or to assure successor management for the business. Without adequate retirement planning, the business may be unable to continue or may be inadequately funded when the owner retires.

Businessowners may be uncomfortable admitting that their personal retirement concerns outrank their altruistic objectives toward their employees, but clients have every right to allocate their retirement dollars in any legal manner they deem appropriate. The owners should have clearly definable objectives and needs that a planner can address when making a planning recommendation. To determine what these needs are, questions must be asked. For example, the planner might ask the following questions.

- What are your objectives for the business when you retire?

- What are your objectives for yourself when you retire?

- Is a plan currently in place?

- If you were to establish a plan, do you want to cover everyone?

- Are you looking for a low-cost plan?

Honest answers to these and other questions will become invaluable tools in the selection of the most appropriate retirement plan.

Product Recommendations

Tax breaks in the form of tax deductions, salary reductions, and tax deferral make a variety of financial products suited to businessowners' needs. Insurance products in many forms (especially permanent life, disability income, and medical expense insurance) play important roles. Securities, particularly mutual funds, are popular with many types of qualified retirement plans. As just mentioned, retirement planners should appreciate the importance of these tax breaks as an incentive in getting owners to set up a plan.

Which type of plan or product is right for a particular businessowner depends on the owner's individual and business needs. Because most employers are interested in current tax breaks as well as their employees' financial security, attention generally turns to some form of qualified retirement plan. Before setting up a retirement plan, though, owners should first consider how the business would be affected upon the death or disability of the owner or even one of its key employees. Maintaining an up-to-date buy-sell plan, properly funded, should be at the top of the list if the businessowner cares about the ongoing survival of the company. Permanent life insurance and disability buy-out insurance (a form of disability income insurance) are ideally suited to funding a buy-sell agreement that assures everyone that the business is sold to the right people at the right time and at the right price upon the owner's death or permanent disability.

Which Type of Plan?

When the subject turns to retirement savings plans, the issue to address would seem to be which type of plan to choose. Addressing this issue first requires an understanding of the owner's individual needs and an honest assessment of his objectives. Once these issues have been clearly identified and defined, the planner then can recommend an appropriate plan or plans. Options for qualified plans include traditional defined benefit and defined contribution plans, profit-sharing plans, 401(k) plans, SEP plans, and SIMPLE plans. Nonqualified plan options might include executive bonus plans, salary continuation plans, or deferred compensation plans. These plans, as well as the issues that must be considered when selecting a plan, are the subjects of Units 7–11.

Whichever type of retirement plan is most suitable for a businessowner, one thing is certain: the employees are going to expect something. A growing uneasiness about Social Security's future and a vanishing sense of company loyalty has made employees all the more sensitive to the need to build nonforfeitable retirement benefits. Businessowners may rank their own needs as the number one priority, but if they want to succeed with top-quality employees they must also respect the needs of those employees. Any business that requires more than average expertise or technical ability and seeks a stable workforce with little turnover must recognize the need for a benefits package that allows employees to build retirement security.

STRATEGIES FOR RETIREMENT PLANNERS

Key Point   The gap between a client's needs and resources can be bridged by increasing savings, increasing investment returns, and lowering retirement lifestyle expectations.

Financial professionals know that their job is to solve problems by meeting the various financial needs of their clients. Those who are new to retirement planning may be concerned about where to begin. In general, the process is no different in retirement planning than it is with meeting any other financial need.

Identify the Market

The first step in the planning process is to determine which markets to target. A good place to start is your current list of clients. You also may choose to prospect within a specific market segment comprised of prospects with similar needs and overall characteristics. To do so, select a geographic area where you would like to work, choose a specific group, learn their needs, and determine which of your products and services fit those needs. For example, you may decide to concentrate on selling annuities to the senior market within a 25-mile radius of your office. Your goal is to become known as someone who specializes in the markets you've chosen. Focusing your efforts in one area, you will increase your effectiveness, productivity, and earnings.

Market and Sell the Product

There are many ways to successfully prospect, market, and sell retirement products and services to both individuals and businesses. You may choose to use natural contacts, direct mail, telephone solicitations, referrals, or a combination of methods. For example, referrals from satisfied clients and colleagues can be a major source of business. But don't be surprised when an older party to whom you have been referred suggests that you contact their children. There may be more concern about retirement security among young consumers than there is among 60-year-olds.

Retirement Planning Seminars

One way to effectively reach large groups of people at a single time is through seminars. The best seminars emphasize information that is supported with data and examples to which the particular audience can relate. There should be no pressure about falling interest rates or one-time-only investment opportunities. Indeed, the seminar itself should be perceived by attendees as an educational opportunity, not a sales presentation. The hard-sell approach at a seminar turns people off.

Most employees are baffled by their employee benefit booklets and by technical explanations of their retirement plans and their options. Professionals who can simplify complex concepts by breaking them into smaller steps and who check for feedback and questions along the way will find themselves a sought-after speaker on the topic of employee retirement benefits.

Some financial companies provide their associates with prepackaged retirement seminar presentation kits, complete with scripts and overhead transparencies or PowerPoint presentations. If you plan on presenting retirement planning seminars, such a kit will save you quite a bit of work. Have your business name and telephone number on all handout literature.

When you make your presentation, think of yourself as a teacher rather than a salesperson. Demonstrating the real possibility for a retirement income gap encourages your participants to listen to the rest of what you have to say. Clients become particularly interested when they can see that their pension, current savings, and Social Security aren't going to give them sufficient income replacement. You may wish to design or purchase work sheets that help the attendees calculate for themselves how great a gap exists between what they have and what they need. You can then show your listeners that this gap can be addressed by:

- increasing savings;

- increasing investment returns; and

- lowering retirement lifestyle expectations.

Encourage your prospects to ask questions about anything they do not understand. Be prepared to answer a variety of questions about diverse topics from options for substantial lump-sum rollovers to maximizing pension benefits. Questions often act as a barometer to measure whether you are on the right track with your presentation and the sales process. A well-designed seminar should lead to a number of appointments.

Determine Financial Needs

When meeting with a prospective client for the first time, the retirement planning process generally begins with identifying the prospect's needs and goals. Only when you know what your client wants or needs can you recommend appropriate products and services. As we've seen, most people facing retirement will have several needs to which you can respond including health care, income needs, final expenses, and estate planning.

Service and Follow-Up

Your clients' retirement planning will not end with the sale of a product. Both before and after retirement, changing needs demand periodic plan reviews to make sure everything is up to date. As people progress through life, their short-term and long-term goals shift. These changes often require a change in products and product usage. Arrange an annual review to compare your clients' current needs with their current plan and make any necessary changes to accommodate new situations or revised goals. Your future depends on your client base. The interest you show in your clients will strengthen the relationship among your company, you, and your clients.

WRAP-UP

A successful, comfortable retirement doesn't just happen—it takes careful planning and continual adjustments. Professional retirement planners can help their clients understand and become more comfortable with the retirement process and gain some control over their financial future. By identifying your market and its needs, you can map out an effective strategy for your clients whether they are part of the baby boom, mature, or senior consumer group.

FIELD EXERCISE

The market segments described in this unit are generalities. It is important to know where you fit into the scheme and where you don't. Make up a spreadsheet of your clients by age, listing the types of products they have bought. Then answer the following questions.

- Does the pattern of your business follow the patterns discussed in this unit?

- If your experience is different, why is that? Are you missing opportunities to serve your clients better?

- If your experience is different than the pattern described in this unit, and you feel that you have not missed opportunities, what factors make your client base different?

UNIT TEST

1. In general, which demographic group has the highest net worth?

   A. Young consumers with families
   B. Mature consumers
   C. Senior consumers
   D. Young singles

2. A financial planner giving a retirement planning seminar should

   A. take the opportunity to sell his products and services
   B. present oneself as an educator
   C. discourage questions from attendees that tend to interrupt the presentation
   D. stir attendees to action with one-time-only investment opportunities

3. Which of these products should be considered when growth is a primary objective?

   A. Stocks
   B. Bonds
   C. Life insurance
   D. All of these

4. Which of these statements regarding retirement planning for the young consumer market is FALSE?

   A. They are more likely to be covered by a company pension than previous generations.
   B. Their investment horizon allows them to take an investment position that is more aggressive than that which older consumers might take.
   C. They are less likely to assume reliance on Social Security than older consumers.
   D. They are awakening to the need to save for retirement.

5. Which of these is least likely to be a product recommendation for a senior consumer client?

   A. Aggressive growth common stock
   B. Blue-chip common stock
   C. Immediate annuities
   D. Government bonds

A N S W E R S   A N D   R A T I O N A L E S

1. **C.** Senior consumers as individuals tend to have the highest net worth of all the age groups. Mature consumers as a group control more wealth, but they don't reach their individual peak until they are ready to retire.

2. **B.** A financial planner's greatest asset is his expertise. He can act as an educator at a retirement planning seminar.

3. **A.** Stocks are growth investments. Bonds and life insurance are not.

4. **A.** Coverage by company pension plans has been declining for some time. Young consumers are less likely to have this type of coverage than older consumers.

5. **A.** Blue-chip common stocks, because of their conservative nature, would be an appropriate recommendation for a senior consumer client as a way to hedge against inflation. Aggressive growth common stocks would normally entail too much risk for this type of client. Both annuities and government bonds would be appropriate for the senior consumer client.

3

Analyzing Retirement Income Needs

There is a saying that has long been used in the financial services field: "People don't plan to fail; they fail to plan." This truism certainly applies to retirement. Although people make plans that affect their education, careers, marriage, and children, many of them fail to adequately plan for the day when they will no longer be working. ■

UNIT OBJECTIVES

As a financial professional, you know that it is never too early for your clients to begin planning for retirement. The longer they wait, the less control they will have over the shape of their lives during retirement. Your goal is to help your clients analyze their long-term retirement objectives and formulate plans to meet those objectives.

On completion of this unit, you should be able to:

- assess the amount of money an individual will need in retirement; and

- describe the sources of income that may be used by a retiree when employment income ceases.

RETIREMENT CONSIDERATIONS

Key Point   The key element in analyzing retirement income needs is time, defined by an individual's life expectancy.

Key Point   Investments can grow over time (as expressed in the time value of money), but their value can be eroded over time by inflation.

Before you can determine how your client should fund retirement, you will have to know how much your client will need for retirement. The amount needed will vary based on your client's desired standard of living after retirement, projected retirement age, and a variety of economic factors. In the following sections, we will discuss how life expectancy, inflation, and the time value of money will affect your client's retirement planning.

Life Expectancy

To adequately fund a retirement plan, certain assumptions must be made that will affect the size of annual contributions that need to be made now to savings accounts and other retirement plans. The sooner your clients begin to save for retirement, the longer they have to invest and earn interest income. But how much they actually need for retirement is also a function of how long they will live.

No one can be absolutely certain how long a person will live, but it is possible to estimate how long the average retiree will live after retirement using past mortality statistics. From there it becomes possible to estimate the total amount of money needed to fund the retirement by multiplying the annual income need by the number of years of remaining life expectancy.

For example, statistics show the current average life expectancy at birth is about 78 to 79 years; however, actuaries know that many people live longer than the average life expectancy. Women tend to outlive men by an average of five to seven years. Individuals who have made it to retirement age tend to do better than the at-birth average and can expect to live into their 80s. But this is only an average. Retirement planning requires conservative projections in this regard; plan for the possibility that your client will live many years past the projected life expectancy when formulating retirement plans.

Inflation

Inflation, a general increase in prices, means that the buying power of a dollar decreases and buys less over time. Even a low rate of inflation can significantly affect the price of things over decades.

The most commonly accepted measure of inflation is the Consumer Price Index (CPI). It is compiled by the Bureau of Labor Statistics and provides an accurate picture of changes in the prices of more than 400 goods and services. According to the CPI, consumer prices have risen in all but two yearssince 1960. Retired persons on fixed incomes are especially affected by inflation because their financial resources are limited. While prices increase, income does not. The conflict is obvious—each year a larger percentage of income is spent for necessities such as food, shelter, and medical care. Although Social Security and many employer-sponsored retirement plans make periodic inflation adjustments to retirement and other benefits based on changes in the CPI, the increases may be inadequate to offset rising costs. What is needed is a way to keep up with inflation during retirement years.

Inflation can seriously erode the purchasing power of a dollar even during periods when the annual rate is relatively low. For inflation rate history, please see the appendix at the end of the book. Compare the average annual rates shown with the total rate for a 25-year period. Remember, many retirees do live for 25 years after retirement.

Time Value of Money

Time is money. As we illustrate later in this unit, there are various ways to save a certain amount of money. One is to wait until the last minute and save a lot of money. Another is to start early, save a little money, and let the power of compound interest pull much of the load. The same math that makes inflation so destructive over time can come to the aid of your client if he starts to save early.

Proper planning relies on the time value of money to do as much of the work as possible; this strategy requires your clients to set aside a certain amount of money in retirement plans, savings accounts, and other investments that will grow in value over the years. As you know, money invested today will increase as a result of earned interest. This concept, called the time value of money, is based on the fact that a dollar received today is worth more than a dollar received a year from now. The dollar received today can be invested immediately and when combined with the interest earned will be worth more a year from now. Conversely, a dollar that will be received a year from now is worth less than a dollar received today.

Calculating Future Value and Present Value

The time value of money centers on two concepts—present value and future value. The present value of a sum of money is simply the amount invested today. The future value, also referred to as compounding, is the amount to which a current sum will increase based on a certain interest rate and period of time.

Future Value

In order to determine how much a client's money will grow if he invests it today and leaves it for a specified number of time periods, assuming it earns a specified rate of return each period, you need to find the future value (FV) of a sum of money.

To determine the FV of a sum of money, you may use the FV formula below or a future value or compound interest table a financial calculator, a spreadsheet program, or proprietary software that shows the future values for various investment periods and rates.

$$FV = PV \times (1 + i)^n$$

where:
FV = future value
PV = present value (amount invested today)
i = interest rate (usually the annual rate)
n = number of periods the money is to be invested at the interest rate (usually the number of years)

ILLUSTRATION 1

Agent's Perspective

I like to think of retirement planning as drawing a line in the sands of time. Time on this side of the line—preretirement time—works to our advantage. Time on the other side of the line—after retirement—works against us. The more time you have on this side of the line, the easier it will be to arrange a comfortable retirement. That's why we urge people to start saving early.

Let's focus on the far side of the line. The essential fact of life for a retiree is that living expenses are a flat-out drain on any assets your client may have. Before retirement, living expenses are offset by income from a job. After retirement, the offset is gone and savings can begin to be eroded.

You have to know, before you do anything, what the drain on the assets will be. That's not meant in a negative sense. Our clients have worked hard, and they deserve a good retirement. It's our job to take their numbers and show them how to make as much of it happen as possible.

For example, $1,000 invested for 10 years earning 5% per year grows to $1,629: $1,000 × (1 + .05)10.

Every financial computer program should be capable of doing this calculation.

Present Value

Present value is the current value of a future sum based on a certain interest rate and period of time. To find the present value, or PV (sometimes referred to as *discounted value*) of a single payment, a formula reversing the process of finding the future value is used:

$$PV = \frac{FV}{(1+i)^n}$$

Again, financial programs or tables can also be used to calculate the PV.

After you have reviewed your prospect's retirement objectives, you can use future values (however you compute them) to illustrate to your clients how investments made today can grow over time to accomplish those objectives.

PROJECTING RETIREMENT INCOME NEEDS

Key Point   Although methods differ, projecting retirement income needs attempts to assess the amount of money needed to maintain an individual's standard of living when employment income ceases.

Key Point   Sources of replacement income include Social Security, employer-sponsored pensions and retirement plans, and personal savings and investments.

An analysis of retirement income needs generally begins with a review of the prospect's existing income and expenses. The current budget is the springboard for creating a retirement budget because it indicates current spending and saving patterns. From this information, you can predict the amount and type of retirement expenses your prospect is likely to have, and forecast the amount of income needed to meet those expenses.

When planning for retirement, a person may make the mistake of thinking that less income will be needed to maintain her current standard of living. Many people realize that expenses such as mortgage payments, transportation, dependent care, and food and clothing costs for work will be eliminated. What they do not consider is that some expenses remain constant or may even increase after retirement. For example, property taxes, repair and maintenance expenses, recreation costs, and medical costs will probably increase and take up a larger portion of a retiree's income. In most cases, overall expenses during retirement remain at no less than 70%–80% of preretirement expense dollars.

Replacement Ratio

There is no universal agreement among retirement planners as to the exact amount of income needed during the retirement years. Many planners simply use a ratio of retirement income to preretirement income called a replacement ratio to estimate the needed amount. Typically, this ratio ranges from 60%–80% of preretirement income. Using this approach, an individual currently earning $75,000 a year would need an annual income of $45,000 to $60,000 (in today's dollars) during retirement to be within this range.

Expense Method

Maintaining one's preretirement lifestyle is an important goal for most individuals. Therefore, some planners feel that a better approach to determine the amount of needed retirement income is to calculate the cost of that lifestyle because it represents the amount the individual currently consumes. This expense method matches current living expenses to future expenses. It provides a more precise estimate of future needs because expenditures— today's and tomorrow's—are analyzed.

For example, an individual's current expenditure for housing may consume 25% of his disposable income, but if the mortgage will be paid off before retirement and there is no plan to purchase a more expensive home, this outlay will not factor into future expenses. By the same token, some expense items will likely increase during retirement. Health care costs are a prime example, as are expenditures for travel and leisure. For many using an expense method, the amount of estimated retirement income will be very close to their current preretirement income.

Reality of Inflation

Both the replacement ratio and the expense method are useful in determining an individual's income needs at and during retirement. However, they represent only the initial step. Inflation must be factored in. The reality of inflation is that, even at low levels, it drastically affects purchasing power over time.

ILLUSTRATION 2

Current and Projected Annual Expenses Worksheet

Current and Projected Annual Expenses (Using Today's Dollars)		
Fixed Expenses	**Current**	**Projected at Retirement**
Mortgage/Rent	$_____	_____
Income Taxes	_____	_____
Property Taxes	_____	_____
Life Insurance	_____	_____
Property Insurance	_____	_____
Automobile Loan	_____	_____
Variable Expenses		
Food	$_____	_____
Clothing	_____	_____
Business Expenses	_____	_____
Utilities	_____	_____
Car Expenses (gas, etc.)	_____	_____
Medical Expenses	_____	_____
Entertainment	_____	_____
Vacations	_____	_____
IRA Contributions	_____	_____
Savings	_____	_____
Charitable Contributions	_____	_____
Gifts	_____	_____
Miscellaneous	_____	_____
TOTAL	$_____	$_____
Notes:		

EXAMPLE

Assume your client, Pat, will be 65 in three months. You have determined that she needs $60,000 of retirement income annually to maintain her current standard of living. But look how inflation affects your calculations.

Even if the rate of inflation is only 3% a year over Pat's retirement, her income will have to increase to almost $70,000 by age 70 and almost $94,000 by age 80 if she is to maintain consistent purchasing power. For individuals whose time lines to retirement are longer, the numbers are even more daunting. At 3% per year inflation, a 45-year-old individual who wants to retire in 20 years with an income equivalent to $60,000 will need more than $108,000 during his first year of retirement.

An important service the retirement planner can provide his clients is an inflation evaluation of retirement resources to determine which are affected by inflation. Social Security and Medicare benefits, for example, are indexed to reflect inflation; most pension benefits, once they begin, are not. A good retirement plan should incorporate an element of inflation protection that accounts for retirement resources (and any shortfalls between what the individual has and what he needs at retirement) that will be eroded by cost of living increases.

ILLUSTRATION 3

Three-Legged Stool: Sources of Retirement Income

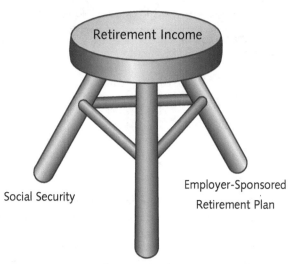

Retirement Income

Social Security

Employer-Sponsored
Retirement Plan

Personal Savings and Investments

Sources of Retirement Income

Determining the amount an individual will need to support a comfortable retirement can be accomplished through financial software programs or financial function calculators. They are the best way to accurately project the return on retirement savings and the impact of an average assumed rate of inflation over periods of accumulation (preretirement) and consumption (post-retirement). No matter how the calculations are accomplished, however, all should take into account the primary sources on which most individuals rely for their retirement funds:

- Social Security benefits

- Employer-sponsored pension and retirement plans

- Personal savings and investments

In creating a visual image of these sources, retirement planners often use a three-legged stool. A person's retirement security rests firmly on this stool when all three legs are in place. If one leg is weak or missing, the stool will collapse, leaving the client without adequate protection—unless steps are taken to strengthen the remaining legs. Many individuals, for example, are not covered by an employer plan; their personal savings and investments and their Social Security benefits will be their only sources of retirement income. In the next few units, we will examine each of these components in detail.

ILLUSTRATION 4
Retirement Tables

The following tables can be used to compute a client's needs for their retirement.

TABLE I (Inflation). This table can be used to project a budget based on today's dollars into the future. Multiply today's figure by the number of years until retirement. This factor is conservatively based on an assumption of 5% annual inflation. Although inflation may be lower at the time the estimate is done, it is unrealistic to assume it will be low throughout a long period of time.

Years to Retirement	Factor
5	1.3
10	1.6
15	2.1
20	2.7
25	3.4
30	4.3
35	5.5
40	7.0

TABLE L (Lump Sum Needed). This table can be used to estimate a lump sum that would be needed to produce an annual income of a specified amount for a specified number of years. If you determine that a client's retirement plan and Social Security will fall short of his needs by $X per year, you can figure out how much he would need to save to make up the difference by multiplying the annual shortfall by a factor based on how long you expect the income to be needed. Here are factors for 20, 30, and 40 years for two different investment strategies: an income portfolio factor, and a growth portfolio factor.*

Years Capital Must Last	Income Portfolio Factor	Growth Portfolio Factor
20	16.8	13.3
30	23.1	16.6
40	28.3	18.6

TABLE R (Retirement). This table will give you an estimate of how a current account will grow before retirement. Multiply the current balance by the factor indicated by the number of years until retirement. Two different investment strategies are shown: income and growth.*

Years to Retirement	Income Portfolio Factor	Growth Portfolio Factor
5	1.4	1.6
10	2.0	2.6
15	2.8	4.2
20	3.9	6.7
25	5.4	10.8
30	7.6	17.4
35	10.7	28.1
40	15.0	45.3

*The income portfolio factor assumes high-quality fixed-income assets (bonds and other debt instruments) at an average growth of 7% annually. The growth portfolio assumes high-quality stocks with the potential to earn an average return of 10% annually. Both factors incorporate a 5% inflation assumption.

ILLUSTRATION 5

Retirement Tables, Continued

The following tables can be used to compute a client's needs for their retirement.

TABLE D (Divisor). Once you determine that your client will need a particular lump sum of money on the day he retires, you can use this table to compute the amount he will have to save each year in order to reach the goal. Simply divide the lump-sum amount by the indicated factor. As with the other tables, it is based on the number of years and whether an income or growth portfolio is assumed.*

Years to Retirement	Income Portfolio Factor	Growth Portfolio Factor
5	6.8	7.4
10	18.1	21.2
15	36.4	46.2
20	65.1	89.6
25	109.2	163.9
30	176.0	288.8
35	276.1	496.9
40	424.5	840.8

*The income portfolio factor assumes high-quality fixed-income assets (bonds and other debt instruments) at an average growth of 7% annually. The growth portfolio assumes high-quality stocks with the potential to earn an average return of 10% annually. Both factors incorporate a 5% inflation assumption.

CASE STUDY: PROJECTING RETIREMENT INCOME NEEDS

Key Point   A detailed comparison of expected expenses with projected values of existing assets could reveal a shortfall at retirement.

Stanley and Laura Rivers, both age 45, plan to retire in 20 years. Stanley is the director of marketing for a garden supply company and is covered by his company's pension plan. Laura, a freelance illustrator of children's books, pays Social Security taxes but is not covered by a formal retirement plan.

Their current combined income is $84,880. At retirement, their expected annual Social Security benefits will be $36,500, and Stanley anticipates $15,000 a year from his pension plan. They recently invested $11,000 in high-quality growth stocks, which they estimate will grow at 10% a year. They have two questions.

1. How much income will they need during their retirement (which statistics show could extend 30 years)?

2. How much money will they need to save to ensure this income?

Creating the Budget in Today's Dollars

As shown in Illustration 6, Stanley and Laura's current annual outlay matches their income: $84,880. They are assuming that certain expenses—the mortgage and business-related expenses—will be eliminated by the time they retire. Other expenses—income taxes and miscellaneous items—will be substantially reduced. Conversely, leisure expenses—entertainment and travel—will increase because they will have more free time during retirement. Based on these anticipated changes, Stanley and Laura have projected their annual retirement expenses to be $61,423 in today's dollars.

At retirement, the Rivers' income—consisting of Social Security benefits ($36,500) and Stanley's pension plan ($15,000)—will fall to $51,500. Based on their projected retirement expenses of $61,423, the Rivers will have a shortfall of $9,923 ($61,423 – $51,500 = $9,923). Of course, their $11,000 stock investment should grow and produce additional income to meet this shortfall, but additional savings will be needed to provide additional retirement income.

How much should the Rivers save each year to meet their retirement needs? As you can see in Illustration 6, by projecting retirement expenses and income and using the factors from the Retirement Tables in Illustration 5, the Rivers have calculated how much additional retirement income they will need.

From Current Budget to Retirement Plan

Let's take a closer look at these calculations. According to the case study, the Rivers have decided to retire in 20 years when they are both age 65. Therefore, their projected retirement expenses (Step 1), employer-sponsored retirement benefits (Step 3), and the amount of their Social Security benefits (Step 5) in today's dollars are multiplied by 2.7, the factor for 20 years to retirement from Table I in Illustration 5. To illustrate, their projected annual retirement expenses in 20 years will be $165,842 ($61,423 × 2.7).

ILLUSTRATION 6

Calculating Retirement Income Needs

Stanley and Laura Rivers
Current and Projected Annual Expenses
(Using "Today's Dollars")

Fixed Expenses	Current	Projected at Retirement	
Mortgage/Rent	$ 12,366	$ 0	(1)
Income Taxes	28,826	17,123	(2)
Property Taxes	3,325	3,800	
Life Insurance	1,178	1,825	(3)
Property Insurance	1,360	1,450	
Automobile Loan (Insurance)	3,825	3,825	(4)

Variable Expenses			
Food	5,800	5,800	
Clothing	5,200	3,200	(5)
Business Expenses	1,200	0	
	1,350	1,650	
Utilities	2,550	1,500	
Car Expenses (gas, etc.)	1,200	4,100	(6)
Medical Expenses	2,400	7,200	(7)
Entertainment	3,500	0	(8)
Vacations	0	2,400	(9)
IRA Contribution	3,000	600	(10)
Savings	1,200	3,000	(11)
Charitable Contribution	3,000	2,000	
Gifts	3,600		
Miscellaneous			
TOTAL	$ 84,880	$ 61,423	

Notes: (1) Mortgage paid off
    (2) Lower taxable income and special deductions
    (3) Premiums will increase when employer-sponsored life insurance is converted
    (4) Auto loan paid off
    (5) No business clothing needed
    (6) No commuting; cost of auto insurance also decreases
    (7) Estimated increase of at least 25% in insurance and out-of-pocket expenses
    (8) More leisure activities
    (9) More time for extended travel
    (10) Currently do not make nondeductible contribution and cannot after retirement
    (11) Reduced income; will save less

ILLUSTRATION 7

Calculating Needed Annual Retirement Savings

Step 1	Enter the amount of the annual projected retirement expenses.	$61,423
Step 2	Multiply the amount entered in Step 1 by the factor shown in Table 1 for the number of years to retirement. (Assumes 5% inflation rate.)	×2.7 $165,842
Step 3	Enter the annual retirement benefit provided by all employer-sponsored retirement plans.	$15,000
Step 4	Multiply the amount entered in Step 3 by the factor used in Step 2. (Assumes 5% inflation rate.)	×2.7 $40,500
Step 5	Enter the amount of any Social Security retirement benefits.	$36,500
Step 6	Multiply the amount entered in Step 5 by the factor in Step 2. (Assumes 5% Social Security cost-of-living increase.)	×2.7 $98,550
Step 7	Subtract the amounts determined in Steps 4 and 6 from the amount determined in Step 2. (Represents annual retirement income shortfall to be provided by personal savings.)	$165,842 −$40,500 −$98,550 $26,792
Step 8	Multiply the amount calculated in Step 7 by the appropriate factor in Table L. (Assume a retirement period of 30 years and a growth portfolio.) (Represents lump-sum amount to provide an annual income of $26,792 for 30 years.)	×16.6 $444,749
Step 9	Enter the total value of all currently owned assets that may be allocated to retirement distribution. (Current growth portfolio.)	$11,000
Step 10	Multiply the amount entered in Step 9 by the factor in Table R for growth portfolios over a 20-year period. (Represents the value of invested assets at retirement.)	×6.7 $73,700
Step 11	Subtract the amount entered in Step 10 from the amount entered in Step 8.	$444,749 −$73,700 $371,049
Step 12	Divide the amount shown in Step 11 by the factor in Table D for growth portfolios over a 20-year period. (Represents the annual retirement savings need.)	÷89.6 $4,141

In Step 7, the Rivers have subtracted their projected Social Security benefits and their income from Stanley's retirement plan from their projected retirement expenses. The resulting number shown in today's dollars is then multiplied by 16.6, the factor for the 30 years that this capital must last from Table L. Based on the calculation in Step 8, the Rivers should save an additional lump sum of $444,749.

Fortunately, the Rivers have already begun to invest for their retirement by purchasing stock. To determine the estimated future value of their stock portfolio, the Rivers multiplied their current investment of $11,000 by 6.7, the growth factor from Table R. Based on this calculation, their investment is projected to grow to $73,700 over the next 20 years as shown in Step 10.

In Step 11, their $73,700 investment value is subtracted from the needed $444,749 savings, leaving a shortfall of $371,049. This amount is then divided by 89.6, the factor for growth portfolios over 20 years, to determine the annual retirement savings need. Based on these calculations, Stanley and

Laura Rivers must save an additional $4,141 annually to meet their projected retirement income needs.

The Rivers should remember, however, that the exact amount of money they will need during retirement is impossible to predict. They should review and revise their plans periodically to assure that they can meet their retirement goals.

When There Is a Shortfall

The case of Stanley and Laura Rivers is typical. For many individuals, a retirement income needs analysis will reveal a shortfall between the amount of income they will need in retirement and the amount of income they will have in retirement, based on their current situation and savings plans. Despite Stanley's pension, their combined Social Security benefits and their stock investment, the Rivers' have a deficit of almost more than $450,000. They need to save an additional $4,141 a year to close that gap and ensure that their retirement income will be sufficient to cover their needs as defined in the needs analysis.

Helping individuals identify and then address their retirement income shortfall, as daunting as it may seem, is a fundamental part of a retirement planner's job. From the planner's perspective, one of the advantages of projecting future income needs and identifying shortfalls is that it urges clients to take action. It turns the vague into the specific. Once the retirement income goal is defined and the shortfall is analyzed, the question becomes, "How can that shortfall be reduced?" Certainly, the best time to address the income gaps is before retirement, when changes in savings and investment strategies can be made.

SOURCES OF RETIREMENT INCOME

Key Point Retirees depend on three main sources for income—Social Security, employer-sponsored retirement plans, and personal savings and investments.

Retirement income rests on three legs: Social Security, employer-sponsored retirement plans, and personal savings and investments. The combined income generated by these three resources will, in large part, determine how comfortable one's retirement years will be. Therefore, a solid retirement plan must include an analysis of all these income sources, evaluating the extent to which each will contribute to the income goal. We will be discussing each in detail in later units; here, we'll point out some important issues which should be considered when mapping the outlines of a plan.

Social Security

Almost everyone who is employed or self-employed is covered by Social Security and will receive benefits when they retire. Social Security benefits are an important source of retirement income, but they are not, in and of themselves, adequate to support a comfortable retirement.

According to the Social Security Administration, if an individual's earnings are equal to the U.S. average, he can expect to receive benefits of about 40% of preretirement earnings. Higher wage earners (those whose pay equaled the maximum earnings base on which Social Security taxes were paid) can expect a benefit that is far less—about 25% of preretirement income. Consequently, for many people Social Security benefits must be viewed as a supplementary source of retirement income, not the primary source.

To some extent, an individual does have some impact over the amount of his Social Security retirement benefit and should consider the following.

- **The date when benefits are claimed**. By delaying claim until after one's full retirement age (currently age 66-67), Social Security benefits are increased. Conversely, early retirement under Social Security (one can claim benefits as early as age 62) will result in permanently reduced benefits.

- **The effect of continued employment on benefits**. Those who continue to work after their Social Security payments begin may see those benefits reduced because Social Security limits the amount of wages one can earn to receive full benefits. This earning limit applies until the individual reaches the full retirement age referenced above.

- **Other sources of retirement income**. Social Security benefits are taxable when an individual's preliminary adjusted gross income exceeds a certain threshold level. By reallocating assets into investments that are tax deferred or otherwise not included in the definition of *provisional income*, the amount of benefits subject to tax could be reduced or eliminated. Provisional income is defined by the Internal Revenue Service (IRS) as the sum of wages, taxable and nontaxable interest, dividends, pensions, self-employment, and other taxable income plus half (50 percent) of your annual Social Security benefits.

Employer-Sponsored Retirement Plans

An important source of retirement income for many individuals is derived through employment-related retirement plans. In the past, the dominant form of employer-provided retirement benefit was the defined benefit pension plan, which promises a specific level of lifelong payments after retirement. However, the trend in employer retirement plans today is away from defined benefit formulas (which are almost always funded by the employer and focus the obligation on providing a specific benefit amount) and toward defined contribution plans, which do not promise any specific benefit and often rely on contributions by the employee. In fact, more and more employer-sponsored retirement plans are looking to the employee to take the lead in contributing and funding these plans and deciding how those funds should be invested.

When putting together the broad outline of a retirement strategy, the following points should be considered so that other aspects of the strategy can operate in tandem with what the individual can expect from her employer program.

- **The type of plan offered**. A defined benefit plan provides a specified level of benefits at retirement. A defined contribution plan focuses the obligation on the funding aspect. Under a defined contribution plan, the amount available to the employee when he retires depends not only on the amount that was contributed but how well the investments performed.

- **The extent to which the individual contributes to the plan.** Many employer retirement plans, such as 401(k)s, 403(b)s, and SIMPLE plans, rely on contributions made by the employee through salary reductions or deferrals. Only if the employee contributes to the plan will the employer match or otherwise contribute, if employer contributions are even an option. If an individual can contribute to a company retirement plan, that should be his first target for retirement savings. Earnings on contributions are tax-deferred so they will grow at a faster rate than if they were taxed each year. Because many plans do provide for matching (e.g., for every $2 the employee contributes, the employer will contribute $1) the employee's contribution is immediately augmented.

- **The investments in which plan funds are deposited.** What kind of investments supports the plan and to what extent does the employee control the investment allocation? Some employer plans—employee stock ownership plans, for example—invest in the stock of the company that sponsors the plan, so the growth of plan assets depends on how well the company does. With other types of plans—401(k) plans and some profit-sharing plans—it is actually left to the employee to determine how plan funds are invested, usually from a menu of different investment vehicles. For better-than-average performance, this requires employing basic investment principles and strategies which, unfortunately, many people are not familiar with.

- **The method of benefit payment.** How will the individual receive his plan benefits? Most pension plans pay out systematically in the form of monthly annuity payments based on the participant's life expectancy or, if married, the joint life expectancies of the participant and his spouse. Under these kinds of arrangements, there is little flexibility. Other types of plans offer no systematic payout structure; the individual is simply given his benefit in a lump-sum amount upon retirement. How he subsequently invests or makes use of that money for what could be 20 or 30 years of retirement must be carefully considered.

Personal Savings and Investments

Depending on the individual's income before retirement, the amount that will be provided by Social Security and an employer-sponsored retirement plan should make up approximately 40%–60% of the amount needed during retirement. In the retirement income needs analysis of Stanley and Laura Rivers, the amount of annual income from Stanley's pension and their combined Social Security benefits will cover much of the couple's needs, but they still have a future income shortfall of more than $26,000. That gap must be covered by augmenting their personal savings and investments, the third leg of the retirement income stool.

When a retirement income needs analysis reveals a shortfall—and many do—the first and obvious step is to start saving more. But saving more does not mean solely more out-of-pocket savings. Saving more can also be accomplished by saving efficiently. This requires a few fundamental ground rules.

- **Savings must be disciplined and budgeted.** They should be considered as important and integral to the monthly budget as the mortgage payment or rent. One of the best ways to enforce strict savings is through payroll deductions and the automatic transfer of money to a savings or investment account.

- **Savings should be tax-advantaged, to the extent possible.** This means directing funds into vehicles that are tax-deductible, tax-deferred, or tax-free. As noted previously, an individual should first take full advantage of any employer-sponsored retirement plan to which he can contribute—401(k) plans, SEP plans, or SIMPLE plans—and then consider individual retirement arrangements such as IRAs and Roth IRAs. Annuities, in or out of a qualified plan, are tax-advantaged, as are certain types of municipal bonds and life insurance.

- **Savings should be allocated among various investments.** This ensures diversification, enhances returns, and reflects an individual's financial profile and investment horizon—conservative or aggressive, short-term or long-term. The mix of investment savings should be reviewed often to make sure they support the individual's goals and risk tolerance. Savings and investments are not static.

Putting It All Together

A financially secure retirement cannot happen without realistic objectives and a plan to achieve those objectives. The analogy of retirement income security as a stool resting on three legs—Social Security, company-sponsored retirement plans, and personal savings and investments—is a good tool because it provides a foundation on which to base that plan. It segments the plan into specific elements, each of which can be scrutinized and analyzed as to what it will contribute to the overall goal. As one element is found to be weak, or as it changes, the others can be altered so that the entire plan remains valid.

WRAP-UP

How a client wants to live during retirement should determine how he prepares for retirement. For most people, the first step is to ask themselves what they will want during retirement and then calculate the amount of money they will need to get it. This can be done by simply assuming a certain percentage of preretirement income or through a more detailed income needs analysis that compares current expenses and lifestyles with those expected or desired during retirement.

Once a retirement income goal is identified, the next step is to analyze the sources from which that income will be derived. For most individuals, those sources are Social Security, employer-sponsored retirement plans, and personal savings and investments—collectively referred to as the three legs of the retirement income stool.

FIELD EXERCISE

Prepare a set of three projected budgets for yourself. The first should pay for a lavish retirement. The second should pay for a shoestring retirement. The third should be the most likely scenario. Then answer the following questions.

■ What types of information did you require in order to prepare the budgets?

■ Which items of expense were need-to-have items and which were nice-to-have items?

■ How much would it cost to go from a poor budget to a rich budget?

Select a client file and repeat the exercise.

UNIT TEST

1. As a rule of thumb, when projecting retirement income needs, the replacement ratio uses what range of preretirement income?
   A. 20%–40%
   B. 40%–60%
   C. 60%–80%
   D. 80%–100%

2. Which of these is NOT a traditional leg of the three-legged retirement income stool?
   A. Retirement plan savings
   B. Social Security benefits
   C. Inheritances
   D. Personal savings and investments

3. When projecting expenses for retirement, all of these would be considered fixed expenditures EXCEPT
   A. IRA contributions
   B. mortgage
   C. property taxes
   D. insurance premiums

4. Which of these statements is TRUE?
   A. For most individuals, Social Security benefits are adequate to provide a comfortable retirement income.
   B. The vast majority of working Americans are covered by an employer-sponsored retirement plan.
   C. Rising inflation creates increased purchase power.
   D. Retirement planning should assume the individual will live many years past his projected life expectancy.

5. One of the advantages of using the expense method to project retirement income needs is that inflation does not have to be a factor.
   A. True
   B. False

ANSWERS AND RATIONALES

1. **C.** Retirees need a good fraction of their preretirement income to maintain their standard of living. It is common to say that a retiree needs 60%–80% of his preretirement income. Some people think even this is too low.

2. **C.** The three legs supporting a retiree's income are Social Security, employer-sponsored retirement plans, and personal savings and investments. An individual who receives an inheritance would count it as part of the personal savings leg. Whether anticipated future inheritances should be counted depends on individual circumstances and is not part of the regular retirement planning process.

3. **A.** Although financial planners advise people to "pay themselves first," savings—including savings to an IRA—are not considered fixed expenditures.

4. **D.** Most people live many years after they retire. Without this assumption, there is no need to plan for retirement.

5. **B.** Because of the length of time involved, both from the time of planning until retirement and from the time of retirement until death, inflation will have a major impact on any calculations.

4

Social Security

Social Security has always played an important role in retirement planning. It is considered one of the three legs of the retirement income stool, representing a source of ongoing income for most retirees and their dependents. However, many people fail to understand its true role, which is to provide a foundation for retirement income. Social Security was never designed to provide a full or complete financial future for American workers; when created, it was described merely as a safety net. Unfortunately, too many people have come to expect Social Security to fill most of their retirement income needs. ■

▌ UNIT OBJECTIVES

In this unit, we will examine Social Security and its proper place in retirement planning. As you will learn, the foundation of benefits it provides must be supplemented by other sources if an individual intends to maintain his current—or even an acceptable—standard of living.

On completion of this unit, you should be able to:

■ list the benefits and limitations of Social Security;

■ explain eligibility requirements for Social Security retirement, disability, and survivor benefits; and

■ describe the process for determining benefit amounts under the Social Security system.

▌ THE SOCIAL SECURITY SYSTEM

Key Point   Social Security provides a basic retirement income but needs to be supplemented by other resources.

In 1935, Congress enacted a federal social insurance program called the Social Security Act, which later became known as the Old-Age, Survivors, and Disability Insurance program (OASDI). More commonly referred to as Social Security, this program is widely quoted but rarely understood by those it serves, namely, American workers. Social Security pays benefits in the form of monthly cash income when a worker retires, becomes disabled or dies. When a covered worker becomes entitled to benefits, other members of the family, including a spouse, children, and other dependents, may also be eligible for benefits.

Myths, Misconceptions, and Realities

Some of the most common myths or misconceptions about the Social Security program include the following (see next table) with an explanation of the reality.

Myths and Misconceptions	Reality
Social Security benefits will cover all the income needs a person has at retirement.	Social Security was never designed to meet all retirement needs. It was established to provide a financial safety net—a floor of income protection for workers who lose their income due to retirement (as well as disability or death). Social Security's benefits are important and should not be dismissed as irrelevant. They comprise an important leg in the retirement security stool. But on their own, they are not sufficient to provide full financial security. Social Security is the basic foundation upon which employer-sponsored retirement plans and personal financial assets stand. Unfortunately, for too many people, Social Security is relied upon to provide more than its intended share—much to their disappointment.
The Social Security taxes an employee pays each year go into an investment fund where they accumulate for that employee's retirement years.	At present, the Social Security taxes that employees and employers pay are used to fund current benefits. They are not earmarked for the employee's personal benefits, however, the amount of taxes paid do play a fairly direct role in the calculation of benefits. In other words, while Social Security taxes do help determine a worker's future benefit, they actually pay for today's retirees. The Social Security tax is simply a transfer of income from working Americans to those receiving Social Security benefits. The system is funded by means of a tax on wages, a tax enacted by the Federal Insurance Contribution Act (FICA). The actual Social Security tax rate and the wage limit to which it applies are frequently revised. Currently, this tax is a little over 15% on wages up to a certain amount (called the maximum taxable wage base), divided evenly between employees and employers. While employers pay half the tax, employees get all the benefits. Self-employed individuals must pay the entire tax themselves.
Every retiree receives the same benefit amount.	In fact, Social Security benefits decrease as a percentage of income as the level of preretirement income increases. Benefits are actuarially structured so that those in the higher income brackets receive a lesser return in benefits per dollar of Social Security tax paid. In other words, Social Security retirement benefits constitute a significantly larger share of a low-income worker's preretirement income than they do of someone who regularly earned more than the taxable wage base. The actual retirement benefit amount is determined by the amount of income earned and taxed over the worker's lifetime. Because taxation stops at the maximum taxable wage base (good news during the working years), it also means a limit to the amount of benefits that can be earned. How to calculate benefits is covered later in this unit.
Retirement benefits begin automatically when a worker retires.	Social Security benefits will not begin until an application is filed. The Social Security Administration's national telephone number (1-800-772-1213) is one place to start. Applications will be sent to the potential retiree or may be taken over the telephone. Another alternative is to apply online at www.ssa.gov.

Answering a Client's Questions

Even those who understand the basics of the Social Security system will have questions about eligibility and the amounts and types of benefits available at retirement.

Social Security plays a crucial role in filling part of a retiree's income needs. For that reason, your clients must understand the basics of the program. But because Social Security cannot meet all or even most of a person's retirement income needs, these clients will also need your assistance in formulating other plans and strategies to fill the gap. This means that you must be as prepared to talk about Social Security as you are to discuss your own products and services.

There are many reasons why the average American does not understand Social Security. Although a great deal of detailed information is available about the subject, few people take time to read and understand the material.

Even the pamphlets provided by Social Security generally go unread because they seem dry or too complicated. Because most people feel that financial professionals understand technical financial material, they look to people like you to answer their questions about Social Security.

Some of the most frequently asked questions about retirement benefits include the following.

- Am I covered?

- How much will my benefits be?

- How do I get Social Security when I retire?

The questions are straightforward enough, but the answers depend on variables that make it impossible to give a simple, universal answer.

ELIGIBILITY FOR SOCIAL SECURITY BENEFITS

Key Point   Most people need 10 years (40 quarters of credit) in the system to be eligible for Social Security retirement benefits.

Key Point   Eligibility for disability or survivor benefits is based on an individual's meeting a minimum requirement for credited services, which depends on age.

Most employed or self-employed individuals contribute to and are covered by the Social Security system. This means that almost all working Americans and their families are covered by the program to some extent and are entitled to benefits. There are a few exceptions.

- Most federal government employees hired before 1984 are excluded but are covered under the Civil Service Retirement Act. They do, however, have limited coverage under Medicare hospital insurance (discussed in Unit 12).

- Some state and local government employees are covered by retirement plans offered by their state or local governments in lieu of Social Security. Each government unit that has such a plan determines whether to join Social Security. All state and local government employees hired after March 1986 are covered by Medicare, even if they are not covered by Social Security.

- Railroad workers are covered by the Railroad Retirement system. However, some workers have coverage and coordinated benefits under both the Railroad Retirement and Social Security systems.

Who Is Eligible?

Although a person may be covered by Social Security, he may not be eligible for benefits. Eligibility for Social Security benefits is based on having attained a required number of credits under the system. These credit requirements differ for retirement, disability, and survivor benefits.

Eligibility for Retirement Benefits

To qualify for retirement benefits, most workers need 40 credits, or the equivalent of about 10 years of work under the program. A credit is earned for a certain amount of wages received during a given year. For the latest Social Security eligibility figures, please see the appendix at the end of the book.

Eligibility for Disability Benefits

Qualification for disability benefits first requires an individual to be so severely impaired, mentally or physically, that the individual cannot perform any substantial gainful work. The disability must be expected to last at least 12 months or to result in earlier death. This determination is based on medical evidence and is made by the government agency in the state where the disabled person applies for benefits.

Second, the individual must have earned a minimum number of credits of Social Security coverage. This number will vary by age.

Eligibility for Survivor Benefits

Survivor benefits under Social Security are payable monthly to the family or spouse upon the death of an eligible participant. In this case, eligibility is based on one's status as either currently insured or fully insured. Currently insured status, which requires earning six credits during the 13 calendar quarters before death, qualifies for payment of benefits to a spouse caring for a child younger than age 16, and to eligible children younger than age 18. Fully insured status entitles survivors to the full range of available benefits. It too is based on number of credits. The longer the period between birth and death, the more credits needed for fully insured status.

In addition to monthly income payments, dependent survivors or a spouse of a deceased worker receive a lump-sum death benefit of $255 when the participant dies. Unlike other Social Security benefits, this amount seldom changes.

▌DETERMINING THE RETIREMENT BENEFIT AMOUNT

Key Point The Social Security retirement benefit is computed based on the individual being qualified by earning 40 credits (10 years work), the individual's preretirement earnings, how old the individual is when benefits are applied for, and whether benefits are payable for a spouse or children. Benefits do not begin automatically, they must be applied for.

Key Point An otherwise eligible individual can receive Social Security retirement benefits even while working.

Key Point   Social Security benefits are taxable if the recipient's income is greater than a given threshold amount.

When asked to determine potential Social Security benefits for retirement (or disability or death), the practitioner will find the process is complicated. Benefits are based on the participant's earnings history, the participant's age at retirement, and number of credits. In addition, benefits are tied to cost-of-living indexes and are subject to annual adjustments.

Factors in Determining Benefit Amounts

The amount of Social Security benefits payable to a retiree (or to the retiree's family as a whole) depends on a number of factors. They include:

- retiree's earnings;

- when the claim is made for the benefits; and

- whether other family members are eligible for benefits.

Average Earnings

The primary factor in determining one's Social Security benefits is the size of the worker's average indexed monthly earnings (AIME), which are based on a lifetime earnings history. (These earnings take into account the wages on which a worker has paid FICA taxes over the years and a weighting factor to account for inflation and cost-of-living increases over those years.) The AIME is then used to calculate the worker's primary insurance amount (PIA) at the time of the claim. The PIA can be defined as the monthly amount a worker would receive as a retirement benefit if the worker retired at full retirement age (currently age between age 66 and age 67).

The PIA is determined by formulas prescribed by Social Security and applied to the participant's credited earnings during certain earnings periods. Basically, the PIA is based on a worker's AIME, which is applied to a benefit formula that depends on the nature of the benefit (e.g., death or retirement). In general, the higher the AIME, the greater the PIA and the larger the benefits (up to stated maximums). However, although those with higher AIMEs will receive larger monthly benefits, these benefits will be proportionately less than benefits paid to individuals who earned less. The fact that Social Security provides proportionately smaller benefits for higher wages is an important concept that many Americans do not understand. Financial professionals who can convey this reality may find their clients more receptive to the need to take charge of their retirement savings.

Retirement Date

Another factor that determines the amount of benefits a retiree receives is when she applies for benefits. Under current Social Security law, normal retirement age depends on when an individual was born, ranging from 65 for individuals born before 1938 to 67 for individuals born after 1959. That is the earliest age at which full benefits are available and is known as the full retirement age (FRA). However, individuals can claim retirement benefits as early as age 62 and receive a (permanently) reduced benefit. The reduction in benefits is based on two things.

1. The individual's average earnings are likely lower because she will have worked fewer years than the normal retiree.

2. Early retirement benefits will, theoretically, extend over a longer period of time.

The amount of the reduction depends on how soon before FRA one claims benefits and is expressed as a percentage of the PIA. Because of the gradually increasing FRA, the percentage of reduction changes from year to year as well.

EXAMPLE

Charlie was born July 1, 1955. His FRA is age 66, which is in July 2021. Charlie retired when he turned 63 in 2018. His benefit was 81.28% of his PIA.

ILLUSTRATION 1

Benefit Reduction for Early Retirement

Year of Birth	Full Retirement Age	Age 62 Reduction Months	Monthly % Reduction	Total % Reduction
1937 or earlier	65	36	.555	20.00
1938	65 + 2 mo.	38	.548	20.83
1939	65 + 4 mo.	40	.541	21.67
1940	65 + 6 mo.	42	.535	22.50
1941	65 + 8 mo.	44	.530	22.33
1942	65 + 10 mo.	46	.525	24.17
1943-1954	66	48	.520	25.00
1955	66 + 2 mo.	50	.516	25.84
1956	66 + 4 mo.	52	.512	26.66
1957	66 + 6 mo.	54	.509	27.50
1958	66 + 8 mo.	56	.505	28.33
1959	66 + 10 mo.	58	.502	29.17
1960 and after	67	60	.500	30.00

ILLUSTRATION 2

Social Security Benefits as a Percentage of Pay

The following chart shows the diminishing significance of Social Security benefits. An individual earning $20,000 would expect to receive Social Security benefits equaling more than 50% of his preretirement income. An individual earning $100,000 could expect just a little over 20%.

Replacement of Preretirement Income

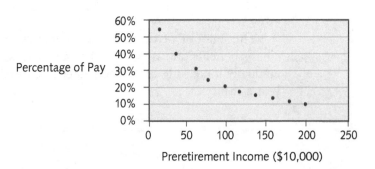

Percentage of Pay

Preretirement Income ($10,000)

Delayed Retirement Credits

By contrast, an individual can delay claiming Social Security retirement benefits beyond FRA and up to age 70 and increase his payments. In these cases, the individual's PIA is increased by a certain percentage for each year of delaying benefits, resulting in larger monthly income payments. The percentage, known as delayed retirement credits (DRCs) depends on the year of birth, as follows:

Delayed Retirement Credits

Year of Birth	Monthly Increase	Yearly Increase
1933–34	11/24 of 1%	5.5%
1935–36	½ of 1%	6.0%
1937–38	16/24 of 1%	6.5%
1939–40	7/12 of 1%	7.0%
1941–42	5/8 of 1%	7.5%
After 1942	2/3 of 1%	8.0%

Family Benefits

Another factor affecting the amount of retirement benefits received under Social Security is whether, in addition to the individual, there are other eligible family members. These include spouses and children, whose benefits are based on the individual's PIA. The benefits paid to family members are in addition to the individual's benefits and are payable only after the individual has applied for benefits.

Spouse

If an individual applies for benefits (is fully insured and married), the individual's spouse, if full retirement age or older, may receive a benefit equal to 50% of the individual's PIA. If the spouse is at least 62, he may receive permanently reduced benefits of 35% of the worker's PIA. If the spouse also qualifies for Social Security benefits under his own record, the spouse will receive either the spousal benefit or the spouse's own benefit, whichever is greater.

A spouse who is caring for an eligible child (as defined in the following) is entitled to a benefit of 50% of the individual's PIA, no matter the age of the spouse.

An unmarried divorced spouse is also entitled to retirement benefits under the worker's account if the divorced spouse was married to the worker for at least 10 years.

Children

Children of a retired worker may also be eligible for benefits. (For this purpose, a child may be a natural child, an adopted child, a stepchild, or a dependent grandchild, if the parents are deceased or disabled.) Eligibility requires that the child be unmarried and under age 18 (or 19, if in high school) or any age if disabled before age 22. Each child's benefit is based on 50% of the greater PIA of either parent but not both.

As you can see, the determination of one's Social Security benefits at retirement can be complicated. This is made even more so due to limitations that may be imposed on benefits.

Limitations on Benefits

Social Security retirement benefits may be limited by one or more restrictions. These include the maximum family benefit and the earnings limitation.

Maximum Family Benefit

The total amount of benefits that all members of one family may receive, based on the earnings records of one person, is limited to an amount that varies with the PIA. This maximum does not apply when both a husband and wife receive only retirement benefits based on their own earnings records.

Earnings Limitation

Collecting retirement benefits under Social Security does not require that an individual actually cease working. However, those who continue to work and earn a wage after their benefits begin may see those benefits reduced, depending on their age and how much they earn. Originally, the purpose of the so-called earnings limit was to restrict Social Security benefits to those who were actually retired or, in the case of dependents, to those who were truly reliant on the worker. Individuals who were self-supporting or who could continue to earn income would receive reduced benefits, it was argued because they had additional sources of income. This thinking held firm until the Senior Citizens Freedom to Work Act was enacted in 2000.

Under previous rules, any individual younger than 70 who collected Social Security retirement benefits was subject to earnings limits. Today, these limits apply only to those who collect benefits before their full retirement age. For current limits on amounts that may be earned by those under full retirement age, please see the appendix at the end of the book. (Family member benefits that are based on the Social Security recipient's work record are also reduced.)

Those who attain full retirement age are not subject to an earnings limitation. They can earn any amount with no reduction in their Social Security retirement benefits.

Special rules apply for the year in which one reaches full retirement age. For current limits on earnings permitted before benefits are withheld, please see the appendix at the end of the book.

ILLUSTRATION 3

Types of Income Exempt From the Earnings Limitation

The limitations and reductions discussed above apply only to "earned" income. For purposes of applying the earnings limitation on Social Security retirement benefits, certain types of earnings or income are not counted. These include the following:

- Pensions and retirement benefits
- Severance pay upon retirement
- Workers' compensation and unemployment compensation
- Dividends and interest on investments (unless in the brokerage business)
- Capital gains
- Contest or lottery winnings
- IRA and 401(k) withdrawals
- Rental income (unless in the real estate business)
- Sick pay if paid more than six months after the last month worked
- Damages, fees, or interest received in a court judgment (except for recovery of back wages)

Benefit Taxation

In addition to the pre-full retirement age benefit reduction facing individuals who earn more than the retirement earnings limit, another form of reduction awaits those whose total income (from virtually all sources, including investment income and a portion of Social Security's benefits) exceeds certain threshold limits.

Social Security benefits are tax-free up to a point. Benefit recipients who are in the upper income level must consider up to 85% of their benefits as taxable income. The formula for determining the benefit inclusion amount involves a two-tier threshold limit, one set for individual filers and one for joint filers. For single individuals, the step-rate thresholds are $25,000 and $34,000. For joint filers, the thresholds are $32,000 and $44,000. In general, those whose total income exceeds the thresholds are subject to taxation on up to 85% of their Social Security benefits.

Use the following worksheet (based on the worksheet found in the instructions for IRS Form 1040) to compute the taxable portion of any Social Security benefits:

1. Social Security benefit	_____
2. One-half of line 1	_____
3. Taxable income items reported on tax return (that is, taxable items other than Social Security benefits)	_____
4. Tax-exempt interest income	_____
5. Total of lines 2, 3, and 4	_____
6. Adjustments to gross income (most "above-the-line" deductions)	_____
7. Modified adjusted gross income (subtract line 6 from line 5) (if line 6 is larger than line 5, stop: none of the Social Security benefits are taxable)	_____
8. Either: ■ Married filing jointly, enter $32,000 ■ Married filing separately, skip lines 8–15, multiply line 7 by .85 and enter on line 16 ■ Single, head of household, qualifying surviving spouse, married but separated for the year, enter $25,000	_____
9. Subtract line 8 from line 7 (if line 8 is larger than line 7, stop: none of the Social Security benefits are taxable)	_____
10. Either: ■ Married filing jointly, enter $12,000 ■ Single, head of household, qualifying surviving spouse, married but separated for the year, enter $9,000	_____
11. Subtract line 10 from line 9. If zero or less, enter zero	_____
12. Enter the smaller of line 9 or line 10	_____
13. Enter one-half of line 12	_____
14. Enter the smaller of line 2 or line 13	_____
15. Multiply line 11 by 85%. If line 11 is zero, enter zero	_____
16. Add lines 14 and 15	_____
17. Multiply line 1 by 85%	_____
18. Taxable Social Security benefits: enter the smaller of line 16 or line 17	_____

EXAMPLE

Mitch and Edna are a retired couple, both age 66. This year, they received $82,000 in income: $27,000 from investment earnings, $35,000 from Mitch's pension plan, and $20,000 in Social Security retirement benefits.

1.	Social Security benefit	$20,000
2.	One-half of line 1	$10,000
3.	Taxable income items reported on tax return (that is, taxable items other than Social Security benefits)	$62,000
4.	Tax-exempt interest income	0
5.	Total of lines 2, 3, and 4	$72,000
6.	Adjustments to gross income (most "above-the-line" deductions)	0
7.	Modified adjusted gross income (subtract line 6 from line 5) (if line 6 is larger than line 5, stop: none of the Social Security benefits are taxable)	$72,000
8.	Either: ■ Married filing jointly, enter $32,000 ■ Married filing separately, skip lines 8–15, multiply line 7 by .85 and enter on line 16 ■ Single, head of household, qualifying surviving spouse, married but separated for the year, enter $25,000	$32,000
9.	Subtract line 8 from line 7 (if line 8 is larger than line 7, stop: none of the Social Security benefits are taxable)	$40,000
10.	Either: ■ Married filing jointly, enter $12,000 ■ Single, head of household, qualifying surviving spouse, married but separated for the year, enter $9,000	$12,000
11.	Subtract line 10 from line 9. If zero or less, enter zero	$28,000
12.	Enter the smaller of line 9 or line 10	$12,000
13.	Enter one-half of line 12	$6,000
14.	Enter the smaller of line 2 or line 13	$6,000
15.	Multiply line 11 by 85%. If line 11 is zero, enter zero	$23,800
16.	Add lines 14 and 15	$29,800
17.	Multiply line 1 by 85%	$17,000
18.	Taxable Social Security benefits: enter the smaller of line 16 or line 17	$17,000

The couple must include $17,000 (85%) of their $20,000 in Social Security benefits as taxable income for the year.

Reducing or Eliminating the Tax on Social Security Benefits

The idea of paying taxes on Social Security benefits rubs many individuals the wrong way. As a planner, you should inform clients who face this tax that there are options that can reduce or even eliminate the taxation of their benefits. The key lies in the portion of the formula that excludes tax-deferred interest from modified adjusted gross income. One possible solution is to shift assets that are currently producing taxable earnings into a fixed or variable annuity. The calculation of modified adjusted gross income does not include annuity earnings. Consequently, by shifting some or all of the income-producing assets into an annuity—to the extent the client can afford to forgo current income—it is possible to substantially reduce or eliminate the taxation of Social Security benefits.

EXAMPLE

If Mitch and Edna were to use the assets that currently generate $27,000 a year in taxable investment earnings to buy an annuity, their modified adjusted gross income would result in a new series of calculations and would drastically lower the amount of Social Security benefits subject to tax.

1. Social Security benefit	$20,000
2. One-half of line 1	$10,000
3. Taxable income items reported on tax return (that is, taxable items other than Social Security benefits)	$35,000
4. Tax-exempt interest income	0
5. Total of lines 2, 3, and 4	$45,000
6. Adjustments to gross income (most "above-the-line" deductions)	0
7. Modified adjusted gross income (subtract line 6 from line 5) (if line 6 is larger than line 5, stop: none of the Social Security benefits are taxable)	$45,000
8. Either: ■ Married filing jointly, enter $32,000 ■ Married filing separately, skip lines 8–15, multiply line 7 by .85 and enter on line 16 ■ Single, head of household, qualifying surviving spouse, married but separated for the year, enter $25,000	$32,000
9. Subtract line 8 from line 7 (if line 8 is larger than line 7, stop: none of the Social Security benefits are taxable)	$13,000
10. Either: ■ Married filing jointly, enter $12,000 ■ Single, head of household, qualifying surviving spouse, married but separated for the year, enter $9,000	$12,000
11. Subtract line 10 from line 9. If zero or less, enter zero	$1,000
12. Enter the smaller of line 9 or line 10	$12,000
13. Enter one-half of line 12	$6,000
14. Enter the smaller of line 2 or line 13	$6,000
15. Multiply line 11 by 85%. If line 11 is zero, enter zero	$850
16. Add lines 14 and 15	$6,850
17. Multiply line 1 by 85%	$17,000
18. Taxable Social Security benefits: enter the smaller of line 16 or line 17	$6,850

As you can see from the worksheet, if Mitch and Edna were to reposition or shift assets from investments that generate taxable earnings into an annuity, the amount of their Social Security benefits subject to taxation would drop more than $10,000, from $17,000 to $6,850.

Other Taxes

In addition to the tax described previously, a worker who is retired and receiving Social Security benefits must pay FICA taxes on income from any work as an employee or self-employed individual. Many states do not tax Social Security benefits, but retirees may want to consult a tax advisor to be certain. Social Security, benefits, however, are not subject to FICA taxes.

APPLYING FOR SOCIAL SECURITY RETIREMENT BENEFITS

Key Point   Benefits do not start until an individual applies for them.

Key Point   An individual may open a "my Social Security" account online or request account information from the Social Security Administration at any time.

Your clients will want to get all the benefits to which they are entitled. You should remind them that Social Security benefits will not begin automatically; they must apply for benefits.

The Social Security Administration recommends that workers periodically check their accrued benefits. Professional retirement planners can enhance their role by helping their clients in this regard. The Social Security Administration mails printed Your Social Security Statement to workers age 25, 30, 35, 40, 45, 50, 55, and 60 or older who have not by then created a "my Social Security" account.

The statement documents a worker's earnings throughout the worker's career and projects the various benefits to which they are (death, disability) or may be (future retirement) entitled. When the statement is received, any errors should be noted and reported to the Social Security Administration. Errors identified early are usually fairly easy to correct. Trying to fix an error after benefits have commenced is significantly more difficult.

Individuals covered by Social Security may open a free "my Social Security" account at any time at SSA.gov. Those opening the account will have to provide a valid email address, have a Social Security number, have a U.S. mailing address and be at least 18 years old. When a person creates a "my Social Security" account, he will no longer receive a paper Social Security Statement in the mail; he will, however, receive an email reminder approximately three months before his birthday to remind him to review his statement on line.

If a person wants to receive her Social Security Statement by mail, she may print and complete a "Request for Social Security Statement" (Form SSA-7004) and mail it to the address on the form. She should receive the paper statement in the mail in four to six weeks.

Information about Social Security can be obtained by calling, toll-free, 1-800-772-1213 or by going online to SSA.gov.

WRAP-UP

Without a doubt, Social Security is an important aspect of an individual's retirement income plan. However, one of the most important things you as a retirement planner can do for your clients is to impart the true nature of the role Social Security plays—that of a foundation or base of income. As this unit points out, the amount of income Social Security replaces for most middle-income and virtually all higher income wage earners will not, in and of itself, provide full financial security. The limitations imposed by the system—in fact, the future of the system itself and the benefits it may or may not be able to deliver—require that individuals have other resources. These include, for example, life insurance, annuities, qualified retirement arrangements, and personal savings and investments. We will cover each of these subjects in later units.

As a retirement planner, you are in a unique position to help your clients understand the Social Security program and the benefits they may receive. You are an important source of information and can use this information to help clients begin to effectively plan for their retirement.

When estimating retirement income for your clients, you must consider the benefit amount that will be payable from Social Security. This amount will depend on a number of things, including the age at which your client plans to retire. Early retirement at age 62 can reduce Social Security benefits by 20%, and that reduction is irreversible. This reduction must be offset by increased savings or investments.

Conversely, delayed retirement can increase Social Security benefits by a certain amount for each year of delay beyond the normal retirement age. The increase is also permanent and has impact on the retiree's total retirement income. You should review current Social Security information annually to determine any changes or limitations in benefits.

In the next unit, we will address how life insurance and annuities can be used to meet retirement income needs.

UNIT TEST

1. For most individuals, the amount of time needed under the Social Security system to qualify for retirement benefits is equal to how many years of work?
   A. 10
   B. 15
   C. 20
   D. 25

2. With regard to Social Security, which of these statements is TRUE?
   A. Retirement benefits begin automatically when an individual retires.
   B. All retirees receive the same benefit.
   C. The Social Security taxes an individual pays are earmarked for his own benefit.
   D. The majority of working Americans are covered by Social Security.

3. Which of the following actions would reduce the amount of Social Security retirement benefits an individual is otherwise entitled to receive?
   A. Postponing the receipt of benefits after age 65
   B. Having a preliminary adjusted gross income below the threshold for benefit taxation
   C. Having more than two dependents
   D. Having income in excess of the earnings limitation

4. Earl and Thelma are a retired couple, both age 67. This year, they received $50,000 in income: $15,000 from Earl's pension plan, $20,000 in Social Security retirement benefits, and $15,000 in investment income. For purposes of determining the potential tax on their Social Security benefits, what is the couple's preliminary adjusted gross income?
   A. $15,000
   B. $35,000
   C. $40,000
   D. $50,000

5. Assuming the facts in Question 4, how much of Earl and Thelma's Social Security benefits is subject to income tax?
   A. $0
   B. $4,000
   C. $8,000
   D. $20,000

6. What is the earliest age at which an individual can receive Social Security retirement benefits?
   A. 59½
   B. 60
   C. 62
   D. 65

7. The amount of Social Security retirement benefits payable when an individual reaches normal retirement age is
   A. the average indexed monthly earnings
   B. the primary insurance amount
   C. the maximum family benefit
   D. the earnings limitation

ANSWERS AND RATIONALES

1. **A.**   An individual needs 10 years of work to become eligible for Social Security retirement benefits.

2. **D.**   Most working Americans are covered by Social Security. Retirement benefits are based on an individual's earning history but do not come from any account earmarked for the retiree.

3. **D.**   Individuals below full retirement age (FRA) can have their benefits reduced by having income in excess of the earnings limitation.

4. **C.**   Before adding the taxable portion of Social Security, you have to determine what the taxable portion is. First, add up other types of income.

5. **B.** $4,000 of the $20,000 in Social Security benefits is taxable.

6. **C.**   An individual can start receiving Social Security retirement benefits at age 62.

7. **B.**   The basic retirement benefit amount is called the primary insurance amount.

5

Product Review I: Life Insurance and Annuities

There is a wide array of financial products available to help Americans prepare for retirement. Most people will do best with a combination of products based on an asset allocation strategy and a systematic approach to savings and investments. In addition to diversification, balancing the savings load on a variety of financial products can help clients pull "double duty" with their savings dollars. Life insurance and certain annuities are prime examples of this. ■

UNIT OBJECTIVES

Permanent life insurance can be used to accumulate retirement capital (through its cash value), but it also satisfies an even more important objective—providing financial protection throughout the client's working years. Annuities offer an excellent way to accumulate retirement funds on a tax-advantaged basis and provide a way to systematically distribute those funds during the retirement years with the assurance that the retiree will not outlive the income.

On completion of this unit, you should be able to:

■ name the ways life insurance values can be accessed for use by retirees;

■ describe the types of annuities and how each can be used to provide benefits during retirement; and

■ explain how Section 1035 of the tax code allows individuals to exchange life insurance or annuity policies on a tax-free basis.

ROLE OF LIFE INSURANCE IN RETIREMENT PLANNING

Key Point Life insurance offers both a guaranteed death benefit and a tax-deferred way to accumulate funds for retirement or other needs.

Key Point Different policy types offer great flexibility in premiums, cash values, and death benefits.

There are two basic forms of life insurance: term and permanent. Simply defined, term life insurance provides death benefit protection only; the absence of a cash value makes term insurance unsuitable for capital accumulation purposes but ideal for meeting pure life insurance needs (at least during one's younger years, when it is generally quite affordable).

Permanent life insurance, on the other hand, in addition to providing death benefit protection, can be used as a means of accumulating capital. Its cash value, which carries important income tax advantages, is a fundamental part of the policy's death benefit, but is also readily available while the insured is alive. For that reason, permanent life insurance can serve an important role in just about any retirement savings plan, provided, of course, the policyowner also needs life insurance protection.

Permanent life insurance includes a variety of forms that range from fixed-premium, guaranteed-interest products to flexible-premium, variable-return products. Whatever the type, all permanent plans have at least one thing in common: a nonforfeitable cash value that is accessible by the policyowner at virtually any time. The cash value is part of the policy's death benefit and would be paid out as such at the insured's death. But the cash value can also be used to meet any financial need while the insured is alive, and it is for this reason that permanent life insurance is an important way to meet retirement needs.

No other product can do what life insurance does, that is, guarantee to pay a (usually substantial) sum of money upon the insured's death and accumulate funds in a tax-favored manner while the insured is alive. This assures clients that even if they die prematurely, their retirement savings plans will be completed, making certain their dependents have a financially secure future. Add these features to the investment nature of a product like variable life insurance and it becomes apparent that permanent life insurance can serve a vital role in providing financial security up to and into retirement.

Needs Change as Retirement Approaches

For most people, life insurance is an important component of a comprehensive financial plan. It provides needed financial protection during child-rearing years and when financial obligations loom large. When coverage is purchased at an early age, the rates are very affordable. Yet even though life insurance may have been purchased to provide protection in the event of death, policyowners who are now facing retirement will find that their coverage can be redirected to meet new and different needs. Retirement does not lessen the need for life insurance; rather, it represents another dimension of this product's use.

As individuals near retirement, many will find that some of their original needs for life insurance, such as paying off a mortgage or ensuring a child's education, are diminishing. They may find that estate liquidity has become a primary concern. Others may require the same level of death protection, yet do not want to divert retirement dollars to premium payments. Businessowners, whose primary focus has been on the day-to-day operation of a company, may find themselves confronted with the issue of what to do with their business upon retirement. Different objectives, brought on by changing circumstances, present an opportunity for financial professionals to serve their clients effectively by updating or expanding the life insurance plan currently in place or by evaluating the need for a new plan.

A Retirement Product From the Beginning

The use of permanent life insurance in retirement planning begins long before the policyowner retires. It begins, in fact, when the policy is purchased. Though a policy should be purchased primarily for its death protection benefits, its accumulation features also allow it to operate as a retirement vehicle in the following ways.

■ **It builds cash value.** The cash value represents the policyowner's non-forfeitable interest in the policy. This money can be obtained, through a loan or withdrawal, virtually any time (though there may be tax consequences in certain cases of withdrawal, as explained later). This makes the cash value a tax-attractive way to supplement the accumulation of capital for retirement. Depending on the type of policy, the cash value growth is either guaranteed (under traditional whole life) or nonguaranteed (under variable life).

■ **The tax-deferred gain enhances accumulation.** The cash value's tax-deferred gain, coupled with compounded interest or investment earnings, can create a sizable sum over time.

■ **Life insurance is safe.** Behind every life insurance policy stand reserve and nonforfeiture laws, state guaranty associations, rating organizations, and the strength of the insurance industry itself. Because of these factors, life insurance is one of the safest, most secure financial products available to consumers.

Because life insurance can serve the dual role of providing protection and accumulating funds, it is a valuable retirement tool. Let's examine some of the ways in which different life insurance plans can be used to meet retirement needs. Though term insurance can play a role in this arena, its lack of a cash value limits its use in retirement planning beyond protection. Our focus, then, will be on permanent life insurance, which is any form of life insurance that generates a nonforfeitable cash value.

Whole Life Insurance

There is nothing new about the role of traditional whole life insurance in retirement planning. The premiums, paid over the life of the insured, remain level over the life of the policy. Whole life policies build guaranteed cash values which, when they are not needed to support death benefits, can be used in a variety of ways for retirement.

Cash values can be accessed through a policy loan or withdrawal to provide income. Upon policy surrender, they also can be used to purchase paid-up insurance or extended term insurance, relieving the insured of premium payments but allowing him to maintain insurance coverage. They can be left intact in the policy, the proceeds of which may be needed for estate liquidity.

Life insurance policies left intact through retirement provide income security to survivors, who might otherwise face an income reduction upon the retiree's death. And finally, they can be used to provide income payments guaranteed for life, through the purchase of an annuity. Life insurance policies can be exchanged for an annuity in a tax-free transaction known as a 1035 exchange (explained later in this unit).

A feature of whole life that is praised by some and criticized by others is the guaranteed nature of its policy values. Traditional whole life insurance is based on fairly conservative interest assumptions (generally 2½%–3½% annually) that permit the policy to guarantee the premium amount, cash value growth, and death benefit.

When one considers that a permanent life insurance contract can obligate a company for up to 100 years (e.g., a policy issued at birth for an insured who lives to policy maturity at age 100), it's easy to see why life insurers have to take a conservative interest position. The debate over guaranteed values and conservative interest returns is unlikely to end, but at least there is an alternative for those who seek insurance protection with higher (nonguaranteed) returns—universal life insurance, variable life insurance, and variable universal life insurance (discussed later in this unit).

Participating Whole Life

Owners of participating whole life insurance policies, which distribute tax-free policy dividends, have an opportunity to realize greater-than-guaranteed death benefit and cash value growth. Policy dividends represent the difference between the premiums charged and the actual costs the insurer incurred during the period for which the premiums were charged, but they also represent actual investment returns that exceed the actuarially assumed rates in the contract.

Owners of participating policies who have been receiving dividends over the years may want to reconsider how they can or should be using these dividends. For example, dividends that have been used to purchase paid-up additions through the years leading to retirement could now be applied to reduce premium payments, if the existing level of coverage is adequate. Conversely, if current levels of life insurance are not enough to meet a survivor's needs or cover estate liquidity, dividends could be used to purchase more coverage, without increasing the insured's out-of-pocket expenditures.

Limited Pay Whole Life

For a number of people, financial obligations are great during the 15- to 20-year period preceding retirement—children are in college, mortgages have not yet been paid off, a business may require additional investment—and their incomes are relatively high. Although these people need and want whole life protection, they are also concerned about maintaining their lifestyle after they retire and their incomes may be drastically reduced. These prospects are candidates for limited-pay whole life policies.

A **limited-payment life insurance policy** is one that becomes paid up before policy maturity (which is typically between age 95 and 100). Common varieties include life paid up at age 65, 20- and 10-pay life (in which premiums are paid up in 20 and 10 years, respectively), and single-premium life (funded by one premium payment).

Generally speaking, the shorter the premium-paying period, the higher the premium will be. However, under the mathematical concept of the present value of money, the sum of premiums under a limited-payment policy will be less (often significantly so) than the sum of premiums under a straight life (to maturity) policy. And, while the cash value will not grow to equal the face amount any earlier under a limited-pay policy than a straight life policy, the rate of cash value growth will be fastest (during the premium-paying period) under those policies that are paid up early.

Those who want to focus on accumulating a cash value for retirement planning purposes should give thought to limited payment policies. Premiums are paid during the insured's most financially productive years, with no premiums due after a specified period. At that time, the insured will have a fully paid-up policy, its values and benefits intact and available, and the premium dollars will be freed up for other needs.

ILLUSTRATION 1

Retirement Planning—A Reason to Call

Middle age is often the time when people begin to seriously consider retirement planning and have the financial resources to start putting their plans into action. A review of your client files will identify individuals who could benefit from your advice and ideas. As a starting point with these clients, review their current life insurance plans with questions like these in mind.

■ Are existing coverages adequate?

■ Are any new policies with different features or different benefits warranted?

■ Does this current plan reflect the needs of this individual today? Are the types and amounts of insurance coverage in line with his current objectives?

■ Are the beneficiary designations and policy ownership structures up to date?

■ Is there another need insurance could address? Is there a need for long-term care coverage?

■ Does this current insurance plan support or counter the person's financial and retirement goals?

Universal Life Insurance

A **universal life policy** can be an attractive alternative to traditional whole life insurance. It too is permanent insurance, but it differs from whole life by permitting flexible-premium payments and adjustable death benefits. These features give the policyowner greater control over his plan.

Quite simply, universal life insurance consists of term insurance coverage and a side fund that serves as the policy's cash value. The term insurance protection may be either level term or decreasing term, which allows the policyowner to select one of two death benefit options:

■ Level death benefit, similar to traditional whole life insurance, equal to the sum of a decreasing term insurance component and an increasing cash value

■ Increasing death benefit, made possible by level term insurance to which is added the accumulating cash value

Based largely on the amount of term insurance (the amount at risk), a target premium rate is established. Policyowners have considerable leeway in paying more or less than the target rate. The minimum premium is the amount necessary to cover the insurance costs and permit the cash value to grow at a minimum rate. The maximum rate, sometimes called the guideline premium, is set by Internal Revenue Code restrictions. Policy charges covering mortality and expense charges are deducted, usually monthly, from the policy's cash value. As long as enough cash value exists to cover monthly charges, the policy will remain in force.

This target rate is what permits the flexible funding that is a key characteristic of universal life. (Funding flexibility is ideal for policyowners who overfund the policy to take advantage of the cash value's tax-deferred growth, but it can be a trap that leads to policy collapse for those who lean the opposite way and try to get away with underfunding the policy.) The cash value is credited with interest that is usually defined as the greater of a contractually guaranteed rate and a rate that reflects current market conditions.

From the policyowner's perspective, the flexibility of universal life centers on the amount and timing of premium payments and the amount of insurance. Because the cost of the insurance is taken from the policy's cash value, premium payments can be increased, decreased, or skipped altogether. As long as the cash values are sufficient to support the cost of insurance protection, the policy remains in force. The amount of the insurance and the death benefit can be increased (as long as the insured is healthy) or decreased to adapt to a policyowner's need. Finally, universal life policies typically allow for partial withdrawals of the cash value (though surrender charges could be applied).

Because of this flexibility, universal life has been described as a "cradle-to-grave" plan. For example, during the years when death protection is most needed, the amount of insurance can be adjusted upward to cover those needs. As the individual nears retirement and perhaps has a greater need for savings and accumulation, the face amount can be decreased. By decreasing premiums, the policyowner can divert the savings to another investment; by increasing the premiums, the insured will enhance her cash value growth. The fact that this growth is tax deferred is another benefit.

Indexed Universal Life Insurance

Indexed universal life insurance is based on universal life insurance with several important additional features. An indexed universal life insurance policy gives the policyholder the opportunity to allocate cash value amounts to either a fixed account or an account linked to an external index. Indexed policies offer a variety of popular indexes to choose from, such as the S&P 500 and the Nasdaq 100.

Indexed policies allow policyholders to decide the percentage of their funds that they wish to allocate to fixed and indexed portions. Also, these types of universal insurance policies typically guarantee the principal amount in the indexed portion. The returns are limited through the use of participation rates, caps on maximums or a combination of these. Since these policies are seen as a "hybrid" universal life insurance policy, they are usually not very expensive as they do not charge management fees.

Indexed universal life insurance has become popular for those seeking returns linked to the market and protection against market downturns.

Variable Life Insurance

Variable life insurance combines the death benefit protection of whole life insurance with investment options that could lead to higher than traditional returns for the policy's cash value (and, accordingly, to a death benefit that is higher than the face amount at policy issue). For some people, variable life insurance could be an ideal retirement planning tool.

Like whole life, variable life has fixed, permanent premiums and a minimum guaranteed death benefit. Unlike whole life, which guarantees a certain rate of return on its cash values, variable life allows the policyowner to choose how the cash value will be invested from a selection of subaccounts (also called portfolios) that are managed in the company's separate account.

Subaccounts generally offer policyowners a variety of investment objectives ranging from conservative to aggressive. To this extent, policyowners assume the risk of variable life's investment returns. Like many investments, a variable life policy's cash value can drop below expectations as well as exceed them. Cash values are not guaranteed with variable life; they will perform in relation to the underlying investment portfolio. If the portfolio does well, the return will be higher than what the policyowner would have received with a traditional policy. However, if the portfolio performs poorly, the policyowner could lose all or a portion of his invested assets.

The death benefit payable from a variable policy is also a function of how well the cash values perform. As noted, a minimum benefit is guaranteed; it is the initial face amount of the policy. The actual amount of the death benefit, however, may be increased based on investment returns that exceed assumed interest rates.

Whether variable life is suitable for a particular client depends largely on the person's risk tolerance. Variable life can be an excellent way to accumulate retirement savings while maintaining needed insurance coverage, as long as the policyowner can accept the risk. Because of the investment risk of these policies, they are considered securities and are regulated by state insurance law and the Securities and Exchange Commission (SEC).

Variable Universal Life Insurance

Universal life insurance features premium and policy flexibility, but no investment choices. Variable life offers investment opportunities but the rigid policy requirements of traditional whole life. Once these two products became available, it was only a matter of time before the best of both came together as variable universal life (VUL). By almost any account, VUL stands as one of the most versatile products offered by insurers today.

Here is a product that can be designed seemingly from the ground up to meet a client's personal needs and situation. It can change in all important respects—premium amount, face amount, type of death benefit, and underlying investments—to accommodate changing needs. As with variable life, policyowners—not the insurer—assume the investment risk for their cash values.

MEETING RETIREMENT NEEDS WITH LIFE INSURANCE

Key Point   Life insurance offers several ways to access funds during retirement in addition to estate planning benefits.

Life insurance products are ideally suited for use in almost any retirement plan but how much, and what kind? In order to answer these questions, financial professionals have to understand their prospects' or clients' financial needs and goals. The selection of the best policy or an appropriate change to an existing plan will depend on an individual's objectives and where he stands financially today. It requires a financial professional to ask, "At this point in life, what does this client want and need, and how can my products and services help?"

Product and service recommendations can be made only after analyzing an individual's financial situation, needs, and goals. While every situation will be different, the following are typical retirement needs that can be met with life insurance:

- Wealth accumulation

- Retirement income

- Medical expenses

- Senior settlements

- Business planning

- Special bequests and charitable gifts

- Estate liquidity and estate protection

Let's examine each of these retirement needs and see how life insurance can be used to meet them.

Wealth Accumulation

A likely retirement priority for most people is to acquire or have access to enough wealth so that they can comfortably and confidently forego the salary or wage they had been earning before retirement. As we have learned, funds for retirement are accumulated through personal savings and investments, employer retirement plans, and Social Security. Through its cash values, permanent life insurance provides an orderly and effective means of accumulating capital, thus supporting the personal savings leg of the three-legged retirement income stool.

Some might argue that the rate of return on life insurance makes it unsuitable as a retirement planning vehicle when compared to other investments that offer potentially higher returns. If the client's sole objective is the accumulation of funds, then that would be a valid argument. Life insurance should not be presented or sold as a savings or investment vehicle. It is, first and foremost, protection against the financial risks associated with death.

To dismiss the cash value accumulation aspect of permanent plans, however, would be a disservice. Life insurance provides a balance to a financial portfolio—reasonable liquidity and, with traditional policies, a guaranteed rate of return and safety of principal. Although many investments can offer a higher rate of return than life insurance, few investments are safer.

In addition, life insurance cash values accumulate on a tax-deferred basis, which enhances their growth. When comparing permanent life insurance to taxable financial products, a proper comparison can only be made by looking at the net (after-tax) return on the taxable investment. Tax-deferred compounded growth can, over time, make life insurance cash values a significant asset for retirement planning or virtually any other financial need.

Finally, certain types of life insurance policies, such as variable life and variable universal life, do offer the potential for higher returns. Through these plans, the life insurance industry has kept its products in pace with the changing needs and expectations of an increasingly sophisticated consumer base that wants insurance protection with greater appreciation potential.

Retirement Income

Being able to count on a certain level of retirement income is an important goal for most people. Social Security benefits will not provide the level of income needed to maintain a comfortable standard of living, nor will most pension plans (if, indeed, the individual is entitled to a pension). Insurance can help provide additional income. For example, a policy's cash value can be used to purchase a single premium annuity, which will create a guaranteed income stream. Or, depending on the type of policy, these values can be withdrawn, surrendered, or borrowed and used to pay off a large debt, such as a mortgage.

Funds to Cover Medical Expenses

Until fairly recently, permanent life insurance policies provided benefits to living insureds in only limited ways: through cash value loans, withdrawals, or surrenders. Even in cases where it was obvious the insured suffered from a terminal illness or permanent confinement to a nursing facility, the death proceeds could not be paid until the insured's death.

Since the mid-1980s, however, a growing number of insurers have started offering—usually at no charge to policyowners—an accelerated benefits rider that allows the payment of some (if not all) of a life insurance policy's death benefit while the insured is alive. The purpose of this benefit is to provide funds to help with final medical expenses.

To qualify for accelerated benefits, the insured must suffer from a medical condition that is expected to result in death within a reasonable period of time. (A physician's certified statement to this effect is required.) Most companies have expanded the eligibility requirement to include insureds who are permanently confined to a skilled nursing facility. Depending on the company and the terms of the provision, an accelerated death benefit may be paid in a single lump-sum or through a series of payments.

One question that remained unanswered for a long time had to do with the tax status of accelerated benefits. Normally, life insurance death proceeds are tax free when paid at the insured's death, but what about payments made when the insured is still alive?

That question was answered in 1996 with legislation that defined such benefits as exempt from income taxation, just as if they were paid at the insured's death. Tax-free treatment of accelerated benefits requires the insured to be terminally ill, with death expected within 24 months. When paid to a chronically ill insured who is confined to a nursing home, accelerated benefits are given a limited tax exemption. The exclusion is limited to actual expenses incurred in receiving long-term medical or nursing care, or to a maximum daily limit, and only to the extent that such care is not covered by any other form of insurance.

For this purpose, chronically ill is defined as a physician-certified condition that prevents the insured from performing at least two activities of daily living (e.g., eating, bathing, dressing, toileting, and walking) for a period of at least 90 days or requires substantial supervision because of cognitive impairment. Many victims of Alzheimer's disease would qualify for accelerated benefits payable under favorable tax status.

Senior Settlements

Another growing trend in the retirement planning field is the senior life insurance settlement, an arrangement whereby an older insured sells his life policy to a company for an amount less than the policy's face but generally far more than the policy's cash value. Life settlements are made by companies (usually referred to as **viatical companies**) that purchase in-force life policies as investments. The investment pays off—or matures, as the industry more delicately calls it—when the insured dies.

For the insured, the reason for entering into a life settlement is to gain funds (more than would be available from the insurance company for a policy surrender) during his life. For the viatical company that purchases the policy, the gain is obviously the difference between the amount paid for the policy and the death proceeds payable when the insured dies.

According to recent studies, the senior settlement market is expanding. This is not surprising, because Americans age 65 and older are the most affluent and fastest growing segment of the population. Furthermore, policyowners in this demographic group own hundreds of billions of dollars of life insurance.

In the not-too-distant past, the principal concern of individuals at this age was not living long enough. Today, with life-extending drugs and medical techniques, the main concern for many is outliving their resources. For older individuals who fear an income or savings shortage, and for whom the original reasons for their insurance purchase no longer apply, a settlement could be appropriate.

The tax treatment of a life settlement is similar to that of a life insurance policy surrender but with a twist. An amount equal to the policy's cash value, less the policyowner's basis (premiums paid) is taxed as ordinary income; the remainder (i.e., the difference between the cash value and the settlement amount received) is treated as a capital gain and taxed at capital gains rates.

Senior life settlements should not be confused with viatical settlements. A viatical settlement is made between a settlement company and a terminally ill individual of any age; senior settlements are made between a settlement company and older individuals, typically in their 70s or 80s, who have suffered some decline in health but are not terminally ill.

Business Planning

Life insurance plays a vital role in the retirement plans of businessowners. For most businessowners, whether they are sole proprietors, partners, or close corporation stockholders, their businesses represent the largest source of their income and the most significant portion of their wealth. Planning for the orderly transition from or succession of their business is a major issue businessowners must address.

Businessowners can choose when to terminate their active involvement in the company. Many plan to remain active until death. Others may choose to withdraw sooner, to make way for a younger family member or to enjoy the leisure of retirement. Regardless of when an owner withdraws, plans must be made so that the owner's departure does not reduce the value of the business or prevent the family from receiving its full interest at the owner's death.

Consequently, retirement planning for a businessowner should take into account that his involvement with the business will eventually cease and his ownership interest will have to be sold or transferred. These two certainties may or may not occur at the same time.

Life insurance is an effective planning tool that can address both eventualities. Though discussed thoroughly in later units, a brief review of its uses in business planning is appropriate here.

Life insurance can be used to do the following.

- Fund plans that provide incentives to a key employee whom the businessowner views as a successor to the owner. These plans include deferred compensation, profit-sharing plans, or split-dollar life insurance, for example.

- Fund a retirement plan (though certain limits apply).

- Fund a business buy-sell agreement, guaranteeing the orderly sale and transfer of the business at the owner's death and providing her family with the assurance that they will receive a full and fair price for the business.

- Provide estate liquidity, an important consideration for businessowners whose assets are tied up in their business.

Special Bequests and Charitable Gifts

Life insurance in retirement can play important roles that are not directly related to providing retirement income. For clients who enjoy contributing to a special charitable concern, life insurance is a way to leverage relatively small annual contributions into a much larger single gift at death. Knowing that their favorite school, hospital, or other charity will benefit upon their death brings a great sense of comfort to many people.

In the past, because of age, illness, or the small amount of coverage needed, applicants in the senior market have found it difficult to obtain life insurance to meet these special needs. However, many companies are now offering a simplified-issue, nonparticipating whole life insurance product created specifically for this market.

The product is designed for healthy prospects who can qualify by answering "no" to a few broad medical questions about their health during the past three to five years. Usually, no medical exam is required, but the issuing company will likely conduct a Medical Insurance Bureau check and a telephone interview at a later date. Many of the policies contain an accelerated benefit provision that allows the policyowner to receive a certain percentage of the face amount upon a physician's confirmation that the insured has six months or less to live.

Estate Liquidity

Everyone has a need for estate liquidity, and a plan to meet that need should be an integral part of any retirement program.

Death brings about certain financial obligations that must be met immediately with cash. Final expenses, hospital and medical costs, funeral and burial costs, unpaid debts, bills, taxes, probate costs, attorney fees—all of these obligations must be paid before an estate can be settled and property and assets can be transferred to the decedent's heirs.

Even the most modest estate will likely be faced with thousands of dollars in final expenses. If there is not enough cash in the estate to cover these costs, assets may have to be sold or liquidated, often at less than fair market value. Life insurance, however, can provide that needed cash, and it is available at precisely the time it will be most needed. In planning to meet the liquidity need, no other vehicle is better than life insurance.

In some cases, a second-to-die policy may be in order. These policies are designed to cover two lives and pay a benefit at the death of the second individual. Such policies are especially useful for married couples who have accumulated substantial estates and who plan to take advantage of the unlimited marital deduction to pass the estate, untaxed, to the surviving spouse at the first spouse's death. It is at the second spouse's death that a large amount of insurance will be needed to provide estate liquidity to pay final expenses and taxes so that property and assets can be passed on intact to heirs.

From this discussion, it is apparent that life insurance plays an important role in retirement planning. It can be used as an accumulation vehicle, a way to distribute retirement income, a means to assist in the orderly transition of a business interest and a way to provide an estate with needed liquidity at an owner's death. But retirement planning professionals have another tool that can play a significant part in helping individuals meet their retirement needs and objectives—the annuity.

THE ROLE OF THE ANNUITY IN RETIREMENT PLANNING

Key Point   Annuities offer structured payments over a lifetime or a specific term of years.

Key Point   Annuities offer a tax-deferred way to accumulate assets.

Annuities, because they accumulate funds on a tax-deferred basis and can guarantee an income flow for life, are also excellent retirement planning tools. From a purely financial perspective, an annuity is simply an arrangement whereby one party makes regular periodic payments to another in exchange for property or a lump sum of cash (which is the basis for the periodic payments).

Financial institutions (primarily life insurance companies) have taken the concept one step further by adding an extra feature—lifetime-guaranteed payments. This insurance protection (annuitants are insured against the risk of outliving their income) explains why those who sell annuities must hold a life insurance license [and in the case of variable annuities, a Financial Industry Regulatory Authority (FINRA) Series 6 or 7 registration].

Annuities have no tax-free features, but they do enjoy tax-deferred gain. This makes deferred annuities (contracts that include an accumulation period as well as a payout period) popular for retirement savings, especially in personal, nonqualified savings plans where there are no tax deductions. Couple this tax feature with the product's ability to provide a lifetime income stream, and it's easy to understand why annuities are so popular.

A Mirror Image of Life Insurance

An annuity is a regular, periodic payment for life or another defined period. It begins with a lump sum of money that is deposited, earns interest over time, and is paid out over time. Annuities are issued primarily by life insurance companies for the simple reason that they involve the same basic factors as life insurance—life expectancy, interest, and expenses. They may not possess insurance qualities that are as obvious as those of life insurance, but the guarantee that payments will continue for life is insurance in its own right—insurance against the risk of outliving one's income.

It can be said that an annuity is a mirror image of life insurance. While both are founded on many of the same actuarial principles, they actually serve opposite purposes. While the principal function of life insurance is to create an estate (an estate being a sum of money) by the periodic payment of money into a contract, an annuity's principal function is to liquidate an estate by the periodic payment of money out of a contract.

Though annuities can be structured to provide benefit payments over any length of time, most are arranged to generate payments over a lifetime. For retirement planning purposes, the advantage of a structured, guaranteed life income is obvious and is perhaps the primary reason annuities are so popular. Many individuals, especially those in retirement, may be reluctant to use the principal of their savings, fearing it may become depleted. However, if they choose to conserve the principal, they run the risk of never deriving any benefit from it at all and ultimately are obliged to pass it on to others at their deaths. An annuity is designed to liquidate principal, but in a structured, systematic way that can guarantee it will last a lifetime.

Besides guaranteeing a lifetime income, annuities make excellent retirement planning products for many other reasons. As accumulation vehicles, they offer safety of principal (except for variable annuities, which may or may not include a guaranteed minimum provision), tax deferral, competitive yields, and liquidity. (Though deferred annuities are considered liquid assets, there may be serious tax consequences and penalties resulting from the withdrawal of funds from a deferred annuity, especially before age 59½.)

As distribution vehicles, they offer a variety of payout options which can be structured to conform to certain payment amounts or certain payment periods. They can cover one life or two. They can be arranged so that a beneficiary will receive a benefit if the annuitant dies before receiving the full annuity principal. Like life insurance, annuities offer the advantage of flexibility, which is important to retirement planning.

Product Variations

Annuities exist to match virtually any need and objective. Immediate annuities are funded with a single, lump-sum premium, and begin to generate periodic benefit payments immediately. Deferred annuities are characterized by an accumulation period, during which time the annuity fund grows tax-deferred for a payout at a future date. Deferred annuities can be funded with a single premium or through a series of periodic premiums over time.

If an annuity is fixed, the insurer guarantees that at least a minimum rate of return will be credited to the annuity funds and the contract holder's principal is assured. If it is a variable annuity, the premiums are invested in separate accounts and subaccounts and the annuity fund performs in relation to the underlying investments. With fixed annuities, the insurer assumes the investment risk; with variable annuities, the annuity owner assumes the investment risk.

Inevitably, an annuity combines two or more of the above features in its design. For example, an individual could purchase a single-premium fixed immediate annuity or a periodic premium variable deferred annuity. Basically, the variables are:

■ when annuity payments are scheduled to begin—immediate or deferred;

■ the method of funding the annuity—single premium or periodic premium; and

■ the underlying investment account that supports the annuity—fixed or variable.

By matching these variables to specific needs, financial professionals can create a product that exactly meets an individual's retirement planning objectives.

Deferred Annuities

When the object is to accumulate retirement funds, the deferred annuity offers a number of advantages. These include funding flexibility, tax deferral, investment options, and liquidity.

The deferred annuity can be funded with a single-premium payment or periodically over time, with a series of premium payments. For single-premium payments, most insurers require a minimum deposit of $5,000 or more; for periodic premium payments, an initial deposit of $500 or $1,000 may be required, but the annuity owner can then make future payments of as little as $25 or $50, as often as he wants. (Unlike life insurance, annuities do not have any pure insurance at risk to the insurer, which explains why insurers are more lax when it comes to making premium payments.)

Another advantage of a deferred annuity—one that is very important in retirement planning—is that the accumulating funds grow within the annuity on a tax-deferred basis. Tax deferral gives the annuity an edge over other products such as CDs or taxable bonds.

A CD that earns 5% will actually yield 3.8% to an individual in the 24% tax bracket. If that same individual purchases an annuity crediting 5%, he would actually realize a 5% return because of tax deferral. The combination of tax-deferred growth and interest earnings on the fund compounded over the deferral or accumulation period can generate significant retirement funds.

EXAMPLE

Assume John, age 50, deposits $50,000 in a certificate of deposit with his local savings and loan. Jane, also age 50, purchases a $50,000 single-premium deferred annuity from ABC Life. Both earn a 5% rate of return. However, because the earnings on the CD are taxed every year, John has fewer funds available for continued growth and compounding than does Jane with her annuity. For the sake of simplicity, say that both the CD and the annuity earn a constant 5% compounded annually over a 15-year period and both John and Jane are in the 24% tax bracket. The result, when John and Jane are ready to retire at age 65, is a fund of $87,484 in the CD and $103,946 in the annuity. The difference is attributed to tax deferral.

Investment Options

Annuities can address different investment objectives. Clients who desire investment control and true investment opportunities would probably be more interested in a variable annuity. Those who seek guaranteed returns and guarantee of principal might feel more secure with a traditional fixed annuity. An equity-indexed annuity is another option. Though it provides for a guaranteed minimum rate of return, its owner is given the opportunity to earn interest at a rate tied to an external index, usually a stock market index. The decision should be based on an individual's objectives and his risk tolerance.

Fixed Annuities

With a traditional fixed deferred annuity, the insurer guarantees that a certain initial interest rate will be credited to the annuity for a specified period of time, such as one, two, or three years. After that initial period, the annuity is renewed and a new interest rate is credited. It may be higher or lower than the initial rate and can never be lower than the guaranteed minimum rate, but it, too, may be guaranteed for a specific period of time. By guaranteeing the interest rate, the insurer absorbs the investment risk with a fixed annuity.

Variable Annuities

Variable annuities shift the investment risk from the insurer to the annuity owner. Variable annuity premium payments are directed into nonguaranteed investments, such as stock, bond, or money-market funds, and the value of the annuity fluctuates in response to how well or how poorly its underlying investments perform. If these investments do well, the annuity owner will likely realize growth that exceeds what a fixed annuity would offer.

On the other hand, the lack of guarantee leaves the owner open to the ups and downs of the market inherent in investment risk. The theory behind variable annuities, which has generally held true over the years, is that by earning market returns they are able to outdistance or at least keep pace with inflation. Like variable life and variable universal life, variable annuities are considered securities because of the investment risk they hold for the consumer.

Equity-Indexed Annuities

An alternative to variable annuities and traditional fixed annuities is the equity-indexed annuity. Though a fairly recent product innovation, the **fixed-indexed annuity** (indexed annuity) has become quite popular. With an indexed annuity, the interest credited to the contract is tied to an independent external market index, such as the S&P 500. As the index moves up or down reflecting the performance of the securities it comprises, the indexed annuity's interest crediting methodology will apply a specified portion of the index's return to the contract.

Underlying the indexed annuity contract for its life—generally, a term of five to seven years—is a guaranteed minimum return (typically 2% or 3%), so the contract holder does not risk loss of principal, even if the index declines over the contract's term. There are many indexed annuity product variations and many ways in which these products work to convert the index performance into interest credit. As retirement planning vehicles, they present yet another choice for today's annuity buyers.

Liquidity

Despite what many people think, the deferred annuity offers a number of liquidity options for those who need access to their funds before retirement. Because most annuities carry some kind of surrender charge (a charge assessed by the insurer for early fund withdrawals or contract surrenders), many people believe that once they purchase an annuity, their funds are out of reach until they retire or the product is annuitized. In fact, surrender charges for most annuities are of limited duration, applying only during the first five to 15 years of the contract. Secondly, for those years in which surrender charges are applicable, most annuities provide for an annual free withdrawal, which allows the annuity owner to withdraw up to a certain percentage of his annuity account each year with no surrender charge.

As our discussion shows, annuities are ideal for accumulating retirement funds, offering many advantages not available with other investments. But they can also serve to create an income flow during retirement through any number of payment or distribution options. In this way, they can address another important retirement need.

Payout Options

Annuities can be used to generate and maintain an income stream during retirement for as long as the annuity owner desires. For this need, there are two options: purchasing an immediate annuity or annuitizing a deferred annuity.

An immediate annuity provides a way to convert an existing sum of money into an income stream very shortly after it is purchased. Most immediate annuities begin generating income payments within a month of purchase; as such, they should be viewed solely as distribution products, not accumulation products. The distribution period is the time during which benefits are drawn from the annuity fund and paid to the annuitant. Deferred annuities can be annuitized and converted from an accumulation mode to a distribution mode.

The payout options are the same for both immediate and deferred annuities. The choice of option will affect the size and amount of the individual benefit payments. These options include:

■ straight life;

■ life with guaranteed refund;

■ life with period certain;

■ joint and survivor; and

■ period certain.

Straight Life Annuity

A straight life annuity pays the annuitant a guaranteed amount of income for life. When an annuitant dies, no further payments are made to anyone. If death occurs before the annuitant receives the return of her full principal, it is forfeited. On the other hand, if the annuitant lives beyond the point at which the principal has been paid out, payments will continue as long as she lives.

Life With Guaranteed Refund Annuity

For those who do not want to risk the loss of principal in the event of the annuitant's early death, a life with refund option may be more attractive. This option offers two guarantees—the annuitant will receive benefit payments as long as he lives and, in the event the annuitant dies before receiving all of the annuity's principal, payment of the balance will be made to the annuitant's beneficiary. This refund of principal can be in the form of a lump-sum cash payment or as continued annuity installment payments until the principal is repaid. In either event, the beneficiary receives an amount equal to the original annuity sum less the amount already paid to the annuitant.

Life With Period Certain Annuity

A life with period certain annuity option provides income payments to the annuitant for life but guarantees the payments for a specific number of years if the annuitant dies earlier. For example, a life with 10-year certain option would make payments to the annuitant for life and guarantee payments for 10 years. If the annuitant dies before 10 years, payments continue to a beneficiary for the remainder of the 10 years. If the annuitant dies after the 10-year period, no more payments are made.

Joint and Survivor Annuity

Joint and survivor annuities are popular because they cover two lives and there are many variations. A joint and 100% survivor annuity makes benefit payments to two people and, at the death of the first, continues the same payments to the survivor until death. A joint and 75%, 66.67% or 50% survivor annuity would pay a joint income to two annuitants and, when the first dies, would pay a reduced income to the survivor.

Period Certain Annuity

Finally, there is the period certain annuity. This option is not based on life contingency; instead, it guarantees benefit payments for a certain period of time, such as 10, 15, or 20 years, whether or not the annuitant is living. At the end of the specified term, payments cease.

Which Option to Choose?

The choice of the best payout option depends, of course, on the annuity owner's needs and objectives. For any given annuity fund, the more guarantees the option offers, the less each benefit payment will be.

EXAMPLE

If Carl, age 60, purchased a $100,000 immediate fixed annuity and chose a straight life payout option, his monthly payments would be about $500. If he chose a life with 10-year period certain option, the payouts would be approximately $490. A joint and 100% survivor option, covering his wife, also age 60, would generate about $375 a month. (In the case of joint and survivor options, the age of the joint annuitant plays as direct a role in the income amount, as does the primary annuitant's age.)

A structured and fixed payout that guarantees a steady income stream for as long as the annuity owner desires can undoubtedly bring peace of mind to many retirees. However, a fixed income is subject to erosion due to inflation. As we have seen, even low inflation levels will significantly reduce the purchasing power of a fixed-income stream over a number of years. For this reason, the variable annuity and its potential for higher annuity payouts may be appealing to some people. Let's take a few moments to consider how the structure of a variable annuity payout differs from that of a fixed annuity and also explore its advantages.

Variable Annuity Benefits

As explained earlier, the value of a variable annuity fluctuates in response to its underlying investments. This is also true after the contract has annuitized and income payments are being made to the annuitant. The amount of each benefit payment will vary, depending on how the contract's investments perform. Because of this, a different method to account for variable annuity premiums and variable annuity benefit payments, involving accumulation units and annuity units, is employed.

During a variable annuity's accumulation or deferral period, premium payments are converted to accumulation units and are credited to the annuity. The value of each unit varies, depending on the value of the underlying investment.

EXAMPLE

If an accumulation unit is initially valued at $15 and the annuity owner makes a $150 premium contribution, he will acquire 10 accumulation units. Six months later, the annuity owner makes another $150 premium payment, but during that time the underlying investments have declined and the value of the accumulation unit is $10. This means the $150 payment will now purchase 15 accumulation units. At any point in time, the value of a deferred variable annuity is equal to the sum of its accumulation units multiplied by the unit value at that moment.

When the time comes to annuitize a variable deferred annuity (i.e., convert it to payout status), the accumulation units are converted into annuity units. This annuity unit calculation is made at the time of annuitization and, from then on, the number of annuity units remains fixed The value of a unit, however, can and does vary from month to month, depending on investment results.

Our annuitant has 1,000 accumulation units in her account when she retires, and these accumulation units have been converted into 10 annuity units per payment. She will always be credited with 10 annuity units; that number does not change. What does change is the value of the annuity units, in response to the underlying funds. Assume that when she retired, each annuity unit was valued at $45. That means her initial benefit payment was $450 (10 × $45). Now assume that for the next three months, the value of an annuity unit was $47.50, $48, and $43.25. The annuitant would receive monthly payments of $475, $480, and $432.50, respectively.

Again, the principle behind the variable annuity and its benefit payment structure is that over a period of years, the benefits will keep pace with the cost of living and thus maintain their purchasing power at or above a constant level. From one month to the next, payments may go down just as easily as they rise, but the historical trend has been up. Like the fixed annuity, a variable annuity offers a variety of payout options, including a life annuity, a life annuity with period certain, a unit refund annuity (similar to a cash refund annuity), and a joint and survivor annuity.

Income Taxation of Annuity Benefits

Annuity benefit payments are a combination of principal and interest. Accordingly, they are taxed in a manner consistent with other types of income—the portion of the benefit payments that represent a return of the contract owner's investment in the contract or cost basis (i.e., premium contributions made by the annuity owner) are not taxed; the portion that represents interest earnings is taxed. The result over the benefit payment period is a tax-free return of the annuitant's investment and the taxing of the interest earnings on that investment.

The method used to determine the taxable and nontaxable portion of annuity benefits is known as the exclusion ratio. The formula is:

$$\frac{\text{investment in the contract}}{\text{expected return}} = \text{amount excluded from taxation}$$

The investment in the contract is the amount of premium contributed by the annuitant; the expected return is the total benefit amount the annuitant will receive. The resulting ratio is applied to the benefit payments to determine the amount of each payment that is not subject to tax.

EXAMPLE

Andy, age 60, invested $50,000 in an immediate fixed annuity and selects a straight life payout option that will provide him with $525 a month for life. Assume that his life expectancy is 15 years. To determine the nontaxable portion of his benefits, we would divide Andy's investment in the contract ($50,000) by the expected return ($525 a month × 15 years = $94,500). The result is 53%, which means that 53% of each $525 payment, or $278, would be considered a nontaxable return of principal, and $247 would be taxable as interest earnings. This exclusion amount would be in effect until the total investment in the contract ($50,000) was distributed tax-free in 15 years, at which point the full value of any and all remaining payments would be taxable income.

Taxation of Annuity Withdrawals and Surrenders

To balance the tax-deferred treatment given to annuities and to encourage their use as long-term retirement savings vehicles and not short-term investments, there are a number of restrictions imposed on the withdrawal of funds (or the surrender of the contract) before annuitization. When either withdrawals or surrenders take place, the money the contract holder receives is considered first a distribution of interest, fully taxable. Only after all credited interest earnings have been paid out will nontaxable principal be considered to be returned.

EXAMPLE

Louise, 40 years old, invested $35,000 in a single premium deferred annuity. Five years later, the contract is valued at $47,000 ($35,000 in principal and $12,000 in interest earnings). At that point, any amount Louise were to withdraw up to $12,000 would be considered 100% interest earnings and fully taxable. Amounts withdrawn above $12,000 would be considered a nontaxable return of principal. If she took a distribution of $25,000, $12,000 of it would be taxable; the remaining $13,000 would be received tax-free. Thus, you can see the difference between the tax treatment of pre-59½ withdrawals and annuitization. Under the former, all withdrawals are fully taxable until all interest earnings have been paid out; under the latter, each payment is only partially taxable until all principal has been paid out.

In addition, when withdrawals or surrenders take place before age 59½, a 10% penalty is imposed on the taxable portion of the money received. Using the example just listed, the $12,000 interest portion of the withdrawal Louise took at age 45 would be subject to a penalty tax of $1,200 in addition to the ordinary taxes owed. The penalty is waived if the withdrawal or surrender is taken due to death or disability or if the contract is annuitized over life.

1035 EXCHANGES

Key Point An individual may exchange life insurance for new life insurance or for an annuity tax free.

Key Point An individual may exchange an annuity for an annuity tax free, but exchanging an annuity for life insurance is taxable.

As this unit has shown, through life insurance and annuities, financial professionals are able to offer their prospects and clients some very important retirement planning products and strategies. However, no discussion of life insurance, annuities, or retirement planning would be complete without mentioning a method by which an insurance plan or an annuity can be exchanged for another annuity plan on a tax-favored basis. This is a 1035 exchange.

Generally speaking, when an individual realizes a gain on an investment, that gain is taxed. For example, an individual who surrenders a life insurance policy after a number of years for its cash value will realize a gain to the extent that the cash value exceeds the premiums paid. That gain is considered ordinary income and will be fully taxed.

However, through Section 1035 of the Internal Revenue Code, certain kinds of policies and annuity contracts can be exchanged without the gain being taxable. Specifically, IRC Section 1035 provides that no gain (or loss) will be recognized when:

■ a life insurance policy is exchanged for another life insurance policy, an endowment policy, or an annuity contract;

■ an endowment policy is exchanged for an annuity contract; or

■ an annuity contract is exchanged for another annuity contract.

Consequently, when an analysis of retirement needs points to the exchange of a life insurance policy for an annuity, this can be accomplished without incurring taxes. However, as is the case when replacing any kind of permanent insurance or annuity plan, financial professionals have a responsibility to initiate such a transaction only when it is in the best interest of the policyowner or annuitant. Also, there are specific steps that must be taken to properly complete a 1035 exchange. Though a detailed discussion of such steps is beyond the scope or intent of this book, they are something the financial professional should understand before undertaking such action.

ILLUSTRATION 2

Agent's Perspective

As we all know, replacing an insurance policy is a transaction fraught with all sorts of ethical implications and related red tape. We're not going to do it lightly. Honestly, a 57-year-old guy is not going to get the deal on insurance he got when he was 35.

But retirement planning has a broad scope. Retirement planners work with people, potentially, over a period of 50 years. Consider your clients. It would not be strange to have clients in their 30s and 80s. That covers many stages in life—from starting a family, to seeing the kids go off on their own, to retirement, and more. These changes require different financial solutions.

It would be a disservice to clients if, for instance, you did not consider replacing a life insurance policy with an annuity when they have reached a stage in life when a steady income is more important than insurance protection. And that's just one example. It is all a question of meeting clients' needs in the most efficient way possible.

WRAP-UP

Life insurance is a key element in any well-formulated retirement plan. Although its primary purpose may be to provide a financial safety net for dependent family members at the premature death of the insured, it can also be used to fund retirement. A variety of policies is available, each with its own premium payment, death protection, and cash build-up structure. In addition, annuities can be used to protect against the possibility that retirees will outlive their income.

FIELD EXERCISE

- Review your client files. Make two lists: List #1 is the names of your clients who have purchased term insurance only; List #2 names your clients who have purchased permanent insurance.

- For List #1 clients, can you determine from your records what financial products they are using to accumulate retirement funds? Do you believe the projected accumulation to be adequate for their retirement needs.

- For List #2, can you determine from your records what other financial products they are using to accumulate retirement funds? Are they doubling up (over-accumulating)? Alternatively, are they impairing the accumulation by taking excessive policy loans? Can you recommend for these clients a different approach to liquidity?

UNIT TEST

1. All of these life insurance policies are characterized by a cash value EXCEPT
   A. life paid up at 60
   B. 30-year term
   C. variable universal life
   D. variable life

2. The primary reason life insurance should be purchased is for
   A. accumulation
   B. tax avoidance
   C. death protection
   D. current income

3. Which of these is indicative of the primary difference between variable life insurance and straight whole life insurance?
   A. Amount of insurance that can be issued
   B. Cost of the insurance
   C. Tax treatment of the death proceeds
   D. Way in which the cash values are invested

4. Larry purchased a deferred annuity and at age 65, annuitized the product under a life with 15-year certain option. His wife, Linda, is the beneficiary. Which of the following statements is CORRECT?
   A. Payments would be made to Larry until he is 80 and then cease.
   B. Payments would be made to Larry until he is 80 and then to his wife for the remainder of her life.
   C. Payments would be made to Larry until his death and then to his wife for another 15 years.
   D. Payments would be made to Larry as long as he lives.

5. Under a variable life policy, the death benefit is equal to
   A. the sum of premiums paid, plus interest
   B. the guaranteed minimum death benefit plus the cash value
   C. the guaranteed maximum death benefit minus the cash value
   D. the guaranteed minimum death benefit plus possible adjustments based on investment performances

6. Which of the following elections for the distribution of a plan participant's pension benefit would produce the largest monthly income payments?
   A. Joint and half survivor
   B. Joint and full survivor
   C. Single life
   D. Joint and 2/3 survivor

7. At the age of 60, Muriel invested $100,000 in a straight life, immediate fixed annuity, which generates $800 a month in income. Her life expectancy is 24 years. How much of her annual annuity income is subject to tax?
   A. $4,166
   B. $6,000
   C. $1,833
   D. $0

8. Section 1035 of the Internal Revenue Code
   A. provides for tax-exempt treatment of annuity benefits
   B. allows life insurance surrenders before the age of 59½ without penalty
   C. allows for the tax-free exchange of an annuity contract for a life insurance policy
   D. provides for the tax-free exchange of a life insurance policy for an annuity contract

ANSWERS AND RATIONALES

1. **B.** Term insurance only has a death benefit. It does not have a cash value like the different varieties of permanent or whole life insurance.

2. **C.** Life insurance should not be sold as an investment, though it has investment features. It should be sold for death protection.

3. **D.** Variable life insurance allows the policyowner to decide how the cash value is invested through a number of subaccounts.

4. **D.** Larry selected the life with 15-year certain option. This pays Larry for his life, regardless of how long, but pays his beneficiary if he dies before the end of 15 years. That is the 15-year certain part.

5. **D.** Although the cash value in a variable life policy can fluctuate based on the performance of the subaccounts, there is a guaranteed minimum death benefit.

6. **C.** Benefits that are paid over more than one life will be smaller than benefits paid over one life.

7. **A.** Muriel's annual annuity income is $6,000. This must be multiplied by the exclusion ratio, which is the $100,000 investment in the contract divided by the $144,000 expected return ($6,000 per year times the 24-year life expectancy). This gives an annual exclusion of $1,836. The balance of $4,166 is subject to tax each year.

8. **D.** Section 1035 allows an individual to trade a life insurance policy for an annuity tax free. It also allows trades of life insurance for life insurance or annuities for annuities. Trades of annuities for life insurance, however, are not tax free.

6

Product Review II: Investment Products

Life insurance and annuities provide guaranteed financial protection and are effective ways to safely accumulate funds for the future and provide a means to systematically distribute income during retirement. But these products are founded on insurance principles, and as such, they carry certain costs that are not present with other noninsurance types of investment products. Furthermore, fixed insurance and annuity products are invested conservatively to preserve their principal and earn a minimum rate of return. On their own, they cannot offer a well-balanced approach to retirement planning. A plan should also include products and investments that address other financial objectives, such as capital growth and accumulation. ■

UNIT OBJECTIVES

In this unit, we consider investment products that should figure prominently in most retirement plans. We will examine investment options and explain the factors that can affect their investment performance. We will discuss the concept of risk and the effect it has on specific investments, which must be accounted for in any kind of financial plan. We will look at different investment objectives, such as growth, income, and liquidity, and discuss how a diversified approach to investing and saving can achieve them all.

On completion of this unit, you should be able to:

- analyze an individual's investment needs for both the short and long term;

- explain the concept of investment risk and how the level of risk relates to the types of returns an investor can expect from different types of investments; and

- discuss the characteristics of stocks, bonds, and mutual funds, and the place those investment types would have in an individual's portfolio.

INVESTMENT BASICS

Key Point An individual needs insurance protection (life, health, property, liability) and an emergency fund before saving for retirement.

Key Point A key factor in determining an investment strategy is the investment horizon—the length of time before the funds will be needed.

A sound retirement plan requires understanding and applying basic investment strategies that would be employed for any successful investment or savings plan. This would include, for example:

- setting a specific goal and measuring how far away that goal is, in terms of both time and money;

- understanding the relationship between risk and return;

- having a basic knowledge of the various types of investment products and what factors affect their performance;

- assessing investment choices and strategies in relation to one's goals, not in terms of what is happening today in the market; and

- diversifying invested assets with a number of different products that have different risk and return potential.

A retirement income needs analysis establishes a specific goal and defines it in terms of what will be needed (money) and when and for how long it will be needed (time). The way in which the goal is achieved is through a planned, methodical approach to saving and investing through a variety of financial products. There is no one right investment plan; what is appropriate depends on the individual's specific dollar needs, the amount of money and time available for investing, and the tolerance for risk in its various forms.

Insurance Should Be in Place First

Most experts recommend that their clients address certain needs before beginning a long-term investment program. First, they should cover their need for financial protection—a program of life insurance, health insurance (including adequate disability coverage), and property and liability insurance should be in place to assure that savings and investments are not derailed due to premature death, sickness, or large property losses. After all, what good is an investment program if an individual's death would mean liquidating savings to meet the current financial needs of surviving dependents?

Once a shield of insurance protection is in place, individuals should set up an emergency fund or short-term savings fund for money that can be obtained quickly and easily in case of immediate need. A standard rule of thumb recommends that six months of after-tax income be set aside in safe, fairly liquid instruments—insured passbook savings, money market accounts and short-term CDs are appropriate investment products for this purpose.

Once a foundation of income and property protection is in place and an emergency fund has been established, an individual can look to investing seriously for her retirement.

Investment Defined

In the broadest sense, an investment is any financial instrument into which funds can be placed with the expectation that they will be preserved, increase in value, or generate some return. Cash stored in a mattress is not an investment because it fails to earn interest and its value will be eroded by inflation. The same cash placed in a savings account becomes an investment because it earns interest over time.

Investment Horizons

As people progress through life, they pass through different financial need phases. Certainly retirement is a need that most everyone should consider—and the younger one begins a retirement plan, the better—but on a financial time line, retirement may be a distant point. Young adults, to the extent they save at all, are naturally inclined to list saving for a home high on the priority list, almost certainly higher than saving for retirement.

They compare the near investment horizon of a house down payment with the long-distance investment horizon of retirement and conclude that retirement savings can wait. Investment horizons are points in the future when a financial need is expected to materialize or a goal is to be met; they mark how much time one has to accumulate or otherwise obtain the resources to meet the need.

For any goal, investment horizons play a central role in helping determine appropriate types of financial products. For example, long-term horizons permit more aggressive investment selections because there is enough time to ride out any downturns in the market. The time value of money and the power of compound growth combine to favor investors who start early.

As the time to the goal grows shorter, a more moderate position may be called for as the need for preservation of assets begins to override the need for growth. With an investment horizon less than eight years, safety of principal may become a dominant objective; therefore, a portion of one's assets are shifted from vehicles that offer the potential for growth into those that provide for preservation of principal.

As individuals' investment horizons change, so too should their investment portfolios. Through the time-tested investment strategies of diversification and asset allocation, investments are shifted into different types of assets or different classes of investments, the selection of which is based on the individual's goals, investment horizon, and risk tolerance.

Through an asset allocation plan, assets are selectively invested into low-risk investments (insured savings accounts, CDs, life insurance, fixed annuities), moderate-risk investments (quality stocks, bonds, and some mutual funds) and aggressive investments (small cap stocks, high yield bonds, and some more aggressive mutual funds). Speculative investments—commodities, precious metals, and collectibles—are usually not recommended for anyone's retirement plan because of the inordinately high risk of loss. But not all risks are the same. Risk has various meanings, and an investment that is regarded as a low risk in one area may represent a high risk in another.

UNDERSTANDING RISK

Key Point Investors looking for high return investments must generally accept high risk of loss.

Key Point Investors looking for low risk of loss must generally accept low returns.

Fundamental to investing and the creation of a sound retirement plan is an understanding of risk and its relation to an investment's return. Most investments yield some sort of return, which can be broadly defined as the (pretax) total return on an investment, expressed as an annual percentage of the investor's original capital. If $1,000 is invested today and one year later it is worth $1,100, the return on that investment is 10%.

Risk is the potential of an investment's actual returns to differ from those expected; it is the degree of uncertainty associated with the expected return. There is a trade-off between the return an investor can expect on an investment and the amount of risk he must assume to earn that return. The greater an investment's potential return, the greater the risk the investor must assume.

When most people think of risk, they associate it with the likelihood of an investment rising or falling in value. This is, indeed, a form of risk known as market risk. But there are many other types of risk that, to one degree or another, are associated with almost every form of investment. A retirement plan that is to include different types of investments must account for risk in its mix of products.

The forms of risk an investor should understand are:

- market risk;

- inflation risk;

- interest rate risk;

- business risk; and

- liquidity risk.

Market Risk

The value of security-type investments (stocks, bonds, and mutual funds, for example) is determined largely by their perceived value by the investors—the market—among whom they are traded. And there is a tendency for security prices (of the same type) to move together—in bull markets, prices of individual securities tend to rise with the market and in bear markets, prices of individual securities tend to fall. This happens regardless of the issuer's financial condition. Thus, market risk is the potential for a security to fluctuate in value due to its inherent tendency to move together with all securities of the same type.

There are a host of reasons why the market fluctuates—social, political, and economic conditions all contribute to the way the market performs. Unrest overseas, for example, may adversely affect the market as a whole, which could cause a fall in the price of stocks in general, which then might bring down the value of the stock of a particular company. This could happen even though that company's prospects for growth and sales are bright.

Inflation Risk

Inflation, which is the general rise in prices during a period of time, tends to reduce purchasing power. Inflation risk is the possibility that the return on an investment will be undermined or eroded by increasing prices; the dollars invested today will purchase less in the future. If inflation is at 3%, an 8% return on an investment will net the investor only 5%. Some investments are more susceptible to inflation risk than others; fixed-rate products such as annuities and CDs have, as a whole, greater exposure to inflation risk than stocks. Historically, equity investments have provided the best hedge against inflation.

Interest Rate Risk

Interest rate risk is associated with the sensitivity of an investment's value to fluctuations in the economy's overall interest rates. Though this risk can affect all kinds of investments, it is typically associated with fixed-income investments such as bonds and preferred stocks. As interest rates rise, the value of bonds drops; as interest rates decline, the value of bonds increases.

Bonds are issued with a fixed rate of return, payable for their duration. Assume that a $1,000 corporate bond is issued that matures in 20 years and pays a 6% rate. That rate was likely competitive when the bond was issued, reflecting the interest rate environment at that time. However, if interest rates since then have increased and newly issued bonds are paying 8%, then the market value of the 6% bond falls because people can purchase higher-yielding bonds. As a result, the 6% bond must be sold for less than $1,000 or held to maturity.

Business Risk

Business risk is the specific risk associated with the underlying business of the particular investment. It is the risk that some event or circumstance affecting the issuer will result in the business performing worse than expected and thus affect the investment's return. Bad or good business decisions or a competitor entering or leaving the market could have an impact on the business, which in turn, would affect the value of its stock or issue.

Liquidity Risk

Liquidity refers to the ease and quickness with which an investment can be sold or otherwise turned into cash at its current value. Different products face different forms or degrees of liquidity risk. Demand deposits in banks have the least liquidity risk, followed closely by money market fund investments. Certificates of deposit can easily be turned into cash; however, if they are cashed in before they have matured, there may be a loss-of-interest penalty. Stocks of publicly traded companies are fairly liquid—the stock can be easily sold on an exchange at the current market value. Other types of investments—real estate, for example—may not be easily liquidated at all.

Investment Pyramid

The risk and return relationship of investment products is often illustrated as a pyramid. The base of the pyramid houses products that are characterized by little risk and comparatively low rates of return. As we move up the pyramid, the products grow riskier but have the potential for greater returns.

The idea behind the pyramid is that a personal financial and investment plan should be developed according to similar proportions. Beginning with a base of financially sound and safe products, the plan then expands to incorporate various types of investments, with varying degrees of risk and return potential. Using the pyramid concept as a guide, a diversified investment portfolio emerges, which spreads risk by mixing invested assets among different types of investments. Let's look at each section of the pyramid in terms of the products' risk, return, and liquidity.

ILLUSTRATION 1

The Investment Pyramid

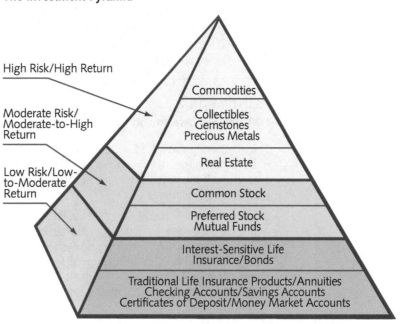

LOW RISK/LOW-TO-MODERATE RETURN

Key Point   Low-risk, low-return investments include passbook savings, money market accounts, traditional life insurance, fixed annuities, and bonds.

At the base of the pyramid are conservative investments that are characterized by low market risk, low-to-moderate returns, and liquidity. These investments—insured savings, checking and money market accounts, certificates of deposit, Treasury bills, traditional life insurance, and fixed annuities—form the base of any sound investment plan. Funds are readily accessible and principal is very safe, if not guaranteed. Low-risk, low-to-moderate return investments include the following:

- Saving accounts

- Money market deposit accounts

- Certificates of deposit

- Treasury bills

- Traditional life insurance

- Fixed deferred annuities

- Money market mutual funds

- Bonds

Savings Accounts

For many, the savings account at a local bank was their introduction to formal saving. Highly liquid with principal backed by the federal government (through the Federal Deposit Insurance Corporation, or FDIC) and dependable, though very conservative, interest rates, these instruments are ideal for keeping cash for emergencies and short-term savings goals.

ILLUSTRATION 2

FDIC-Insured Investments

The FDIC was established in 1933 to insure bank deposits and protect the assets of bank depositors. As expensive as it is for the federal government to provide this protection, it has created stability in the banking system that in turn has allowed the economy to prosper.

Under current law, the FDIC insures each individual's account up to $250,000. An individual may have an account in his name, an account in a spouse's name, and a joint account in both their names; each is separately insured up to $250,000 for a total of $750,000. The protection of federal deposit insurance does not extend beyond this limit; therefore, individuals should be cautioned against retaining more than $250,000 in one account at a time. It should be spread among various accounts at various banks.

Money Market Deposit Accounts

Banks and other financial institutions also offer money market deposit accounts, a combination of savings and checking accounts. A sound savings base can be built with these accounts. They offer unregulated money market rates, may require a minimum deposit and permit only limited withdrawals so funds in the account cannot easily be depleted. Funds are federally insured (within certain limits) and may be accessed through automated teller machines (ATMs).

Certificates of Deposit

The certificate of deposit (CD) was designed with safety of principal in mind. CDs are federally insured, redeemable debt obligations issued by banks and other depository institutions. Money is effectively frozen and must be left in the account for a specified period of time or interest will be forfeited. In return for this longer commitment (and reduction of liquidity), rates are generally higher with CDs than with passbook savings accounts.

Treasury Bills

Treasury bills, or T-bills, are short-term obligations of the U.S. government that mature in one year or less. Because they are backed by the full faith and credit of the federal government, they are the safest investment that can be made.

Traditional Life Insurance

Life insurance in any form is not an investment per se and should be purchased only if there is a need for protection. Once the decision has been made to own life insurance, the purchaser should consider the additional benefits offered by a permanent plan, a product that accumulates cash values, which in time can rival the growth of a number of other investment products. This is possible due to the fact that no taxes are imposed, so the interest credited to the values, though modest, steadily compounds. The risk that life insurance owners face is that the company that issued the contract may default. As long as the issuing company is financially sound, there is very little risk associated with owning a life insurance policy.

Fixed Deferred Annuities

Fixed deferred annuities are based on long-term contractual guarantees that require conservative returns. Most fixed-rate annuity contracts sold today provide for an interest rate that is declared in advance upon each contract anniversary and is guaranteed payable for the next year. Underlying the contract for its life is a guaranteed minimum rate; the rate declared annually is never lower than the minimum. The interest credited to an annuity contract is tax deferred, which leverages the otherwise modest interest return paid by most contracts.

A fixed indexed annuity provides an additional option for fixed-annuity buyers. The interest rate credited to an indexed annuity is tied to an external index like the S&P 500. The interest credited to the indexed annuity is linked to the performance of the index. However, a fixed indexed annuity guarantees against loss of principal because like a traditional deferred annuity, the contract provides for a minimum rate of return over the life of the contract.

Though very safe investments (the main risk is the financial security of the issuing company), fixed annuities are not designed for short-term investment goals. A contract that is cashed in before a certain number of years (it varies by contract) would be subject to surrender charges assessed by the insurer. Furthermore, if cashed in before the owner is 59½, there could be adverse tax consequences.

Money Market Mutual Funds

Money market mutual funds, sponsored by nonbank financial institutions, offer small investors attractive yields on short-term, highly liquid securities. These funds pool the resources of many investors to purchase short-term securities issued by the U.S. Treasury, large commercial banks, and financially strong corporations. Although not federally insured, these investments are considered very safe.

Bonds

A bond is a debt obligation (usually long-term) in which the borrower promises to pay a set interest return until the issue matures, at which time the principal is repaid. These investments include corporate bonds and government bonds (including Series EE savings bonds and Treasury bonds). Bonds are fairly illiquid and are normally purchased for modest interest income.

Corporate bonds are offered to raise money for a company's growth. Usually sold in $1,000 units, corporate bonds carry varying degrees of risk and interest. Typically, investors receive a fixed-interest payment twice a year, except for bonds like Series EE bonds which earn compound interest and accumulate. Bonds are discussed further later in this unit.

MODERATE RISK/MODERATE-TO-HIGH RETURN

Key Point   Moderate-risk, moderate-return investments include preferred and some common stocks and some mutual funds.

The middle section of the risk pyramid consists of investments that are purchased for growth, income, or speculation. With the foundation securely in place, this is money that can be exposed to more risk in return for the potential of greater returns. Depending on the investment product selected, there is modest risk/modest return to high risk and potentially high return.

For example, an investor may choose a blue-chip stock (safe and conservative), income stock (usually utility stock that pays higher than average dividends), or cyclical stock (speculative stock that follows business cycles).

Preferred Stock

Although any stock represents a share of corporate ownership, preferred stocks are shares whose stated dividends and par values must be paid before common shareholders receive any dividends or liquidation payments. The risk and income levels may range from moderate to high.

In general, preferred stock is fairly liquid; however, investors may not be able to sell their preferred stock when they want, at the price they want. When stock prices are falling, an investor may have to take a loss by selling below the original purchase price.

Mutual Funds

A mutual fund is a pooled investment in which professional managers buy and sell assets with the income, gains, and losses accruing to the mutual fund shareholders Mutual funds are diversified so that an occasional loss in one security is often offset by gains in other securities. Mutual funds range from long-term, conservative investments to highly speculative investments. They may be either load (with a sales charge) or no-load (with no sales charge) funds. Some funds impose a deferred sales charge (i.e., surrender charge) on monies withdrawn during a certain period of time after being paid in. In all cases, mutual funds stand ready to buy back their shares at their net asset value. Mutual funds are discussed further later in this unit.

Common Stock

Common stock represents proportional ownership of an incorporated enterprise. Stockholders share the possibility of a company's gain as well as its loss. Common stockholders are the residual claimants for earnings after all holders of debt and preferred stock have received their contractual payments. More information about investing in stocks, bonds, and mutual funds is found later in this unit.

HIGH RISK/HIGH RETURN

Key Point   High-risk, high-return investments include real estate, precious metals, and commodities.

The top of the risk pyramid includes speculative investments that might return large profits in short periods of time. However, there are no guarantees a profit will be made and there is a real danger that there will be no gain and the principal may be lost. In general, high-risk investments are not appropriate for retirement planning because the risk of losing everything usually outweighs the potential return.

Real Estate

Land is a limited resource, so real estate is often considered a good investment. Real estate includes raw acreage, vacation property, second homes, and apartment or office buildings, not all of which are wise investments.

Although it can be profitable for seasoned investors, investment property can create problems for the beginner. The value of the property may decrease because of changing economic conditions. Because managing rental property is time-consuming and difficult, a professional property manager may be needed. When the investor wishes to sell, the real estate market may be soft and the selling price may fluctuate widely, depending on economic conditions.

Precious Metals, Gemstones, and Collectibles

This category includes gold, silver, other precious metals, gemstones, and such collectibles as stamps, coins, fine art, and antiques. Assets listed in this section are tangible items that have substance and can be seen and touched. These items are acquired not only for their financial gain but for their intrinsic value. The value of the asset is relative and based, in part, on the tastes of the viewer.

Precious metals, gemstones, and collectibles produce no income. Such assets involve all of the risk inherent in traditional investments and, in addition, not very liquid, very speculative, and subject to fraud risk. Because of their high risk, these investments are not recommended for retirement planning. Furthermore, investors interested in these speculative investments should deal with only reputable dealers and investment firms.

Commodities

Investors can make relatively large profits in the commodities market. Commodities are a select group of items—cotton, silver, corn, pork bellies, and many others—traded on one of the commodity exchanges. Commodity contracts are traded in either the spot (for immediate delivery) or the futures market (for delivery at a prescribed future date).

Trading is quite risky and requires substantial expertise, time, and financial resources. The commodity's performance depends on weather conditions, government intervention, consumer attitudes, and a variety of other factors. Generally, commodities are not recommended as retirement investments because the potential for loss is great, they pay no interest, and tax advantages are limited.

A CLOSER LOOK AT STOCKS

Key Point Market risk makes stocks unsuitable for short-term investments but perfectly suitable for mid- to long-term investments.

Many of your clients, especially those with 10 years or more before retirement, will want to lean into the moderate risk/return investment range. Because stocks, bonds, and mutual funds are what usually come to mind at this level, it is important that retirement planners be familiar with these investment vehicles. The chance to pull in higher investment returns is especially attractive to mid-life investors who are starting to realize they have too few years to save all they should for a secure retirement. In the following sections, we will discuss the features, advantages, and disadvantages of each investment.

Equity Investments: Common and Preferred Stock

Stocks represent ownership in a company. Corporations issue units, or shares, of common and preferred stock to raise equity capital in order to grow and expand. Those who buy the stock actually acquire a share of the company, and the value of their shares will rise and fall with markets and with the company's fortunes. Both types of stock provide the opportunity for dividend income, appreciation of value.

A dividend is a dollar amount that a company pays its stockholders (usually quarterly) and which represents a portion of the corporation's earnings. Although the corporation's board of directors is under no legal obligation to pay dividends, most boards like to keep stockholders happy by declaring dividends in the form of cash or additional stock. Dividends represent actual profit earned by a company. (So important are dividends in many investors' plans that an announced drop in a dividend amount is likely to cause a company's stock value to fall.)

Changing economic conditions can cause the value of the stock to appreciate in value. If the market value of the stock increases, the stockholder may continue to hold the stock or sell it at the higher price (and thus realize a gain). The difference between the purchase price and selling price represents gain. Unlike dividends, which are cash disbursements, gain is unrealized until a share is sold, at which point the gain becomes realized.

Stock splits are also attractive to shareholders. For example, in a 2-for-1 stock split, two new shares of stock are exchanged for each old share. Stock splits are used when a company, believing the price of its stock is too high for many consumers, wants to enhance the stock's trading appeal by lowering its market price. While stock splits intrinsically have no value (because the value of each share decreases proportionately to the split), the potential for future gain is attractive. As each new (lower priced) share becomes suddenly more attractive to a larger market, the price may rise higher than it would have when it was twice as expensive before the split.

Equity Investments: Moderate- to Long-Term Investment Horizon

Their higher market risk factor makes equity investments generally unsuitable for short-term investment horizons. Clients who need a specific sum of money within five years or less are usually best advised to seek a safe, fixed-interest investment. But when the investment horizon is longer than 5 or 10 years, there is enough time to ride out the inevitable dips in asset value, and so equity investments may be more suitable. Stocks have, over the long term, significantly outperformed fixed-interest investments. For clients whose retirement investment horizon is still a decade or more away, equity investments should play a leading role in their savings program.

Advantages of Common Stock Ownership

Millions of people invest in common stock because it enables them to participate in the profits of a firm. Regardless of fluctuations in the market, stocks usually provide an attractive, competitive return over the long run. Therefore, common stocks can be the basis of a long-term wealth accumulation plan. Stocks can also provide a steady stream of retirement income from the dividends they provide.

Common stock ownership carries three primary rights or privileges.

- **Residual claim to income.** All funds not paid out to other classes of securities automatically belong to the common stockholder; the firm may then choose to pay these residual funds out in dividends or reinvest them for the benefit of common stockholders.

- **Voting privileges.** Because common stockholders are the ultimate owners of the firm, they are accorded the right to vote in the election of the board of directors and on other major issues.

- **Preemptive right to purchase new securities.** Through a procedure called a rights offering, common stockholders may have the privilege to purchase new shares somewhat below current market price.

Advantages of Preferred Stock Ownership

Most corporations that issue preferred stock do so to achieve a balance in their capital structure. It is a means of expanding the capital base of the firm without diluting the common stock ownership position or incurring contractual debt obligations.

Preferred stock has the following advantages.

■ **Cumulative dividends.** Some but not all preferred stock is cumulative. If dividends on cumulative preferred are not paid in any one year, they accumulate and must be paid in total before common stockholders can receive dividends.

■ **Conversion feature.** Some preferred stock may be convertible into a certain number of common shares.

■ **Cash dividends.** An investor in preferred stock receives cash dividends before common stockholders are paid. This is especially important when a corporation is experiencing financial problems and cannot pay dividends to both common and preferred stockholders.

Disadvantages of Stock Ownership

Stocks are subject to several types of risk that can affect their earnings and dividends, price appreciation, and rate of return. For example, foreign competition can affect a company's sales and profits and cause the value of its stock to fall. Because the performance of a stock is subject to outside forces, it may be difficult to determine the true value of a stock. Preferred stock is especially susceptible to inflation and high interest rates.

A CLOSER LOOK AT BONDS

Key Point Bonds are generally safer investments than stocks, but returns may be more moderate.

Bonds are competitive investments that have the potential for attractive returns. Many corporations along with state, local, and federal governments issue bonds to finance their operations. In general, bonds are safer than common stocks and usually pay a higher annual income. They are especially appealing to retired investors or pension funds that must plan for the retirement of its participants. Unlike stocks whose return varies based on market conditions, bonds provide a fixed return if they are held to maturity.

Corporate bonds are negotiable, long-term debt instruments that carry certain obligations on the part of the issuer. Bondholders have no ownership in the organization that issues the bond. In essence, bondholders are lending money to the issuer in return for its promise to return that money (with interest) at some point in the future.

Bond Basics

The bond agreement specifies the following basic terms.

- **Par value** (face value)—Initial value of the bond. Most corporate bonds are traded in $1,000 units.

- **Coupon rate**—Actual interest rate on the bond, usually payable in semi-annual installments. To the extent that interest rates in the market go above or below the coupon rate after the bond is issued, the market price of the bond will change from the par value.

- **Maturity date**—Final date on which repayment of the bond principal is due.

All bonds fall into two major classes: secured or unsecured debt. Bonds may be secured or collateralized by a lien on a specific asset such as equipment or other real property. Mortgage bonds are issued by corporations and secured by mortgages on properties owned by the issuing corporations. The bond itself is secured by a pledge of real property. An unsecured bond (one that is backed by the good faith and credit of the issuing company) is called a debenture.

Government and Municipal Bonds

Bonds are also issued by different levels of government. Like corporate bonds, they are basically IOUs of the issuing government agency. Common government bonds include the following:

- **Treasury bonds**—Issued to fund the needs of the U.S. government and backed by the full faith and credit of the U.S. government

- **Agency bonds**—Issued by organizations of the U.S. government such as the Resolution Funding Corporation (RFC) or the Tennessee Valley Authority (TVA)

- **Municipal bonds**—Issued by state, county, city, and other political subdivisions (most of these bonds are tax-exempt, so no federal income tax is payable on interest income)

How Bonds Are Retired

The method of repayment for bond issues may not necessarily call for a lump-sum disbursement at the maturity date. Although a bond may be retired in that way, bonds are more commonly retired in a number of other ways.

- **Serial payments**—The bonds are paid off in installments over the life of the issue.

- **Sinking fund provision**—Semiannual or annual contributions are made by the corporation into a fund administered by a trustee for the purpose of debt retirement. The trustee may hold the funds to refund the bonds when they mature, or the proceeds may be used in the market to purchase bonds from willing sellers.

■ **Conversion**—Debt may be converted into common stock, but there may be penalties for this conversion.

■ **Call feature**—A call provision allows the corporation to call in or force in the debt issue before maturity. A lottery system may be used to select among current bondholders in the event of a partial call.

The corporation will pay a premium over par value to redeem the debt. This option may be used when interest rates on new securities are considerably lower than on previously issued debt.

Series EE Savings Bonds

Series EE savings bonds, or U.S. savings bonds, have long been popular with long-term savers for their safety (they are backed by the U.S. government). These are nonmarketable securities that cannot be bought or sold in any manner other than directly from the U.S. Treasury Department or through their agents, including most banks. Since May 1995, savings bond interest rates have been totally variable; they are no longer issued with guaranteed rates.

Advantages of Investing in Bonds

Investors purchase bonds for interest income, possible increases in value, and repayment at maturity. The interest and principal payment are legally binding obligations and must be met regardless of the economic position of the issuing organization. Bond prices will fluctuate as the overall interest rates in the economy change. If overall interest rates rise, the market value of the bond will fall. Conversely, if interest rates fall, the market value of the bond will rise.

Disadvantages of Investing in Bonds

There are two major risks that bond investors face—default risk and interest rate risk. Default risk is the risk that a debt security's contractual interest or principal will not be paid when due. Interest rate risk is the risk that a rise in interest rates will take place, thereby reducing the market value of fixed-income securities such as bonds.

ILLUSTRATION 3

Bond Ratings

Standard & Poor's	Moody's	Interpretation
		Bank grade (investment-grade) bonds
AAA	AAA	Highest rating. Capacity to repay principal and interest judged high.
AA	Aa	Very strong. Only slightly less secure than the highest rating.
A	A	Judged to be slightly more susceptible to adverse economic conditions.
BBB	Baa	Adequate capacity to repay principal and interest. Slightly speculative.
		Speculative (noninvestment-grade) bonds
BB	Ba	Speculative. Significant chance that issuer could miss an interest payment.
B	B	Issuer has missed one or more interest or principal payments.
C	Caa	No interest is being paid on board at this time.
D	D	Issuer is in default. Payment of interest or principal is in arrears.

ILLUSTRATION 4

Features of Various Securities Issues

	Common Stock	Preferred Stock	Bonds
Ownership and control of the firm	Belongs to common stockholders through voting rights and residual claim to income	Limited rights, may include a participation feature	Possible limited rights under default in interest payments
Obligation to provide return	None	Must receive before common stockholder	Contractual obligation
Claim to assets in bankruptcy	Lowest claim of any security holder	Bondholders and creditors must be satisfied first	Highest claim
Risk-return trade-off	Higher risk, higher return	Moderate risk, moderate return (dollar amount of dividend is known before stock purchase)	Low risk, moderate return
Tax status of payment to recipient	Taxable as dividend in most cases	Taxable as dividend in most cases	Taxable as ordinary income in most cases

A CLOSER LOOK AT MUTUAL FUNDS

Key Point   Mutual funds offer investors reduced risk by diversification.

A mutual fund is an arrangement whereby a group of investors pool their money to buy (usually equity) investments, sharing proportionately in the assets' gains and losses. Of course, this simple definition hides the true size and complexity of most mutual funds, which can have many billions of dollars under management and provide a full range of administrative support services.

Assets held in the funds (which are technically called open-end investment companies, signifying that people can buy and sell shares at will) are selected and managed by professional investment advisors who base their decisions on the funds' investment objectives. By their very nature, mutual funds offer diversification, which provides a degree of safety for the investors.

Range of Investment Objectives

Mutual funds allow investors to choose from a wide variety of risk, liquidity, and tax-treatment alternatives. A diversified portfolio may contain only low-risk stocks or speculative stocks, taxable bonds, tax-exempt securities, short-term highly liquid securities, or a combination of these investment vehicles.

Every prospective investor must receive a fund's prospectus, which clearly spells out the fund's investment objectives.

Common investment objectives include the following.

- **Capital appreciation.** Objective is to build up investment capital through long-term growth.

- **Aggressive growth.** Objective is to target stocks that are poised for high growth.

- **Current income.** Objective is income, so the targets are bonds, preferred stock, and blue-chip stocks that have a solid history of paying dividends.

- **Balanced.** Objective is to balance capital gain and current income by a combination of stocks and bonds.

Advantages of Mutual Funds

In addition to a professionally managed and well-diversified portfolio, mutual funds also offer a variety of services that may be appealing to investors. In most cases, investors can automatically reinvest the fund's dividends in additional shares of the fund, withdraw money from one fund and invest it in another within the same family of funds, or switch funds into IRA accounts. Many funds can be acquired with limited capital, and additional shares can be purchased in small amounts.

Disadvantages of Mutual Funds

A major disadvantage of a mutual fund is its market risk. In addition, some mutual funds may be fairly expensive because of sizable sales commission (or load) charges. There are also annual operations charges for management and the professional services provided. Finally, the fund's performance reflects the performance of the market in general and may be substantially less than expected.

INVESTOR OBJECTIVES

Key Point   Investors should select investments that best match their objectives for four factors: safety, income, liquidity, and growth.

Millions of Americans will invest in some or all of the items listed on the risk pyramid. The investments they select should be determined by their objectives. Investors whose savings goals are short-term will put funds into investments that are easy to liquidate and whose liquidation would cause no adverse tax consequences. When people are saving for the future, however, they may choose to invest in order to take advantage of growth opportunities in some higher risk, higher return investments.

Trade-Off Between Return and Risk

Although most investors would like to earn the highest possible return, many people are risk-averse. They may take an occasional risk if they feel the potential return is worth it. For example, these people may be comfortable betting $1 in a state lottery with a potential return of $20 million. In general, however, they avoid higher risk investments and are willing to accept lower returns. These investors often invest their funds in bank savings accounts, CDs, and other market risk-free investments.

Other people, however, are aggressive investors who expect to earn a higher return for taking part in riskier investments. Their aggressive investment strategies might include purchasing precious metals, gems, or commodities. In general, these investors are willing to sacrifice some safety to achieve greater returns. It is this mix of risk-averse and aggressive investors that allows the market to function effectively.

Investment decisions must be based on several factors, including safety, expected income, liquidity, and growth potential. Let's look at how each factor affects investment decisions.

ILLUSTRATION 5

Asset Classes and Diversification

There are many ways to classify investment and financial products. The investment pyramid, for example, categorizes products according to their risk and return potential. Another way is to group similar products into specific classes. These classes are generally defined as the following:

- **Cash and cash equivalents**—passbook savings and checking accounts; money market accounts; money market funds; certificates of deposit; T-bills
- **Fixed-income investments**—corporate bonds; municipal bonds; Treasury bonds; bond funds; mortgage-backed securities, preferred stocks
- **Equities**—common stocks of all kinds: growth, income, growth and income; stock mutual funds
- **Tangible (hard) assets**—real estate, collectibles, precious metals, and stones

Each of these asset classes, as a whole, responds differently to different types of risk; therefore, diversifying or allocating investment resources among these classes is a proven way to reduce risk overall, dampen volatility, and improve the performance of one's portfolio. Fixed-income products, for example, are a hedge against deflation; equities are a hedge against inflation. To minimize market risk, one could diversify among all four asset categories (with additional diversification within the equities category). To minimize interest rate risk, one could diversify within the fixed-income category by staggering bond maturity dates. To minimize business risk, one could allocate among the four categories and purchase mutual funds. To reduce liquidity risk, one would keep a sufficient portion of assets in cash or cash-equivalent assets.

The Safety Factor

Safety in an investment means a minimal risk of loss. When determining whether to invest in something, individuals must determine how much risk they are willing to assume by asking a very basic question: "Can I afford to lose this money?"

During the retirement years and just before them, the major objective of most people is to preserve the value of the investments or savings they already have. Therefore, these people prefer safe investments—savings accounts, municipal bonds, and preferred stock. Common stocks, commodities, options, and collectibles are just a few of the investments many consider too risky.

The Income Factor

The second factor investors consider is the amount of income generated by the investment. The amount of return is usually dependent on the degree of risk the investor wishes to assume. Safe investments, such as CDs, will yield predictable income, and riskier investments, such as mutual funds, will yield less predictable results.

If your clients are supplementing Social Security and an employer-sponsored retirement plan, they may seek investments with the highest current yield. As we have seen, these investments will include money instruments, long-term bonds, preferred stocks, rental real estate, or utility common stock. However, if their income needs are met by other sources, they should probably choose investments that maximize their total returns. These investments include common stocks and investment real estate.

The Liquidity Factor

The third factor investors consider is liquidity, or the ease with which an asset can be converted into cash. Investments range from cash (the most liquid) to real estate and collectibles (the least liquid because of market or economic conditions).

During the retirement years, liquidity is quite important because budgets are geared for expenses. Clients who are retired will need available cash for emergencies and, therefore, may be interested in more liquid investments. During their working years, clients may earmark some of their funds for investments, but they could also use those funds for emergencies.

After retirement, savings accounts, money market funds, and short-term government obligations are safe choices. They may lack high yields, but they are highly liquid. Although stocks, real estate, and bonds are also good investments and may be sold quickly, your client may be unable to regain the amount of money originally invested.

The Growth Potential Factor

There is inherent risk in any investment that grows and increases in value. In general, the greater and faster the growth, the higher the risk, and each investor must decide how much risk is acceptable in relation to potential return.

Investors may purchase stocks issued by certain corporations to provide capital for their future growth and expansion. Those interested in growth stocks should study the market, diversify, and take advantage of opportunities open to them. In general, investors who purchase growth stocks forego immediate cash dividends for greater dollar value in the future. As the corporation grows and prospers, the dollar value of the investor's stock increases.

Substantial growth opportunities are also afforded by some mutual funds and real estate investments. More speculative investments—commodities and options—emphasize more immediate returns rather than continued growth. Precious metals and collectibles offer even less predictable growth potentials.

WRAP-UP

Financial security in retirement depends on the adequacy of your clients' financial resources. Even if their actual retirement date is 30 or more years in the future, it is never too early to begin a retirement plan for them. Part of that plan will include capital accumulation and investment planning for their investment fund. Financial professionals usually recommend starting any savings program with a solid base of insurance protection, most notably some form of permanent life insurance, which can provide current death benefit protection as well as long-term cash value accumulation. From there, a variety of investment alternatives can be used to provide your clients with needed income during their retirement years.

In addition to Social Security benefits and personal investments, your clients will likely also have an employer-sponsored retirement plan. We will discuss this third leg of the retirement income stool—qualified employer and individual retirement plans—in the next several units.

UNIT TEST

1. The longer an individual's investment horizon
   A. the more aggressive he can be with the choice of investment products
   B. the more conservative he should be with the choice of investment products
   C. the less need there is for a retirement plan
   D. the less risk he can afford to take

2. Some risk is involved in almost all investments. In general, the greater the risk
   A. the greater the potential return
   B. the more expensive the investment
   C. the longer the period until a return will be realized
   D. the smaller the potential return

3. Which of these is the technique for reducing risk by spreading investment dollars among different investments?
   A. Pyramiding
   B. Denomination
   C. Pooling
   D. Diversification

4. The potential for a security to fluctuate in value due to its tendency to move with all securities of the same type represents what kind of risk?
   A. Business
   B. Interest rate
   C. Market
   D. Inflation

5. In the event of a company's insolvency, which of the following has first claim on assets?
   A. Officers and members of the board of directors
   B. Common stockholders
   C. Preferred stockholders
   D. Bondholders

6. By their very nature, mutual funds offer investors
   A. diversification
   B. current income
   C. tax deferral
   D. guaranteed returns

7. Which of these types of investments would have the lowest liquidity risk?
   A. Real estate
   B. Mutual funds
   C. Preferred stock
   D. Money market funds

8. Which of these is generally NOT an appropriate product for retirement planning?
   A. Life insurance
   B. Commodities
   C. Mutual funds
   D. Bonds

ANSWERS AND RATIONALES

1. **A.** Over a long period of time, losses in riskier investments tend to be made up by gains. Investments that are high risk in the short term are consequently a lower risk in the longer term.

2. **A.** Risk and potential return tend to go together. Low risk investments usually produce low returns. High risk investments offer the hope of high returns.

3. **D.** By diversifying an investment portfolio, an investor can expect that losses in one holding might be offset by gains in another, thus reducing overall risk.

4. **C.** Changes in the value of a security due to movement in the market, rather than changes in the underlying business, is the subject of market risk.

5. **D.** Bondholders have contractual rights to the assets of a business that must be honored on insolvency before claims of stockholders, officers, or directors.

6. **A.** Mutual funds invest in a broad range of securities, giving their investors diversification.

7. **D.** Money market funds are, by definition, invested in cash and cash equivalents, and are the most liquid.

8. **B.** Commodities are among the most risky investments and are usually inappropriate for retirement planning.

7

Qualified Employer Retirement Plans

Retirement security rests on three legs—Social Security, personal savings and investments, and qualified retirement plans. With this unit, we begin a study of the greatest potential source of retirement income of the three, which is qualified retirement plans. A qualified retirement plan is one that complies with a host of Internal Revenue Code requirements that, in turn, qualify the plan for favorable income tax treatment. ■

UNIT OBJECTIVES

In this unit and the next, we discuss employer-sponsored qualified retirement plans. Most employers are interested in getting the most for their contribution and will usually consider a qualified plan before a nonqualified arrangement. (Nonqualified employer-sponsored arrangements are examined in Unit 11.) Our review of employer-sponsored qualified retirement plans begins with an overview of qualified plans. (Individual retirement plans, such as the IRA, are reviewed in Unit 9.)

On completion of this unit, you should be able to:

- describe the tax advantage of qualified retirement plans;

- compare the features of the main types of qualified plans, including simplified plans;

- explain what plan qualification means; and

- describe the types of dollar limitations that apply to contributions and benefits of these plans.

OVERVIEW OF QUALIFIED PLANS

Key Point Legal requirements governing employer-sponsored retirement plans come from the Employee Retirement Income Security Act of 1974 (ERISA) and the Internal Revenue Code.

Key Point Funds contributed to a qualified retirement plan are generally sheltered from tax until they are withdrawn.

The law governing qualified retirement plans emerges from two sources—the Employee Retirement Income Security Act of 1974 (ERISA) and the Internal Revenue Code. ERISA sets up compliance rules for plans, and the tax code sets up the tax-saving rules that make retirement plans attractive, but there is considerable overlap between the two. To be eligible for the tax advantages, a plan must be in compliance.

ERISA introduced the modern era of retirement planning. By establishing rules and strict standards for employer-sponsored retirement plans (including guidelines for employee coverage, funding, and contributions), ERISA gave much-needed structure to employee pension plans. It also imposed a significant burden of paperwork for plan sponsors, causing many to reconsider how they would provide such plans to their employees. The growth in popularity of defined contribution plans, which generally require less compliance paperwork, is based largely on this factor.

When a retirement plan meets all of the Internal Revenue Code (IRC) requirements, it may qualify for the favorable tax treatment provided through the IRC. Qualified employer plans entitle those who make contributions to realize immediate tax benefits (in the form of tax-deductible contributions) and future tax benefits (through the plan's tax-deferred earnings).

Employers who perceive a need to provide their employees with a retirement plan—a fact of life today for just about any employer who is looking to stay competitive in the hiring market—are usually interested in realizing as many benefits for themselves as possible. This generally means getting a tax break on contributions paid and structuring the plan so that the owner and other key employees benefit most from it.

ERISA limits the degree to which businessowners can favor their key employees and still qualify for favorable tax treatment, but there are ways for owners to make sure they receive the lion's share of benefits. Often this is accomplished merely by choosing the right type of plan to suit the owner's needs.

Of course, there are other, less tangible benefits to employers who implement qualified retirement plans. Retirement plans can boost employee morale. (Because most employees have come to expect retirement plans as part of their compensation package, perhaps it is more accurate to say that the absence of a plan will lower morale.) A good retirement plan can lead to longer terms of employment by quality employees and enhance their company loyalty. These benefits notwithstanding, the bottom-line financial benefits to the company are, in most cases, the driving force behind the implementation of most qualified plans.

No Discrimination—Financial Soundness

In general, an employer retirement plan must meet the following requirements in order to qualify for favorable tax treatment, it must:

- be established by the employer for the exclusive benefit of employees and their beneficiaries;

- be permanent in nature;

- be in writing and communicated to all current employees;

- be financed or funded by the employer, the employees, or both;

- provide contributions and benefits that are not discriminatory under ERISA or IRC rules;

- comply with contribution and benefit limits guidelines; and

- comply with regulations affecting minimum participation, coverage, separation from the sponsor's general assets, vesting, funding, disclosure, etc.

These requirements are intended to ensure that qualified plans are maintained for the exclusive benefit of the employees or their beneficiaries, do not discriminate in favor of highly compensated employees and that they are operated in a financially sound manner.

Tax Advantages of Qualified Plans

The trade-off to the sponsoring employer for accepting heavy compliance and reporting responsibility is the availability of several tax advantages that go along with qualified plans. With a qualified plan, an employer can provide benefits to employees under conditions that reduce current taxes for both parties. The tax advantages of a qualified plan include the following.

- The employer's contribution is generally deductible in the year it is made, assuming that the contribution is made no later than the date on which the employer's income tax—including extensions—is filed.

- Expenses incurred to establish and maintain the qualified plan are considered to be deductible business expenses to the employer.

- The employer's contribution to the plan on behalf of the employee is not included in the employee's current income.

- Earnings or gains from investments held in qualified plans accumulate tax free until they are actually distributed to plan participants (this includes earnings attributable to employee contributions).

- Employee contributions can reduce an employee's personal taxes by reducing the amount of his taxable income.

ILLUSTRATION 1

Agent's Perspective

Retirement plans and retirement planning go together, right?

Most retirement planning clients will never need to concern themselves with retirement plans, other than looking at their annual statements. For most employees, retirement plans are really just another financial product. The decision may be to participate or not participate or how much to invest. Think about your client's 401(k) plans. There is no more need for your clients to know about how to set up a qualified plan than they have to know how to set up an insurance company before they buy insurance.

But some of your clients own businesses. For these clients, the line between a private retirement plan and the employer plan is blurred. For these clients, the employer and the employee are the same person.

Plan design and installation is a specialized area. You may not have the expertise to guide your clients through the entire compliance process, but you need to know the issues if you want to be able to serve your clients' retirement needs.

TYPES OF QUALIFIED PLANS

Key Point Defined contribution plans accumulate funds in an account for the employee.

Key Point Defined benefit plans provide a traditional pension for an employee.

Qualified plans generally fall into one of two basic categories—defined contribution or defined benefit plans. It is important to understand the distinction between these two approaches.

Plans that shelter otherwise taxable income without promises of specific future benefits are called defined contribution plans; that is, the plan defines the amount of contribution or the manner in which contributions will be made, with no promises made with respect to ultimate retirement income amounts. Under these plans, the employer's or employee's contribution rate is defined.

Plans that promise specific retirement benefit amounts are termed defined benefit plans. Under these plans, the employee's retirement benefit amount is defined by formula, and annual contributions will be whatever amount is actuarially determined as necessary to support those future benefit payments.

Defined Contribution Plans

The most popular approach to offering qualified retirement benefits today is the defined contribution plan. These plans provide for an individual account for each participant into which employer and employee contributions will be paid. Retirement benefits are based on the contributions and interest earnings allocated to an employee's account. Consequently, the amount of future benefits that the participant will actually receive is not currently known; those benefits will ultimately depend on contributions, plus any income, expenses, gains, losses, and forfeitures of accounts of other participants. The length of the employee's participation and the employee's retirement age will also affect the amount of future benefits to which he will be entitled.

The most common types of defined contribution plans include 401(k) plans, profit-sharing plans, money purchase plans, target benefit plans, stock bonus plans, employee stock ownership plans (ESOPs), and thrift or savings plans. Each of these plans is discussed in more detail later in this unit.

Defined Benefit Plans

Defined benefit plans are more complex and costly to administer than defined contribution plans. These plans promise a specific retirement benefit to each participant, typically utilizing a formula to determine the amount. For example, the plan could adopt a relatively simple formula, providing benefits equal to 3% of the participant's average monthly compensation, or it could use a more sophisticated approach, providing benefits equal to average compensation of the highest five years during the 10-year period immediately before retirement.

Because the benefits are predetermined, the employer is liable for contributions based on the actuarially determined amounts needed to fund the present value of future benefits. This uncertainty can make some employers uncomfortable. There is a commitment to make contributions even when company profits aren't doing well along with the possibility that future contribution amounts may need to rise higher than expected in order to cover shortfalls in asset earnings.

Despite the drawbacks, defined benefit plans have their uses. Small-business owners who want to put a lot of money away in a hurry can use defined benefit plans to exceed limits that apply to defined contribution plans. Other employers feel that a true pension plan is an important benefit for their employees. In some cases, these advantages can outweigh the regulatory burden, but the trend is definitely away from this type of plan.

The specific plan provisions of both defined contribution and defined benefit plans will be discussed in more detail later in this unit.

COMPLIANCE RULES FOR QUALIFIED PLANS

Key Point Employees must have a vested right to their benefits after a minimum period of employment.

Key Point Qualified plans may not discriminate in favor of owners or highly compensated employees.

It is not the intent of this course to cover the technical requirements for establishing and maintaining qualified retirement plans. In general, though, financial professionals should know that the IRC and ERISA require a plan to meet minimum standards that are intended to ensure most if not all employees the chance to benefit to some degree from the plan. In essence, the IRS is telling employers that in exchange for tax breaks, a qualified plan must benefit the common worker as well as owners and key executives.

Specific issues that must be addressed in all qualified plans include the following.

■ **Exclusive benefits**. Who can benefit under a plan? In order for a plan to be qualified, it must be established by an employer for the exclusive benefit of its employees or their beneficiaries. Plan assets may not be used for any other purpose.

■ **Plan eligibility and coverage**. Who participates, and how do they get in? Though there are some exceptions, the general rule is that an employee is eligible to participate in most types of plans if he is 21 or older and has completed one year of service with the employer. Moreover, in operation, a qualified plan must benefit a certain proportion of non-highly compensated employees in relation to highly compensated employees.

■ **Vesting**. When does a participant's employer-funded benefit become nonforfeitable? A plan's vesting schedule (a term used to describe how a participant accrues rights to contributions made on his behalf by the employer) must conform to certain minimum requirements. In general, a plan may use one of two approaches:

— **Immediate vesting**, under which participants gain 100% ownership of the employer's matching money as soon as it lands in their accounts

— **Three-year cliff vesting**, under which the participant is 100% vested after completing three years of service with the employer and has no entitlement to employer contributions before completion of the three years

— **Graded vesting**, under which the participant gradually attains vested rights to the plan sponsor's contributions in stages over no more than six years (a common graded vesting schedule is a five-year plan.)

Years of Service	Percentage Vested
1	20%
2	40%
3	60%
4	80%
5	100%

It should be noted that qualified plan participants are always immediately and fully vested in any contributions they make to a plan.

Nondiscrimination requirements. To what degree may a plan favor owners or key employees over the rank and file? In addition to the coverage requirements noted here, a qualified plan must conform to certain nondiscrimination standards. Basically, these standards prohibit plans from favoring highly compensated employees in terms of contributions or benefits, or any rights, features, or changes under the plan.

Contribution and benefit limits. To what extent can a participant expect to benefit from a plan? All qualified plans must conform to IRC provisions that place limitations on the amounts that may be contributed on behalf of or received by any participant. For defined contribution plans, the limit is imposed on the amount that may be contributed to a participant's account in any year; for defined benefit plans, the limit controls the amount of benefit a participant may receive in any year.

Distribution requirements. How and when will a plan participant receive payment of benefits? In order to meet qualification standards, a plan must comply with rules regarding the timing, amount, and manner in which a participant can receive benefits. These rules can be complex; they are discussed in detail in Unit 10.

DEFINED CONTRIBUTION PLANS: HOW THEY WORK

Key Point Employee accounts in defined contribution plans accumulate from employer contributions, employee contributions (as in a 401(k) plan), investment earnings, and forfeitures from accounts of departing employees who were not yet vested.

Key Point Contributions are subject to two main annual limits—a limit on annual additions (all additions to the account other than investment earnings) and a limit on employee contributions.

Key Point Employees age 50 and older may make limited additional employee contributions under a catch-up rule.

Defined contribution plans are based on contributions made by the employee, and in many cases the employer, and the earnings these contributions generate. In a defined contribution plan, the amount of retirement benefit that will be available is not known until retirement actually begins. The rate of return earned on the invested assets of a defined contribution plan directly affects the employee's ultimate retirement benefit. Obviously, greater investment earnings will produce larger retirement benefits. If greater yields are applied to larger contributions, the retirement benefit will be greater.

The age of an employee participating in a defined contribution plan also affects the amount that will be available to produce retirement income. It is clear that defined contribution plans favor younger participants because the lower the employee's age when he becomes eligible to participate, the longer will be the time over which assets allocated to the employee may accumulate and earn interest.

Younger eligibility translates into a greater number of initial contributions. Younger eligibility combined with sufficient length of participation in the plan may also provide the participant with a large amount of forfeitures. Forfeitures are employer contributions left in the plan by employees who leave the employer before becoming fully vested. The former employee's forfeited amounts are simply left in the plan and proportionally distributed to the remaining employees.

Types and Limitations of Defined Contribution Plans

In most defined contribution plans, each participant has an account to which annual additions are made. Annual additions may come from any one of three sources:

- The employer's annual contribution

- The employee's contribution (if any)

- Nonvested forfeitures allocated to the participant's account

The maximum annual contribution to an employee's account, from all sources, in a defined contribution plan (known as the IRC Section 415 limit) is the lesser of 100% of the employee's compensation or a dollar amount adjusted annually for inflation. For current contribution limits for qualified plans, please see the appendix at the end of the book.

Contributions may be made to several types of defined contribution plans. These plans generally provide that the employer will regularly contribute a certain amount to the plan for each employee.

Money Purchase Plans

A money purchase plan is a popular type of qualified plan in which the employer's contributions are pre-established either in terms of dollars or, more commonly, fixed percentages of employee compensation. Contributions may also be based on a point or unit formula allocating a specified dollar amount or percentage of salary to be contributed for each year of a participant's service with the employer. The employer must make annual fixed contributions in accordance with the plan's documents; contributions cannot be related to the employer's profits.

Profit-Sharing Plans

A profit-sharing plan is a type of defined contribution plan funded by profits that exceed a certain level. IRC rules mandate that contributions to profit-sharing plans be "recurring and substantial," which generally means they must be based on a realistic formula that makes it more than likely that contributions will be made. But—and this is an important bottom line for many employers—contributions are not required when the company's profits fail to exceed the defined level. If earnings are poor or the employer has a pressing need for funds, a year's contribution may be skipped.

Employers (and employees) who want a plan that allows employees to add to the pot may combine profit-sharing features with elective employee contributions. This feature is the defining characteristic of a 401(k) plan.

The IRC Section 415 limit on annual contributions that applies generally to defined contribution plans needs to be coordinated with a deduction limit on contributions applicable to profit-sharing plans. This limit is 25% of compensation, but not all contributions to profit-sharing plans are subject to this limit, so total annual additions even to profit-sharing plans may exceed 25% of compensation. Employee elective contributions, for example, do not count against the 25% limit.

401(k) Plans

In recent years, 401(k) plans have achieved great popularity. The term 401(k) has almost become synonymous with tax-advantaged retirement savings. People speak of having a 401(k) in a way that almost makes the term a generic reference to a personal savings plan.

A 401(k) plan is a cash or deferred arrangement (CODA) that can stand alone or operate in tandem with another type of defined contribution plan, including profit-sharing plan (most commonly), stock bonus plan, thrift plan, or money purchase plan established before the enactment of ERISA. Newer money purchase plans may not have 401(k) provisions.

With a cash or deferred arrangement, an employee may elect either to take a part of their salary in cash—with an immediate tax liability—or defer the salary by having it shunted into a 401(k) account. That is, employee contributions are regarded not as payments by them, but as the deferral of salary. This means that the immediate tax advantage to an employee comes not from tax-deductible contributions, but from a reduction in income tax due to a reduction in salary.

Limits on Elective Deferrals

Participants in a 401(k) plan are subject to dollar limits on their elective deferrals that change from year to year. Participants age 50 or older can add an additional amount referred to as catch-up contributions.

For current contribution limits to 401(k) plans, please see the appendix at the end of the book.

The catch-up deferrals are available even if other restrictions apply. If, for instance, the terms of a plan restrict elective deferrals to an amount less than the amount allowed by law, a 50-year-old or older participant can still make the additional catch-up deferral.

Seyda, age 52, participates in a 401(k) plan that allows employee deferrals of up to 10% of their compensation. If Seyda's compensation is $80,000, the maximum contribution she would be able to make to the 401(k) plan would be $8,000. However, the catch-up provision will allow Seyda to make an additional $5,500 contribution to the plan for that year.

Any elective deferral by the employee is tax-deductible to the employer just as if it had been paid out in wages. Like wages, the amounts deferred are immediately subject to Social Security (FICA) taxation and federal unemployment (FUTA) tax.

Vesting, Matching Contributions, and Nondiscrimination

Elective employee contributions, made in the form of salary reductions, are 100% vested from the moment they are made. If the employer matches employee contributions (either on a one-for-one basis or a fractional basis), the matching contributions must vest on an accelerated basis: either on a three-year cliff vesting schedule or on a two- to six-year graduated schedule.

A plan may require that a certain percentage be deferred as a condition of participation, but most plans avoid this requirement because it might lead to discriminatory contributions favoring the highly paid. Many employers provide matching contributions that are pegged to the employee's elective deferral percentage or amount. For example, an employer might contribute $1 for every $2 the employee defers, up to a specified maximum.

When an employer offers a matching contribution, lower-paid employees have an increased incentive to participate in the plan. This is important because 401(k) plan nondiscrimination rules require, among other things, that a minimum percentage of rank-and-file employees elect to participate in the plan in order for key employees to participate. Increasing the rank-and-file employees' incentive to participate can do much to prevent disqualification of the plan.

Nondiscrimination testing—the process of proving that a 401(k) plan's contributions do not excessively favor highly compensated employees over the rank and file—is one of the biggest administrative challenges to sponsoring a 401(k) plan. Compliance with this rule is determined by meeting an actual deferral percentage (ADP), which compares the percentage of deferrals made by highly paid employees versus rank-and-file employees.

A 401(k) plan may allow for loans, though certain procedures must be established so that the loan will not be treated as a taxable distribution. These rules are explained in Unit 10.

Safe Harbor 401(k)

Safe harbor 401(k) plans are very similar to traditional 401(k) plans; both are available for employers of any size and can be combined with other plans. However, there are some differences. Safe harbor 401(k) plans require that employers make contributions for all eligible employees and that all contributions must be immediately 100% vested. Safe harbor plans are easier to administer given they are not subject to many of the complex tax rules that apply to traditional 401(k) plans, such as annual nondiscrimination testing.

The IRS issued proposed regulations that provide employers experiencing a substantial business hardship an alternative to terminating their safe harbor plans. Under the proposed regulations, qualifying employers can lower or suspend mandatory nonelective contributions without losing the qualified status of the plans.

Automatic Enrollment 401(k)

Automatic enrollment 401(k) plans do just that—they automatically enroll employees in the plan and deduct a certain percentage from each employee's salary for contributions to the plan unless the employee opts out or selects a different percentage. However, at one point in time, many employers were unwilling to sponsor automatic enrollment 401(k) plans because many state garnishment laws banned such plans and employers needed assurance that they would be protected as fiduciaries. The Pension Protection Act resolved these employer concerns; automatic enrollment is protected from conflicting state law and employers sponsoring these plans receive fiduciary protection granted under ERISA.

An automatic enrollment 401(k) that satisfies the requirements of a qualified automatic contribution arrangement (QACA) is not subject to the nondiscrimination and top-heavy testing that applies to traditional 401(k) plans. The QACA has special contribution and vesting requirements. For instance, while the automatic enrollment 401(k) vests employer contributions pursuant to the plan's schedule, employer contributions to a QACA must be 100% vested after two years of service.

The automatic enrollment feature not only applies to 401(k) plans, but also 403(b) plans and 457(b) plans.

Roth 401(k)

401(k) plans can incorporate a program in which employee contributions to the plan may be treated as Roth IRA contributions (i.e., after-tax contributions and tax-free distributions). Roth 401(k) contributions are considered salary-deferral contributions; therefore, all salary deferral rules apply.

Roth 401(k) plans are beneficial to participants because not only is the 401(k) contribution limit higher than the Roth IRA limit (for current amounts, please see the appendix at the end of the book), but also persons with any income can contribute to Roth 401(k) plans. The one disadvantage to this plan is that it is somewhat difficult to administer; Roth 401(k) contributions must be held in separate accounts in the plan.

SIMPLE 401(k)

The SIMPLE 401(k) plan was created to benefit small employers. Unlike the traditional and safe harbor 401(k) plans, only employers with 100 or fewer employees are eligible to set up a SIMPLE 401(k) and no other retirement plans can be maintained when a SIMPLE 401(k) is in place. However, similar to the safe harbor 401(k), the SIMPLE 401(k) is not subject to the discrimination rules applicable to the traditional plans and all employer contributions must be fully vested immediately. The SIMPLE 401(k) is similar to the SIMPLE IRA; however, the 401(k) plan is not as popular among employers as the IRA because the SIMPLE IRA is easier to maintain.

You will learn more about the SIMPLE 401(k) plan later in this unit.

ILLUSTRATION 2

Actual Deferral Percentage Test

The nondiscrimination test that a 401(k) plan has to pass is known as the **actual deferral percentage**, or ADP, test. It compares the rates of elective deferrals by highly compensated employees to those of the rank-and-file. A 401(k) plan will satisfy the ADP test if:

■ the actual deferral percentage for eligible highly compensated employees for the plan year does not exceed 1.25 times the actual deferral percentage of all other eligible employees for the preceding plan year; or

■ the actual deferral percentage for eligible highly compensated employees for the plan year does not exceed the actual deferral percentage of all other eligible employees for the preceding plan year by more than 2%, and the actual deferral percentage for highly compensated employees for the plan year is not more than two times the actual deferral percentage of all other eligible employees for the preceding year.

The ADP for either group (highly compensated employees or all other employees) is the average of ratios (calculated separately for each employee) of the amount electively deferred to the plan for the year to the employee's compensation for the year.

Thrift and Savings Plans

Thrift and savings plans are qualified plans that have a structure similar to profit-sharing plans with 401(k) provisions. However, thrift plans incorporate after-tax employee contributions rather than the before-tax salary reductions or deferrals used under 401(k)s. Employee participation is voluntary and the participant chooses the amount of his contribution within the plan's guidelines. The employee may generally choose investment options from a menu of investments available through the plan.

Employers may provide full or, more commonly, partial matching contributions; typically, employee contributions account for the larger proportion of the total amount contributed. In-service distributions, which occur while the participant is still employed, are permitted under some plans, but may generate taxation on amounts exceeding the participant's cost basis. Most plans offer withdrawal provisions only after a minimum of two years of participation.

Thrift and savings plans must satisfy many of the requirements generally associated with qualified plans. These include minimum age and service eligibility requirements, vesting standards, nondiscrimination rules, and use of a trustee to oversee plan assets.

Generally, forfeitures under thrift and savings plans are used to reduce the employer's future contributions. However, thrift and savings plans may reallocate forfeitures among continuing participants on a percentage of payroll ratio.

Employee Stock Ownership Plans and Stock Bonus Plans

Employee stock ownership plans (ESOPs) and **stock bonus plans** are similar to profit-sharing plans in many ways. Annual employer contributions are not required, future account balances are not guaranteed, and forfeitures may be reallocated.

Under an ESOP, the employer contributes company stock to a participant's account. Both the employer and employee benefit. An employer who sponsors an ESOP or a stock bonus plan delivers employer securities—not cash—to the plan trustee. Cash can be preserved for other business uses, including expansion.

Under most circumstances, there is no limit to the amount of employer securities that can be held by the plan. Employees benefit because they own shares in the company for which they work. As a rule, increased corporate profits translate into increased revenue or appreciation for stockholders. Employees covered under an employer stock program usually experience increased pride and productivity.

Distributions to participants may be made in the form of cash, which is immediately taxable. More commonly, distribution is made in the form of stock and taxation occurs when the stock is ultimately sold by the retired participant. For terminated participants, tax exposure occurs when the stock is distributed to the terminated participant based on the employer's cost basis.

If the former participant chooses to hold the stock in anticipation of further appreciation, the appreciation will not be taxable until the stock is sold and a capital gain is realized. If the employer securities are not tradable on a stock exchange, the employee must have the right to have the securities repurchased by the employer. This required feature is known as a put option. The employee puts the securities up for sale to the sponsoring employer, who must redeem them.

▌DEFINED BENEFIT PLANS: HOW THEY WORK

Key Point   Defined benefit plans compute a salary-replacement benefit, often as a percentage of an employee's final or average salary, with the percentage determined based on the number of years of employment.

Key Point   Although funds are not earmarked for individual employee accounts, employers are required to make annual contributions to defined benefit plans in an amount determined by an actuary to be adequate to meet future benefit obligations.

A defined benefit plan is a retirement plan under which benefits are determined in advance by a formula in the plan and the employee-participant is guaranteed a specified pension benefit at retirement. The level of contributions required can only be determined by an actuary on a year-by-year basis. Benefits may be designed as a specific dollar amount or, more often, as a specific percentage of wages to be replaced at retirement.

The amount of contributions an employer makes under a defined benefit plan is determined by actuarial calculation. The plan administrator, often with the help of an actuary, considers a number of significant variables and calculates the amount that the employer should contribute periodically (generally monthly or yearly) so that adequate dollars will be available to distribute the promised benefits when each employee reaches retirement age.

The amount of contribution that the employer is permitted to deduct is substantially different under a defined benefit plan than under a defined contribution plan. Under a defined contribution plan, as we have seen previously, the maximum annual contribution that the plan-sponsoring employer may contribute—and deduct—for any one employee is limited to the lesser of 100% of the employee's compensation or a dollar amount that is adjusted for inflation. With a defined benefit plan, the maximum contribution that an employer may deduct is the amount necessary to fund the plan benefits that have been determined under the terms of the plan document. In fact, the contribution must be sufficient to fund those benefits assuming it is to be invested over the expected time until the employee retires.

Generally, a defined benefit plan is more cumbersome and costly to administer than a defined contribution plan. Annual contributions have to be calculated each time they are made. Actuaries must be engaged periodically to certify the accuracy of the contribution amounts. Compliance and reporting requirements are much more extensive and expensive. But for an employer whose objective is to maximize retirement funding contributions for the owner and key employees, especially older ones, the financial and administrative trade-offs may well be worth the extra trouble. To understand how a defined benefit plan really works, it is necessary to look at how benefits are determined and how predicted earnings compounded over time can be used to determine a reasonably correct annual funding contribution.

Determining Benefits Under a Defined Benefit Plan

Defined benefit plans are designed to replace a percentage of preretirement earnings during the retirement years. However, there is some variance among plans as to just how earnings are defined. Two working definitions of earnings, both of which include an average of the employee's compensation over a set period of time, are used in determining benefits in defined benefit plans.

- The **career average method** averages a worker's earnings over his employment with the company. Because of inflation and potential salary raises for long-term employees, the career average method may leave substantial gaps in preretirement income replacement during the retirement years. (Some plans do make adjustments for inflation.)

- The **final average method** typically factors the retirement benefit by calculating an average of earnings over the final three, five, or 10 years of employment before retirement. This method will provide the retired employee with a larger pension because an average of a retiree's final, and generally highest, years of pay produces a higher number than will an average of compensation throughout the years of a worker's employment.

Virtually all defined benefit plans will use one of four formulas to calculate future annual retirement benefits:

■ The **flat amount formula** determines benefits according to a specified amount. For example, all employees will receive $600 per month. Generally, employees covered under a flat amount benefit formula who earn the same compensation receive the same retirement benefit. However, a plan document may include a provision that reduces the flat amount of an employee's benefit if his service is less than a certain time period (often 10 years) as specified in the document.

■ The **flat percentage of earnings formula** provides benefits based on a stated percentage of the employee's preretirement average compensation. Length of service does not come into play in this formula. An example of this formula would be a defined benefit plan that provides a benefit of 50% of preretirement pay. The final average method of defining earnings is generally used with this formula to address inflation.

■ The **flat amount per year of service formula** provides a retirement benefit in the form of an established dollar amount for each year of employment covered under the plan. This formula is commonly used by union pension plans. Federal tax laws define a year of service as 1,000 hours worked in a 12-month consecutive period. For example, a flat amount per year of service formula plan that offers a benefit of $30 per month for each year of participation or covered service for a worker with 30 years of participation under the plan would provide a monthly pension of $900.

■ The **percentage of earnings per year of service formula** provides a percentage unit of compensation for each year of participation in the plan. If each unit is 3%, a covered worker with 25 years of service will have a benefit of 75% of compensation. Both career average and final average methods are used under this system that tends to favor younger workers who have the potential for many years of future service.

Limit on Annual Benefits

The IRS has set limits on the amount of retirement benefit allowed under a defined benefit plan. The intent of this rule is to restrict highly compensated employees from reaping inordinate benefits under this type of qualified plan.

Under a defined benefit plan, the maximum annual retirement benefit permitted is the lesser of an annually indexed dollar amount (for current annual benefit limits, please see the appendix in the back of the book) or 100% of an employee's average pay over the highest three (high-three) years of preretirement earnings. Furthermore, if benefits begin before an employee attains a certain age (currently 62), the law requires that this maximum amount be reduced by a reasonable rate of interest. Conversely, when retirement begins after the Social Security retirement age, the benefit is to be adjusted upward using a reasonable interest rate.

Determining Contributions in a Defined Benefit Plan

The ultimate cost of benefits under a defined benefit plan will be affected by the actual experience of the plan, taking into account such events as employee turnover, true investment earnings, and the ages of participating employees.

A rate of return or interest must be assumed to determine the amount of the employer's annual funding responsibility. A high interest rate assumption translates into a smaller funding contribution because it is anticipated that earnings on contributions will provide a significant percentage of the dollars needed to provide a full retirement benefit under the terms of the plan instrument. However, if plan assets fail to earn at least the assumed return, the employer will still have an obligation to provide the promised benefit and must make up for the shortfall when the employee retires. If a low rate of return on plan assets is assumed, larger contributions by the employer will be required to make up for lower earnings.

Employee turnover also affects contributions made to a defined benefit plan. The turnover rate expresses the statistical probability of the severance of employment for a given group of employees. Employee age has the greatest impact on turnover rates: younger workers change jobs more often. Turnover rate is also affected by sickness (morbidity) and death (mortality) within a workforce.

A high turnover rate means that only a small proportion of employees will actually be around to receive benefits at retirement. This translates into lower required funding contributions because forfeitures under a defined benefit plan are generally used to reduce the employer's subsequent contributions.

Mandatory Minimum Funding Requirements

Employers that sponsor defined benefit pension plans must prefund the benefits that employee participants earn each year. Under prior law, many plans became underfunded because employers were allowed to spread out the costs over the life of the plan and pay lower costs at the plan's inception.

The Pension Protection Act of 2006 (PPA) changed all of that when it revamped the funding requirements for defined benefit pension plans, particularly single-employer plans. A defined benefit pension plan must be adequately funded each year. Employers must contribute to the plan each year in an amount adequate to pay the plan's costs for the year (i.e., accrued benefits). Employers have seven years to pay off with interest any funding shortfalls. Employers that fail to comply with the minimum funding requirements will be subject to a 10% penalty tax.

While the funding rules for the defined benefit plan are the most complicated, other pension plans, including defined contribution plans such as the target benefit and money purchase plans, are also subject to the Act's minimum funding requirements. However, 403(b) plans, ESOPs, profit-sharing plans, SEPs, SIMPLEs, and stock bonus plans are not subject to the rules. Note these differences in applicability of the minimum funding rules as you study these various retirement plans in this unit.

Accounting for Variances From Assumptions

What happens if investment income, mortality and morbidity, administration expenses, turnover, and other actuarial variables differ from what the plan administrator or actuarial consultant estimated? The dollar amount accumulated in the plan may be less or more than the actual retirement benefits to be paid.

To maintain control, a plan uses a single funding method. A plan is considered to have an unfunded liability if the plan's current assets are not sufficient to cover the funding target (i.e., present value of an employee's accrued benefits). The employer must correct any funding shortfall by paying off any unfunded liability within seven years (formerly, a period of 5 to 30 years was allowed). If a surplus shows, the plan trustee can instruct the sponsor to reduce upcoming periodic contributions.

Government rules require a defined benefit plan sponsor to periodically engage the services of an actuary to oversee the computation of contributions. The annual contributions must be adequate but not excessive. The plan's actuary must implement a formal, government-approved method for establishing a sponsoring employer's annual actuarial costs.

HYBRID PLANS

Key Point   Hybrid plans, including cash balance plans, age-weighted profit-sharing plans, and target benefit plans, aim to meet employer needs by grafting features of defined benefit plans on defined contributions plans or vice versa.

Hybrid plans are plans that combine features of defined benefit and defined contribution plans in different ways. Plans still must be characterized as one or the other, so that compliance and tax rules can be applied properly, but various drawbacks of the traditional plans are reduced for some employers in these plans.

Cash Balance Plans

A **cash balance plan** is a defined benefit plan that has become increasingly popular among employers because the benefit accrual formula generally results in lower plan costs. However, along with popularity has come controversy over whether the cash balance plan is legitimate and not age discriminatory.

Employers have always been cautious in implementing cash balance pension plans because these plans have been subject to public and legal scrutiny from the outset. Older employees distrusted the conversion of their defined benefit plans to cash balance plans because employers usually failed to clearly communicate the changes and fully explain to older employees that their total benefits under the new plan would be reduced. Older employees whose plans were converted to cash balance plans were beginning to file age-discrimination suits, many of which resulted in the employees' favor. The IRS decided at one point to suspend issuing determination letters on cash balance plans because the legality of the plans was questionable.

However, the tide turned in 2003 when the U.S. Court of Appeals for the Seventh Circuit overturned the lower court's decision in *Cooper v. IBM Personal Pension Plan*, ruling that cash balance plans do not discriminate against plan participants based on age. The PPA thereafter solidified the federal court's decision confirming the legality of cash balance plans. Although the court's decision and the PPA put to rest some legal issues surrounding the cash balance plan, some pension practitioners and employers are still wary of the validity of the plan.

Unlike the traditional accrual formula, which is based on an employee's length of service and salary, cash balance plans use a *hypothetical* separate account for each plan participant. The employer credits a certain amount to each account and also credits each account with interest. However, because all account funds are pooled together, participants cannot direct how their accounts are invested.

Because a cash balance plan is a defined benefit plan required to have definitely determinable benefits, a fixed-interest rate must be used. The interest rate may be a specified rate or may be tied to Treasury bill rates or some other outside standard. The promised benefit for a participant is based on credits in the hypothetical account. These credits accrue in a manner similar to a defined contribution plan based on a percentage of pay and interest credits under the plan's assumed interest rate. This is a mathematical construct, however, because there is no separate account and the promised benefit must be paid regardless of the investment experience of the plan.

As in other defined benefit plans, plan participants may elect to receive their benefits either as lump sums or annuities.

Contributions

The amounts an employer contributes to a cash balance plan are determined by an actuary. The actuary uses certain assumptions concerning mortality, interest, and participant turnover to calculate how much the employer must contribute to ensure sufficient funds to provide the benefits promised by the plan.

From the employee's perspective, one of the advantages of cash balance plans is that investment risks are borne by the employer. In these plans, just as in any other defined benefit plan, the employer is exclusively responsible for investment decisions, and employees do not direct the investments in their individual accounts.

Cash Balance Plans: Pension Protection Act

In addition to legitimizing the cash balance pension plan, the Pension Protection Act established concrete rules for age-discrimination testing, conversions, and vesting.

Age-Discrimination Testing

A cash balance plan does not discriminate against employee participants based on age if the employee's accrued benefit is equal to or greater than that of any other employee similarly situated in all regards except age. The employees are considered to be similarly situated if they are identical with respect to compensation, years of service, date of hire, position, work history, and any other factor affecting pension benefits other than age.

Conversions

When an employer decides to convert a defined benefit plan to a cash balance plan, the minimum benefit under the cash balance plan must not be less than the employee's accrued benefit before the conversion plus the benefit earned after the conversion. In other words, the employee's earned benefits under the defined benefit plan may not be reduced, or "wear away," after the plan is converted to the cash balance plan. Also, any early retirement benefits or retirement-like subsidies to which an employee was entitled under the old plan must be incorporated into the cash balance plan.

Vesting

Employees who are participants in cash balance pension plans or other hybrid pension plans must be 100% vested in the accrued benefit from employer contributions after completing three years of service.

Age-Weighted Profit-Sharing Plans

Traditionally, profit-sharing plans use compensation as the basis for allocating participants' shares of contributions, forfeitures, and earnings. Participants with equal compensation are given equal allocations. The result, however, is often more favorable for younger employees, who have more years to accumulate those allocations.

EXAMPLE

Carl, age 55, and Lucy, age 35, both earn the same salary and are given a 6% pay allocation to ABC, Inc.'s profit-sharing plan this year. The value of this allocation will be significantly less for Carl at his retirement in 10 years than it will be for Lucy at her retirement in 30 years.

Age-weighted plans attempt to overcome this disparity by providing participants with equal benefits at retirement, as opposed to making equal contributions during participation. This means that the plan takes into account not only a participant's compensation but his age as well.

EXAMPLE

If ABC, Inc. were to adopt an age-weighted plan, it would allocate more of the current year's contribution to Carl than to Lucy in order to provide equal benefits to both at retirement. In fact, all the older employees at ABC, Inc.—a group that happens to include its owners and key executives—would receive a substantially larger share of this year's contribution.

Age-weighted plans are the result of IRS regulations that allow defined contribution plans to be tested on projected benefits as well as contributions, for purposes of meeting the nondiscrimination rules. Using an assumed interest rate, each participant's allocation is projected to retirement age and then converted into a benefit. This benefit is then tested against the general nondiscrimination rules for defined benefit plans.

Thus, by combining the simplicity and flexibility of traditional profit-sharing plans with the benefits-oriented approach of defined benefit plans, the age-weighted plan has many advantages that would appeal to older corporate businessowners and executives.

Target Benefit Plans

A target benefit plan is a hybrid of the best features of the defined contribution and defined benefit approaches to retirement planning. Although the combined approach is sometimes difficult to understand, the availability of larger contributions (without corresponding guaranteed future benefits) makes a target benefit plan attractive to employers, while employees appreciate the fact that contribution amounts are intended to support a potential (targeted) retirement benefit amount.

Although a target benefit pension plan is technically classified as a defined contribution plan, it shares many characteristics with defined benefit plans. The lump sum necessary at an employee's normal retirement age is established for each participant. The employer's contribution is based on this future value, the time remaining until the employee's normal retirement age according to the plan instrument, and the assumed rate of return.

Like defined benefit plans, target plans implement a benefit formula to determine the employer's annual contribution. However, the targeted benefit is not guaranteed. Once the amount of the annual employer contribution needed to support the estimated benefit has been determined, the employer's contributions remain largely fixed. Most target benefit plans are designed with a provision that helps to maintain the stability of the employer's cash outflow corresponding with annual contributions to the plan. Such a provision has excess earnings or losses allocated to each participant's account. In traditional defined benefit plans, variances from expected returns become the sponsoring employer's concern because benefits are guaranteed.

Under a target benefit pension plan, it is the participating employee who is directly affected by the rate of return earned on plan assets. The ultimate benefit that plan participants will receive will be directly affected by investment performance on the plan's assets. Most target benefit plans invest wholly or partially in such vehicles as variable annuities or mutual funds. When the rate of a target plan's actual investment performance exceeds the rate (element) used in the actuarial calculations originally applied to determine the targeted benefit, the true benefit that the employee receives can be greater than the target amount. Like a defined benefit, a target benefit plan tends to favor older employees because it allows for heavier contributions on their behalf.

New Comparability Profit-Sharing Plans

New comparability plans, first introduced in the 1990s, provided even more flexibility to employers in the design of employer-sponsored retirement plans. In these plans, the employer's contributions to employees' accounts are allocated by a formula specified in the retirement plan document. Plan participants are divided into categories such as job classification (including the owner of the business), age, or age and service. Each category or group receives its own level of employer contributions. This allows larger contributions to be made to the accounts of higher paid, older, longer term employees, and even owners, and lower contributions to the accounts of younger, lower paid employees.

Because of the greater allocation flexibility of this type of plan it is subject to stringent cross nondiscrimination testing. Generally, whether or not plans are nondiscriminatory is based on a benefits, rather than contribution, basis.

New Comparability vs. Age-Weighted Plans

Generally speaking both types of plans are similar in that they allow a business to maximize contributions to the accounts of older, higher paid employees and owners and minimize contributions to younger employees' accounts. The new comparability plans, however, differ in that employees are placed into different groups or categories with a different contribution formula for each group rather than strictly by age.

SEPs, SIMPLEs, AND KEOGH PLANS

Key Point Under a SEP, an employer contributes to employee IRAs under relaxed qualification and nondiscrimination rules.

Key Point Under a SIMPLE plan, small employers can establish a retirement plan on the IRA or 401(k) plan model with reduced contribution limits.

Key Point Keogh plans may be established by unincorporated employers under rules and contribution limits that are similar to full-scale qualified plans.

In addition to the traditional defined contribution and defined benefit plans, there are many other types of qualified plans, most of which were originally created to encourage small businesses or small employers to establish retirement plans. These include SEP plans, SIMPLE IRA and SIMPLE 401(k) plans, and Keogh plans.

Simplified Employee Pension (SEP) Plans

Simplified employee pension (SEP) plans were created as an outgrowth of two other programs—IRAs and Keogh plans. SEPs were introduced by the Revenue Act of 1978 to encourage small employers to provide retirement benefits for their employees. With a SEP, employers can establish a retirement plan without much of the paperwork and administrative burdens of qualified plans or profit-sharing plans.

Basically, a SEP is an employer-sponsored plan that uses an individual retirement account (IRA) for each eligible employee. The employer makes contributions to these accounts. (Note that the employee may be a self-employed individual.) Thus, the plan provides the benefits of deductible contributions, tax-deferred earnings, and no current taxation to plan participants on contributions made on their behalf. Today, many employers—large and small, corporate and noncorporate—prefer a SEP plan over a qualified pension or profit-sharing plan because administration, operation, and installation are much simpler and contributions can be more flexible.

Advantages of a SEP

To encourage retirement savings, SEPs have several distinct advantages for both the employer and employee. The advantages to the employer include:

- ease of plan creation and operation;

- establishment of a specialized retirement plan that will help attract and retain employees;

- increased productivity due to reduced employee turnover and reduced recruiting and training costs; and

- attractive tax advantages because SEP contributions can be deducted as an ordinary and necessary business expense.

For the employee, SEP contributions are excluded from gross income for income tax purposes and are tax deferred until the savings are withdrawn. Also, because the SEP-IRA is owned by the individual employee who can control the account, plan participants have the ability to select the investment options that best meet their budgets and retirement goals.

If there is a disadvantage to a SEP, it is the mandatory nature of coverage. Every employee who meets the very liberal qualification requirements must have a SEP-IRA established on his behalf, and for every year a contribution is made under a SEP agreement, the employer must contribute on behalf of every employee who:

- is age 21 or older;

- has worked for the employer during at least three of the past five years; and

- has received at least an indexed dollar amount of compensation for the year (for the current minimum compensation amount for SEP plan participation, please see the appendix at the end of the book).

Employees who have not met these eligibility rules may be excluded from the SEP. In addition, the law also allows the exclusion of union employees and nonresident aliens who have no U.S. income.

Contribution Limitations

A SEP is similar to a profit-sharing plan because the employer does not have to make a contribution to the plan each year. The law also limits the amount an employer may contribute for any eligible employee. For current annual employer contribution limits to SEPs, please see the appendix at the end of the book.

In addition, the employee can treat the SEP-IRA account as an individual retirement account and make deductible or nondeductible contributions to it according to the rules that govern IRAs (see Unit 9).

If the employer maintains other qualified plans, a SEP will be treated as a defined contribution plan, and any contribution by the employer to the SEP must be aggregated with all other contributions by that employer for the purpose of applying the Section 415 limit.

That is, the total annual addition that can be made on behalf of any employee is limited to 100% of the employee's compensation or the annual limit on additions to defined contribution plans, whichever is less. For the annual limit on additions to defined contribution plans, please see the see the appendix at the end of the book.

Salary Reduction SEPs

An alternative to the simplified employee pension is the **salary reduction SEP**, or **SARSEP**. SARSEPs employ a deferral (or salary reduction) approach in that the employee can elect to have employer contributions directed into the SEP or paid out as taxable cash compensation. The limit on the elective deferral to a SARSEP is the same as a 401(k). For current employee contribution limits, please see the appendix at the end of the book.

SARSEPs are reserved for employers with 25 or fewer employees and must have been established before 1997. Plans that were already in place before 1997 may continue to operate and can accept new employee participants.

SIMPLE Plans

Another type of qualified employer retirement plan is the Savings Incentive Match Plan for Employees, or SIMPLE, plan. As the name suggests, these are simplified retirement plans that allow eligible employers to set up a tax-favored retirement savings plan for their employees without having to address many of the usual qualified plan requirements.

SIMPLE plans are available to small businesses (including tax-exempt and government entities) that employ no more than 100 employees who received at least $5,000 in compensation from the employer during the preceding year. In addition, to be eligible to establish a SIMPLE plan, the employer must not have a qualified plan in place.

SIMPLE plans may be structured as IRAs or 401(k) cash or deferred arrangements.

SIMPLE IRAs

Under a SIMPLE IRA plan, contributions are made under a salary reduction arrangement that allows an eligible employee to elect to receive payments as (taxable) cash compensation or contribute them to a SIMPLE IRA account. For participation purposes, an eligible employee is one who received at least $5,000 in compensation during any two preceding years and who is reasonably expected to receive $5,000 in the current year. All eligible employees must be allowed to make the cash or salary reduction election. The amount to which the election applies can be defined as a percentage of compensation, but cannot exceed a specified annual indexed amount. Individuals age 50 or older can make additional contributions. For contribution limits for individuals age 50 or older, please see the appendix at the end of the book.

For each employee who elects to participate, the employer must also make contributions, according to one of two formulas.

- **Matching contribution formula**. The employer is required to match the employee's elective contribution, dollar for dollar, up to an amount equal to 3% of the employee's compensation for the year. (A rate as low as 1% can be used, provided the same matching contribution rate is used for all employees and that the lower rate would not result in less than 3% in more than two of the preceding five years.) There is no limit on the amount of the employee's compensation that may be taken into account in determining the employer's matching contribution. For example, if Brett earned $400,000, he could reach the maximum employer match of $12,000 ($12,000 = 3% of $400,000).

- **Nonelective contribution formula**. The employer may contribute an amount equal to 2% of each eligible employee's compensation for the year. (The eligible employee must have earned at least $5,000 that year.) The nonelective contribution formula places a limit on the amount of an employee's compensation that may be taken into account for this purpose; this amount is indexed for inflation.

All contributions to a SIMPLE IRA account are nonforfeitable; the employee is immediately and fully vested. Taxation of contributions and their earnings is deferred until funds are actually withdrawn or distributed, under the rules applicable to regular IRA distributions (see Unit 10).

SIMPLE 401(k)s

The Small Business Job Protection Act also added provisions to the tax code that created **SIMPLE 401(k)** plans. These provisions are similar to the SIMPLE IRA requirements; however, the nondiscrimination tests that have proved so burdensome with traditional 401(k) plans are alleviated somewhat. The ADP test will be satisfied by meeting the SIMPLE plan requirements.

A SIMPLE 401(k), like a SIMPLE IRA, must provide for elective employee contributions (per the same schedule above). The employer must make mandatory contributions on a matching basis (dollar for dollar for the amount the employee contributes up to 3% of the employee's compensation) or under the nonelective contribution formula, whereby the employer makes a contribution equal to 2% of compensation on behalf of each employee who is eligible to participate.

Employees are immediately and fully vested in all contributions made to a SIMPLE 401(k); there can be no restrictions requiring employees to keep the funds in the plan or limiting their withdrawal. However, any withdrawals or distributions will be subject to the general distribution restrictions imposed on regular 401(k) plans (see Unit 10).

One of the advantages of a SIMPLE 401(k) plan is that it is not subject to the top-heavy requirements that apply to traditional 401(k) or SEP plans. A plan is top-heavy when the accrued benefits or account balances of key employees exceed those of rank-and-file employees by certain levels. Some small employers, due to the mix of their workforce, the number of key employees, and the differences in pay scales among its employees will see a traditional 401(k) plan or SEP become top-heavy. For those years in which a plan is top-heavy, additional qualification requirements (such as accelerated vesting and adjustments to contributions or benefit levels) will have to be met. SIMPLE 401(k) plans are not subject to these requirements.

Keogh Plans

Years ago, when laws and regulations pertaining to qualified plans were established, the provisions requiring that plans be established by employers for the benefit of employees failed to account for a large portion of the working population. The self-employed (owners and partners of unincorporated businesses) were not considered employees for this purpose and consequently could not participate in such plans. To correct this inequity, Congress passed the Keogh Act, enabling self-employed individuals to establish and participate in a tax-qualified plan. These plans are known as Keogh plans.

Keogh plans provide that self-employed individuals are to be treated for qualified retirement purposes as employees of their particular enterprise. Such people would include a sole proprietor who owns an unincorporated business or an individual professional (a physician, attorney, or dentist) who is the sole or part-owner of an unincorporated professional practice. In addition to having an ownership interest, the individual must also be actively involved in the operations of the business.

Eligibility

Because a qualified plan must be established by an employer for the benefit of its employees, the law confers the status of both employer and employee to those who are self-employed. For example, the owner of a small unincorporated business is also considered an employee of that business. As an employer, he can deduct the contributions made to the qualified plan (provided the contribution meets all qualification requirements), and as an employee, he is not taxed on either the contributions made on his behalf or on the investment gains in the plan fund.

Even though the owner may be the only employee, the plan must provide for the eventual inclusion of additional employees at a later date. If the self-employed person has employees, they must be included in the plan, subject to permissible age and length-of-service limitations.

Active partners are also considered to be self-employed and eligible to participate in a Keogh plan on a tax-favored basis. However, limited partners who do not contribute any personal services to the company are not considered self-employed and may not participate.

A self-employed person's spouse must participate in the plan if he is a bona fide employee and meets the same tests applied to other employees. However, an employer-employee relationship is not formed by simply filing a joint income tax return.

Earned Income and Compensation

Earned income and compensation have a direct bearing on the allowable contribution that can be made to a Keogh plan. **Earned income** can be defined as earnings attributed to personal services that constitute a meaningful income-producing factor for the business. As noted, net income received by a limited partner who does not provide personal services to a business will not be considered earned income for Keogh contribution purposes. For self-employed individuals, **compensation** is defined as earnings from self-employment. It is a self-insured's compensation that will determine allowable contributions.

Plan Overview

As far as plan design and qualification, there is no distinction between plans established for Keogh purposes and those available to corporations. Self-employed individuals may select a defined contribution, a defined benefit, or a profit-sharing plan approach. The steps involved are then determined by the funding medium used under the type of plan to be installed. For example, a plan investing wholly in annuity contracts may be established without either a trust or a custodial account, but those requiring greater investment latitude should be administered by a bank or other competent entity as trustee.

Prototypes or master plans are normally used to install a Keogh plan, and plans must be in writing before the end of the taxable year for which the deduction is claimed. The plan must provide procedures for establishing a funding policy that complies with ERISA, describe procedures for operating and administering the plan, detail procedures for amending the plan, and specify how and when payments to and distributions from the plan will be made.

ILLUSTRATION 3

Lower Wage Earners: Credit for Qualified Deferrals and Contributions

To encourage more low- to middle-income wage earners to contribute to their own retirement, Congress, under the Pension Protection Act of 2006, established a credit for contributions or elective deferrals to a personal IRA (traditional or Roth) or employer-sponsored plan. The amount of the credit varies, depending on the amount contributed and the taxpayer's filing status and adjusted gross income (AGI), and is adjusted annually for inflation.

The amount of the credit is equal to the amount the individual contributes multiplied by 10%, 20%, or 50%, depending on AGI not to exceed $2,000 ($4,000 if married filing jointly). The credit can be applied dollar-for-dollar against the individual's or couple's regular tax. To be eligible for this credit, an individual must be at least 18 years old, cannot be a full-time student and cannot be claimed as a dependent on someone else's tax return. The credit is adjusted annually for inflation. For 2018 the credit is as follows:

Joint Filers AGI	Single Filers AGI	Allowable Credit
$0–$38,000	$0–$19,000	50%
$38,001–$41,000	Over $19,001–$20,500	20%
Over $41,001–$63,000	Over $20,501–$31,500	10%
Over $63,000	Over $31,500	0%

EXAMPLE

Karen is single, and her adjusted gross income for 2018 was $24,000. If she deferred $1,000 to her 401(k) plan, she would be able to claim a $100 tax credit for that year. The credit is in addition to any deduction or exclusion from gross income that is otherwise available.

For the purpose of calculating the credit, any and all amounts contributed by or for an individual to a qualified plan, IRA, 401(k) plan, 403(b) plan, or 457 plan will be considered a sum amount.

TAX-SHELTERED ANNUITY (TSA)

Key Point   Tax-sheltered accounts, also known as 403(b) plans, are similar to 401(k) plans set up for employees of public schools and certain nonprofit, charitable, education, or religious organizations.

A tax-sheltered annuity (TSA) is a retirement plan designed to meet the needs of employees of public schools and certain nonprofit, charitable, educational, and religious organizations. These plans are permitted under IRC Section 403(b), and so are often called 403(b) plans. (They are sometimes called 501(c)(3) plans, in reference to the IRC section that describes the types of organizations that qualify for such plans.)

Contributions to a TSA are used as premiums to fund an annuity contract or purchase shares in a mutual fund. They are excluded from a participant's gross income, and his earnings in a TSA accumulate tax-deferred until distribution. To ensure that TSAs are used for long-term savings for retirement, TSAs (like IRAs and other retirement plans) are subject to penalties if the savings are withdrawn before the participant reaches a certain age.

A TSA may seem like an employer-sponsored plan, and from a purely administrative standpoint it is (i.e., employees of eligible institutions may only participate in a TSA through their employers). But TSAs are also like individual retirement plans that happen to be provided through an employer arrangement. They are funded primarily by employee contributions (in the form of salary reduction) and are not subject to the eligibility requirements typical of a true employer-sponsored plan.

Qualifying Requirements for TSAs

TSAs are qualified plans and, as such, are subject to certain qualifying requirements. One of the requirements deals with the type of employer that can establish a TSA. To be eligible, an employer must qualify as a public educational institution, a tax-exempt 501(c)(3) organization, or a church organization. Eligible entities include:

- elementary and secondary schools (public and private);

- colleges and universities (public and private);

- zoos and museums;

- research and scientific foundations;

- private hospitals and medical schools; and

- churches and religious organizations.

Some tax-exempt employers, such as fraternal orders, credit unions, and chambers of commerce, are not eligible to establish TSAs for their employees. The TSA plan must satisfy certain eligibility requirements.

- The funding vehicle must be purchased by the employer for the participating employee's benefit and must be nonforfeitable.

- There may be only one salary reduction agreement per eligible employee per year.

- The TSA must be nontransferable and may not be sold, assigned, or pledged as security for a loan, except to the issuer of the annuity contract funding vehicle.

- The premium amount (which translates into contributions to the plan) must fall within certain guidelines.

The two types of funding vehicles that are permissible for TSAs are annuity contracts (either fixed or variable) and mutual funds.

Pretax Contributions

A TSA plan may be employee elective, nonelective, or a combination of the two. Most plans today are elective, enabling employees to make contributions by means of salary reductions. When the contribution is attributable to a prearranged salary reduction, the contribution amount does not constitute reportable income (for federal income tax purposes) to the employee since it is not constructively received. Rather, the amount of the agreed-upon elective contribution is shunted into the employee's TSA account. Although not currently federally taxable, any salary reduction amounts are still subject to FICA (Social Security withholding) taxes. Contributions that come from the sponsoring employer (rather than from an elective salary reduction) are not deemed to be wages and are not subject to FICA taxes.

Limits on Contributions

For the maximum annual salary reduction and catch-up contribution limits for employees age 50 or older under a TSA (Section 403(b) plan), please see the appendix at the end of the book. These amounts are subject to IRC Section 415 limits and an exclusion allowance (which operate independently to limit available contributions). The amount is scheduled to increase gradually over the next few years on the same schedule as 401(k) plans.

The annual limit applies collectively to contributions for all such salary reduction plans in which an individual participates. For example, if an individual is covered by both a 403(b) plan and a 401(k) plan, the maximum salary reduction that the individual could take and contribute to both is the limit for one or the other but not for both combined.

Withdrawals and Loans

Loans are available with many TSA plans; however, such loans must meet the same requirements that generally apply to loans from qualified plans. These rules are explained in Unit 10.

Withdrawals of amounts attributed to salary reduction contributions from TSAs are permitted only in instances of death, disability, severance, a loan, attainment of age 59½, or financial hardship. Any earnings credited to such salary reduction contributions may not be withdrawn for reasons of financial hardship. The amount of any withdrawal for reasons other than those mentioned will be considered ordinary income that is not only taxable to the participant but subject to a 10% penalty tax as well.

Distributions From TSAs

The rules governing distributions from TSAs are, for the most part, the same as those that apply to other qualified plans. For example, distributions from TSAs are generally subject to a 10% penalty tax if made before the participant reaches age 59½. After the age of 59½ and before the age of 72, distributions may be taken, but they don't have to be. At the age of 72 (or when the participant retires, if later), distributions must begin. (The distribution rules for all qualified and individual plans are discussed in detail in Unit 10.)

Any amount or portion distributed from a TSA that is not attributable to the participant's basis (employee's taxable contributions) is taxable at the employee's ordinary income tax rate. An employee's basis may have come from excess contributions that were taxed or premiums on life insurance within the TSA plan that were taxable to the participant in previous years. Generally, distributions attributable to mutual fund shares are taxed as ordinary income. If distribution from the plan takes the form of an annuity and is paid out for reasons other than the death of the participant, special rules apply for taxation. The tax-free portion of the annuity income is spread evenly over the annuitant's life expectancy by the calculation of the exclusion ratio, discussed in Unit 5, to determine the split between the taxable and nontaxable portions.

For TSAs, the exclusion ratio can be easily calculated using the following formula for the exclusion ratio:

$$\frac{\text{employee contributions}}{\text{life expectancy} \times \text{annual annuity benefit}}$$

EXAMPLE

To determine the income tax actually owed on periodic annuity payments, assume that a client has made $40,000 of after-tax contributions to an annuity that distributes $4,000 annually. According to the Pension and Annuity Income tables found in IRS Publication 575, the client has a life expectancy of 15 years. The exclusion ratio would be:

$$\frac{\$40,000}{15 \times 4,000} = .67$$

Based on this calculation, 67% of the distribution is excluded from current taxation; 33% of the $4,000, or $1,320, is currently taxable. The tax-free portion of the annuity is spread over the annuitant's anticipated lifetime of 15 years. Any undistributed amounts in a decedent/participant's TSA will be included in his gross estate.

In general, when an annuity contract is used to fund a TSA (and there is no life insurance protection), all benefit payments are fully taxable to the TSA owner. This is because most TSAs are funded by salary reductions or deferrals that are excluded from tax when deferred to the plan.

WRAP-UP

In this unit, we discussed the basics of qualified plans and focused on specific types of plans used primarily by corporate employers. In the next unit, we'll continue our discussion of employer-sponsored retirement plans by addressing the question, "Which plan should the businessowner choose?"

FIELD EXERCISE

Review your files to determine how many of your clients are participants in an employer-sponsored retirement plan. For each client, answer the following questions.

■ What type or types of plans are used?

■ Is the client taking maximum advantage of the plan or would the client be able to increase his investment in the plan?

■ Is the client an owner of the business? What would the consequences be if your client were to change the type of plan used?

U N I T   T E S T

1. All of these are tax advantages of an employer-sponsored retirement plan EXCEPT

    A. employees are allowed to deduct contributions made by the employer on their behalf

    B. employers can deduct their contributions in the year they are made

    C. expenses incurred in establishing and maintaining a plan are considered a deductible business expense

    D. earnings realized on the plan are tax-deferred until distributed

2. Which of the following statements regarding simplified employee pension plans is FALSE?

    A. They are relatively easy to establish and administer.

    B. They involve many of the same tax advantages as any other qualified retirement plan.

    C. Employers may pick and choose employees who will be allowed to participate in the plan.

    D. Employees are immediately and fully vested in all contributions made on their behalf to the plan.

3. Which of the following could NOT participate in a Keogh plan?

    A. Self-employed individual who owns an IRA

    B. Limited partner who does not contribute any personal services to the partnership but has invested money

    C. Spouse of a self-employed individual who works for the business

    D. Employee of a self-employed individual

4. All of these types of qualified plans specify a dollar limit on the amount that may be contributed annually on behalf of any participant EXCEPT

    A. profit-sharing

    B. SEP

    C. 401(k)

    D. defined benefit

5. With regard to SIMPLE IRA plans, which of these statements is TRUE?

    A. Once a SIMPLE plan is established, the employer must make contributions on behalf of every employee who is eligible to participate.

    B. Employees can elect to make tax-deferred salary reduction contributions to the plan or receive an equivalent amount in cash tax free.

    C. Under the matching contribution formula, only the first $100,000 of an employee's compensation may be taken into account for employer contributions.

    D. All contributions to an employee's SIMPLE IRA are nonforfeitable.

6. Which of these is NOT a qualification requirement for an employer retirement plan?

    A. The plan must be established for the exclusive benefit of the employees.

    B. The plan must be funded by the employer, the employees, or both.

    C. The plan must be permanent.

    D. The plan must provide for inflation-adjusted contributions or benefits.

7. Defined contribution plans

    A. tend to favor younger employees

    B. must use a graded vesting schedule

    C. can be overfunded with excess contributions so long as the contributions do not exceed 15% of covered payroll

    D. will be disqualified if they become top-heavy

8. Gerry participates in a 401(k) plan to which he has contributed $6,000 and his employer has contributed $4,000. Gerry is 40% vested. To what amount is Gerry currently entitled?

    A. $4,000

    B. $2,400

    C. $6,000

    D. $7,600

9. Tax-sheltered accounts (TSAs) are available to
   A. anyone who is not covered by an employer-sponsored retirement plan
   B. all nonprofit organizations
   C. public and private elementary schools
   D. credit unions

ANSWERS AND RATIONALES

1. **A.** Employers may deduct their own contributions, but employees don't get that deduction. What employees get is an addition to their account without having to pay taxes on the amount. Employee tax liability is postponed until withdrawals are taken.

2. **C.** Nondiscrimination rules prevent employers from picking and choosing employees who will be allowed to participate in the plan. Broad participation is required for the plan to be qualified.

3. **B.** Keogh plan participants must work for the business. This may include a sole proprietor, a partner who works in the business, or an employee, but not a limited partner who contributes no personal services.

4. **D.** Defined benefit limits focus on benefits, not contributions. Contributions are set in order to meet the plan's future obligation to pay benefits.

5. **D.** Contributions to an employee's SIMPLE IRA are nonforfeitable (as are contributions to any IRA).

6. **D.** Employer-sponsored retirement plans are required to have a definite formula for determining contributions (for a defined contribution plan) or for determining benefits (for a defined benefit plan), but there is no requirement that those formulas include an inflation adjustment. Inflation adjustments are found in federal contribution or benefit limits, but generally not in the plans.

7. **A.** Defined contribution plans function like any savings vehicle or investment that accumulates assets. The earlier you start, the more you will have at the end.

8. **D.** Employees are fully vested in their own contributions to a 401(k) at all times, so Gerry's $6,000 contribution is vested. Employer contributions may be subject to a deferred vesting schedule. Gerry's $4,000 contribution is 40% vested for an amount of $1,600. The total of both is $7,600.

9. **C.** To be eligible to set up a TSA, an employer must qualify as a public educational institution, a tax-exempt 501(c)(3) organization, or a church organization. Not all nonprofit organizations are tax-exempt under 501(c)(3).

8

Choosing the Right Plan for the Small-Business Owner

With the variety of qualified plan options available to businessowners, which type to choose is often a consideration in the installation of a plan. Large corporations usually don't face this challenging question, for several reasons. First, their options are more limited (they can't implement SIMPLE plans, for example). Second, they usually have a team of financial advisors or benefit specialists who make this decision for them. And third, most large employers already have a plan; although there is a trend toward replacing defined benefit plans with defined contribution plans. ■

UNIT OBJECTIVES

Small employers have a wider range of options to choose from than do large employers. Because most businesses being started today are small, they are less likely to have a plan in force. Furthermore, there are many small companies that have existed for a number of years without having established any kind of qualified plan. In this unit, we will focus on meeting the needs of the small-business owner.

On completion of this unit, you should be able to:

■ describe the types of retirement plans that could be used by the owner of a small business and the benefits of using a business-based plan rather than an individual plan; and

■ explain the costs and limitations of a business-based plan.

SETTING RETIREMENT PLAN PRIORITIES

Key Point   A small-business owner must decide (within legal limits) the classes of employees who will benefit most from the retirement plan, whether to allow employee contributions, and the level of the business's financial commitment to the plan.

Ideally, businessowners might be motivated to set up a retirement plan by a desire to do right for their employees. While doing the right thing is certainly a factor in prompting businessowners to action, their leading motivation is usually a desire to benefit their own bottom-line needs. Retirement planning professionals who recognize the basic truth in this statement will find it easier to understand their prospective clients' needs than will those who push an idea that favors the company's employees.

Fortunately, the Internal Revenue Code permits businessowners to set up plans that target their personal needs while at the same time benefiting their employees. There are, however, limits to the extent to which owners, highly compensated executives, and other key employees can favor themselves. These limits take the form of nondiscrimination rules. As long as they do not violate these nondiscrimination rules, businessowners can arrange their plans to meet their personal and business needs.

Key Issues in Setting Up a Retirement Plan

When deciding whether or not to establish a qualified plan and which type of plan makes the most sense, businessowners need to assign priorities to several key issues central to the decision process. These priorities can be stated in the form of questions.

■ How important will the plan be to assure a financially secure retirement for the businessowner?

- How important is it that the new retirement plan maximizes benefits for older employees rather than younger ones? This question is especially pertinent when the owner is older than most other employees.

- How important is it to maximize retirement benefits for employees with many years of service rather than those who will have been with the company for a relatively short period of time?

- How important is it to give employees the chance to contribute toward their retirement security?

- How important is a plan that has predictable costs rather than variable costs?

- How important is it to avoid an annual financial commitment?

- How important is it for employees to be able to gain access to their money while employed?

- How important is administrative convenience?

As these questions are answered, a picture will emerge illustrating the right type of plan for a businessowner. Let's examine them.

The Businessowner's Needs

Rarely (if ever) will businessowners disregard their own retirement income needs when deciding which type of plan to install. Therefore, it is appropriate to proceed on the assumption that taking care of oneself is priority number one. This will influence not only the type of plan but the plan formula, too.

When meeting with businessowners, retirement planning professionals should verify up front that taking care of the owner's retirement income needs is a top priority.

Maximizing Benefits for Older Employees

Is the businessowner approaching retirement, or is the businessowner one of the many young entrepreneurs who is reshaping the face of business in America?

Older businessowners won't have as many years to accrue benefits as younger employees. Defined contribution plans, which promise nothing in the form of retirement income but instead rely on the accumulation of individual employee account balances, heavily favor younger employees who have many years in which to do so. Young businessowners are much more likely to be attracted to defined contribution plans than those who are older and have relatively few years in which to accrue benefits.

Defined benefit plans, on the other hand, can be set up so that older employees can retire with a meaningful benefit despite their relatively brief period of plan coverage. By setting up a benefit formula based on years of service or final average earnings, an employee (or businessowner) can be assured of retiring with a benefit that is not shortchanged by the few years remaining to retirement. Defined benefit plans allow (in fact, require) plan sponsors to pay whatever amount is necessary to fund anticipated benefits.

If the businessowner is 10 years from retirement while other employees are younger, the lion's share of plan funding will be directed to covering the owner's accruing benefit.

One of the drawbacks of a defined benefit plan is the much higher degree of administrative expense (measured in time and money) compared to a defined contribution plan. It is unlikely that younger businessowners will be interested in defined benefit plans, especially because they can accrue just as meaningful a benefit (with lower plan costs and administrative hassles) using a defined contribution approach.

Rewarding Years of Service

All other factors being equal, most businessowners naturally want to reward employees who have been with the company for a long time over those who will have been there for a short time. If the group is relatively young as a whole, meaning everyone has plenty of time remaining before retirement, a defined contribution plan fits this objective (because there will be plenty of time in which to accrue benefits). If rewarding years of service is important and key employees or the owner are nearing retirement, a defined benefit plan will probably be more appealing. Remember, a defined benefit plan can look backwards and recognize service before the effective date of the plan; a defined contribution plan cannot.

Permitting Employee Contributions

If employee contributions are to be part of the plan, a defined contribution plan is in order. Even if a defined benefit plan is in place or will be installed, employee contributions call for a defined contribution plan, even if it means existing side by side with the defined benefit plan. Employee contributions must be fully vested from day one and must be allocated on a per-participant basis, a defining characteristic of a defined contribution plan. A 401(k) plan (regular or SIMPLE) is an ideal way to accommodate employee contributions, as are SIMPLE IRAs.

Reminder: Under the SIMPLE plan rules, a SIMPLE 401(k) plan will not satisfy nondiscrimination rules if employer contributions were made on an employee's behalf under any other form of qualified plan.

Cost Predictability

Most small employers will consider cost predictability to be a high priority. This fact alone points to defined contribution plans as the right choice, all other factors being equal. Defined benefit plans are characterized in part by the uncertainty of future costs, while defined contribution plans assure businessowners that future contribution levels will be predictable.

Businessowners who wish to accrue a certain benefit at retirement but also want the predictability of a defined contribution plan may consider a target benefit plan (see Unit 7).

Avoiding an Annual Financial Commitment

Retirement plans cost money, and employers who are not ready for the financial commitment such plans entail might consider delaying or forgoing them. They might consider a 401(k) plan (regular or SIMPLE), which shift some or all of the contribution burden to the employees.

Employers who are prepared to assume the contribution responsibility on a normal basis, but who want the freedom to suspend contributions in particularly lean years, could consider a profit-sharing plan. While contributions to profit-sharing plans must be recurring and substantial and must be allocated on a formula basis when made, they can be skipped in years when profits slip below minimum levels.

Employee Access to Plan Funds

Qualified retirement plans are intended to provide financial security in retirement. Giving employees the opportunity to tap into their vested benefits before retirement would seemingly defeat this purpose. The federal government agrees with this logic and penalizes workers who withdraw qualified plan funds before retirement with serious tax penalties.

But occasionally, the need for current funds outweighs the benefits to be gained at retirement. Employers who recognize that their employees might need their accrued benefits before retirement, and who want to allow them access to the money while avoiding tax penalties, may want to consider installing a 401(k) plan. Unlike other types of qualified retirement plans, a 401(k) plan may allow for loans, though certain procedures must be established so that the loan will not be treated as a taxable distribution. The rules for plan loans are addressed in Unit 10.

ILLUSTRATION 1
Agent's Perspective

Unless your client is in a one-person business, part of the cost of installing a retirement plan is providing benefits for employees. Some people don't like this, but others don't mind.

The fact is: your clients pay their employees in many ways. There are salary and health benefits, and there are retirement benefits. Adjusting the mix may be a way to give a raise to employees without incurring additional cost. This is accomplished in a qualified retirement plan by reducing the employees' taxes on the benefit. Point out to your clients that their competitors are using this tax leverage to reward employees. Your clients are at a competitive disadvantage if they don't put the same deal to use.

Administrative Convenience

When it comes to administrative convenience, small employers have a clear advantage over larger ones. While defined contribution plans in general have fewer administrative requirements than defined benefit plans, nothing beats a SEP plan or a SIMPLE plan for administrative convenience. In both cases, there are no reporting requirements and practically no employee disclosure rules.

DEFINED BENEFIT VS. DEFINED CONTRIBUTION

Key Point   Defined benefit plans typically favor owners and long-term employees, but impose a high financial and compliance commitment on the business.

Key Point   The financial and compliance burden of a defined contribution plan tends to be lower than for a defined benefit plan, but contribution limits keep these plans from being used to fund owner and key-employee retirements in a short period of time.

Deciding on the type of retirement plan to install usually comes down to comparing the advantages and disadvantages of defined benefit and defined contribution plans.

The Advantages of a Defined Benefit Plan

Defined benefit plans are especially attractive when the desire is to reward employees who have many years of service, or to replace a percentage of the participant's preretirement compensation, regardless of administrative requirements or funding commitments. Replacing salary (that is, retiring with a benefit that reflects a worker's income immediately before retirement) is especially important, because this is, in bottom-line terms, the truest measure of a quality plan. After all, of what significance is a retirement plan if the retirement benefit is a mere fraction of the income being taken home just before retirement?

The income that a retirement benefit seeks to replace can be an average of the compensation paid over an employee's total career. However, because compensation changes over the years (upwards, one hopes), a plan that replaces a worker's earnings nearest retirement will more accurately reflect the standard of living enjoyed at that time. For that reason, most defined benefit plans base their formula on the participant's final average earnings (typically, the average of earnings during the five to 10 years preceding retirement).

EXAMPLE

A plan could be based on a formula that promises to pay a monthly benefit equal to 20% of the participant's average monthly compensation during the five years preceding retirement. If a participant's final five-year average compensation is $50,000 a year ($4,167 per month), the plan would pay $833 per month at retirement. If the plan formula is based on career average earnings, lower compensation in a worker's earlier years will naturally reduce the average compensation and, accordingly, will reduce the retirement benefit.

A defined benefit plan may recognize years of service as well as final average compensation.

EXAMPLE

A formula might read, "2% of final five-year average compensation times years of service." In this case, an employee whose average earnings are $50,000 and who has 35 years of service would receive a monthly benefit of $2,917 ($4,167 × .02 × 35 = $2,917). An employee with the same average earnings but who only has 20 years of service at retirement would realize a benefit of $1,667 per month ($4,167 × .02 × 20 = $1,667).

The advantage described here may not seem quite so attractive to a businessowner who is younger than the company's other workers. For example, the owner is 40 years old and most of his employees are in their 50s. In this case, a defined benefit plan that recognizes either years of service or final average earnings will shift the funding weight in favor of those older employees. This might be agreeable to the owner, but it is more likely that he will want to balance the plan funding so that he and the other younger employees will benefit more by the funding. If so, he could use a formula that recognizes only years of service commencing with the plan's effective date. It's even more likely the owner will simply decide that a defined contribution plan makes more sense.

The Advantages of a Defined Contribution Plan

As attractive as defined benefit plans are for replacing employment income at retirement, most employers favor a defined contribution plan because:

- these plans are relatively easy to understand because they work like other investment scenarios; money is invested, and the end result depends on how well the investments do;

- investment risk is borne by the participating employee who makes decisions on how his account funds are invested;

- these plans are subject to less stringent funding and compliance requirements than their defined benefit counterparts;

- plan sponsors may choose from several types of qualified defined contribution plans to meet the specific needs of the employer and its participating employees; and

- defined contribution plans can offer at least one of the advantages of a defined benefit plan: rewarding employees with long terms of service (although this presumes the long-term employee participated in the defined contribution plan for the full length of his employment).

Money purchase plans often appeal to medium-sized and larger businesses. The employer must make a commitment to fixed contributions, which may make it easier to budget annual contributions

Profit-sharing plans are especially attractive to businessowners who are looking to avoid financial commitments when profits are low. However, profit-sharing plans can also be useful in motivating employees, especially when they are offered in addition to another plan. Knowing that their efforts (and the company's profits) can lead directly to a contribution on their behalf, employees are likely to view profit-sharing plans very favorably.

ILLUSTRATION 2

Comparing Defined Benefit and Defined Contribution Plans

	Defined Contribution	Defined Benefit
Contributions	Plan contains formula for determining annual contributions	Contributions computed based on the actuarial cost to fund the benefit obligation of the plan
Benefits	Amount accumulated in participant's separate account	Plan contains formula for determining retirement benefit
Individual accounts	Yes	No
Who contributes	Employer, employee, or both	Usually only employer
Benefits for past service	None	May be provided if called for in plan
Predictability of costs	High predictability	Lower predictability
Age of worker gaining most benefit	Younger workers (longer time to accumulate funds)	Older workers (benefits based on their higher salaries, years of service)
Administration	Simple and relatively inexpensive	Cumbersome and expensive
Understandability	Easy to explain to employees	More difficult to explain to employees

OTHER CONSIDERATIONS IN SETTING UP A RETIREMENT PLAN

Key Point   Qualification rules allow highly paid owners some leeway to skew benefits in their own favor through integration with Social Security.

Key Point   If Social Security integration does not meet owner needs, a nonqualified plan may be used.

When deciding which type of qualified retirement plan is best for a businessowner, several other factors should be considered.

Social Security Integration

Though it provides little more than a floor of basic protection, Social Security is an important source of retirement income. And, because employers pay half the tax used to support Social Security, they have every right to recognize this fact when determining how their retirement plan will be structured. The IRC and ERISA also recognize this and allow employers to integrate their plans with Social Security. That is, qualified retirement plans may use a benefit formula that offsets plan benefits (to a certain degree) by the amount of income a retiree receives from Social Security.

Integration provides a way to give highly paid employees a larger portion of plan benefits or contributions without being discriminatory. This is in recognition of the fact that Social Security weights benefits in favor of lower-paid workers. Social Security integration rules are an important planning tool for retirement planners. Integration is a logical extension of needs selling because Social Security will partially supplement efforts to provide a satisfactory income replacement level at retirement.

However, integration rules are fairly complex and may be confusing. These rules must be thoroughly understood by the planner before any discussion takes place with a prospect. It is beyond the scope of this course to fully explain the integration rules.

Nonqualified Plans for Key Employees

While nondiscrimination rules limit the extent to which employers can favor themselves and their key employees in a qualified retirement plan, there is an alternative approach they can take—step outside the qualified plan arena. Once an employer accepts the fact that immediate tax benefits will not be available, there are plenty of ways to provide additional retirement income to key employees without regard to ERISA's nondiscrimination rules.

As long as several basic rules are followed (namely, employees must not gain any economic benefit or have any constructive receipt of money used to fund the arrangement), employees will not be subject to income taxation on plan benefits until they are distributed.

Common nonqualified arrangements include deferred compensation plans and salary continuation plans. The basic difference between these two types of nonqualified arrangements lies in whose dollars are funding them. With a deferred compensation plan, the employee funds the plan (by foregoing the receipt of current income), while a salary continuation plan is funded by the employer. In either case, employers do not realize tax advantages until benefits are actually paid out, at which time they are recognized as income paid to employees, and may be deducted as such.

Within these two basic categories of nonqualified plans, there are several varieties. Nonqualified plans are the subject of Unit 11.

WRAP-UP

In retirement planning, there are rarely pure examples of right and wrong choices. Determining the best plan for a particular businessowner depends on a variety of factors, including the owner's age, personal needs, and business objectives (e.g., whether the company should fund the plan or have employees participate in funding it). One thing is certain—no retirement planner should approach a businessowner with a preconceived idea of the right plan. Deciding on the proper course to take requires a thoughtful analysis of the businessowner's needs, both personal and business.

Not all qualified plans are employer-based. In the next unit we examine individual qualified retirement plans, including the well-known (though not always well-understood) IRA.

UNIT TEST

1. Which of these statements regarding defined benefit plans is FALSE?

   A. They are generally less complicated to administer than defined contribution plans.
   B. They can recognize an employee's years of service before the plan was implemented.
   C. They are usually funded entirely by the employer.
   D. They cannot allocate employer contributions into individual employee accounts.

2. Which of these statements regarding defined contribution plans is FALSE?

   A. They are generally less complicated to administer than defined benefit plans.
   B. They can recognize an employee's years of service before the plan was implemented.
   C. They can be funded jointly by the employer and employees.
   D. They allocate employer contributions into individual employee accounts.

3. A businessowner who wants to set up a qualified retirement plan that allows employees to borrow from their accounts would have to establish which of the following plans?

   A. Simplified employee pension
   B. Defined benefit pension
   C. 401(k)
   D. SIMPLE IRA

4. If the owner of a small business is age 52 and the average age of the other employees is 40, which type of plan would probably most benefit the businessowner (all other factors being equal)?

   A. 401(k)
   B. SEP
   C. Defined benefit pension
   D. Profit-sharing

5. A businessowner who wanted to benefit highly paid employees as much as possible through one or more types of retirement plans might consider all of these approaches EXCEPT

   A. using a Social Security integration formula within the qualified retirement plan
   B. setting up a deferred compensation arrangement exclusively for selected key employees
   C. setting up a nonqualified salary continuation plan for selected key employees
   D. excluding employees who earn less than $30,000 per year from participating in the company's 401(k) plan

ANSWERS AND RATIONALES

1. **A.** Defined benefit plans are generally much more complex than defined contribution plans.

2. **B.** A defined contribution plan simply accumulates funds in an employee's account. There is no way to go back and give credit for time put in before the plan was adopted, but this is possible with a defined benefit plan.

3. **C.** A 401(k) plan may have a loan provision. IRA-based plans and defined benefit plans may not.

4. **C.** Defined benefit pension plans tend to benefit older employees more than younger employees.

5. **D.** An employer who wants to direct benefits to highly paid employees may integrate a qualified plan with Social Security or use a nonqualified deferred compensation or salary continuation plan. Excluding low-paid employees would disqualify a 401(k) plan or any other type of otherwise qualified plan.

9

Individual Retirement Plans

While employer-sponsored retirement plans help people meet their retirement income needs, many people are not covered under the umbrella of an employer plan. For them, the task of accumulating retirement assets can be daunting. Fortunately, the federal tax laws recognize this situation and make it possible for these individuals to enjoy the benefits of a tax favored retirement plan. ■

UNIT OBJECTIVES

In this unit, we study three retirement plan options that are available to individuals: the traditional IRA, the Roth IRA, and the 403(b) plan. We will explore what they are, the rules under which they operate, and the tax benefits associated with each.

On completion of this unit, you should be able to:

- discuss the basic rules underlying individual retirement accounts or individual retirement annuities;

- explain how traditional IRAs and Roth IRAs differ;

- determine whether individuals are eligible to deduct contributions to a traditional IRA; and

- determine whether individuals are eligible to contribute to a Roth IRA.

INDIVIDUAL RETIREMENT ACCOUNTS (IRAs)

Key Point IRAs may be set up as individual retirement accounts or as individual retirement annuities.

IRAs were created in 1974 to encourage retirement savings by people who were not actively participating in qualified pension, profit-sharing, or Keogh plans. IRAs allow qualified individuals to save for their retirement and enjoy some of the same tax advantages—tax-deductible contributions and tax-deferred accumulation—as are given to employer plans. Since their creation, IRAs have been subject to several changes affecting contributions, deductions, and eligibility. In 1998, the Roth IRA was introduced, providing yet another option to save for retirement. These two types of IRAs (the traditional and the Roth) are similar in many ways, but have a number of distinct characteristics and are governed by different tax rules.

To put the IRA in context, we'll begin with a few basic definitions.

Individual Retirement Accounts/Annuities

An IRA is a program available to working individuals as a personal retirement savings plan. As noted, IRAs were designed to encourage individuals to save for their own retirement by allowing for tax-deferred accumulation of the retirement funds and in some cases, tax deductibility of contributions to the plan. Depending on their particular situation, working individuals may also be able to make contributions on behalf of their spouses.

Basically, there are two approaches to establishing an IRA: individual retirement accounts and individual retirement annuities. Individual retirement accounts are established with qualified custodians or trustees, such as banks, savings and loans, credit unions, or brokerage houses. Some trustees charge a small annual fee, typically ranging from $25 to $50 for their custodial services. Allowable investments for individual retirement accounts provided by these trustees include stocks, bonds, CDs, mutual funds, government securities, and a variety of other investments.

Individual retirement annuities are annuities issued by an insurance company in compliance with certain standards and guidelines. For example, the annual premium for any individual cannot exceed the IRA contribution limit (discussed shortly), and no individual retirement annuity can require fixed premiums.

In making a decision about where to invest their money, individuals should know that, because each annual contribution is independent of any other, changes can be made in the investment of IRA funds. It is possible, therefore, that a person could have several different investments as a result of the separate individual annual deposits being placed in different accounts. Under certain circumstances, it is also possible to roll IRA funds from one investment into another.

Although the prevailing IRS rules that govern IRAs have been on the books for many years, much confusion remains as to who can establish an IRA, the amount that can be contributed each year, and exactly how much of that contribution is deductible. The introduction of the Roth IRA added to the confusion.

ILLUSTRATION 1

Excluded Investments for IRAs

The investments not permitted for IRAs are:

- commodity futures contracts (although units of commodity limited partnerships are permitted);
- tangible personal property, with some exceptions;
- investments in collectibles (art, antiques, gemstones);
- gold and silver coins minted outside the United States; and
- life insurance policies.

TRADITIONAL IRAs

Key Point Qualified individuals may deduct contributions to traditional IRAs on their federal income taxes, earnings are tax deferred as long as they are in the account, and distributions are generally taxable.

Key Point Individuals who are covered by an employer's retirement plan may not deduct contributions to a traditional IRA if their incomes exceed specified limits that change from year to year.

A traditional IRA can be established by anyone who receives compensation. For this purpose, compensation includes wages, salaries, tips, bonuses, and professional fees. It does not include investment earnings, pension benefits, Social Security benefits, disability payments, or unemployment compensation. A person whose income is derived solely through these means would not be eligible to establish or contribute to an IRA.

Contributions to a traditional IRA are not taxed while they remain in the account. This tax deferral of growth adds greatly to the amount of funds that accumulate in an IRA.

EXAMPLE

Assume that Anne and Cedric, both age 30, are each in the 24% tax bracket. Anne deposits $5,000 in an IRA account; Cedric invests $5,000 in a taxable vehicle. Both investments earn a constant 10% return compounded annually over the next 35 years. When they are 65, Anne's IRA will be worth $140,512; Cedric's investment will be worth $64,923. The difference is attributable to tax deferral. Because no tax is imposed on her earnings, Anne's rate of return is 10% each year; because Cedric's earnings are taxed at 24% each year, his annual net rate of return is only 7.6%.

It should be noted that Anne will have to pay tax when she withdraws the funds. If she withdraws them at age 65, she will owe $33,723, leaving $106,789, but this is still almost twice as much as Cedric. Anne doesn't have to withdraw anything until age 72 and even then doesn't have to withdraw it all at once, thus mitigating the tax that will be due.

Amount of Contributions

Each year of eligibility, a person may contribute to an IRA up to a specified amount, or 100% of compensation, whichever is less. Individuals age 50 or older may also make additional catch-up contributions. For the latest annual IRA contribution limits, please see the appendix at the end of the book.

A married couple filing jointly, whether only one spouse works or both spouses work, can set up two IRAs and contribute up to the annual limit to each of the two IRAs. A nonworking spouse's IRA is known as a spousal IRA.

EXAMPLE

Todd and Sara are a young married couple. Todd is the manager of a local hardware store; Sara does not work outside the home. A regular IRA could be established for Todd, and a spousal IRA could be established for Sara if they file a joint tax return.

Ongoing Contributions

Once an IRA has been established, contributions are made at the owner's discretion. They may be made as frequently or as infrequently as the owner desires. As long as contributed amounts do not exceed the annual limit, the account owner does not have to meet any other ongoing funding requirements. Financial institutions that offer IRA accounts may, however, impose their own limits. They may, for example, require a minimum amount to be contributed, such as $25 or $50, each time a contribution is made. Contributions for any year can be made up to the individual's tax filing deadline (typically, April 15 of the following year) and still apply to the prior year.

ILLUSTRATION 2

IRA Tax-Deferred Accumulation

If an individual invests $5,000 each year in an IRA, interest earnings accumulate tax-deferred and do not increase the individual's gross income until the savings are withdrawn. There is considerable benefit to contributing consistently because compounding of interest can increase savings dramatically over a long period of time.

The following shows how the balance of an IRA increases with consistent $5,000 annual contributions and tax-free accumulation (assumes 7% rate of return).

Starting Age	Total Deposited by Age 65 at $5,000 Per Year	IRA Value at 65
30	$175,000	$691,184
35	$150,000	$472,304
40	$125,000	$316,245
45	$100,000	$204,977
50	$75,000	$125,645
55	$50,000	$69,082
60	$25,000	$28,754

Deductibility of IRA Contributions

Although traditional IRAs are thought of as deductible IRAs (when compared to Roth IRAs), not all contributions to them are deductible. While any working individual may contribute to an IRA and enjoy tax-deferred growth, the ability to deduct traditional IRA contributions is based on a number of factors. These factors include:

■ whether or not the individual is an active participant in a qualified employer plan;

■ the individual's tax filing status (single or married filing jointly); and

■ the individual's modified adjusted gross income.

The combination of these factors determines whether a traditional IRA contribution will be fully deductible, partially deductible, or nondeductible. Regardless of deductibility, all funds contributed to an IRA grow tax deferred.

Active Participant Status

For purposes of the IRA rules, an active participant is an individual who:

■ was covered under a defined benefit plan in the current tax year;

■ had an allocation made to his account under a defined contribution plan during the current tax year; or

■ was entitled to (but did not necessarily receive) contributions or reallocated forfeitures to an employer-sponsored money purchase pension plan during the current tax year.

Filing Status

For the purposes of IRA deductibility, the two main categories for federal income tax filing status are:

- single—for unmarried, divorced, or legally separated individuals; or

- married, filing jointly—for a husband and wife filing one return for their combined incomes.

Modified Adjusted Gross Income

Modified AGI is compensation, interest and investment income, and Social Security benefits reduced by certain adjustments such as alimony, contributions to Keoghs, and early withdrawals penalties. For this purpose, IRA contributions are not subtracted in calculating modified AGI.

With these definitions of active participant, filing status, and modified AGI in mind, let's look at the steps involved with determining the deductibility of IRA contributions.

Step 1: Apply the Active Participant Test

A worker must pass two tests to qualify to deduct traditional IRA contributions. The first is the active participant test. Quite simply, if a worker is not an active participant (as defined previously), the worker may deduct the full contribution made to a traditional IRA regardless of compensation earned.

If the worker is an active participant, there is a second step based on compensation and modified adjusted gross income.

Step 2: (For Active Participants) Apply the Modified AGI Test

For active participants, the next step in determining the deductibility of traditional IRA contributions is to compare their modified adjusted gross income to the phaseout range that applies to the individual's filing status. (These ranges are different for single and joint filers. For the latest phaseout limits that apply to traditional IRAs, please see the appendix at the end of the book.)

If AGI is below the minimum of the phaseout range, the contribution is fully deductible; if AGI is above the maximum of this phaseout range, the contribution is not deductible at all. If AGI falls within the range, a partial deduction is allowed. A worksheet for calculating partial deductions is as follows:

1.	Enter the top of the phaseout range based on filing status (taken from the phaseout limit table)	_____
2.	Enter modified AGI (without reduction for any IRA contribution or certain other deductions)	_____
3.	Subtract line 2 from line 1 (If answer is zero or less, STOP; no deduction is allowed.) (If answer is greater than $10,000, enter $10,000 [including age 50 catch-up amount if applicable].)	_____
4.	Enter the maximum deductible amount for the year divided by $10,000. For 2013, enter 0.55 ($5,500 ÷ $10,000), or 0.65 if the individual is age 50 or older and entitled to make a catch-up contribution ($6,500 ÷ $10,000)	_____
5.	Multiply line 3 by line 4	_____

Deductible vs. Nondeductible Contributions

It is important to keep in mind that IRA owners can make contributions up to the annual contribution limit, even if the whole amount may not be deducted. Do not confuse the amount that may be contributed with the amount that may be deducted. For this reason, and to account for the tax treatment that contributions will receive when distributions are taken, traditional IRA contributions must be designated as either deductible (in which case a current tax deduction is taken and the amount contributed will be taxed upon distribution) or nondeductible (in which case no current deduction is taken and the amount contributed is received tax free upon distribution). A single contribution can be both deductible and nondeductible.

Individuals who may deduct any part of a traditional IRA contribution may still make nondeductible contributions; at the same time, they may elect to treat contributions that would otherwise be deductible as nondeductible. Deductible contributions are claimed on IRS Form 1040 or 1040A when one files his income taxes for the year; nondeductible contributions are designated on IRS Form 8606. Failure to report nondeductible IRA contributions will result in severe tax consequences for the owner when withdrawals are made: they will be treated as though they had been deducted and will be fully taxed.

Individuals who are ineligible to deduct their full contribution should consider contributing to a Roth IRA, if they are eligible (high-income taxpayers are not; see the following).

Spousal Rule

The limitation on the deductibility of contributions is determined separately for each spouse. Under prior law, spouses of active participants were themselves considered active participants for purposes of applying the phaseout rules for IRA deductions. However, today an individual is not considered an active participant simply because his spouse is. However, the deductibility of the spouse's contribution is phased out if the adjusted gross income exceeds a certain amount. Consult the appendix at the end of the book for the phaseout limits.

A spousal IRA is available when the spouse of an employed person has no taxable compensation or has a minimal amount of income. Spouses may also elect to be treated as if they have no income and, therefore, be eligible for the spousal IRA if desired. Under this arrangement, two separate IRA accounts are established: one for the employed person and the other for the spouse. No more than the maximum annual limit may be contributed to either account, but no other restrictions apply to the proportions that may be allocated. The combined IRA contribution, however, cannot exceed the combined taxable compensation of the couple. For the latest annual contribution limits that apply to traditional and spousal IRAs, please see the appendix at the end of the book.

Taxation of Traditional IRAs

Funds accumulated in a traditional IRA are generally not taxed until they are actually withdrawn. When this occurs, the taxation rules prescribe a rather simple approach—that which was not taxed before will be taxed now. If it was taxed before, it won't be taxed again. In other words, any IRA funds on which taxes were deferred will be taxed when they are distributed. This includes any contributions that were deducted by the IRA owner as well as earnings that accumulated in the account. Keep in mind that a traditional IRA is a tax-deferred device, not a tax-free device.

Distributions from traditional IRAs are taxed according to the annuity rules of Internal Revenue Code Section 72. These rules provide for a share of the distribution, representing a proportion of the account owner's cost basis, to be received tax free; the balance, representing currently untaxed earnings or previously deducted contributions, is taxable.

EXAMPLE

Lydia, 60 years old, has a traditional IRA valued at $50,000. Of that amount, $15,000 is attributed to nondeductible contributions she made over the years; $35,000 is interest the account accumulated. Now suppose she took a $10,000 distribution from the IRA. The nontaxable amount of that distribution is proportionate to the amount that previously taxed funds (the nondeducted contributions or cost basis) bear to the entire account value. This would be expressed as:

$$\frac{\text{cost basis (nondeductible contributions)}}{\text{total account balance}} = \frac{\$15,000}{\$50,000} = .30$$

The .30 is known as the exclusion ratio. The exclusion ratio is applied to the distribution and the result is the amount of the distribution that represents a nontaxable return of basis. In our example, Lydia's cost basis is 30% of the account balance. Applying this to the $10,000 distribution, Lydia will take $3,000 as a nontaxable return of basis; the $7,000 balance is attributed to interest earnings and is taxable.

If an IRA consists totally of deductible contributions, then there is no cost basis. The total value of each distribution is fully taxable. This is frequently the case, but it would be wrong to assume that it is always true. It is not true whenever nondeductible contributions have been made to the IRA.

Timing of Distributions

Distributions from traditional IRAs must follow certain rules if they are to stay within accepted tax guidelines and avoid penalties. Though this subject is discussed in detail in Unit 10, an overview of the rules is appropriate here.

■ Distributions from a traditional IRA taken before the owner is 59½ are subject to a 10% tax penalty unless the distribution qualifies as an exception.

■ Distributions from a traditional IRA must begin by the time the owner turns 72 and must be taken in at least minimum amounts every year. The purpose of this required minimum distribution rule is to prevent IRA funds from being perpetually tax sheltered and to force them into a distribution mode whereby they will be taxed.

■ IRA distributions are subject to ordinary income tax at ordinary rates, not capital gains at capital gains rates.

ROTH IRAs

Key Point   Contributions to a Roth IRA are not deductible, earnings are tax-deferred as long as they are in the account, and qualified distributions are tax-free.

Key Point   High-earning individuals are not eligible to contribute to a Roth IRA.

Key Point   Traditional IRAs and most qualified plans may be converted to Roth IRAs, but the transaction (alone among rollovers) is taxable.

Those who have been in the business a long time consider the Roth IRA to be a newcomer, but it is not so new. Introduced in 1998, Roth IRAs provide a different slant on the normal tax rules for retirement funds. No deduction can be taken for contributions made to these plans, but the earnings on those contributions may be entirely tax free when they are withdrawn. The tax benefits are said to be back-loaded as compared to the front-loaded benefits of an IRA or qualified employer plan. As one might imagine, tax-free accumulation and distribution of funds hold great appeal for many individuals.

Contributions

The tax treatment of Roth IRAs differs markedly from that of traditional IRAs. Contributions to Roth IRAs are not deductible. However, the earnings in Roth IRAs (which, like traditional IRA earnings, are tax-deferred while they remain in the account) may be withdrawn on a tax-free basis—subject to certain restrictions.

To make tax-free withdrawals from a Roth IRA, a Roth IRA account must have been held for at least five years and one of the following requirements must be met:

■ The account owner has reached age 59½.

■ The account owner has become disabled.

■ The account owner has died.

■ The funds are used to make a qualifying first-time home purchase (subject to a $10,000 lifetime limit).

Roth IRA contributions are subject to the same contribution limits we discussed earlier in connection with traditional IRAs. A taxpayer may contribute to both a traditional IRA and a Roth IRA, as long as the total contributions don't exceed these limits. Availability of Roth IRAs is phased out if a taxpayer's adjusted gross income exceeds certain limits. For the current phaseout limits that apply to Roth IRAs, please see the appendix at the end of the book. Availability of the Roth IRA is not affected by participation in an employer-sponsored retirement plan. Roth IRAs are not subject to the age 72 required distribution rules that apply to traditional IRAs. And contributions may be made to a Roth IRA as long as there is qualifying compensation.

When Roth IRAs were first introduced, only taxpayers with less than $100,000 of AGI, married or single, could convert existing traditional IRAs to Roth IRAs. This income cap was eliminated in 2010, and all taxpayers are now eligible to convert their traditional IRAs to Roth IRAs. It is important to keep in mind that conversions are taxable events for federal tax purposes. This involves paying income tax on all nondeductible contributions and earnings converted from the traditional IRA to a Roth IRA.

Modified AGI Phaseout Limits for Roth IRAs

Eligibility to contribute to a Roth IRA is based on modified adjusted gross income and filing status. Individuals with AGIs above specified limits will find that the maximum amount they can contribute is phased down from the specified limit and then eliminated entirely once AGI reaches a certain point. For the current phaseout limits for contributions to Roth IRAs, please see the appendix at the end of the book.

Individuals with modified adjusted gross income (MAGI) below the phaseout range may make a full contribution to Roth IRAs (reduced by any contributions to traditional IRAs for the year) measured by the annual contribution limit for the year plus the age 50 or above catch-up amount if applicable. Individuals with MAGI above the phaseout range may not make a contribution to a Roth IRA. Individuals with MAGI within the phaseout range can determine their allowable contribution using the following worksheet:

1.	Enter modified AGI (without reduction for any IRA contribution or certain other deductions)	_____
2.	Enter the bottom of the phaseout range (taken from the phaseout limit table)	_____
3.	Subtract line 2 from line 1	_____
4.	Enter ■ $10,000 for married (joint or separate returns) or qualifying widow or widower ■ $15,000 for all others	_____
5.	Divide line 3 by line 4 (rounded to at least 3 decimal places)	_____
6.	Enter the IRA contribution limit for the year (including catch-up amount for age 50 or older)	
7.	Multiply line 5 by line 6	
8.	Subtract line 7 from line 6. Round the result up to the nearest $10. If the result is less than $200, enter $200.	

This amount is reduced by any funds contributed to other IRAs.

It should be noted that Roth contributions that are phased down due to income levels can be made up with corresponding contributions to traditional IRAs.

EXAMPLE

If Dean and Diane each contributed the maximum they could ($2,600) to a Roth IRA, each could also contribute $2,900 to traditional IRAs. Combined, the contributions would equal the $5,500 limit. (If they were active participants, the traditional IRA contributions would be nonde-ductible because their AGI would exceed the threshold for deductible contributions to traditional IRAs.)

Taxation of Roth IRAs

The primary benefit of the Roth IRA is that it provides for tax-free accumulation and distribution of funds. In this way, it differs from the traditional IRA, which only defers taxation. With a Roth IRA, contributions are not deductible; taxes are paid up front. Theoretically, once a contribution is made to a Roth IRA, there are no future taxes to pay as long as the rules are followed.

To qualify for the tax-free advantages of the Roth IRA, two requirements must be met—the funds have been held in the account for a minimum of five years and:

■ the account owner has reached age 59½;

■ the account owner has died;

- the account owner is disabled; or

- the funds are used to purchase a first home.

If these requirements are met, no portion of Roth funds is taxable. If, however, funds are withdrawn before the end of five years or under circumstances other than those cited here, the earnings portion of any withdrawal could be subject to tax and possibly a 10% premature distribution penalty. (These rules are discussed in more detail in Unit 10.)

Be aware, however, that individuals concerned about liquidity in their IRAs can access funds on a tax-free basis so long as they have a cost basis in their account. Cost basis is equal to the sum of all contributions (which are nondeductible and therefore part of basis) minus any withdrawals. In other words, contributions may be withdrawn tax free on a first-in first-out basis. Withdrawals of earnings are subject to tax and possible early withdrawal penalty only after all contributions have been withdrawn.

Unlike traditional IRAs or any other qualified plan, Roth IRAs are not subject to minimum distribution requirements. The funds can remain in the account as long as the owner desires. The account can be left intact and passed on to heirs or beneficiaries. However, upon the death of a Roth IRA owner, any funds that do remain in the account must be distributed to the beneficiary in accordance with minimum distribution requirements.

Conversion to Roth IRA

When Roth IRAs were created, provisions were included to allow traditional IRA owners to convert their funds to a Roth IRA. Certainly the Roth offers benefits that the traditional IRA does not—tax-free withdrawal of funds, no age limit on contributions, and no required distributions are just some of the reasons IRA owners might want to shift their funds from a traditional account to a Roth. Most qualified plans can also be converted to a Roth IRA. When Roth IRAs were first introduced, only taxpayers with less than $100,000 of AGI, married or single, could convert existing traditional IRAs to Roth IRAs. This income cap was eliminated in 2010, and all taxpayers are now eligible to convert their traditional IRAs to Roth IRAs. It is important to keep in mind that conversions are taxable events for federal tax purposes. This involves paying income tax on all nondeductible contributions and earnings converted from the traditional IRA.

Converting funds from a traditional IRA or qualified plan to a Roth IRA entails two requirements:

- The taxable portion of the converted funds is included in the owner's gross income for the year in which the conversion takes place. This would include any previously deducted contributions and all account earnings.

- Once funds are distributed from the traditional IRA or qualified plan, they must be converted to a Roth IRA within 60 days.

EXAMPLE

Steve, age 42, has a traditional IRA worth $42,000 that he wants to convert to a Roth IRA. All of the contributions he made over the years were deducted. Steve is a 30% taxpayer (combined federal and state) and earns $65,000 a year. The full value of the IRA, $42,000, would be includable in Steve's income for the year, generating a tax liability of $12,600. Going forward, however, the converted funds will not be subject to taxation again, nor will their earnings. As long as Steve does not withdraw his funds before he turns 59½ (thereby satisfying the five-year holding requirement as well), he can look forward to tax-free accumulation and distribution of the money he converted.

The question of whether or not a client should convert traditional IRA funds to a Roth IRA usually centers around the question, "Which will produce the greater future benefit—paying taxes now and allowing the funds to accumulate for tax-free distribution or continuing to defer taxes and paying them in the future?" The answers to the following questions might help.

- Will the client's tax bracket be higher or lower in the future than it is now? An anticipated higher future tax bracket might be one reason to convert.

- How will the conversion affect the client's current tax liability? Will it push the client into a higher bracket?

- Where will the money to pay the tax on the converted funds come from? If the tax is to be paid from the IRA funds, that much less will actually be deposited into the Roth. Furthermore, distributed amounts used to pay the income tax and not converted will be taxed and may be subject to the 10% early distribution penalty.

- Does the client want or need greater flexibility after age 72? With traditional IRAs, distributions must be taken. Roth IRAs have no required distributions while the owner is alive.

- What is the client's age now and will he need the funds before the end of five years? Traditional IRAs require only that the owner be 59½ before withdrawals can begin (at least without penalty); Roth IRAs require that the funds be held in the account for a minimum of five years, even if the owner turns 59½ before the end of that time.

- What is the likelihood that the client will want to take advantage of the first-time homebuyer option? Both traditional IRAs and Roth IRAs allow withdrawals for this purpose without penalty; however, such withdrawals would be income taxable under an IRA and tax free under a Roth, as long as the account had been held for five years or longer.

IRA FUNDING OPTIONS

Key Point IRAs may be funded with annuities, stocks, bonds, mutual funds, and other similar investments.

Key Point IRAs may not hold life insurance or collectibles

There are few restrictions on the types of investments one can use to fund an IRA, traditional or Roth. Allowable options include passbook savings, money-market accounts, fixed and variable rate certificates of deposit, stocks, bonds, mutual funds, annuities, and even certain U.S.–minted gold, silver, or platinum coins or bullion of a type that is traded on the futures market. IRA funds cannot be invested in collectibles—artwork, rugs, antiques, gems, rare books, or stamps—or in life insurance. The appropriate funding option for an IRA should be determined by the individual's risk tolerance, investment horizon, and what is required in an asset allocation strategy.

Changing IRA Investments

When it comes to reallocating or switching IRA funds from one type of investment to another (from a CD to a mutual fund, for example, or from a money market to stocks) the laws allow much leeway. Depending on the type of IRA account, various investments may be bought or sold within the account. However, it is important to know the difference between a transfer and a rollover. A transfer is the direct shift of funds from one trusteed account to another. The IRA owner never takes receipt of the money; he simply directs that the transfer be made. The IRS imposes no restrictions or penalties on direct transfers; they can be done as often as the individual desires. The only penalty that might arise would be imposed by the financial institution that offers the investment. For instance, a withdrawal from an IRA CD before the CD's maturity date might trigger a loss-of-interest penalty.

A rollover takes place when an IRA owner (or qualified plan or 403(b) plan participant) actually withdraws funds from the IRA or plan and deposits them in another IRA. With a rollover, the IRA owner or plan participant takes receipt of the money and is given 60 days to deposit that money into another IRA. If the deposit is not made within that time, the transaction will be deemed a distribution and will be subject to tax and penalty. Rollovers are limited to one per 12-month period, regardless of the number of IRA accounts held by the owner.

WRAP-UP

IRAs represent excellent ways to save for retirement. IRAs are extremely flexible—they can be funded with a wide variety of investments or financial products, they are tax-advantaged and due to the penalties for early withdrawals, they encourage individuals to stay the course and keep the money intact for retirement. The main criticism of IRAs is the relatively small amount that can be contributed on an annual basis. However, consistent and steady contributions to an IRA account—traditional or Roth—can create substantial amounts over the years. The quality of an individual's life during retirement will depend as much, if not more, on the savings the individual builds as on what the government or an employer can provide.

FIELD EXERCISE

Make a list of clients and divide them into four categories:

- Eligible to contribute to both a Roth and traditional IRA and eligible to deduct the traditional IRA contribution

- Eligible to contribute to both a Roth and traditional IRA but not eligible to deduct the traditional IRA contribution

- Eligible to contribute to a traditional IRA only and eligible to deduct the contribution

- Eligible to contribute to a traditional IRA only but not eligible to deduct the contribution

UNIT TEST

1. Which of these would NOT be eligible to contribute to a traditional IRA?

    A. Sheila, age 55, is covered by an employer-sponsored pension plan at her current employer.
    B. Ron, age 32, is self-employed.
    C. Darlene, age 18, works part time and attends college.
    D. Bob, age 72, receives a pension income and Social Security.

2. Anyone with earned income can establish and contribute to a Roth IRA.

    A. True
    B. False

3. Which of these would NOT be considered an active participant when determining deductibility of IRA contributions?

    A. Self-employed consultant with an adjusted gross income of $85,000
    B. Employee for whom an annual addition is made in a profit-sharing plan
    C. Employee for whom a forfeiture is allocated in a 401(k) plan
    D. Employee who is covered by a defined benefit pension plan but who is 0% vested

4. Under what circumstance would a contribution to a traditional IRA always be fully deductible?

    A. An individual is an active participant in a qualified employer plan.
    B. An individual is not an active participant in a qualified employer plan.
    C. An individual's earnings for the year are more than a specified amount.
    D. An individual's earnings for the year are less than a specified amount.

5. In 2014, Barry made the maximum contribution to his traditional IRA. He deducted half that amount. What portion of his contribution will accumulate on a tax-deferred basis?

    A. None of the contribution
    B. Half of the contribution
    C. Dependent on Barry's age at the time of the contribution
    D. The entire contribution

6. Contributions to a Roth IRA are subject to income tax

    A. when contributed
    B. when distributed
    C. as they accumulate within the account
    D. never

7. This year, 45-year-old Barry opened a Roth IRA and made the maximum contribution. What is the earliest date he can take a withdrawal from the account without tax or penalty?

    A. After 5 years
    B. When he retires
    C. After age 59½
    D. Immediately

8. Which of these is subject to the 60-day rollover rule?

    A. Roth IRA-to-Roth IRA rollover
    B. Traditional IRA-to-Roth IRA conversion
    C. Qualified plan-to-Roth IRA conversion
    D. All of these

ANSWERS AND RATIONALES

1. **D.** Individuals who do not have earned income may not contribute to a traditional IRA.

2. **B.** Unlike traditional IRAs, Roth IRAs have a maximum income level for eligibility to contribute.

3. **A.** To be considered an active participant, an individual must be covered by a plan and eligible for contributions to be made on his behalf for benefits to accrue.

4. **B.** An individual who is not an active participant in an employer's retirement plan is always eligible for deductible IRA contributions.

5. **D.** The entire account accumulates on a tax-deferred basis. Earnings are sheltered in an IRA until withdrawn regardless of whether the contributions were deducted or not.

6. **A.** Contributions to a Roth IRA are not deductible, so they are taxed before the contribution is made.

7. **D.** An individual may take tax-free withdrawals from a Roth IRA at any time, provided that total withdrawals do not exceed total contributions to the account. Once all contributions have been withdrawn, however, earnings will be subject to tax unless the account has been held for five years and one of the qualifying conditions exists.

8. **D.** Rollovers from Roth IRAs and conversions from traditional IRAs and qualified plans to Roth IRAs are subject 60-day rollover rules.

10

Distributions From Qualified Plans

A retirement distribution may be one of the largest sums of money most people will ever receive. What people decide to do with this money has a significant impact on their financial security and that of their family in retirement. It is natural, therefore, for people to have questions about how they can receive this income, whether before or during their retirement years.

Any discussion or study of the subject of qualified retirement plans places much emphasis on the funding or accumulation aspect of these vehicles. What type of plan is appropriate, how it should be funded, how it should be structured—all of which are important considerations with which planners must be familiar. However, equally important is an understanding of the distribution aspect of these plans—how and when accumulated retirement funds may be taken or withdrawn.

Qualified plan distributions represent a very complex area of retirement planning and one that raises many questions. Answers to a client's questions about his qualified plan distributions must be framed within the context of the plan in which the individual participates—employer plan versus IRA, for example—for they are very different. The introduction of the Roth IRA further complicates the issue; it is no longer possible to present a one-size-fits-all explanation of IRA distributions because the rules for Roths are different from those for traditional IRAs.

The distribution rules also vary according to the age of the individual when the distribution is taken. Distributions taken before the age of 59½ are treated differently than those taken after that age; distributions taken after age 72 are treated differently than those taken before that age. This timeline sets up its own terminology—before age 59½, distributions are considered premature; after age 72, they are, for most plans, required. What happens or what may happen between age 59½ and 72 usually depends on the type of plan in question and whether it has a specified normal retirement date. In addition, many types of employer plans allow for in-service distributions (i.e., withdrawals during employment) for other than retirement purposes, such as hardship and loans. ■

UNIT OBJECTIVES

In this unit, we will explore many of the issues that influence retirement distribution decisions. As a financial services professional, you should be prepared to discuss the most common distribution options available to your clients and the tax consequences of these options.

On completion of this unit, you should be able to:

■ describe the normal tax treatment of retirement plan distributions;

■ explain the penalty that applies to distributions taken before age 59½ and exceptions that may allow a client penalty-free access to retirement account money;

■ describe the requirement for taking distributions after age 72 and the method for computing the required distribution amount; and

■ list alternative ways a client can access funds in a retirement account, including hardship withdrawals, loans, and rollovers and explain the conditions under which each might be used.

NORMAL RETIREMENT DISTRIBUTIONS

Key Point   Distributions may be taken from employer plans or IRAs in the form of an annuity or as a lump sum.

Key Point   Distributions taken before age 59½ may be subject to a 10% penalty in addition to tax; minimum distributions are required after age 72 or a tax is imposed on the shortfall.

Key Point   Distributions taken between ages 59½ and 72 are subject to tax but not penalties or restrictions.

Formal employer-sponsored retirement plans are designed to include provisions that address the point at which a plan participant is entitled to receive his benefits. Under most plans, this is accomplished simply by defining the earliest age at which an employee may receive full retirement benefits. This is known as the plan's normal retirement age. Most pension plans, for example, give this age as 65. Participants may elect a later distribution date, though generally this date cannot be deferred past age 72 or the individual's actual retirement date, whichever is later.

Under an employer plan, when a participant reaches normal retirement age, his plan benefit is payable. Under most pension plans, the benefit is paid out systematically in the form of monthly annuity payments based on the participant's life expectancy or, if married, the joint life expectancies of the participant and spouse. A plan may make provisions for an early retirement, such as 60 or 62, in which case the benefits will be actuarially reduced or, as noted above, a delayed retirement, in which case they will be increased. Annuitized pension benefits are fully taxable to the extent the participant did not contribute after-tax dollars to the plan.

ILLUSTRATION 1

Forward Averaging

For some participants, qualifying lump-sum distributions may be 10-year forward averaged, which lowers the rate at which the distribution is taxed. Forward averaging works to spread the distribution as if it had been received more than 10 years ago as opposed to a single year. The tax is still payable at once for the year of the distribution; however, the tax rate that is applied may be lower. The marginal rate at which a single $250,000 distribution is taxed is likely higher than the rate at which 10 annual distributions of $25,000 would be taxed.

To qualify for 10-year forward averaging treatment:
- the participant must have been born before January 1, 1936;
- the distribution must be from a qualified pension, profit-sharing, or stock plan (individual plans such as IRAs or SEP plans do not qualify);
- must have been of the entire balance of the plan and made in a single tax year;
- must have been made on account of the participant's death, disability, attainment of age 59½, or separation from service; and
- the participant must elect forward averaging treatment on all lump-sum distributions received during a single year (for example, if an individual received lump-sum distributions from a pension plan and a 401(k) plan and rolled one of them over to an IRA, the other would not be eligible for forward averaging).

The taxation of lump-sum distributions under the forward averaging rules can be extremely complicated. Unless he thoroughly understands these rules, the practitioner should confine the advice he gives a client to simply pointing out the options and should then refer the client to a qualified tax consultant.

Alternatively, depending on the type of plan the employer sponsors, benefits may be payable in a lump sum. Lump-sum distributions are common for 401(k) and profit-sharing plans, which are based on individual employee accounts. A lump-sum distribution is one that is made in a single year of the entire balance in a participant's account. Lump-sum distributions are fully taxable to the extent that the participant never made after-tax contributions to the plan. Individuals born before January 1, 1936, may take advantage of 10-year forward averaging to potentially reduce that tax on a lump-sum distribution.

Many individuals will choose to take their lump-sum distributions and roll them into another qualified plan, usually an IRA. This enables the funds to continue to accumulate on a tax-deferred basis under the umbrella of a new qualified plan or account. Once rolled over, the funds operate under the provisions of the new rollover account and the participant must follow the distribution rules as they apply to that account.

ILLUSTRATION 2

Agent's Perspective

A major issue for clients approaching retirement is distribution planning. You don't want the money coming out of an IRA or retirement plan too early or too late. Either way, your client could be hit with penalties.

Avoid the penalties with planning.

The 10% early withdrawal penalty creates a potential liquidity problem. A client who puts all his savings into an IRA or employer plan is asking for trouble. People need an emergency fund so they don't have to tap tax-qualified funds for every little thing.

On the other end, planning can mitigate problems that can be created after age 72 when minimum distributions are required. Remember this requirement when considering an annuity for a retired client. Will the required minimum distribution (RMD) rules result in your client drawing too much once he reaches age 72. For example, say your client is retiring at age 60. Knowing that he will be required to draw funds from his retirement accounts starting at age 72, it might be a good idea to buy a 10-year term annuity to provide income until then, after which withdrawals from the retirement accounts will replace the annuity as a source of retirement income.

If you think about it in advance, there are many things you can do to maximize the value of the tax deferral in these accounts.

Individual Retirement Plans

For IRA plans (and employer plans that use IRA accounts, such as SEP and SIMPLE IRA plans) there is really no such thing as normal retirement distributions. Under these plans, which are fully controlled by the individual, the period between the owner's age 59½ and 72 represents a time when distributions may be taken—in any amount and in any manner—but they are not required to be taken. If funds are withdrawn during this time (to the extent they represent previously deducted contributions or earnings), they will be taxed as ordinary income. Funds withdrawn from a Roth IRA any time after age 59½ are completely tax free, as long as they were held in the account for at least five years.

PREMATURE DISTRIBUTIONS

Key Point   A 10% tax penalty is imposed to encourage plan participants to leave their money in the plan until they are retired (at least until age 59½).

Key Point   Exceptions to the penalty allow penalty-free access to funds for many important lifetime needs as they occur before age 59½.

All qualified retirement plans—employer and individual—are subject to early distribution rules, which were designed to encourage the use of these plans as long-term retirement vehicles, not short-term tax savings plans. In this context, early is defined as any point before the individual reaches age 59½. Thus, any distribution received or withdrawal taken from a qualified plan before this age is considered early or premature. Premature distributions are subject to a penalty in addition to any income tax they generate. Specifically, as set forth in IRC Section 72(t), the penalty is 10%, applied to the taxable portion of the distribution.

EXAMPLE

Randy, age 44, takes a $20,000 distribution from his IRA plan to purchase a new car. Because the contributions he made to the IRA were fully deducted over the years, the $20,000 distribution is fully taxable. Consequently, in addition to the income tax he owes on the distribution, Randy will be faced with a $2,000 penalty. (For SIMPLE IRAs, the penalty is 25% if premature distributions are taken during the first two years of participating in the plan. After two years, the penalty is 10%.)

Exceptions to the Penalty

There are a number of exceptions to the 10% penalty exposure. For various reasons and under various circumstances, individuals can take distributions from their qualified plans before the age of 59½ and escape the penalty. These circumstances include:

- the death or disability of the participant;

- when the distribution is taken in substantially equal payments over life;

- to correct or reduce an excess contribution or deferral;

- when the participant separates from the employer's service after age 55;

- when the distribution is rolled over into another qualified plan or account;

- when the distribution is required per the terms of a qualified domestic relations order (QDRO);

- for payment of qualifying medical expenses;

- for payment of health insurance premiums while unemployed;

- for purchase of a first home ($10,000 lifetime limit);

- to cover qualified education expenses;

- for distribution of dividends from an ESOP;

- when the IRS has placed a levy on the plan;

■ for any reason, if taken out of *contributions* accumulated in a Roth IRA, but not earnings (we cover this in greater detail later in this unit.); or

■ for qualified reservists called to active duty after September 11, 2001.

Complicating the issue is the fact that these exceptions do not apply equally to all types of plans. Some are applicable only to qualified employee plans; others apply only to IRAs and IRA-based plans (such as SEPs and SIMPLE IRAs). The following chart can be used as a guide.

ILLUSTRATION 3

10% Early Distribution Penalty Exceptions by Plan Types

	Qualified Pension, Profit-Sharing, ESOPs, and TSAs (403(b) Plans)	401(k) and SIMPLE 401(k) Plans	Traditional and Roth IRAs, SEP IRA, and SIMPLE IRA
Death	X	X	X
Disability	X	X	X
Separation from service after age 55	X	X	
Certain medical expenses	X	X	X
QDROs	X	X	
To reduce excess contributions or deferrals	X	X	X
As substantially equal payments over life	X	X	X
First-time home purchase			X
Higher education expenses			X
Health insurance premiums while unemployed			X
Dividends from ESOPs	X (ESOPs only)		
IRS levy on plan	X	X	X
Roth IRA contributions			X (Roths only)
Qualified reservists called to active duty post-9/11	X	X	X

Death or Disability of the Participant

Under all types of plans, the premature distribution of funds is exempt from the 10% penalty if paid to a beneficiary due to the participant's death or to the participant if he is totally disabled. To qualify under the disability exception, the individual must meet the Social Security definition of disability (i.e be unable to engage in any substantial gainful activity).

Substantially Equal Payments Over Life

Also applying to all types of plans is the exception for premature distributions that are structured to be paid as a series of substantially equal payments over the participant's life or over the joint lives of the participant and his beneficiary. The payments must be made annually and cannot be modified before the participant reaches age 59½ or within five years of the date of the first payment, whichever is later. The consequence of altering the payment structure before that date is severe—the 10% penalty will be retroactively and cumulatively applied, going back to the first payment.

Correct or Reduce Excess Contributions or Deferrals

No premature distribution penalty is assessed if the distribution is taken to reduce or correct excessive contributions. For example, an individual who contributed more than $5,500 to an IRA could withdraw the excess and not be penalized. (If, in fact, the IRA owner did not withdraw the excess, he would be faced with a 6% excess contribution penalty.)

Separation From Service After 55

This exception to the penalty recognizes that early retirement is a fact of life. Consequently, if an individual leaves an employer's service after the age of 55 and the plan in which the individual participated allows for early distributions, a distribution can be made without penalty.

This exception applies to distributions from employer plans; it does not apply to IRA plans.

Rollovers

Distributions that are rolled over from a qualified plan to an IRA or from one IRA to another IRA are not subject to the 10% premature distribution penalty, as long as they qualify as legitimate rollovers and follow the rollover rules explained later in this unit. If a qualified plan contains life insurance, the life insurance may not be rolled over to an IRA.

Qualified Domestic Relations Orders (QDROs)

Premature distributions that are taken pursuant to a qualified domestic relations order (QRDO) are exempt from the 10% penalty. A QDRO is a court-issued order that gives someone the right to an individual's qualified plan assets, typically an ex- (or soon-to-be-ex-) spouse, and the QDRO is usually issued in the course of divorce proceedings or to satisfy child support obligations.

A QDRO applies only to assets in a qualified employer plan; it would not be applicable to an IRA or a SEP.

Qualifying Medical Expenses

Also exempt from the 10% penalty are distributions taken for certain qualifying medical expenses. Qualifying medical expenses are listed in Section 213 of the IRC; they include the unreimbursed cost of diagnosis, treatment, transportation, prescription drugs, and insurance premiums that exceed 10% of an individual's adjusted gross income.

The qualifying medical expense exception used to apply only to early distributions from qualified employer plans. The law was changed to extend the exception to include distributions from IRAs and SEPs as well.

Health Insurance Premiums

Unemployed IRA owners who take premature distributions from their IRAs to pay premiums on their health insurance will not be penalized by the early distribution tax. To qualify for this exception, the owner must have:

- received unemployment compensation for at least 12 weeks; and

- taken the distribution during the year in which unemployment compensation was received, or the year following.

Once an individual has been back in the workforce for 60 days, the exception no longer applies.

Self-employed individuals also qualify for this exception, even though they may not receive unemployment compensation.

First-Time Home Purchase

For IRA owners, there is an exception to the premature distribution penalty that exempts up to $10,000 in distributions taken for qualified first-time home purchase expenses, including the cost of acquiring or constructing the home as well as settlement, financing, and closing costs. Although most people acquire a first home only once, the tax laws as they apply in this case allow a person to acquire a first home again if it has been two years since the previous home ownership. The $10,000 distribution allowance is a lifetime limit.

Qualified Education Expenses

Available only to IRA owners is a premature penalty exception for distributions taken for qualified higher education expenses. These expenses include tuition, books, supplies, and fees for college, graduate school, or other post-secondary educational institutions. The expenses may be for the IRA owner, his spouse, children, grandchildren, parents, or grandparents. The amount of qualified expenses to which the distribution applies (and for which the exemption would pertain) would be reduced by any scholarship or educational assistance.

Qualified Reservists

Members of a reserve component who are ordered or called to active duty after September 11, 2001, may receive penalty-free early distributions from their IRAs, 401(k)s, or 403(b) plans if the reservists are on active duty for over 179 days or for an undetermined time and the distribution was made while the reservists are on active duty.

The term *reserve component* includes the Air Force Reserve, Army Reserve, Coast Guard Reserve, Marine Corps Reserve, Naval Reserve, Reserve Corps of the Public Health Service, U.S. Air National Guard, and U.S. Army National Guard.

Reservists who receive qualified reservist distributions can repay these amounts back to their IRAs even if the repayments would cause the total annual contributions to the IRAs to be higher than the annual contribution limit. Qualified reservist repayments are not deductible.

Premature Distributions and Roth IRAs

Distributions from Roth IRAs are different from those that apply to regular IRAs. Accordingly, the premature distribution rules apply differently as well. The general rule is that distributions of Roth contributions are not subject to income tax since these contributions were not deducted to begin with; therefore, there is no penalty imposed on distributed contributions, even if received before age 59½. What is subject to potential tax is the earnings portion of a Roth distribution, which also makes it subject to the 10% penalty if taken before age 59½.

One issue that causes confusion when discussing Roth IRAs is the tendency to equate premature distributions or withdrawals with the five-year holding requirement. In other words, some might contend that a premature distribution from a Roth IRA account is one taken before the end of the five-year period. For purposes of our discussion, the two are separate. The five-year holding requirement applies no matter what the circumstance—if funds are withdrawn before five years, the distributed earnings are subject to income tax no matter how old the owner is or why the distribution was taken.

When Roth funds are withdrawn before age 59½, the distributed earnings could be subject to income tax plus an additional 10% penalty, regardless of how long the account was held. This is an important distinction and must be considered in any planning process. For purposes of the premature distribution rules as they pertain to Roth IRAs, age 59½ can be used as the defining point—any withdrawal before age 59½ is considered premature and potentially subject to tax and the 10% penalty.

The exceptions to the 10% penalty for Roth IRAs are the same as for traditional IRAs—death, disability, first-time home purchase, qualifying medical expenses, payment of health insurance premiums while unemployed, payment for higher education expenses, and distributions taken as substantially equal payments over life. Depending on how long the account was held, however, these same distributions—though exempt from penalty—

could be subject to income tax. The following chart summarizes the taxation and penalty rules for Roth distributions as they compare to traditional IRAs:

	Roth IRA				Traditional IRA	
	Held less than 5 years		Held 5 years or more			
	Earnings taxed	*10% penalty*	*Earnings taxed*	*10% penalty*	*Earnings taxed*	*10% penalty*
Before age 59½ and no exception applies	Yes	Yes	Yes	Yes	Yes	Yes
Death	Yes	No	No	No	Yes	No
Disability	Yes	No	No	No	Yes	No
First-time home purchase	Yes	No	No	No	Yes	No
Substantially equal payments	Yes	No	Yes	No	Yes	No
Medical expenses	Yes	No	Yes	No	Yes	No
Health insurance while unemployed	Yes	No	Yes	No	Yes	No
Higher education expenses	Yes	No	Yes	No	Yes	No
After age 59½	Yes	No	No	No	Yes	No

ILLUSTRATION 4

Calculating Taxable and Nontaxable Portions of a Traditional IRA Distribution

In 1980, Dan, age 42, opened an IRA account. Over the next few years, he made annual contributions that were fully deductible. In 1986, the tax laws changed and Dan, who was also a participant in his company's profit-sharing plan, could no longer make deductible contributions. However, realizing the benefits of tax-deferred compounding, he continued to make annual deposits to his account. Many years later, his IRA had grown to $100,000. His deductible contributions totaled $9,000; his nondeductible contributions totaled $39,000. If he took a $20,000 distribution from his IRA at this point (his first), how would it have been taxed?

Distributions from IRAs that contain both deductible and nondeductible contributions are taxed under the annuity rules of IRC Section 72, which provide that a portion of each payment is treated as a nontaxable return of basis, with the balance being taxable. The formula for determining this is fairly straightforward—divide the IRA owner's investment (or basis) in the contract by the IRA account value as of the end of the previous year and then apply that ratio to the distributed amount. The result is the nontaxable portion of the distribution. Let's see how this calculation would apply to Dan's $20,000 distribution:

$$\frac{\text{basis in contract}}{\text{IRA account value as of 12/31 of previous year}} \times \frac{\text{distribution}}{\text{amount}} = \frac{\text{nontaxable portion}}{\text{of distribution}}$$

$$\frac{\$39,000}{\$100,000} \times \$20,000 = \$7,800$$

This calculation must be done every year to account for the changing proportion of cost basis to the changing value of the plan. For example, the year after taking his first distribution, Dan takes an $8,000 distribution (his second) from his IRA. His value in the account as of December 31 of the prior year was $84,000. He would calculate the taxable and nontaxable portions of the second distribution as follows:

$$\frac{\$32,000}{\$84,000 + \$8,000} \times \$8,000 = \$2,783$$

As you can see, the contract basis for the second calculation was reduced by the amount that Dan recovered tax free when he took his first distribution.

It should be noted that for purposes of determining the taxable and nontaxable portions of an IRA distribution, all traditional IRAs owned by an individual are treated as one plan by the IRS; therefore, the value of all of an individual's traditional IRAs are included when determining account value. This rule applies even if a distribution is taken only from one plan.

REQUIRED DISTRIBUTIONS

Key Point   Once an individual reaches age 72, a minimum amount must be distributed from the retirement account each year.

Key Point   The distribution amount is determined by dividing the account value by the owner's life expectancy, as determined under an IRS table.

Just as there are rules and penalties to discourage the early withdrawal of qualified plan funds, there are rules and penalties to discourage the use of qualified plans as perpetual tax shelters. With the exception of Roth IRAs, every type of qualified plan requires distributions to begin by a certain date and in at least certain minimum annual amounts. These are known as required minimum distributions (RMDs).

The exact date by which required distributions must begin varies by the type of plan. Generally, distributions from IRAs (including SEP and SIMPLE IRAs) must begin no later than April 1 following the year the owner turns 72. Distributions from qualified employer plans must begin no later than April 1 following the year the participant:

■   turns 72; or

■   retires, whichever is later.

However, a participant in a qualified employer plan who is more than 5% owner does not have the option to wait until retirement. These individuals must start their distributions by April 1 of the year following the year they turn 72, whether or not they have retired.

The date on which distributions must begin is known as the **required beginning date** (RBD). Though the first required distribution can be delayed until April 1 following the year the participant turns 72 (or retires, if that option is applicable), all subsequent distributions must be taken by December 31 for the year in which they are required.

EXAMPLE

Lonnie, the owner of an IRA, turned 72 on August 1, 2021. He must take a distribution for 2021 no later than April 1, 2022. He must also take the distribution for the year 2022 no later than December 31, 2022. Clients who are reluctant to begin minimum distributions are likely to change their minds when they realize that the IRS imposes a 50% penalty on the difference between the amount that should have been distributed and the amount that was actually distributed.

EXAMPLE

If a participant has a minimum distribution of $10,000 but elects to receive only $4,000, the penalty for failing to take the minimum due is calculated as follows:

$10,000	Required minimum distribution
− 4,000	Amount actually distributed
$6,000	Shortfall
× .50	Penalty rate
$3,000	Penalty

As this calculation demonstrates, failure to comply with minimum distribution rules can result in serious penalties for the participant.

The Distribution Period

The purpose of the required distribution rules is to prevent perpetual tax sheltering of plan assets by forcing them to be distributed and then taxed. Consequently, to the extent that there are funds remaining in a participant's qualified plan (or plans) as of the required beginning date, they must be taken by a certain period of time prescribed by law. Previously, this period was based on the participant's single life expectancy or the joint life expectancy of the participant and beneficiary. The choice was up to the participant and would vary from individual to individual. The objective was to help ensure that a participant's qualified plan interest was fully distributed over life and required that the distribution period—single or joint life—be selected before RMDs began.

A single uniform distribution period is to be used by virtually all participants. (The exception is a participant with a beneficiary spouse who is more than 10 years younger.) These periods are as follows:

Uniform Lifetime Distribution Table			
Age of Participant	Distribution Period (Years)	Age of Participant	Distribution Period (Years)
70	27.4	86	14.1
71	26.5	87	13.4
72	25.6	88	12.7
73	24.7	89	12.0
74	23.8	90	11.4
75	22.9	91	10.8
76	22.0	92	10.2
77	21.2	93	9.6
78	20.3	94	9.1
79	19.5	95	8.6
80	18.7	96	8.1
81	17.9	97	7.6
82	17.1	98	7.1
83	16.3	99	6.7
84	15.5	100	6.3
85	14.8		

(The complete uniform distribution table extends to age 115.)

EXAMPLE

Carl celebrated his 72nd birthday in April this year, so he must begin taking minimum distributions from his IRA. Per the Uniform Lifetime Distribution Table, the time period for the distribution of his IRA money is 25.6 years. The following year, when Carl is 73, the remaining time period for the distribution of his IRA money is 24.7 years.

These time periods are based on the joint life expectancies of an individual and a beneficiary 10 years younger at each age, beginning at age 72. In other words, the distribution period of 25.6 years reflects a joint life expectancy of a 72-year-old and a 62-year-old; the distribution period of 24.7 years reflects a joint life expectancy of a 73-year-old and a 63-year-old; and so on.

The uniform lifetime distribution periods are used whether or not the participant has named a beneficiary, with one exception.

The Spousal Beneficiary Exception

The only exception to the use of the universal distribution period is when the participant's beneficiary is a spouse who is more than 10 years younger. In those cases, the distribution period may be determined using the couple's actual joint life expectancy from IRS tables. This period will always be longer than the uniform lifetime distribution period.

EXAMPLE

Carl had named his wife Marie as the beneficiary of his IRA. When Carl turned 72, Marie was 58. Their joint life expectancy (based on IRS tables) is 28.4 years, which can be used as the distribution period for Carl's RMDs. If the age of a spousal beneficiary is within 10 years of the plan participant, the universal distribution period based solely on the participant's age is used.

The Required Distribution Amount

The significance of the distribution period is that it establishes the amount that must be taken as a required minimum distribution for any given year. The formula is simple:

$$\frac{\text{account balance as of 12/31 of prior year}}{\text{prescribed distribution period factor}}$$

This formula is used every year to determine the required minimum distribution for that year. The prescribed distribution period factor is taken from the table and applies to everyone, whether or not they have named a beneficiary. Again, the only exceptions are cases where the beneficiary is a spouse who is more than 10 years younger than the participant. For these individuals, the actual joint life expectancy period may be used as the denominator in the formula. Let's look at a couple of examples.

EXAMPLE

Ramone turns 72 this year and must begin taking minimum distributions from his IRA. As of December 31 last year, the IRA was worth $475,000. Ramone's beneficiary is his 65-year old wife, Loni. His RMD for the current year is:

$$\frac{\$475,000}{25.6} = \$18,555$$

(The factor of 27.4 comes from the uniform distribution table. It is the factor applicable to a 70-year-old.)

Assume it is one year later. The balance in Ramone's IRA as of December 31 the following year is $484,282. His required minimum distribution for the second year is:

$$\frac{\$484,282}{24.7} = \$19,607$$

As you can see, Loni's age does not enter into the RMD calculation (it would have under rules in effect before 2001).

This is not to say that a participant is limited to only the required amount. At any time, if more is wanted or needed, more can be taken; there is no ceiling on the amount a participant may take after the required beginning date. The minimum distribution rules are just that—rules that govern the minimum amount that must be taken.

Now let's look at an example that shows what the RMD would be if the participant named a spousal beneficiary who is more than 10 years younger than the participant. In these cases, the actual joint life expectancy of the two lives can be used.

EXAMPLE

John turns 72 this year and must begin taking distributions from his 401(k) plan. He retired some time ago but had not needed the 401(k) money, choosing to let it remain in the plan and continue to accumulate tax-deferred. As of December 31 last year, the account was worth $475,000. John's 58-year-old wife, Nancy, is the beneficiary of his 401(k) plan. Because Nancy is his spouse and more than 10 years younger than John, he can use their actual joint life expectancy factor (28.4 years) to determine his RMD:

$$\frac{\$475,000}{28.4} = \$16,725$$

As you can see, though the amounts in Ramone's and John's retirement plans were the same when they began their required distributions, John's RMD for the first year was almost $2,000 less than Ramone's. Because John was able to use the actual joint life expectancy for a 72-year-old and a 58-year-old (28.4 years compared to 26.4 years), the longer distribution period produces a lower RMD. The benefit to a lower RMD is lower taxes.

Selecting the Beneficiary

Under the old required distribution rules, the plan participant had to choose either a single life payout period or a joint life payout period. Consequently, for joint life payouts (which always produced lower RMDs than single life payouts), the beneficiary had to be designated before the required beginning date because there was no other way to calculate the RMD amount. This was a major flaw in the old rules because it hampered beneficiary changes after age 72.

Now, because required minimum distributions are calculated based only on the age of the participant (with the sole exception given to those who want to take advantage of the longer distribution period for spousal beneficiaries who are more than 10 years younger), it is not necessary to designate a beneficiary for RMD purposes. In fact, beneficiaries do not need to be identified until the end of the year following the year of the participant's death. Under the old rules, a change of beneficiary could increase the required minimum distribution. Under the new rules, a change of beneficiary has no effect on the participant's RMD amount because the age of the beneficiary is no longer taken into account in that calculation.

For RMD purposes, the beneficiary of a participant's qualified account will be determined based on those designated as of December 31 of the year following the year the participant died. Consequently, any individual who was a beneficiary as of the date of the participant's death but not a beneficiary as of the later date (having disclaimed entitlement to the benefit in favor of another or having cashed out of the plan) will not be considered for purposes of determining the distribution period and RMDs after the participant's death.

Distributions at Death

In the event a participant dies before the funds in his plan (or plans) have been fully distributed, the remaining monies must be withdrawn according to guidelines set forth in IRS regulations. These regulations vary, depending on whether the participant dies before or after his required beginning date and the type of plan involved.

The rules, which are quite complicated, are shown in the following chart.

	Account owner dies before RBD	Account owner dies after distribution has begun
Year of death	No RMD is required for the year of death since the account owner did not reach her RBD.	In the year of an account owner's death, RMD is paid to the estate in amounts equal to the amount that would have been paid to the account owner had she lived to the end of the year.
Spouse is sole beneficiary	If account is an IRA, the spouse may treat IRA as her own and compute RMD as the account owner (rather than beneficiary) when the time comes. Otherwise, RMD for a spousal beneficiary is determined either by (a) following provisions in an employer's plan requiring application of the five-year rule that otherwise applies when no beneficiary is named or (b) by dividing the appropriate account balance by the following period: ■ The spouse's life expectancy from IRS single life table (Table I) for the year after the year of death and continuing to use the single life table for each following year based on the spouse's age for that year). Note that since the RBD was never reached by the account owner, a new start date applies. The first RMD payment must be made by the later of (a) the end of the calendar year following the year of death or (b) the end of the calendar year in which the account owner would have reached age 70½ if she had lived.	If account is an IRA, the spouse may treat IRA as her own and compute RMD as the account owner (rather than beneficiary) when the time comes. Otherwise, RMD for a spousal beneficiary is determined by dividing the appropriate account balance by the following period: ■ Longer of— — spouse's life expectancy from IRS single life table (Table I) for the year after the year of death and continuing to use the single life table for each following year based on the spouse's age for that year); or — IRA owners age during the year of death and continue using the single life table for each following year using the age of the prior year plus 1. — the period determined as if no beneficiary were named.
Other eligible designated beneficiaries ■ The IRA owner's minor child.* ■ An individual who is not more than 10 years younger than the IRA owner. ■ Disabled (as defined by the IRS). ■ Chronically ill (as defined by the IRS).	Distribute the entire balance by end of the 10th year after the year of the owner's death, or take a lifetime distribution based on Table I. ■ NOTE: Minor children of the IRA owner may take a lifetime distribution based on Table I, until they reach the age of majority. Upon reaching the age of majority, the 10-year rule applies.	Take entire balance by end of the 10th year after the year of the owner's death, or take a lifetime distribution using Table I based on younger of beneficiary's age as of end of year after the owner's death or owner's age as of year of death. ■ NOTE: Minor children of the IRA owner may take a lifetime distribution based on Table I, until they reach the age of majority. Upon reaching the age of majority, the 10-year rule applies.

	Account owner dies before RBD	**Account owner dies after distribution has begun**
Nonspousal beneficiary	Take entire balance by the end of the 10th year after the year of the IRA owner's death.	Take entire balance by the end of the 10th year after the year of the IRA owner's death.
Other designated beneficiaries (e.g., charities or estate)	If no beneficiary is designated, RMD must be paid out by the end of the calendar year containing the fifth anniversary of the account owner's death. This is known as the *five-year rule*.	If no beneficiary is designated, RMD must be paid out by the end of the calendar year containing the fifth anniversary of the account owner's death. This is known as the *five-year rule*.
No beneficiary is designated	If no beneficiary is designated, RMD must be paid out by the end of the calendar year containing the fifth anniversary of the account owner's death. This is known as the *five-year rule*.	If no beneficiary is designated, RMD must be paid out by the end of the calendar year containing the fifth anniversary of the account owner's death. This is known as the *five-year rule*.

Minimum Distributions and Multiple Plans

It is not uncommon for one's retirement savings to be invested in a number of different accounts or plans. For example, a person may participate in his company's 401(k) plan, be covered by a profit-sharing plan and own two or three IRAs. How do the minimum distribution rules apply in these situations? Must a minimum distribution be made from each? Or can separate accounts and separate plans be aggregated for this purpose?

The IRS allows only limited aggregating. IRAs may be aggregated with IRAs and TSAs may be aggregated with TSAs. Pension or profit-sharing plans may not be aggregated with IRAs, TSAs, or even other pension or profit-sharing plans. Minimum distributions must be calculated and taken from each plan.

Note that in this sense, *aggregation* is a mathematical, not a physical, combining of accounts. With multiple IRAs or TSAs, a minimum distribution is calculated separately for each, but then these amounts may be totaled and taken from any one of the accounts or from any combination of the accounts.

EXAMPLE

Jill is a 72-year-old retiree with a number of retirement plans, including three traditional IRAs. Assume the following minimum distribution options apply for each:

Plan	Minimum Distribution Due
IRA in bank CD	$500
IRA in annuity	$733
IRA in mutual fund	$ 11,132
Profit-sharing plan	$ 17,307
Pension plan	$ 23,116
TSA in annuity	<u>$1,346</u>
	$54,134

What are Jill's options? She must take $17,307 from the profit-sharing plan, $23,116 from the pension plan, and $1,346 from the TSA. The remaining amount due for the IRAs—$12,365—may be taken from any one IRA or from any combination of IRAs.

TAXATION OF REQUIRED DISTRIBUTIONS

Key Point   Required distributions are taxed in a manner similar to any other distribution from a retirement account.

As mentioned earlier, the primary reason that the RMD rules were enacted was to force qualified plan money into a distribution mode during the life of the participant so that it could be taxed. In this last section, we will look at the income tax rules that apply to RMDs as well as the estate tax rules.

Income Taxation

The income taxation of required distributions is fairly straightforward and, with the exception of Roth IRAs, follows a basic rule of thumb—that which was not taxed before distribution is taxed upon distribution. This means that any contributions and any interest earnings that were not taxed on the front end will be subject to tax when distributed from the plan. Conversely, any contribution that was taxed to the participant before it was deposited in the plan is recovered tax free.

Thus, a distribution from a plan that consists entirely of deductible contributions is fully taxable. This would be typical for a 401(k) account, for example, because the account likely consists of pretax contributions by the participant and account earnings. A distribution from a plan that contains nondeductible contributions is partially taxable and partially tax free. This might be the case with some traditional IRAs. Nondeductible contributions represent the participant's cost basis or investment in the contract; these amounts are not taxed when they are distributed. Only the portion of the distribution that represents deductible contributions and interest earnings, never previously taxed, is taxed upon distribution.

EXAMPLE

Myron has two IRAs. He opened IRA #1 in 1985 and contributed $11,000 to it over the years. These contributions were fully deductible. Myron opened IRA #2 in 1992 and made deposits totaling $16,000 ($12,000 in deductible contributions and $4,000 in nondeductible contributions). A number of years ago, he ceased making contributions entirely.

Myron must take his first required distribution this year. As of December 31 last year, the value of IRA #1 was $31,500; the value of IRA #2 was $26,600. Myron's RMD is $2,120 ($58,100/27.4), which he takes from IRA #2. The following shows how Myron will determine the taxable and nontaxable portions of that distribution when he fills out his tax return for this year:

1.	Value of all IRAs as of December 31 last year plus any distribution taken last year	$58,100
2.	Myron's total IRA cost basis	$4,000
3.	Cost basis as a percentage of total IRA value ($4,000 / $58,100)	6.9%
4.	Nontaxable portion of distribution (.069 × $2,120)	$ 146
5.	Taxable portion of distribution ($2,120 − $146)	$1,974

Notice how the calculation ignores which IRA account has a cost basis and from which IRA account the distribution is taken. For purposes of determining the taxable and nontaxable portions of an IRA distribution, all IRAs are considered as one.

Estate Taxation

For purposes of determining the value of an estate for estate tax purposes, any funds remaining in any qualified plan accounts at the time of the participant's death are included in the estate. Also included in the estate is the present value of any annuity payments that would continue to a surviving spouse.

Annuitized Payments

The above discussion pertains to the distribution of qualified plan funds that were not annuitized. If a participant had retired under the terms of an employer's plan and her benefit was being distributed in the form of annuity payments when she died, those payments would continue for the remainder of the annuity period. This period would usually extend over the life of the surviving spouse, since the option typically used for an annuitization period is joint life and survivor.

Roth Distributions at Owner's Death

Though Roth IRAs do not require that distributions be taken from the account while the owner is alive, they do impose requirements at the owner's death. These are similar to those that apply to traditional IRAs when the account owner dies before his RMD date. For one, the entire amount remaining in the Roth account must be fully distributed within 10 years of the owner's death or, for some beneficiaries, over the life expectancy of the beneficiary. If the latter is elected, the distributions must begin by December 31 of the year following the year the owner died. If the surviving spouse is the named beneficiary, the surviving spouse can choose to treat the account as their own Roth IRA and make contributions to it and take distributions from it.

Special Situation

Distributions from a Roth IRA to a beneficiary are tax free, as long as the account was held for at least five years. In the event a Roth owner dies before satisfying this five-year holding requirement, income tax will be due on the earnings portion of the account's value. Because death is a qualifying exception to the 10% early distribution penalty, no penalty will be due regardless of the owner's age at death.

The beneficiary could take a distribution equal to the total of all contributions (cost basis) immediately which is tax free and then wait until the five-year holding requirement is met to take the earnings, which would also be tax free at that time.

OTHER TYPES OF DISTRIBUTIONS

Key Point Hardship provisions in employer plans allow employees access to their accounts in emergencies but do not override tax penalty rules.

Key Point Employer plans may allow employees to borrow from their retirement accounts.

Key Point Rollovers can be used to transfer funds from one retirement account to another without tax (except in the case of a transfer from a traditional to a Roth IRA).

There are other types of distributions that are common to qualified plans, which we will discuss briefly. These include hardship withdrawals, in-service withdrawals for profit-sharing plans and pension plans, loans, and rollovers.

Hardship Withdrawals

A number of qualified employer plans, notably the 401(k), often contain provisions that allow participants to make in-service withdrawals or distributions from these plans due to hardship. Hardship withdrawals are not exempt from the 10% early distribution penalty and they are taxable. However, in some cases and for some participants, they may be an appropriate way to gain access to needed cash. It is important for the practitioner to understand the basic rules applicable to hardship distributions.

First, hardship distributions are allowed only if the participant has an "immediate and heavy financial need" and no other resources are available to meet the needs. Second, the amount of the distribution is limited to the amount required to relieve the hardship and cannot be more than the amount the participant electively contributed to the plan.

Whether a participant has an immediate and heavy financial need is based on the facts and circumstances of the individual case. Medical expenses, the down payment on a principal residence, college tuition, and funds necessary to forestall foreclosure or eviction are examples of acceptable needs. (A vacation home or a new boat is not considered an acceptable need.) In addition, a distribution must be the only resource available to satisfy such needs. If the participant has other assets, would be compensated by insurance, or could obtain a nontaxable loan, it's likely a distribution would be denied.

An individual who receives a hardship distribution cannot make any contributions to the plan for at least six months.

In-Service Withdrawals: Profit-Sharing Plans and Pension Plans

Certain employer-sponsored retirement plans allow a participant to withdraw from the plan while still employed for reasons other than hardship, even if the participant has not reached normal retirement age.

For example, profit-sharing plans (401(k) plans, ESOP, stock bonus plan) allow participants to withdraw funds while employed under certain circumstances—participant reaches a certain age, fixed number of years has passed, or a specific event has happened (e.g., death, disability, financial hardship, illness, layoff, retirement, severance, termination of employment).

Pension plans (money purchase plans, cash balance plans), on the other hand, do not allow participants to withdraw funds while employed, with one exception—employed participants may withdraw funds starting at age 62. This exception was put in place by the PPA of 2006 to help older employees who are increasingly choosing to continue to work but reduce hours. Under prior law, distributions from pension plans could occur only when the participant's employment ended or the participant reached normal retirement age.

Loans

Another method of distribution from a qualified plan is through a plan loan. Qualified pension and profit-sharing plans, 401(k) plans, and 403(b) plans may offer loans to participants as long as certain guidelines are followed. Basically, such loans must be adequately secured, bear a reasonable rate of interest, carry a reasonable repayment schedule, and be available on a nondiscriminatory basis.

For a loan not to be deemed a taxable distribution to the plan participant, its term and amount must meet the following requirements.

■ It must be repaid within five years, unless it is to be used to acquire a principal residence.

■ The amount is limited to the lesser of

    — $50,000 minus the amount, if any, by which the highest outstanding loan balance during the year preceding the loan exceeds the outstanding loan balance on the date of the loan, or

    — one-half of the participant's vested plan benefit or $10,000, whichever is greater.

Any loan that does not meet these requirements will be considered a taxable distribution to the participant. In addition, if the plan provides for spousal benefits and the participant wants to pledge his account as security, the spouse must consent to the loan in writing.

IRA and SEP owners cannot take loans from their individual retirement accounts.

Rollovers

Rollovers were created by ERISA to encourage savings programs for retirement and to make provisions for the continuation of tax-deferred qualified savings if participation in a plan is discontinued. A rollover is actually a transaction in which a distribution of qualified plan funds (typically from an employer-sponsored plan) is deposited in another plan (typically an IRA). When a distribution is rolled over, the participant avoids paying taxes now and ensures that the savings will continue to grow tax-deferred. Given the trend toward early retirement and the fact that many employees leave an employer before they retire, rollovers have become a common occurrence.

Rollovers can also be used to protect retirement funds from taxation after an employee has left one employer, received a distribution, and is waiting to become eligible to participate in the new plan. Many qualified plans will accept funds from other plans; however, some qualified plans have certain waiting periods that affect an employee's eligibility to participate. An employee may receive a distribution from a former employer's qualified plan but may not yet be eligible to join a new employer's plan. In these cases, rollover IRAs are used as conduits to hold retirement funds until they can be moved to a new qualified plan.

Under the rollover provisions, the IRS permits the participant to roll over either the entire amount of a distribution or any part of it. Only the amounts not rolled over become taxable; the remaining amounts contributed to the rollover IRA continue to grow tax-deferred. It is important to remember that any part of the distribution not rolled over may be subject to the 10% early withdrawal penalty as well as ordinary income tax. Once the funds are rolled over, they are governed by the rules of the plan into which they have been deposited.

There is no restriction on the amount that may be deposited into a rollover. Although IRAs are limited to maximum annual contributions, an IRA rollover account is not subject to maximum contribution limitations. In addition, active participant status has no bearing on the ability to make a rollover. A rollover may be made from one qualified plan even though the individual is an active participant in another plan.

Rollovers must be accomplished within 60 days of the distribution; otherwise the funds are subject to taxes and any applicable penalties. This 60-day period does not include any time during which the amount transferred is "frozen" (i.e., cannot be withdrawn because of bankruptcy or insolvency of the financial institution). If the distribution is made in two or more installments, the individual has 60 days from the final payment or installment in which to make a rollover. For example, if a participant receives a partial distribution on February 1 and the remaining distribution on July 1, the 60-day period begins on July 1, the date of the final payment. If after 60 days the participant has not reinvested the funds in a rollover account, the distribution will be taxed as current income and, if the participant is younger than 59½, he may also have to pay the 10% penalty.

As a general rule and under most circumstances, rollovers are allowed only once in any 12-month period.

Distributions Ineligible for Rollover Treatment

Rollover treatment is allowed for distributions from qualified employer plans, 403(b) TSA plans, and individual retirement plans. However, not all distributions are eligible to be rolled over. For example, none of the following would qualify for rollover treatment:

■ Any distribution or portion of a distribution that would not be included in the participant's taxable income (i.e., a distribution that contains deductible contributions)

■ Any distribution that is taken to correct an excess contribution or excess deferral

■ Any distribution that is part of a series of substantially equal payments payable over the life of the participant or a period of 10 years or more

■ Required distributions

A nonspousal death beneficiary is now entitled to rollover distributions from a qualified plan, 403(b) plan, or 457 plan into an inherited IRA on a trustee-to-trustee basis, but only if provided for in the plan. For plan years starting after 2009, all eligible plans must offer rollovers to nonspousal beneficiaries. Under prior law, qualified funds inherited by a nonspousal beneficiary did not qualify for rollover treatment; only spousal beneficiaries were allowed to take advantage of rollovers; though the rollover could be made only to an IRA.

In addition, the rules for SIMPLE IRAs indicate that the distribution of funds from these plans during the first two years of participation (while the increased 25% early withdrawal penalty applies) cannot be rolled over to regular IRA accounts.

Direct Rollover Option

When a distribution eligible for rollover treatment is made from a qualified employer plan, the participant must be given the option to have the funds transferred directly to the rollover plan or account. Under a direct rollover, the participant does not take receipt of the funds; they are transferred directly by the trustee of the (old) distributing plan to the trustee of the (new) rollover plan.

In most cases, a participant would be wise to take advantage of the direct rollover option. If he does not, and takes possession of the funds personally, the distribution will be subject to an automatic 20% income tax withholding. The 20% withheld will be considered a distribution subject to tax and the 10% early distribution penalty unless the participant rolls over the full amount distributed. For example, 48-year-old Joe takes a $100,000 distribution from his 401(k) plan and declines the direct rollover option. The amount actually distributed to him will be $80,000; $20,000 will be withheld by the employer (just like income tax withheld from salary). Furthermore, unless Joe deposits the full $100,000 into a rollover account, he will face taxes and a 10% penalty on the deficit. If Joe deposits only $80,000, the $20,000 withheld will be considered a premature distribution and will be assessed a $2,000 penalty tax.

The 20% withholding requirement applies only to rollover amounts distributed from qualified employer plans and 403(b) plans; it does not apply to IRA distributions.

Roth Conversions

Prior to 2010, rollovers from a traditional IRA to a Roth IRA were not allowed if the investor's adjusted gross income in the year of the rollover exceeded $100,000 or if the investor was married and filed her tax return separately. However, these two restrictions on traditional IRA-to-Roth IRA conversions were eliminated as of 2010. As a result, persons with higher incomes can now convert their traditional IRAs into Roth IRAs.

WRAP-UP

Though they have been simplified, the tax laws affecting the distribution of funds from qualified and individual retirement plans can still be confusing. Accordingly, specific advice regarding a client's distribution options—what can be done, what should be done, and what must be done—should probably come from a qualified tax attorney, tax accountant, or the plan's benefits specialist.

As a financial professional, your primary role is to assist clients in making decisions with respect to the use of financial products for retirement planning purposes and point out some options that might be available to the client when he retires. It is not necessary to be an expert in every aspect of a qualified plan and its distribution alternatives. The most important things for you to remember about retirement distributions are:

■ the participant must take some action within 60 days of the date he receives the distribution or some tax advantages will be lost;

■ what to do with the distribution will depend on the participant's age and how the money will be used;

■ the typical distribution options include a lump-sum distribution, annuitized payments or a rollover IRA; and

■ funds rolled over into an IRA keep growing, tax-deferred, until they are withdrawn.

As a financial professional, you can be an important source of retirement information and advice for your clients. Of course, you can assist your clients in preparing for retirement by offering employer-sponsored retirement plans. You also have a number of other products that can help your clients fund an adequate retirement income. Mutual funds, annuities, stocks, bonds, and life insurance can all play an important role in retirement planning.

Regardless of which retirement plan your client selects, remember that he looks to you for advice about the best plan. Every individual's circumstances will be different, and some will be more complex than others. If you need additional assistance in designing a plan or understanding the tax consequences of a plan, you should always seek specialized help.

In the last few units, we concentrated on qualified retirement plans that primarily involve the employer as the initiator of the plans and the provider of the funds needed for the employee's benefit at retirement. These qualified plans provide substantial tax advantages and other benefits to both the employer and the employee. And when the funds are distributed, at least for most people, they usually represent the most significant source of income.

UNIT TEST

1. Under the terms of most formal employer-sponsored retirement plans, at what age is an employee entitled to full retirement benefits?
   A. 59½
   B. 60
   C. 65
   D. 72

2. Under which of these circumstances would a premature distribution from a traditional IRA be exempt from the premature distribution penalty?
   A. A distribution taken to satisfy the terms of a court-ordered property settlement
   B. A distribution taken at age 55 if the owner is retired
   C. When the account is fully funded with nondeductible contributions
   D. When the distribution is paid in equal annual amounts over the owner's life

3. Lena died at the age of 50 with $100,000 in her traditional IRA account. In addition to income taxes due on the distribution, her beneficiary will have to pay a premature distribution penalty tax of how much?
   A. $0
   B. $6,000
   C. $10,000
   D. $15,000

4. For traditional IRA owners, minimum distributions must begin no later than
   A. April 15 of the year they turn 72
   B. April 1 following the year they retire
   C. April 1 following the year they turn 72
   D. April 15 following the year they retire or turn 72, whichever is later

5. Which of these would be exempt from a premature distribution penalty under an IRA but not a 401(k) plan?
   A. Premature distribution due to death
   B. Premature distribution due to disability
   C. Premature distribution used to cover higher education expenses
   D. Premature distribution to correct an excess contribution

6. At what point must funds be distributed from a Roth IRA?
   A. April 1 following the year the owner turns 72
   B. April 15 following the year the owner turns 72
   C. After the owner's death
   D. Never

7. For purposes of required distributions at a participant's death, which of these could claim the fund as his own and designate new beneficiaries?
   A. Rolfe, the beneficiary of his wife's 401(k) plan
   B. Scott, the beneficiary of his father's IRA account
   C. Herb, the beneficiary of his wife's IRA account
   D. All of these

8. As a general rule, required minimum distributions are based on
   A. the uniform lifetime distribution period based on the age of the participant alone
   B. the joint life expectancy of the participant and his beneficiary
   C. the joint life expectancy of the participant and his beneficiary if the beneficiary is more than 10 years older
   D. the life expectancy period that will produce the smallest RMD

9. All of these plans can include provisions for loans
   EXCEPT

   A. 401(k)
   B. IRAs
   C. 403(b)
   D. profit-sharing

10. Hardship withdrawals are usually associated with
    401(k) plans.

    A. True
    B. False

11. Gail's required distribution this year is $5,000. If
    she takes $8,000, the penalty will be

    A. $0
    B. $1,500
    C. $2,000
    D. $2,500

ANSWERS AND RATIONALES

1. **C.** Most employer-sponsored retirement plans use 65 as the normal retirement age.

2. **D.** A distribution from an IRA taken in equal annual amounts over the owner's life is not subject to the 10% premature distribution penalty even if started before age 59½. This is one of the exceptions that apply to IRAs. The exception for QDROs and for retirement at age 55 apply to employer-sponsored plans but not to IRAs.

3. **A.** The premature distribution penalty does not apply if the distribution is made after the death of the account owner.

4. **C.** Distributions from a traditional IRA must begin by April 1 of the year following the year in which the owner turns 72.

5. **C.** IRA owners may withdraw funds before age 59½ to cover higher education expenses without being subject to the 10% premature distribution penalty. The same is not true of a 401(k) plan.

6. **C.** A Roth IRA owner is never required to take distributions during his lifetime, but distributions must begin after the Roth IRA owner's death.

7. **C.** A spouse who inherits an IRA may treat it as his own.

8. **A.** Except when a beneficiary spouse is more than 10 years younger than the account owner, all minimum distribution amounts are determined under the IRS uniform lifetime distribution table based on the age of the participant alone.

9. **B.** Loans are not allowed from IRAs.

10. **A.** Hardship withdrawal provisions are found in 401(k) plans.

11. **A.** There is no penalty if a participant withdraws more than the required minimum distribution.

11

Nonqualified Executive Benefits

Most employers offer some form of group health, life, and long-term disability insurance, and a formal pension or profit-sharing plan to attract new employees and prevent employee turnover. Many employers are particularly anxious to offer upper-level management additional benefits to reduce employee turnover at that key level. However, because such discriminatory practices could jeopardize the tax-advantaged status of an entire qualified plan, companies must offer alternative benefit plans to key employees and executives. ■

UNIT OBJECTIVES

To provide additional incentives to select employees on a discriminatory basis, employers may offer discretionary benefit plans, or nonqualified plans. A plan is called nonqualified when it is not eligible for the tax benefits of a pension, profit-sharing, or other qualified plan. Nonqualified plans do enjoy advantages of their own, but these advantages are not as substantial as those granted to qualified plans. Nonqualified plans are used to:

- attract and retain key employees;

- provide supplemental benefits beyond existing qualified plans;

- provide a plan in lieu of a qualified plan for selected employees; and

- take advantage of provisions in the Internal Revenue Code to the advantage of certain employees.

On completion of this unit, you should be able to:

- describe the varieties of nonqualified executive benefits;

- explain the types of plans used to structure deferred compensation or salary continuation plans; and

- discuss the use of life insurance, annuities, and other funding mechanisms used in nonqualified plans.

DEFERRED COMPENSATION PLANS

Key Point A deferred compensation plan provides nonqualified retirement benefits to employees who are comfortable enough to set aside part of their compensation.

Key Point Although deferred compensation plans lack the full range of tax incentives that apply to qualified plans, they may be structured to defer tax for the employee through the use of life insurance, trusts, or both.

A deferred compensation plan is a contractual arrangement entered into by an employer and a selected employee, typically one who is highly compensated. The employer agrees to pay the employee compensation in the future, usually at retirement, for services the employee renders currently. In this way, it is the employee who funds the plan. By reducing current salary, foregoing a raise or bonus or simply deferring a portion of the total compensation package until retirement, the employee lowers his current tax liability and supplements retirement savings. These deferred compensation arrangements may include payment in the event of disability as well as payments to the employee's spouse should the employee die before or after retirement.

A deferred compensation arrangement has a twofold objective:

1. For the employer, it provides a means to attract or retain the services of the selected employee.

2. For the employee, who is already comfortably compensated, it is a way to lower current tax liability by deferring compensation until retirement (when he may be in a lower tax bracket), and to supplement retirement benefits.

Unfunded, Informally Funded, and Formally Funded Plans

Deferred compensation plans fall into three broad categories: unfunded, informally funded, and formally funded. The distinction is important because the tax consequences vary by plan.

With an unfunded plan, the employee has only an unsecured contractual right to the benefit payments. No assets are set aside to fund the obligation. In effect, the employee becomes a creditor of the employer at the time he satisfies the conditions necessary to receive benefits, and the employer finances its obligation on a pay-as-you-go basis.

An informally funded plan is one in which the employer sets aside and accumulates assets to meet its future obligation; frequently, these assets take the form of life insurance. However, because they are assets of the employer, they are attachable by creditors; the employee does not have a secured right to these funds.

A formally funded plan is one in which the employer sets aside special assets, often in an irrevocable trust or escrow account, to meet its future obligation. These assets are shielded from the claims of the employer's general creditors.

From a tax standpoint, there is an important distinction between these types of plans. With an unfunded or informally funded deferred compensation arrangement, the employee is not taxed on the plan's benefits until they actually receive them. By the same token, the employer cannot take a deduction for the benefits until they are actually paid out. In contrast, a formally funded plan will result in the compensation being taxable to the employee and deductible by the employer as soon as the employee's rights to the deferred benefits become nonforfeitable, which is usually when the plan is implemented.

ILLUSTRATION 1

The Doctrines of Constructive Receipt and Economic Benefit

Two income tax concepts are particularly pertinent to deferred compensation arrangements. They are known as the doctrine of constructive receipt and the doctrine of economic benefit.

Doctrine of Constructive Receipt. Under our tax laws, income that has not been received may be taxed as if it had been received in those cases where the individual constructively received the income. This happens when income is set aside for the individual, credited to an account established for him or otherwise made available, without any substantial restrictions on the individual's control over the income. The theory of the constructive receipt doctrine is that a person cannot, for tax purposes, ignore income he has a right to receive.

Doctrine of Economic Benefit. A general rule of tax law is that an individual is deemed to have received income if property has been handled or arranged in such a way that a cash-equivalent benefit has been provided to him. With regard to a formally funded deferred compensation plan, this economic benefit doctrine results in taxation to the employee at the time his right to the benefits becomes nonforfeitable or nontransferable. This does not apply to arrangements whereby benefits are payable from assets that can be attached by the employer's general creditors.

Life Insurance and Deferred Compensation

Deferred compensation plans appeal to highly compensated executives who are faced with the unique problem of too much income today relative to future retirement income needs. Because these plans are actually a substitute for currently taxed compensation, they offer a way to achieve a better balance between the employee's present income and future income needs. If the plan is not funded or is informally funded, the benefits, instead of being paid and taxed today, are received during retirement, when the need for them is more acute and when the employee may be in a lower tax bracket.

Life insurance fits neatly into a deferred compensation plan and is a widely used funding vehicle for these kinds of arrangements. The particular type of policy to recommend depends on the employer's financial situation and the age of the key employee. A life paid-up at 65 policy, for example, could be recommended. The employer applies for life insurance on the life of the executive, and insurance premiums are then paid up to the employee's normal retirement date. The employer is the owner, premium payor, and beneficiary of the policy; the employee should have no rights to the policy, currently or after retirement. Any incidents of ownership attributable to the employee could constitute income and become taxable. As with all deferred compensation arrangements, the employer gets no deduction until payment or other benefits are transferred to the employee or become no longer subject to risk of forfeiture.

At retirement, the employer can provide the promised benefits by making payment from current earnings or accumulated surplus, or the policy's cash value could be used to make the promised benefit payments. For example, the employer could elect to receive the cash surrender value under a fixed period of year option, the duration matched to the term of its deferred benefits obligation. As the employer receives the payments from the insurer, they are paid to the employee. In this way, the employee's tax liability is limited to the amount received in the taxable year.

In other instances, the employer may desire to keep the policy intact. If the company has sufficient earnings and profits to pay the promised benefit, the policy can remain undisturbed so that the employer receives the face amount upon the death of the employee. These death proceeds would, for the most part, be an income tax-free addition to the company's surplus and, assuming the company has a continuing obligation to the deceased employee's spouse or beneficiary, would offset this liability.

ILLUSTRATION 2

The Advantages of Life Insurance as a Funding Medium

While any form of cash accumulation may be used to build the pool of money to pay promised retirement benefits, life insurance, because of its unique nature, is ideally suited for this role.

In fact, permanent cash value life insurance is the medium of choice for companies to informally fund salary continuation and deferred compensation plans. Funding is informal when it does not provide any vested or nonforfeitable rights or interest to employees.

Funding a deferred compensation or salary continuation plan with life insurance on an informal basis provides the employer with at least three benefits.

- The cash values accumulate income tax-free and the tax on the growth is deferred until the policy matures.
- Death proceeds from the policy are received income tax-free to the beneficiary (the employer).
- The benefits are paid as an expense to the corporation, which then takes an income tax deduction for the benefits when they are paid at retirement.

Although there are other ways to fund a deferred compensation plan, no other funding vehicle provides this leverage as economically or as practically as life insurance.

When using a life insurance policy to provide benefits, it is important to properly arrange the ownership and beneficiary designations of each policy. In most cases, the employer is the beneficiary, as well as the owner of all incidents of ownership in the policy. The insurance cash values become part of general company assets and the proceeds are payable to the company. The insured has no interest in or rights to the insurance policy, either presently or in retirement.

It must be remembered that the deferred compensation or salary continuation agreement has no direct relationship to insurance. In fact, an effective agreement could be carried out whether or not there was life insurance. At retirement, the employer may use the cash value of the policy to meet its retirement benefit promise or draw on its other assets to make the deferred compensation payments. If the policy remains in force, the company may still collect the proceeds upon the employee's death.

From the corporation's point of view, the use of life insurance means that the business will be in a sound financial position when new liabilities are created for amortizing the future cost of paying benefits to a retired employee. This means greater peace of mind for the insured executive who realizes that the deferred compensation agreement has set up a substantial future liability in their favor.

The Market for Deferred Compensation Plans

The motivation to enter into a deferred compensation agreement comes from two directions:

- **The employer.** The employer has an employee whom it wants to recruit or retain and sees a deferred compensation arrangement as an additional employee benefit to induce that person to come to, or stay with, the organization.

- **The employee.** The employee is well compensated but wants future retirement security (and perhaps a current tax break as well) and is willing to defer a portion of his current income.

Prospects for deferred compensation plans can be found in tax-paying corporations, partnerships, and sole proprietorships as well as in nonprofit organizations such as service organizations, trade associations, hospitals, and charitable organizations. The individual covered under the plan may be an employee—an important general manager, engineer, or sales manager, for example—or an independent contractor, such as a clinic-associated physician or a manufacturer's representative. In fact, one advantage of deferred compensation over a qualified plan is that it may be used where the relationship is one of principal and independent contractor, as is the case with many professional people and the organizations they serve.

Deferred compensation plans are a good choice for businessowners who want a strong incentive for their key employees to stay with the business. Because benefits are received only if the employee remains with the company until retirement, they are called golden handcuffs. If the employee accepts other employment, the benefits are lost. To further prevent movement to the competition, a noncompetition clause can be added to the deferred compensation agreement.

SALARY CONTINUATION PLANS

Key Point   Salary continuation plans are similar to deferred compensation plans, but rather than being funded out of a salary reduction, they are funded by an additional commitment from the employer.

Planners often use the terms *deferred compensation* and *salary continuation* synonymously. However, there is one major difference between the two plans—a deferred compensation plan uses the employee's income to provide the promised benefit; a salary continuation plan uses the employer's dollars.

A salary continuation plan is an arrangement in which the employer agrees to continue a portion of the executive's salary upon the executive's death, retirement, or disability. These plans are also referred to as sick pay plans. Salary continuation plans differ from deferred compensation plans because salary continuation payments are made in addition to, rather than in lieu of, a current raise or bonus. In this way, a salary continuation plan is funded with the employer's dollars.

Like a deferred compensation arrangement, the salary continuation plan is primarily a fringe benefit used by an employer to help retain key personnel and to encourage performance. But the plan offers other advantages.

- The employer's promised future payments are not currently taxable. Furthermore, when the employee does receive the payments at retirement, he may be in a lower tax bracket.

- The plan is not subject to the majority of ERISA requirements, so it is easier to establish and administer.

- The employer receives an income tax deduction when the benefits are actually paid.

- The employer may be selective in rewarding key personnel.

When life insurance is used as the funding mechanism, two additional benefits apply.

■ Policy proceeds are not included in the employee's gross estate.

■ When the employee dies, the employer receives death proceeds that are, for the most part, income tax-free to aid in funding other obligations.

Yet another advantage to the employer is its ability to retain the executive through the use of golden handcuffs that encourage executives to join the company and make it difficult for competitors to lure them away. In exchange for future benefits, the employee must comply with certain conditions of employment before, and sometimes after, retirement. The conditions are set forth in a written agreement with the employer and may include the executive's promise to:

■ remain with the company for a specified number of years;

■ refrain from employment or any other service with a competing company; and

■ act as a consultant to the company after retirement.

A salary continuation arrangement enables a company to provide substantial retirement benefits for top management on a selective basis. Although certain minimal reporting procedures must be followed, a salary continuation plan requires no qualification with the IRS.

The Market for Salary Continuation Plans

An excellent candidate for salary continuation plans is the small-business owner who relies on a few key employees. The loss of those employees, due to retirement, disability, or death, could be a huge financial drain on the company. To solve this problem, employers can set up a salary continuation plan funded by insurance. These plans can be used to replace a percentage of the employee's income after retirement by transferring the long-term financial obligation to a life insurance company.

Salary continuation plans are also excellent choices for publicly held corporations with several levels of management. These plans help both the corporation and its key executives meet their objectives. In addition, a salary continuation plan may be marketed to private corporations, an S corporation, or a nonprofit organization. Such a plan can broaden an employer's retirement options for its key employees and do so in both a cost- and benefit-effective manner.

TYPES OF DEFERRED COMPENSATION AND SALARY CONTINUATION PLANS

Key Point Supplemental employee retirement plans (SERPs), top hat plans, excess benefit plans, and rabbi or secular trusts are different arrangements used to structure deferred compensation or salary continuation plans.

Key Point Life insurance is frequently used as a funding medium, providing retirement benefits out of cash values, and a death benefit in the event of an untimely death.

As stated earlier, the key distinction between a salary continuation and a deferred compensation plan is whose dollars are being used to provide the promised benefit. A salary continuation plan uses employer dollars; a deferred compensation plan uses employee dollars.

Both salary continuation plans and deferred compensation plans are commonly structured in one of the following ways: as supplemental employee retirement plans, top hat plans, excess benefit plans, or rabbi or secular trusts.

Supplemental Employee Retirement Plans

To provide salary continuation, employers often establish a nonqualified plan called a supplemental employee retirement plan (SERP). These plans are frequently funded with life insurance contracts. Typically, a SERP contains the following three provisions.

- The corporation is the owner and beneficiary of life insurance on the key employee's life.

- The benefit is based on an unsecured promise. The employee reports no taxable income, nor does the employer receive a tax deduction, until the benefit is received at retirement.

- The corporation funds the employee's benefit at retirement with policyholder loans against the cash value of the policy.

A SERP satisfies the employer's objective of bringing retirement benefits up to desired levels in an already existing qualified plan. However, an employer may also use deferred compensation plans or executive bonus plans to accomplish its objectives. (These are discussed later in this unit.)

ILLUSTRATION 3

Features and Benefits of a Deferred Compensation or Salary Continuation Plan

How is it executed?	Employer and employee enter into a written agreement under which the employer agrees to pay certain retirement, survivor, or disability benefits to the employee or heirs. The employer indemnifies its obligation by purchasing insurance on the employee's life and naming itself as beneficiary.
Who is the participating employee?	The employer has complete freedom to pick and choose who and how many of its employees may participate. A different plan can be designed for each selected employee.
Does the plan have to comply with ERISA?	There is minimal ERISA compliance required, dealing only with reporting and disclosure rules.
What are the tax implications for the employer?	If the plan is informally funded, no current deduction is available; however, benefits are deductible when paid and any insurance death proceeds are received tax free. Formally funded deferred compensation contributions are deductible in the taxable year in which the employee includes an amount attributable to the contribution in gross income.
What are the tax implications for the employee?	If the plan is informally funded, there is no current tax; however, benefits will be taxable as income when they are received. In a formally funded plan, the fair market value of the contribution is included in gross income if the right to the contributions is transferable and not subject to substantial risk of forfeiture.

Top Hat Plans

Either the employer or the employee may initiate a top hat plan during employment contract negotiations. Under such a plan, the executive forgoes receipt of currently earned compensation such as salary or commissions, and directs these funds to be paid out at retirement. A top hat plan is typically set up as a defined contribution plan, with the amount deferred and investment gain credited to an account set up for the executive. The executive's retirement benefit is an aggregate amount of all contributions and earnings.

Excess Benefit Plans

The employer may legally exceed the maximum contribution and benefit limit for qualified plans (the IRC Section 415 limits) by establishing an excess benefit plan. An excess benefit plan provides additional benefits for executives who will already be receiving the maximum benefit under their employer's qualified plan.

Rabbi Trusts and Secular Trusts

Assets intended to provide the promised benefits to executives can be placed in irrevocable trusts. The rabbi trust, originally developed by and named for a rabbi concerned about his future retirement income, segregates assets in a trust with conditions that the funds be used for unfunded deferred compensation obligations. In the rabbi trust, contributions are made to an irrevocable trust and are not taxed to the employee as current taxable income; the employer receives no tax deduction. To avoid current income taxation, the assets in the trust are subject to the claims of the employer's general creditors.

A secular trust may also be used to fund nonqualified deferred compensation benefits. In an employer-funded secular trust, all employer contributions to the trust are currently taxable to the employee because the opportunity for forfeiture of assets is sufficiently reduced by a trust provision to create current income to the employee. Funds are not subject to the claims of general creditors, and the employer is entitled to a tax deduction.

Secular trusts are appealing to executives who feel that the income tax rate may increase in the future, or when it appears that the existing corporation will be merged or sold to unfriendly future owners. However, in certain cases, highly compensated employees are taxed not only on employer contributions but also on the earnings of the trust from those contributions, making the secular trust less attractive.

EXECUTIVE BONUS PLANS

Key Point An executive bonus plan can give an executive permanent cash value life insurance or an annuity contract at little cost to the employee through employer bonuses of the premiums on these contracts.

Another commonly used discretionary employee benefit plan is called an executive bonus plan. This plan meets a number of corporate and executive needs, is relatively simple to establish, and is easy to understand. An executive bonus plan, also known as an insured bonus plan or an IRC Section 162 plan, is a nonqualified plan that provides benefits to both the employer and the employee.

Basically, an executive bonus plan is a simple life insurance fringe-benefit program in which an employee is given ownership of a policy on his life, with the employer paying the premiums either directly or indirectly through a salary increase to the employee. The employee owns the plan from the start and has control over the policy's cash values and the beneficiary designation.

An executive bonus plan benefits the employer because it chooses who will participate in the plan and may use the plan to attract, motivate, and reward employees. In addition, the plan provides a simple way to buy personal life insurance for key executives (including owners) using tax-deductible business dollars. Finally, the employer can fix the costs of the plan in advance, which helps to assure proper cash management.

The executive also benefits from an executive bonus plan because he receives permanent cash value life insurance at a very low personal cost. Though the premium payments made on the executive's behalf are considered a taxable benefit, his out-of-pocket cost is only the additional income tax generated on the bonus received. Furthermore, executive bonus plans are flexible, so options may be selected at later dates to meet the executive's needs. The employee could choose to take the policy's cash value at retirement under a payout option, or leave the policy intact for its death benefit. Finally, the executive may feel rewarded by the company for his personal efforts.

Executive Bonus Plan Structure

Most executive bonus plans are designed to fit into ERISA's safe harbor for welfare benefit plans. By qualifying for safe harbor treatment, the plan is exempt from all of the participation, funding, and vesting requirements of ERISA. The plan document can be as liberal or as restrictive as the employer desires.

The actual plan design is limited only by the imaginations of the financial advisor, the attorney, and the employer involved in its creation. Although it may be tempting to create a rather formidable document, a simple plan is easier to understand, administer, and amend at a later date.

An executive bonus plan may be funded by any form of permanent cash value life insurance other than modified endowment contracts (MECs). This class of contracts, once used to provide tax shelters, was defined by the Technical and Miscellaneous Revenue Act of 1988 (TAMRA). Passage of TAMRA ended what some felt was an abusive application of the tax advantages afforded the life insurance transaction. To avoid being labeled an MEC and losing the advantage of tax-free policy loans, a policy's premiums cannot be paid more rapidly than necessary to provide the paid-up death benefits that seven level annual payments can purchase.

Annuity contracts are another popular funding alternative for an executive bonus plan. Although they lack the advantage of a preretirement death benefit, they can be issued to any executive, regardless of health. Also, annuity contracts may maximize future additional income when compared with some forms of permanent life insurance.

Income Taxation

Most executive bonus plans are considered welfare benefit plans under ERISA because they provide death benefits as well as other benefits. IRC Section 162 sets out three requirements that must be met if an expense is to be deductible for the employer. The expense must be:

- "ordinary and necessary" in the normal course of business and must be helpful in the business;

- "paid or incurred" in the year it is deducted; and

- "a reasonable allowance for services actually rendered" in the course of an employment relationship.

The executive has a single requirement—the amount of the premium payment or the bonus must be included in his gross income as compensation for services. Even if the benefit is something other than cash, if it has a measurable value, it must be included as income.

The Market for Executive Bonus Plans

Executive bonus plans are especially appealing to new or struggling businesses with limited funds. The owner can select both the participants and the amount to be spent on each participant. The company can use tax-deductible business dollars to make modest premium payments to purchase substantial life insurance. Unlike the restrictions and golden handcuffs imposed by deferred compensation plans, executive bonus plans are portable. If a covered employee leaves the company, he may pick up the premium payment, so there is no loss of coverage. This may be appealing to an employee since the employer's premium dollars and policy cash values built up to that point also go with the employee.

GOLDEN PARACHUTES

Key Point   Golden parachute plans protect executives against termination by providing a substantial payment upon termination, often occasioned by an acquisition or merger.

A relatively new addition to executive compensation arrangements are plans called golden parachutes. These plans are arrangements for allowing terminated, highly paid executives to maintain relatively affluent lifestyles in exchange for agreeing to leave his corporate employ. Such agreements are commonly sought when a corporation is acquired by another corporation.

A golden parachute is characterized by extremely generous benefits to the executive, owner, or employee. Parachute distributions in conjunction with a change in ownership or control of a business are not looked upon with a kind eye by the IRS. The IRS is concerned with excess parachute payments, a term which generally refers to payments that exceed three times the recipient's average annual compensation. When an excess parachute payment is made to a disqualified individual (officer, shareholder, highly compensated individual, and others specified in the regulations), the employer cannot deduct this excess payment. Furthermore, the recipient of the excess parachute payment is subject not only to income tax, but also to a 20% excise tax on the excess amount.

WRAP-UP

In today's highly competitive business environment, employers must find a way to recruit and retain productive, loyal employees. The successful retirement planning professional knows special perks for officers, executives, and other highly compensated employees can be provided with nonqualified plans. Your job and your opportunity are to understand nonqualified plans so that you can help your clients decide which plans best suit their needs.

In addition to concerns about adequate retirement income, many of your clients will be concerned about adequate health care after they retire. In the next unit, we will discuss health care planning for retirement, including Medicare, Medicaid, and long-term health care.

FIELD EXERCISES

- **Review your portfolio of products.** What do you offer that would be suitable for a deferred compensation or salary continuation plan?

- **Make a list of your clients.** How many of your clients are currently covered by deferred compensation or salary continuation plans? How many of your clients own businesses or are key executives in businesses that lack these types of nonqualified executive benefits? What other retirement income arrangements do they participate in? Are they adequate?

UNIT TEST

1. Under a formally funded deferred compensation plan, the employee is taxed on the benefits
   A. when the benefits become nonforfeitable
   B. when the benefits are paid out
   C. at death
   D. never

2. Which of these statements about salary continuation plans is TRUE?
   A. They are based on the promise of future benefits to which a key employee will be entitled.
   B. They allow the employer to currently deduct the cost of funding the plan.
   C. They create a currently taxable benefit for the key employee.
   D. They must conform to the majority of ERISA requirements.

3. Which of these statements regarding nonqualified deferred compensation arrangements is FALSE?
   A. These arrangements usually are unsecured promises made by an employer to an employee to pay the employee part of his compensation in the future.
   B. Under such arrangements, the employee can rely on guaranteed future benefits.
   C. The employer cannot take a tax deduction for the compensation deferred until it is paid out or otherwise taxable to the employee.
   D. Most deferred compensation arrangements are unfunded.

4. Which of these statements regarding salary continuation plans is TRUE?
   A. They are subject to most of the provisions of ERISA.
   B. They cannot discriminate in coverage or eligibility.
   C. The employer takes a tax deduction when benefits are paid out to the employee.
   D. The employee is currently taxed on the present value of the future benefits.

5. Which of these is TRUE under a typical executive bonus plan?
   A. An executive is provided with life insurance, the cost of which he can deduct.
   B. A company purchases and controls a life insurance policy on an executive and deducts the cost.
   C. An executive is provided with life insurance, the cost of which is taxable income to him.
   D. A company purchases and owns a life insurance policy on an executive but cannot deduct the premium payments.

ANSWERS AND RATIONALES

1. **A.** As long as benefits are forfeitable, the employee is not taxed.

2. **A.** An employee may not deduct the cost of funding a salary continuation plan until the employee is subject to tax on the benefit. Neither occurs until the benefit is paid or becomes nonforfeitable. These plans may discriminate.

3. **B.** A basic feature of a nonqualified plan is that the benefits are not guaranteed. If they were, the tax characteristics of the plan would change.

4. **C.** In a salary continuation plan, the employer may take a tax deduction when benefits are paid to the employee.

5. **C.** Under a typical executive bonus plan, an executive is provided life insurance, the cost of which is a taxable benefit.

12

Meeting the Retiree's Health Care Needs

The U.S. Census Bureau estimates that the average 65-year-old can look forward to an additional 20 or so years of life. This increased life expectancy means both good news and bad news for all of us. First, the good news: with a positive attitude and adequate health care, people may eventually expect to live an estimated life span of 115 years. Now, the bad news: for most people, with increasing age come illness, more frailty, and medical costs that may be only partially covered by insurance.

The need for adequate health care coverage translates into an opportunity for a retirement planner specializing in life and health insurance to offer clients both an education and well-chosen insurance products. Your knowledge of what types of policies a client might currently have, and whether those policies are adequate to meet the client's retirement needs, is vital. ■

UNIT OBJECTIVES

In this unit, you will find a brief discussion of available private and government health care programs, Medicare and Medicaid benefits, Medicare supplement insurance programs, and long-term care insurance. This overview will assist you in helping your clients understand and choose the best retirement health care options for their needs.

On completion of this unit, you should be able to:

- describe the financial risks to a retiree's financial security posed by ill health or disability;

- discuss the role of Medicare in paying the health care costs of a retiree, including both coverage and gaps in coverage;

- explain Medicare supplement insurance;

- list the costs and benefits of long-term care insurance; and

- define disability income insurance and explain its use.

PRIVATE AND GOVERNMENT HEALTH CARE PROGRAMS AND HEALTH CARE REFORM

Key Point   Uncovered health care costs are a serious financial risk for current and future retirees.

Key Point   The Affordable Care Act of 2010 (ACA) is making complex changes to the U.S. health care system, including private and government programs.

The purpose of health insurance is to reduce the financial burden that individuals face when illness occurs. Your clients will expect you, as a retirement planning professional, to apply your knowledge of financial products to help them select the proper kind of health protection within their financial boundaries. Whether you work with individuals or groups, you will probably be asked to advise clients about which insurance policies to choose.

After retirement, many people will face chronic health problems and become dependent on formal or informal caregiving systems. The cost of this care will be paid for in a number of ways. Most of the private insurance coverage in the U.S. is group coverage related to the past or current employment of a family member. As part of an employment benefit package, employers often purchase group insurance policies to cover employees and their dependents. Group health insurance is offered by private insurance companies, service plans like Blue Cross/Blue Shield, health maintenance organizations (HMOs), or preferred provider organizations (PPOs). In addition to medical benefits, the plans may also offer dental and vision care. Group insurance plans provide about 90% of private health insurance with employers paying a large portion of the cost.

In many cases, group coverage may be continued after the employee leaves the company. Employees who would have lost their benefits upon termination of employment, divorce, or a number of other events are now protected under the law. The Consolidated Omnibus Budget Act of 1986 (COBRA) requires that employers offer terminated employees the option of continuing their group coverage for a set period of time, provided the employee pays the entire cost.

Affordable Care Act of 2010

The Affordable Care Act of 2010 (ACA), also referred to as health care reform, is the most complex and extensive health care legislation in decades. The act is administered by the U.S. Department of Health and Human Services (HHS), with key provisions implemented and enforced by the Labor Department and the IRS. Although some provisions became effective soon after enactment, others are being implemented on a rolling basis. Many regulations implementing the act have not been finalized, and other provisions are not fully funded. Some dates are also subject to change. Therefore, it is especially important to stay up-to-date on how this law will affect your clients and prospects. The website www.HealthCare.gov, which is maintained by HHS, is a good source of information.

A major goal of the ACA is to transform the U.S. health care system from one that focuses on treating the sick to a system focused on keeping people healthy. Many provisions of the act focus on wellness, early care, and screenings to prevent chronic illnesses.

Another goal is to cover the uninsured. Unless an individual is exempt or is covered by Medicare or Medicaid, everyone will be required to obtain health insurance or pay a tax. Group insurance provided by employers will satisfy the universal health insurance mandate. Lower-income individuals and certain middle-income families may qualify for premium assistance tax credit, cost sharing, or vouchers to help pay for health insurance premiums. Insurance exchanges will be established to help individuals and small businesses shop for coverage and will offer various levels or tiers of coverage.

Limits and Caps on Essential Health Benefits

The ACA prohibits insured and self-insured health plans from imposing lifetime limits on the dollar value of essential health benefits. After January 1, 2014, plans can still impose lifetime or annual per-beneficiary limits on the dollar value of *nonessential* health benefits.

Essential health benefits fall under the following broad general categories:

- Ambulatory patient services

- Emergency services

- Hospitalization

- Maternity and newborn care

- Mental health and substance use disorder services, including behavioral health treatment

- Prescription drugs
- Rehabilitative and habilitation services and devices
- Laboratory services
- Preventive and wellness services and chronic disease management
- Pediatric services, including oral and vision care

These essential health benefits, which are the basis for the coverage that will be provided to people enrolled in exchange plans and the individual and small group insurance markets, will be defined in more detail by the Secretary of Health and Human Services.

Annual waivers are available for a class of group health plans and health insurance coverage, generally known as *limited benefit* plans or *mini-med* plans that often have annual limits well below the restricted annual limits set out previously. These group plans and health insurance coverage often offer lower-cost coverage to part-time workers, seasonal workers, and volunteers who otherwise may not be able to afford coverage. The waivers are available to ensure that individuals with certain coverage, including coverage under limited benefit or mini-med plans, would not be denied access to needed services or experience more than a minimal impact on premiums.

The following plans are not subject to the restriction on annual limits: such account-based plans as health savings accounts (HSAs), flexible spending account plans (FSAs), and medical savings accounts (MSAs); retiree-only group health or health reimbursement accounts (HRAs) and Medicare supplements; HRAs integrated with group coverage; stand-alone vision/dental; on-site medical clinics; long-term care; and certain limited scope plans, such as for specific disease.

Free Preventive Care

Beginning September 23, 2010, qualified health plans must cover preventive services that have strong scientific evidence of their health benefits. These plans cannot charge patients co-payments, coinsurance, or deductibles for these services when they are delivered by a network provider. Employers can continue to require cost sharing for preventive services employees receive from out-of-network providers. The preventive care requirements are intended to provide easier access to services such as blood pressure, diabetes, and cholesterol tests; many cancer screenings; routine vaccinations; and tobacco cessation counseling.

Retiree Reliance on Government Health Care Programs

As the retirement market swells, more and more people will look to the government to provide for their basic health care needs. After retirement, most people use Medicare, the federally sponsored health care program, to meet their medical cost.

However, Medicare coverage is subject to deductibles, co-payments, and limitations that must be satisfied by recipients or their insurance companies.

In the next few pages, our discussion will focus on Medicare and Medicaid—two of the most commonly used (and least understood) government health care programs.

ILLUSTRATION 1

Agent's Perspective

The single factor most likely to undermine every element of the retirement plans that you work on so diligently with your clients is unexpected major illness. Hospitalization, drug costs, and long-term care have to be paid for. Retirement incomes that may already be stretched won't be adequate. Even if your client recovers, severely reduced retirement savings may be unable to support the type of retirement originally planned.

Unexpected illness is not really unexpected. What we don't know is when it will strike and how prolonged it will be. It is a cost that should be provided for in any retirement plan.

Because of the unpredictability of the cost, the ideal solution is insurance. The government covers part of that through Medicare, but many of the illness-related costs that strike retirees are not covered by this program.

The question that needs to be answered by you and your client is the same as any other insurance issue—how much risk do you want to cover and how much will it cost?

MEDICARE PARTS A AND B: THE ORIGINAL MEDICARE PLAN

Key Point   Medicare Part A pays for medically necessary inpatient care in a hospital, skilled nursing facility, psychiatric hospital, or hospice.

Key Point   Medicare Part A also pays for the cost of medically necessary home health care and 80% of the approved cost for durable medical equipment supplied under the home health care benefit.

Key Point   Medicare Part B pays for covered medically necessary services no matter where they are received—at home, in a doctor's office, in a hospital, or in a nursing home.

Medicare is a government insurance entitlement program that provides basic health insurance protection to about 50 million Americans age 65 and older plus an additional 9 million who are disabled. In addition to providing medical benefits, the program attempts to hold down the cost of medical care by limiting the scope of its coverage and its benefit amounts, thus making the health care consumer and the service provider more cost conscious and less likely to overuse or overcharge the program.

The Affordable Care Act of 2010 (ACA) contains substantial payment and delivery reforms designed to reward efficiency in the delivery of care and to change the incentives in the current system to contain costs and to encourage prevention and quality care. To improve efficiency and save costs, many health care reform provisions are also designed to improve payment accuracy so Medicare pays the right amount for health services; to eliminate overpayments to private Medicare plans; and to fight waste, fraud, and abuse.

Contrary to popular belief, Medicare does not cover all medical expenses. In addition, many long-term health problems requiring custodial or private nursing care (such as Alzheimer's disease) are not covered. Medicare coverage is also subject to deductibles, co-payments, and limitations.

The original Medicare plan (sometimes called fee-for-service) has two parts: Hospital Insurance (Part A) and Medical Insurance (Part B). Part A provides hospitalization insurance for inpatient hospital care, inpatient care prescribed by a doctor at a skilled nursing facility, home health care, and care at a recognized hospice. Part B provides medical insurance for required doctors' services, outpatient services and medical supplies, and many services not covered by Part A hospitalization coverage.

Eligibility for Medicare

Eligibility for Medicare benefits is not determined by financial need. Practically everyone age 65 or older, as well as many people classified as disabled, is eligible for Medicare Part A and Medicare Part B. A person is eligible for Medicare benefits if that individual is (was):

■ 65 or older and has qualified for Social Security or Railroad Retirement monthly cash benefits;

■ entitled to benefits under the Social Security program for 24 months as a disabled worker, disabled widow or widower, or as a child age 18 or older who was disabled before age 22;

■ diagnosed as having permanent kidney failure and requiring dialysis or a kidney transplant; or

■ born before 1929 and has few or no quarters of coverage under the Social Security system.

Coverage Under Medicare Part A

Coverage under Medicare Part A is automatic and premium-free if individuals or their spouses are entitled to benefits under either the Social Security or Railroad Retirement systems or if they have worked for a prescribed period of time for a local, state, or federal government. Part A coverage is financed through part of the Social Security (FICA) tax paid by workers and their employers. People who do not qualify for premium-free Part A coverage may purchase the coverage if they are at least age 65 and meet certain other requirements. People younger than age 65 may also purchase coverage but only if they were previously entitled to disability benefits under Medicare, have the same disability, and their benefits were terminated because of the recipient's work and earnings.

Coverage Under Medicare Part B

Medicare Part B is voluntary and may be elected or rejected as the recipient wishes. Enrollment in Part B is automatic when the recipient is enrolled in Part A coverage. However, people may choose not to participate in this program by filing a "nonelection of Part B benefits" on a special government form mailed to all individuals qualifying for Part A. Part B coverage requires payment of a monthly premium that is deducted from Social Security benefits. These premiums fund only about one-fourth of the cost of the program; the federal government pays approximately 75% of the total program costs.

What Services Are Covered

Medicare performs its health care function through a series of carefully laid out steps. There are rules, regulations, and procedures that must be followed to ensure that the claim is paid, either to the Medicare recipient as reimbursement or to the care provider as direct payment. Now let's look at how Parts A and B of Medicare function, what they cover, and what they don't.

Part A—Hospital Insurance

Medicare hospital insurance (Part A) pays for medically necessary inpatient care in a hospital, skilled nursing facility, psychiatric hospital, or hospice. In addition, Part A pays for the cost of medically necessary home health care and 80% of the approved cost for durable medical equipment supplied under the home health care benefit. Certain deductibles, co-payments, and limitations apply to Part A coverage.

Part A hospitalization benefits cover:

- semiprivate room and board;

- regular nursing services;

- drugs furnished by the hospital;

- lab tests, X-rays, and medical supplies such as dressings, splints, and casts;

- blood transfusions, except for the first three pints, which are paid for by the Medicare recipient;

- use of durable medical equipment such as wheelchairs;

- use of the operating room, recovery room, and special-care units, such as intensive care; and

- rehabilitation services, including physical therapy.

Part A covers basic inpatient hospital care, skilled nursing facility care benefits, home health care, hospice care, and to a limited extent, inpatient psychiatric care. Although coverage is fairly comprehensive, there are limitations, deductibles, and co-payments for each benefit period.

Medicare Part A coverage is summarized in Illustration 2. The current amounts are outlined in the appendix.

ILLUSTRATION 2

Medicare Part A: Hospital Insurance—Covered Services Per Benefit Period[1]

Services	Benefit	Medicare Pays**	Patient Pays**
Hospitalization— Semiprivate room and board, general nursing, and miscellaneous hospital services and supplies	First 60 days	All but deductible	Deductible
	61st to 90th day	All but daily deductible	Daily deductible
	91st to 150th day*	All but daily deductible	Daily deductible
	Beyond 150 days	Nothing	All costs
Post-Hospital Skilled Nursing Facility Care— Patient must have been in a hospital for at least three days, enter a Medicare-approved facility generally within 30 days after hospital discharge, and meet other program requirements*	First 20 days	100% of approved amount	Nothing
	Additional 80 days	All but daily deductible	Daily deductible
	Beyond 100 days	Nothing	All costs
Home Health Care— Medically necessary skilled care, home health aide services, medical supplies, etc.	Part-time or intermittent nursing care and other services for as long as patient meets criteria for benefits	100% of approved amount; 80% of approved amount for durable medical equipment	Nothing for services; 20% of approved amount for durable medical equipment
Hospice Care— Full scope of pain relief and support services available to the terminally ill	As long as doctor certifies need	All but limited costs for outpatient drugs and inpatient respite care	Limited cost-sharing for outpatient drugs and inpatient respite care
Blood	Blood	All but first three pints per calendar year	First three pints***

* 60 reserve days may be used only once.

** These figures are subject to change each year.

*** To the extent the blood deductible is met under Medicare Part A during the calendar year, it does not have to be met under Medicare Part B.

A benefit period begins on the first day a patient receives services as an inpatient in a hospital and ends after he has been out of the hospital or skilled nursing facility for 60 days in a row or remained in a skilled nursing facility but did not receive skilled care there for 60 days in a row. Neither Medicare nor Medigap insurance will pay for most nursing home care.

Part A—Inpatient Hospital Care

When an eligible person enters the hospital, Part A pays for all Medicare-covered services in a hospital (over the deductible) for the first 60 days of each benefit period. The benefit period begins on the first day a patient enters a hospital and ends when the patient has been discharged for 60 consecutive days. If a patient is discharged but returns to the hospital during the benefit period (that is, within 60 days of discharge), the deductible does not have to be paid again. On the other hand, if a patient is released from the hospital and returns 61 days later, Medicare deems that a new benefit period has begun and the deductible must be paid again.

If a hospital stay lasts longer than 60 days during one benefit period, Medicare continues to pay for covered services from the 61st to the 150th

1 Source: The National Association of Insurance Commissioners and the Health Care Financing Administration of the U.S. Department of Health and Human Services.

day. During this period, however, the patient also absorbs a portion of the cost by paying a daily amount called a daily deductible. From the 61st to 90th day of hospitalization, one co-payment is applied; from the 91st to 150th day of hospitalization, another higher co-payment is assessed. After 150 days of hospitalization, the patient pays for all hospitalization charges.

Inpatient hospital care also provides a lifetime reserve of 60 days. These lifetime reserve days may be used whenever the eligible patient needs more than 90 days of inpatient hospital care in a benefit period. When a reserve day is used, Part A pays for all covered services except for a higher daily deductible. Once exhausted, reserve days are not renewed.

Part A—Skilled Nursing Care Facility (Nursing Home) Benefits

A skilled nursing care facility is an institution that treats people with complex nursing and rehabilitative needs, such as physical, occupational, or speech therapy. In many cases, patients in skilled nursing care facilities have suffered a stroke or have had major surgery. They do not require as much care as a hospital provides, but they do need around-the-clock supervision and skilled treatment from trained personnel. Others are admitted to such facilities because of a need for custodial or assisted care. For the purposes of Medicare, understanding the distinction between skilled care and custodial care is essential.

Care at a skilled nursing facility is covered by Medicare if both the facility and the patient's diagnosis and treatment plan meet Medicare's strict standards. Medicare nursing home benefits are available only if the following three conditions are met.

- The patient must have been hospitalized for at least three days (measured as 72 consecutive hours in the hospital) before entering the nursing home, and the patient must have been admitted to the nursing home within 30 days of the hospital discharge.

- A doctor must certify that skilled nursing is required.

- The services or care must be provided by a Medicare-certified skilled nursing facility (SNF); assisted living facilities, board-and-care homes, rest homes, and homes for the aged are not covered.

As a result of these requirements, the number of nursing home stays covered by Medicare is quite limited. To begin with, only about half of those entering a nursing home were previously in a hospital. Furthermore, coverage for most chronic and cognitive impairments is ruled out because the nursing home care must be for the same condition for which hospital care was needed. These conditions typically do not require a hospital stay before nursing home care is needed.

The requirement that the patient receive skilled nursing care further restricts Medicare's coverage. Usually, individuals receiving skilled care are recovering from an injury or illness that required a hospital stay. Such care is administered for short periods of time, decreasing recently to an average of 23 days.

Custodial and assisted care—less intensive, yet the most often utilized—are not covered. Care is considered custodial when the care primarily meets personal needs rather than medical needs or when the care can be provided by individuals without professional training. It includes help in walking, getting in and out of bed, bathing, dressing, and taking medicine. Medicare will not pay for this type of care; it pays for skilled nursing care only.

Those who meet Medicare's strict qualification standards will find that Medicare's benefits are quite limited. Medicare pays for 100% of all covered charges for the first 20 days. For the next 80 days, the patient is responsible for a daily co-payment. After 100 days, the patient is responsible for all charges.

Part A—Home Health Care Benefits

Health care benefits for homebound patients are also available under Medicare Part A. Here again, Medicare imposes strict standards on these. The following four eligibility rules must be met.

■ A physician must prescribe and periodically review the need for home health care.

■ The patient must be homebound.

■ The care must be intermittent or part time.

■ The care must be provided by a skilled nurse who works for a Medicare-certified home health care agency.

If these requirements are met, the full cost of part-time skilled nursing, physical therapy, or speech therapy are covered. Part-time or intermittent home health aide services, occupational therapy, medical social services, and medical supplies are also covered. Durable medical equipment, such as hospital beds, wheelchairs, and oxygen equipment, if ordered by a physician, is also covered at 80% of the cost.

Normally, home health care under these guidelines is only needed for short periods of time. The typical Medicare home health user receives 51 visits.

Part A—Hospice Care Benefits

A **hospice** is an organization that furnishes a coordinated program of inpatient, outpatient, and home care for terminally ill patients. Hospice care includes counseling, control of disease symptoms, and pain relief.

Terminally ill patients can elect to receive hospice care but only in lieu of other Medicare benefits. Under hospice care benefits, the full cost of physician and nursing services, medical appliances, and supplies is paid for by Medicare. Medicare benefits for this care are available for as long as a doctor certifies the care is needed, up to 210 days for patients who are terminal (although, in some cases, patients may be recertified for benefits). The patient pays 5% of the cost of prescription drugs (not to exceed $5 for each prescription) and 5% of the cost of respite care (not to exceed five consecutive days or the current Part A deductible).

Part A—Psychiatric Hospital Care Benefits

Inpatient care in a Medicare-participating psychiatric hospital is covered for up to 190 days. After the 190 days are used or inpatient hospital coverage is exhausted, Part A will not pay for additional inpatient care. However, if psychiatric care is received in a general hospital rather than a psychiatric hospital, Medicare treats it the same as other inpatient hospital care.

Part A Exclusions

As noted earlier, Medicare does not cover all hospital or medical expenses. Specifically, Part A of Medicare excludes:

- personal convenience items such as television sets, radios, and telephones;

- private duty nurses;

- private rooms (unless deemed medically necessary);

- custodial care in a skilled nursing facility; and

- full-time nursing care, drugs, homemaker services, and meals delivered to the patient's home for home health care benefits.

Part B—Supplementary Medical Insurance

Part B is the medical expense part of Medicare. Part B pays for covered medically necessary services no matter where they are received—at home, in a doctor's office, in a hospital, or in a nursing home. Although people are automatically enrolled in Part B when they enroll in Part A, they may elect to decline this coverage. If an individual elects Part B coverage, the individual must pay a monthly premium for that coverage.

People may enroll during the three months before their month of initial eligibility and become covered the month they become eligible. People who enroll during the month that they are first eligible for coverage or during the three months following will be covered in the following month. People who do not elect Part B during those initial seven months may sign up for this coverage during an annual general enrollment period from January through March. For people who enroll during this period, the coverage becomes effective in July of the year in which they sign up.

If eligible persons who are not covered by employer-provided coverage or other active group coverage do not enroll at the earliest opportunity or if they drop out and enroll again, they must pay a 10% higher premium for each 12 full months of nonparticipation. The 10% penalty lasts for life.

Part B covers the following:

- Surgeon and physician fees

- Outpatient services

- Medical lab fees

- Ambulance costs

- Some outpatient psychiatric care

- Annual wellness visits

In addition to a monthly premium, the recipient must pay an annual deductible before Part B benefits begin. After the annual deductible is met, Medicare will pay 80% of allowable charges for covered medical services and 100% of some costs, such as clinical diagnostic lab tests. Please see the attachment in the appendix for Medicare premium and cost-sharing amounts.

Part B Exclusions

As noted earlier, not all medical services are covered under Part B. Items and services that are excluded include:

- eyeglasses, hearing aids, or dental care;

- services not medically necessary;

- full-time private nursing care in the home;

- homemaker services provided by a relative or household member; and

- most prescription drugs taken at home.

It is clear that the coverage and benefits provided by Medicare are by no means comprehensive or complete. Because of deductibles, co-payments, and other limitations, there are many gaps in coverage. Many of the most obvious gaps are found in Medicare Part B. The first of these is the annual deductible. The next gap is the difference between the actual fee that a doctor charges and the allowable charge that Medicare covers. Any remaining excess charge within Medicare's legal limit must be paid entirely by the Medicare recipient. The third gap is the patient's 20% co-payment charge of the allowable expense. The most popular way to fill these gaps is with a Medicare supplement or Medigap policy, sold by private insurance companies.

ILLUSTRATION 3

Medicare Part B: Medical Insurance—Covered Services Per Benefit Period[2]

Services	Benefit	Medicare Pays	Patient Pays
Physicians' services, inpatient and outpatient medical and surgical services and supplies, physical and speech therapy, diagnostic tests, durable medical equipment, etc.	Medicare pays for medical services in or out of the hospital	80% of approved amount (after deductible)	Deductible* plus 20% of approved amount and charges above approved amount**
Clinical Laboratory Services	Blood tests, biopsies, urinalysis, etc.	Generally 100% of approved amount	Nothing for services
Home Health Care— Medically necessary skilled care, home health aide services, medical supplies, etc.	Part-time or intermittent nursing care and other services for as long as patient meets criteria for benefits	80% of approved amount; 80% of approved amount for durable medical equipment	20% of approved amount
Outpatient Hospital Treatment— Reasonable and necessary services for the diagnosis or treatment of an illness or injury	Part-time or intermittent nursing care and other services for as long as patient meets criteria for benefits	80% of approved amount medical equipment	20% of approved amount
Blood	Blood	80% of approved amount (after deductible and starting with fourth pint)	First three pints plus 20% of approved amount for additional pints (after deductible)***

*   The Part B deductible is applied only once annually.

**   The amount by which a physician's charge can exceed the Medicare-approved amount is limited by law.

*** To the extent that blood deductible is met under one part of Medicare during the calendar year, it does not have to be met under the other part.

MEDICARE SUPPLEMENT INSURANCE

Key Point   Medicare supplement insurance or Medigap policies supplement Medicare's benefits by paying most, if not all, coinsurance amounts and deductibles and paying for some health services not covered by Medicare.

Medicare supplement insurance or Medigap is designed to pick up coverage where Medicare leaves off. The purpose of these policies is to supplement Medicare's benefits by paying most, if not all, coinsurance amounts and deductibles and paying for some health services not covered by Medicare, such as outpatient prescription drugs. Let's begin by looking at how Medigap policies were designed.

In 1990, Congress required the National Association of Insurance Commissioners (NAIC) to address the subject of Medicare supplement insurance policies. Specifically, this group's task was to develop a standardized model Medicare supplement policy, which would provide certain core

2   Source: The National Association of Insurance Commissioners and the Health Care Financing Administration of the US Department of Health and Human Services.

benefits, plus as many as nine other policies. These model policies could then be adopted by the states as prototype policies for their insurers. The intent of this law was to reduce the number of Medicare supplement policies that were being offered for sale. It was also intended to help consumers understand and compare Medicare supplement policies (thereby helping them make informed buying decisions) by:

- standardizing coverages and benefits from one policy to the next;

- simplifying the terms used in these policies;

- facilitating policy comparisons; and

- eliminating policy provisions that could be misleading or confusing.

Medigap Standard Policy Forms: Legacy Plans A-L

The NAIC developed 12 Medicare standard supplement plans, ranging from the basic core policy with a minimum of supplemental coverage, to policies with increasingly more comprehensive coverage. These 12 so-called legacy Medicare supplement plans were available through May 31, 2010. They are no longer available for purchase, but plans purchased before June 2010 may remain in force and are guaranteed renewable for life.

Each of the 12 legacy Medicare supplement plans has a letter designation ranging from A (the most basic policy) to L (the most comprehensive policy). Plan A is the core benefits plan; each of the remaining 11 plans incorporates these core benefits and adds various other benefit combinations. Insurers could not alter these combinations of benefits nor could they change the letter designations (though insurers could add names or titles to the letter designations).

MEDIGAP STANDARD POLICY FORMS: CHANGES IN THE MEDICARE MARKETPLACE

Beginning June 1, 2010, the previous existing 12 Medigap plans, labeled Plan A through Plan L, underwent dramatic changes to reflect changes that occurred in the Medicare marketplace, including passage of the Affordable Care Act of 2010 (ACA). The following are a few of the changes:

- The preventive care and at-home recovery benefits were eliminated from Medigap policies. Also, Medicare Part B added many more preventive benefits.

- Plans E, H, I, and J are no longer offered.

- Two new plans, Plans M and N, are available. Plan N offers similar benefits to Plan F along with co-payments for visits to the doctor and the emergency room. Although Plan M also offers benefits similar to Plan F, Plan M will cover only 50% of the Part A deductible and none of the Part B deductible.

■ All Medigap policies added a hospice care benefit as part of the core benefits, and Plan G has 100% coverage for excess charges.

Starting January 1, 2020, Medigap plans sold to people new to Medicare are not allowed to cover the Part B deductible. Because of this, Plans C and F are no longer available to people who are new to Medicare on or after January 1, 2020. People new to Medicare are those who turned 65 on or after January 1, 2020, and those who got Medicare Part A (Hospital Insurance) on or after January 1, 2020. If the insured already has either of these two plans (or the high deductible version of Plan F) or are covered by one of these plans prior to January 1, 2020, they are allowed to keep the plan. Now, let's look briefly at each of the plans and the benefits each plan provides.

Plan A: Core Benefits

The basic plan, Medicare Supplement Plan A, is the core plan. It includes coverage for the following:

■ Part A coinsurance for inpatient hospital care

■ Coverage for Parts A & B reasonable cost of the first three pints of blood

■ Coverage for the coinsurance amount for Part B services after the deductible is met

■ Coverage for hospice care

Plan B

Plan B includes the Plan A core benefits, plus coverage for the Medicare Plan A inpatient hospital deductible.

Plan C

Plan C includes the Plan A core benefits, plus coverage for the following:

■ Part A inpatient hospital deductible

■ Coverage for skilled nursing facility care coinsurance

■ Coverage for Medicare Part B deductible

■ 80% coverage for medically necessary emergency care in a foreign country, after a deductible

Plan D

Plan D includes the Plan A core benefits, plus coverage for the following:

■ Part A deductible

■ Coverage for skilled nursing care facility coinsurance

■ Coverage for foreign travel emergency

Plan F

Plan F includes the Plan A core benefits, plus coverage for the following:

- Part A deductible
- Part B deductible
- Coverage for skilled nursing care facility coinsurance
- Coverage for Part B excess charges
- Coverage for foreign travel emergency

Plan G

Plan G includes the Plan A core benefits, plus coverage for the following:

- Part A deductible
- Coverage for skilled nursing care facility coinsurance
- Coverage for Part B excess charges
- Coverage for foreign travel emergency

Plan K

Plan K includes the Plan A core benefits, plus coverage for the following:

- Part A coinsurance and all costs after hospital benefits are exhausted (100%)
- 50% of Part A deductible
- 50% of skilled nursing care facility coinsurance
- 50% of Part B deductible
- 50% of cost of first three pints of blood
- 50% of cost of hospice care
- Will only pay for a portion of the cost that Medicare does not cover until you reach an annual out-of-pocket limit

Plan L

Plan L includes the Plan A core benefits, plus coverage for the following:

- Part A coinsurance and all costs after hospital benefits are exhausted (100%)
- 75% of Part A deductible
- 75% of skilled nursing care facility coinsurance

- 75% of Part B deductible

- 75% of cost of first three pints of blood

- 75% of cost of hospice care

- Will only pay for a portion of the cost that Medicare does not cover until you reach an annual out-of-pocket limit

Plan M

Plan M is the same as Plan D but with 50% coinsurance on Part A deductible.

Plan N

Plan N is the same as Plan D but with 100% Part B coinsurance benefit, less $20 per physician visit and $50 for each emergency room visit unless the patient is admitted.

ILLUSTRATION 4

Standard Medicare Supplement Plans: Effective June 1, 2010

The following chart shows the benefits included in each of the new, modernized standard Medicare supplement plans. Every company must make Plan "A" available. Basic benefits include the following:

- Hospitalization—Part A coinsurance plus coverage for 365 additional days after Medicare benefits end
- Medical Expenses—Part B coinsurance (generally 20% of Medicare-approved expenses) or co-payments for hospital outpatient services. Plans K, L, and N require insureds to pay a portion of Part B coinsurance or co-payments
- Blood—First three pints of blood each year
- Hospice—Part A coinsurance

Plan Benefits	National Medigap Plans									
	A	B	C[4]	D	F[1,4]	G	K	L	M	N
Part A coinsurance and hospital costs up to additional 365 days after Medicare benefits are exhausted	Yes	Yes	Yes	Yes	Yes	Yes	Yes	Yes	Yes	Yes
Part B coinsurance or co-payment	Yes	Yes	Yes	Yes	Yes	Yes	50%	75%	Yes	Yes[3]
Blood (first three pints)	Yes	Yes	Yes	Yes	Yes	Yes	50%	75%	Yes	Yes
Part A hospice care coinsurance or co-payment	Yes	Yes	Yes	Yes	Yes	Yes	50%	75%	Yes	Yes
Skilled nursing facility coinsurance	No	No	Yes	Yes	Yes	Yes	50%	75%	Yes	Yes
Part A deductible	No	Yes	Yes	Yes	Yes	Yes	50%	75%	50%	Yes
Part B deductible	No	No	Yes	No	Yes	No	No	No	No	No
Part B excess charges	No	No	No	No	Yes	Yes	No	No	No	No
Foreign travel exchange (up to plan limits)	No	No	Yes	Yes	Yes	Yes	No	No	Yes	Yes
Out-of-pocket limit[2]	N/A	N/A	N/A	N/A	N/A	N/A	$5,120	$2,560	N/A	N/A

[1] Plan F also offers a high-deductible plan. If you choose this option, this means you must pay for Medicare-covered costs up to the deductible amount of $2,200 for 2017 before your Medigap plan pays anything.

[2] After you meet your out-of-pocket yearly limit and your yearly Part B deductible, the Medigap plan pays 100% of covered services for the rest of the calendar year.

[3] Plan N pays 100% of the Part B coinsurance, except for a co-payment of up to $20 for some office visits and up to a $50 co-payment for emergency room visits that don't result in inpatient admission.

[4] Plan F and Plan C are scheduled for elimination for Medicare enrollees in 2020 and later

Qualifying for Medigap Coverage

According to a federal law, people age 65 or older who enroll in Medicare Part B are afforded a six-month open enrollment period for purchasing Medigap insurance coverage. They may select any of the Medigap policies available in their state and cannot be denied coverage because of health problems. In fact, insurers may not discriminate in the pricing of the policy or condition the issuance of the policy on good health. However, the insurer may exclude certain preexisting conditions, such as health problems treated within the six months before the policy went into effect. It is important, therefore, that agents carefully check their policies for any exclusions in order to explain such restrictions to their prospects and clients. In general, people under age 65, disabled, and enrolled in Medicare Part B are not eligible for open enrollment unless their state mandates otherwise.

MEDICARE PART C: MEDICARE ADVANTAGE

Key Point   Medicare Advantage plans include Medicare managed care plans and Medicare private fee-for-service plans.

Key Point   Tax-advantaged accounts (MSAs and HSAs) are available to allow individuals to save for medical expenses.

While Medicare is facing many challenges, the most pressing are the financial pressures resulting from changing demographics. Today, and in the future, the number of people becoming eligible for Medicare will increase rapidly and the number of workers paying taxes to support Medicare will decrease. Innovative solutions to this financial challenge must be developed and tested.

In 1997 and 2003, Congress passed laws intended to reduce the financial strain on Medicare funds and provide Medicare beneficiaries with a variety of new health plan options. The original Medicare plan and Medicare supplement insurance, which is purchased from private insurance companies, are still available. Options are also available through the Medicare Advantage Program. These options include a variety of Medicare Managed Care choices and a private fee-for-service plan (PFFS). Medicare MSAs and HSAs are also available.

As part of a broad set of reforms aimed to control the cost of Medicare, the Affordable Care Act of 2010 (ACA) eliminated certain subsidies that the federal government first used to establish the Medicare Advantage program. Reductions in Medicare payments to Medicare Advantage plans began in 2012, with changes being phased in over two to six years. A significant reduction in enrollment in Medicare Advantage plans is expected as a result of these changes

It is clear that one of the ACA's many reforms is that it encourages more collaboration and accountability among providers by bundling payments and advancing Medicare Accountable Care Organizations (ACOs). A Medicare ACO includes a hospital, primary care physicians, specialists, and other health care professionals. The hospital and the health care professionals are paid to keep patients well, not just treat them when they're sick. Hospitals benefit from keeping patients out of the hospital. Doctors and hospitals have financial incentives to limit unnecessary tests as well as to encourage patients to exercise and eat better. Services will still be billed under the fee-for-service system, but the ACO's members coordinate care for their shared Medicare patients with the goal of improving quality. Because ACO members are held jointly accountable for the care provided, they share in any cost savings that stem from improved quality.

In addition, the ACA requires Medicare Advantage plans to spend at least 85% of revenue on medical costs or activities that improve quality of care rather than on profit and overhead. Provisions in the law create an incentive system to increase payments to high-quality plans. Quality is measured by beneficiary satisfaction ratings on a one-to-five-star system. Starting in 2012, plans with at least a four-star rating will receive an increase in payments.

Medicare Managed Care Plans

Medicare's Managed Care system consists of a network of approved hospitals, doctors, and other health care professionals who agree to provide services to Medicare beneficiaries for a set monthly payment from Medicare. The health care providers receive the same fee every month, regardless of the actual services provided. As a result of this arrangement, health care providers try to manage care in such a way that they achieve a balance between budgetary and health care concerns. The options available to Medicare beneficiaries include HMOs, PPOs, and provider-sponsored organizations (PSOs). Some HMOs and all PPOs offer a point-of-service option (POS). With a POS option, beneficiaries can use providers outside the network for an additional fee. HMOs and PSOs provide incentives for beneficiaries who use only the doctors and hospitals in the plan's network.

Although likely to be more expensive than managed care plans, a **private fee-for-service plan** (PFFS) offers a Medicare-approved private insurance plan. Medicare pays the plan for Medicare-covered services while the PFFS plan determines, up to a limit, how much the care recipient will pay for covered services. The Medicare beneficiary is responsible for paying the difference between the amount Medicare pays and the PFFS charges.

Tax-Advantaged Savings for Health Care: MSAs

Medicare beneficiaries have the most control over their health care expenditures with **Medicare Medical Savings Accounts** (MSAs). MSAs are available to self-employed people and to individuals employed by employers with fewer than 50 employees, provided the individual lives in the service area of the plan. A Medicare Advantage MSA consists of two parts—a high-deductible insurance policy (the policy) and a savings account (the account). The policy pays for at least all Medicare-covered items and services after an enrollee meets the annual deductible. Medicare pays the premium for the policy and deposits the difference between the premium and the fixed amount Medicare allots for each Medicare Advantage enrollee in the individual's account. Money in the account may earn interest or dividends. Money can be withdrawn from the account tax free to pay for services covered under the Medicare benefit package, as well as services listed as qualified medical expenses in the Internal Revenue Code. MSA funds also can be used to purchase long-term care insurance.

If a beneficiary does not use all of the money in the account during the year, the money, including interest, is carried over into the next year. A beneficiary who needs a lot of medical care may not have enough money in the account to meet the policy's deductible. In that case, the beneficiary will have to use his own money for medical bills until the policy's deductible is met. After that, the policy will pay some or all of the medical bills.

It should also be noted that health care providers can charge any amount above what is paid by the Medicare MSA policy. Individuals may sign up for a Medicare MSA plan when they are first eligible for Medicare, or during the annual election period each year. Furthermore, unlike other Medicare Advantage options, individuals who choose an MSA must enroll in the Medicare MSA Plan for at least a year, from January to December. They can then withdraw by December 15 of the following year.

Tax-Advantaged Savings for Health Care: HSAs

A program known as HSAs began in 2004. The purpose of an HSA is to serve as a tax-favored way to accumulate funds to cover medical expenses. An HSA lets a person set aside pretax money for medical expenses. If money in an HSA is not used by the end of the year, the money in the account grows tax deferred for future expenses. An individual can keep the account even if the individual switches jobs. Note, however, that a person cannot contribute to an HSA once becoming eligible for Medicare.

Any individual younger than age 65 is eligible to establish and contribute to an HSA if the individual has a qualified health plan. A qualified health plan is one with a high minimum deductible and a high annual cap on out-of-pocket expenses. Both employees and employers can contribute to HSAs on a tax-free basis. Individuals age 55 or older can make an additional catch-up contribution. All of these amounts are indexed for inflation and change annually. For current minimum deductibles, maximum out-of-pocket limits, and contribution limits for individuals and families, please see the appendix at the end of the book.

The tax advantages of HSA contributions are that they lower the contributor's taxable income, grow tax deferred, and can be used tax free for qualified medical expenses. Qualified expenses include retiree health insurance premiums, Medicare expenses (but not Medigap), qualified long-term care services, and COBRA coverage. Prescription drugs are also qualified expenses, but the Affordable Care Act of 2010 (ACA) prohibits over-the-counter drugs not prescribed by a physician from being paid from HSAs on a tax-free basis. Exceptions are made for insulin, even if purchased without a prescription, or other health care expenses such as medical devices, eye glasses, contact lenses, copays, and deductibles.

Nonqualified withdrawals are subject to income taxes and a 20% penalty tax.

HSAs are fully portable, and assets can accumulate over the years. Upon death, HSA ownership may be transferred to a spouse tax free.

Employers can offer HSAs through cafeteria plans. Employer contributions are made on a pretax basis and are not taxable to the employee.

MEDICARE PART D: PRESCRIPTION DRUG PLAN (PDP)

The voluntary Medicare prescription drug program began in 2006 and continues today, with changes still being phased in under the Affordable Care Act of 2010 (ACA). Prescription drug coverage is provided through private prescription stand-alone drug plans (which offer only prescription drug coverage) or through Medicare Advantage prescription drug plans (which offer prescription drug coverage that is integrated with the health care coverage they provide to Medicare Part C beneficiaries).

Medicare beneficiaries who wish to participate in a Part D prescription drug plan get an initial enrollment period of seven months (including month of eligibility) and three months before and three months after. A penalty of higher premiums is imposed on persons who fail to enroll during the initial enrollment period unless they are eligible for subsidized coverage or had prior creditable prescription drug coverage [i.e., drug coverage under other insurance plans that is at least as beneficial (actuarial equivalency) as Medicare's standard prescription drug plan].

Medicare law sets out a standard benefit structure under the Part D benefit that contains four types of costs: premiums, deductibles, co-payments, and the so-called donut hole (coverage gap during which participants pay a larger percentage of their prescription drug costs). The cost of premiums depends on the plan but continues to average about $30 to $35 per person per month nationally. Please see the attachment in the appendix for more details on Medicare Part D.

The standard Medicare Part D structure has four stages:

- The recipient is responsible for the initial deductible ($405 in 2018).

- The recipient is responsible for copays until total negotiated retail costs (including deductible) of medications equal a specified amount ($3,750 in 2018).

- During the coverage gap (a.k.a. donut hole), the recipient is responsible for a larger percentage of the prescription drug costs. The donut hole will be closing in 2019, which means that Part D participants will pay 25% of the costs of all prescription drugs until they reach the catastrophic coverage level.

- After recipients pay the specified amount ($5,000 in 2018), catastrophic coverage begins under which recipients pay only small amounts for generics and preferred drugs (greater of 5% or $3.35 in 2018) and others (greater of 5% or $8.35 in 2018).

Generic Drugs and Brand Drug Discounts

Under the ACA, brand name drug manufacturers must provide a 50% discount off the negotiated price for Medicare beneficiaries in the coverage gap. However, the full negotiated price will count toward determining whether a Medicare beneficiary has made it out of the donut hole. Medicare beneficiaries who have employer-provided coverage or who are eligible for low-income subsidies are generally not eligible for the 50% discount.

Medicare Part D Changes

Other changes to Medicare Part D under the ACA include the following:

- High-income beneficiaries with adjusted gross income in excess of specified amounts pay additional premiums through Income Related Monthly Adjustment Amount (IRMAA).

- Consumer protections have been expanded for Part D enrollees. For example, a centralized system will be developed to handle complaints regarding Medicare Advantage and Part D plans or their sponsors. In addition, Part D plans will be required to use a single, uniform exceptions and appeals process.

▮ MEDICAID

In addition to Medicare, governmental assistance for health care is offered through Medicaid. Medicaid is a joint federal and state health program that provides medical assistance to certain low-income individuals and families. Typically, the services will include inpatient and outpatient services, prescription drugs, medical supplies, and nursing home care. However, because each state designs its own Medicaid program within federal guidelines, the extent of coverage and the quality of services vary widely from state to state.

Medicaid is most often used by people who, because of long-term debilitating illness or insufficient assets, are unable to pay for medical services. Each state has different Medicaid rules.

Medicaid is currently the primary source of long-term care assistance for one out of every seven people in the United States. This proportion has expanded under new requirements in the Affordable Care Act of 2010 (ACA). The Medicaid expansion was one of the major provisions at stake in the ACA cases decided by the Supreme Court in 2012. The Supreme Court upheld the Medicaid expansion but limited the federal government's ability to penalize states that don't comply. Most states are predicted to expand their programs.

Under current Medicaid rules, states are not required to provide Medicaid coverage to adults without dependents, and most states do not provide such coverage. However, the ACA could bring up to 20 million additional people into the program, most of whom are low-income adults. Under the ACA, the federal government will give a state more money if it covers everyone who's not on Medicare and who has an income below certain limits. The ACA makes no changes for eligibility for persons who are aged, blind, or disabled ("classic Medicaid").

According to the American Association of Retired Persons (AARP), about 9 million people qualify for both Medicaid and Medicare (so-called "dual eligibles"). These people make up only 15% of the Medicaid program but account for 39% of all Medicaid spending. The ACA creates a new office within the Centers for Medicare & Medicaid Services (CMS)—the Medicare-Medicaid Coordination Office, to coordinate care for dual eligibles. The office is charged with making the two programs work together more effectively to improve care and lower costs.

Many people older than age 65, because of increased medical costs, longevity, and a decreased income, are turning to Medicaid as a last resort. Under the current system, a person can qualify for Medicaid only when they meet certain income and asset tests. Financial assistance is available only if a person has divested himself or herself of all nonexempt assets. These assets include cash over $2,000 (in most states), stocks, bonds, IRAs, Keoghs, CDs, Treasury notes, savings bonds, and certain other items depending on the state involved. Medicaid does not count certain exempt assets in determining eligibility for financial assistance. Although the definition of exempt assets will vary from state to state, they often include a house used as a primary residence, a car, personal jewelry, and term life insurance. Exempt assets are not counted as things of value and do not have to be sold in order to qualify for Medicaid.

Medicaid Planning

Under the Health Insurance Portability and Accountability Act of 1996 (HIPAA) and the Deficit Reduction Act of 2005 (DRA), an individual's eligibility for Medicaid assistance will be delayed if the individual transfers assets for less than their market value within five years of applying for Medicaid benefits or entering a nursing home. This five-year period is known as the look-back period. The length of the delay in becoming eligible for Medicaid—what is commonly known as the penalty period—is determined by dividing the amount of the asset transferred by the average monthly cost of nursing home care in the state. For example, if George were to transfer $35,000 in assets during the look-back period and the average monthly cost of nursing home care in his state is $3,500, he would be ineligible for Medicaid assistance for 10 months ($35,000 / $3,500 = 10). The result is that the Medicaid applicant is responsible for paying for nursing home care for the same amount of time that the transferred assets would have covered.

Clients who consider transferring personal assets—whether in anticipation of applying for Medicaid assistance or not—should be aware of the look-back restrictions. Advisors need to understand the potential penalties they face discussing Medicaid and long-term care. The intent of the law was to promote the use of long-term care insurance and discourage the use of Medicaid as a strategy or planning tool for those who have available funds.

Medicaid is the country's largest purchaser of long-term care services, but the program spends far more on institutional care than in community-based care. Several provisions of the Affordable Care Act were designed to provide more Medicaid funds to noninstitutional care, specifically home and community-based services. These include an enhancement of the home and community-based services state plan benefit authorized by the Deficit Reduction Act of 2005 (DRA). However, a program established in the ACA known as CLASS (Community Living Assistance Services and Supports) is not currently being implemented due to legal, political, and solvency issues.

In sum, Medicaid will pay for long-term care but only after certain assets are used up. Purchasing long-term care insurance, which we talk about in the next section, may allow a client to pay for necessary care while preserving assets and income and increasing their choice of and access to services.

LONG-TERM CARE (LTC) INSURANCE

Key Point Long-term care includes a range of services provided to care for individuals who cannot care for themselves due to illness or age.

Key Point Long-term care (other than strictly medical services) is not covered by Medicare, but insurance is available to provide long-term care benefits.

As beneficial as Medicare and Medicare supplement insurance plans are to the elderly in protecting them against the costs of medical care, there still exists a critical risk that neither of these covers—long-term custodial or nursing home care.

The cost of the extended daily care some older people need can be staggering—$84,000 a year or more for nursing home care and upwards of $1,000 a month or more for aides who come to one's home. A study by the U.S. Department of Health and Human Services indicates that about 43% of people who are age 65 and older today will enter a nursing home.

How can these costs be paid? The solution for many is long-term care insurance.

What Is Long-Term Care?

Long-term care is the broad range of medical and personal services for individuals who need assistance with activities of daily living (ADLs) for an extended period of time. The need for such ongoing assistance is usually a result of a physical or mental impairment brought on by the aging process. Depending on the severity of the impairment, assistance may be given at home, at an adult day care center, or in a nursing home.

The responsibility of paying for this kind of care usually falls on those who need the care of their families. Neither Medicare nor Medicare supplement policies are designed to cover long-term, ongoing assisted living. Furthermore, the cost of such care could easily wipe out an individual's lifetime savings. Thus, for many, the answer is long-term care insurance.

What Is Long-Term Care Insurance?

Long-term care insurance is a relatively new type of insurance product. What began as simply nursing home coverage has expanded greatly to incorporate the full array of medical, custodial, and personal care services provided on an extended, daily basis.

Long-term care insurance is similar to most insurance plans; the insured pays a premium for specified benefits in the event that he requires long-term care, as defined by the policy. Most long-term care policies are reimbursement plans. This means they reimburse the insured for the actual cost of the care received, up to the policy limits.

Insurers offer a wide range of policy limits, ranging from $50 a day to $350 a day for nursing home care. The daily benefit for community and at-home care is typically half the nursing home benefit. Many policies include an inflation rider or option to purchase additional coverage, enabling the policies to keep pace with increases in long-term care costs.

The need for LTC insurance has grown steadily. However, it was not until 1996, with the passage of the HIPAA, that the tax treatment of LTC insurance was settled. The Act clarified, once and for all, that LTC insurance would be treated like all other accident and health insurance plans, as long as coverage conformed to certain qualifying standards.

Long-Term Care Coverages

There are a variety of long-term care policies on the market, some of which are characterized by innovative coverage concepts. The following is a brief discussion of some typical coverages that may be found in a long-term care policy. Note that the definition of the kind of care provided is a determining factor in where it is administered. It is important to understand the distinctions among the levels of nursing home care as well as the extent and limitations of other kinds of care.

ILLUSTRATION 5

Levels of Long-Term Care

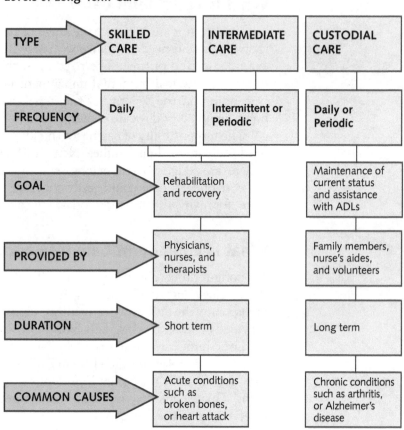

Long-Term Care Coverages

Skilled Nursing Care

This is daily nursing care ordered by a doctor and necessary for certain medical conditions. It can only be performed by, or under the supervision of, skilled medical professionals and is available 24 hours a day. Skilled nursing care is typically administered in nursing homes.

Intermediate Nursing Care

Intermediate nursing care is occasional or rehabilitative care ordered by a doctor. This too can only be performed by skilled medical personnel. Intermediate nursing care is typically provided in nursing homes for stable conditions that require daily, but not 24-hour supervision.

Custodial Care

Custodial care can be defined as care given to meet daily personal needs, such as bathing, dressing, getting out of bed, etc. It does not require the same level of medical training as skilled or intermediate nursing care, but it must be given under a doctor's order. Custodial care is usually provided by nursing homes, but can also be given by adult day care centers, respite centers, or at home.

Home Health Care

This is care provided in the insured's home, usually on a part-time basis. It can include skilled care (such as nursing, rehabilitative, or physical therapy care, ordered by a doctor) or unskilled care (such as help activities of daily living, cooking or cleaning).

Adult Day Care

Adult day care is designed for those who require assistance with various activities of daily living, while their primary caregivers (usually family or friends) are absent. These day care centers offer skilled medical care in conjunction with social and personal services, but custodial care is usually their primary focus. Some communities have established day care centers that specifically serve the special needs of those with Alzheimer's disease.

Respite Care

This type of coverage is designed to provide a short rest period for a family caregiver. There are two options—either the insured is moved to a full-time care facility or a substitute care provider moves into the insured's home for a temporary period, giving the family member a rest from his caregiving activities.

Residential Care

A fairly new kind of long-term care coverage, residential care, is designed to provide a benefit for elderly individuals who live in a retirement community. Retirement communities are geared to senior citizens' full-time needs, both medical and social, and are often sponsored by religious or nonprofit organizations.

ILLUSTRATION 6

Defining LTC Tax Treatment

The Health Insurance Portability and Accountability Act of 1996 addresses a variety of concerns dealing with the availability and portability of health insurance coverage. While it centers on medical insurance, the Act also covers key issues pertaining to long-term care insurance. In summary, it formally recognizes long-term care insurance as medical expense insurance for federal tax purposes, thus affording it the same tax treatment as medical expense policies. It also allows chronically ill individuals to cash in their life insurance policies on a tax-free basis to pay for long-term care. By providing these tax breaks, the Act encourages the purchase of private LTC insurance, with the hopes that the burden on Medicaid will be eased.

Highlights of the Act, as they affect long-term care prospects, include the following.

- Qualified LTC policies are treated like medical expense policies. This means that the LTC premiums are included in the definition of medical care under IRC Section 213 and thus can be deducted under the rules of Section 213. In addition, benefits received under LTC policies are considered payments for personal injuries and sickness and, therefore, are not included in income. There are, however, limitations imposed on the tax deductibility of premiums and the tax-free receipt of benefits; these are explained in the following.

- In order to be considered qualified, an LTC policy must meet certain provisions of the NAIC long-term care insurance model regulations. These regulations address issues such as underwriting, replacement coverage outlines, reporting requirements, marketing practices, and suitability of purchase standards.

- Employers may deduct premiums paid for qualified LTC coverage for their employees, and the employees will not be taxed on the cost of coverage.

- It sets criminal penalties for advisors who help clients transfer assets with the intent of qualifying for Medicaid assistance. This clearly illustrates the government's intent to reserve Medicaid assistance for those who genuinely need it. It also underscores the role and importance of LTC insurance in helping people conserve assets when the need for long-term care arises.

As previously noted, premiums for LTC policies now formally fall under the definition of medical expenses as set forth in Section 213 of the Internal Revenue Code. Section 213 allows for the deductibility of such medical expenses to the extent that they are not reimbursed by insurance and to the extent that they exceed 10% of an individual's AGI beginning in 2013. (The former in excess of 7.5%-of-AGI limitation continues to apply for individuals age 65 and older through 2016.) Deductions for qualified long-term care premiums are subject to additional dollar amount limitations that vary depending on the insured's age (adjusted annually for inflation). No income tax is owed on qualified long-term care benefits unless the benefits are provided on a per diem basis, in which case only a certain amount per day is tax free. For the current maximum deductible amounts, please see the appendix at the end of the book.

When Do LTC Benefits Begin?

Some of the older long-term care policies required that the insured first be hospitalized before benefits for nursing home care would be paid (or required a prior nursing home or hospital stay before home care benefits were paid). This is no longer permitted. Indeed, even the use of the so-called medical necessity trigger (in which a physician certified that long-term care was medically necessary) is no longer allowed.

The benefit trigger that must occur to qualify for tax-free LTC benefits is the insured must be chronically ill. Chronic illness is defined as:

- being unable to perform at least two **activities of daily living (ADLs)** for a period of at least 90 days; or

- severe cognitive impairment that requires substantial supervision to protect the individual's health or safety.

The general tax treatment of long-term care insurance is summarized in Illustration 6.

Activities of daily living measure levels of physical ability; cognitive impairment indicates lessened capacity to think, reason, or remember. Absent from the definition of chronically ill is any trace of the medical necessity trigger. Note also that the ADL trigger now has a minimum 90-day period assigned to it. This 90-day requirement needs to be only the expected impairment duration. An insured who suffers an impairment that is expected to last more than 90 days (say, a heart attack) but recovers, unexpectedly, before the end of 90 days, will not see his benefits adversely affected.

Policies may use either five or six ADLs, but cannot require insureds to be unable to perform any more than two. The six possible ADLs include—eating, bathing, dressing, toileting, continence, and transferring.

Long-Term Care Policy Provisions and Limits

There are a number of long-term care policies on the market today, each characterized by some distinguishing feature or benefit that sets it apart from the rest. However, there are enough similarities to discuss the basic provisions of these policies and their typical limits or exclusions.

ILLUSTRATION 7

Typical Long-Term Care Coverage Offered by Insurers

Services covered	Skilled, intermediate, and custodial nursing home care
Home health care	Health-related and personal care
Adult day services	Optional
Daily benefit	Per diem amount for nursing home care or home health care
Benefit eligibility	Physical or severe cognitive impairment
Maximum benefit period	Various periods or unlimited
Alzheimer's disease	Covered
Elimination periods	0–20 and 90–100 days
Renewability	Guaranteed
Preexisting conditions	6 months
Age limits for purchasing	50–84 (some companies issue at age 40)
Inflation protection	Optional
Waiver of premium	Standard
Free-look period	30 days
Marketing	Company or independent agents

Long-Term Care Policy Provisions and Limits

Benefit Limits

Almost all long-term care policies set limits to how long the benefits are paid and the dollar amount of the benefit for any one covered care service or combination of services. Maximum dollar amounts and coverage periods vary considerably from policy to policy. In fact, it is not unusual for one policy to include separate maximum coverage periods for nursing home care and home health care. Maximum daily benefits range from $50 to $320; coverage or benefit periods extend anywhere from two to six years to unlimited lifetime coverage.

Age Limits

Long-term care policies typically set age limits for issue, the average being about age 79. However, some newer policies can be sold to people up through age 90. Many policies set a minimum purchase age, typically age 40.

Renewability

Long-term care policies must be guaranteed renewable, meaning that the insurance company cannot cancel the policy and must renew coverage each year, as long as premiums are paid. A guaranteed renewable policy allows the insurer to raise premiums, but only for entire classes of insureds.

Elimination Periods

An elimination period is the specific time from the beginning of a benefit period during which benefits will not be paid. It is also known as a deductible period or waiting period. Long-term care elimination periods can range from 0 to 365 days, and many insurers give the policyowner the option of selecting the deductible period that best serves his needs. The longer the elimination period is, the lower the premium is.

Exclusions

Most long-term care policies exclude coverage for drug or alcohol dependency, acts of war, self-inflicted injuries, and nonorganic mental conditions. Organic cognitive disorders, senile dementia, and Parkinson's disease are almost always included. In fact, Alzheimer's disease must be covered if the policy is to conform to qualifying standards.

Premiums

The cost for a long-term care policy is based on a number of factors: the insured's age and health; the type and level of benefits provided; the inclusion or absence of an elimination period and the length of that period; and the options or riders included with the policy. Such options include the right to purchase additional coverage in the future or the inflation-adjustment rider, which automatically increases the policy's coverage to match inflation levels. Generally, the more beneficial the policy's terms are for the insured, the more expensive it will be.

DISABILITY INCOME INSURANCE

Key Point   For individuals younger than age 65, the financial risk of a disability is greater than the financial risk from death.

Key Point   Disability insurance can provide income if earnings are interrupted by a disability.

We conclude our discussion of health care needs with a look at one of the greatest financial risks facing working Americans: total disability. One might not think that a discussion of disability belongs in a course on retirement planning, unless when one considers that the disability of an individual can thwart retirement savings plans therefore, derailing hopes of a financially secure retirement.

The odds of a person suffering a long-term disability are greater than death at any age before 65. In addition, the costs of disability are often greater than the costs resulting from death. When a person becomes disabled, it may not be possible to set aside adequate funds for retirement. Therefore, attention must be paid to the need for income protection in the case of disability.

Sickness or an accident can impose tremendous burdens on an individual or a family. If a person cannot return to work for an extended period of time after an accident or illness, the income protection provided by disability income insurance will be necessary. Disability income insurance replaces lost income when a person is disabled on a total or partial basis. Payments are made for various lengths of time based on the policy's definition of disability.

To your client, disability income and income replacement are one and the same—you are providing income if disability occurs, and you are replacing income that has been lost. However, disability income usually refers to all policies that pay a stated benefit. Income replacement refers to those in which the benefits payable are tied to the actual amount of income lost. As a financial professional, you must pay close attention to the terms of a particular contract, because neither of these names truly describes the policy's scope.

Most disability income policies provide for both long-term and short-term disability benefits. In addition, they may provide optional coverages such as cost-of-living benefits, under which benefits are adjusted annually to reflect changes in the cost of living. Another optional benefit is for coverage of rehabilitation or relocation. This benefit covers the cost of retraining, locally or in another geographical location, in order to reenter one's profession or to enter a new profession following a period of disability.

Types of Policies

Disability insurance comes in many forms including individual policies, riders on life insurance policies, group insurance, employers' sick pay plans, governmental plans, and union-administered plans. Businesses use disability insurance to protect businessowners and key employees, to ensure business continuation and to fund buy-sell agreements. Individuals use disability insurance to replace earnings that are lost when a person becomes sick or injured.

What Is a Disability?

When is a person considered disabled? The definition depends on the government plan, workers' compensation, and disability policies. The term *disability* may be broadly or narrowly defined in the policy. A broad definition allows benefits for disabled persons who are unable to perform some or all duties of their chosen occupation. A narrow definition restricts benefits to insureds who cannot work in any gainful employment. In other words, if the person is able to do any type of work, he is not considered disabled and is not eligible for benefits.

Disability policies may be grouped by the way in which they define disability and determine benefits based on that definition. In addition, disability benefits may be limited by a narrow definition, as in the case of Social Security, by the policy's definition of occupation or by whether a loss of earnings has occurred because of injury or sickness.

Social Security

Social Security is one source of disability income. However, as stated in Unit 4, Social Security narrowly defines disability as "the inability to engage in any substantial gainful activity by reason of any medically determinable physical or mental impairment which can be expected to result in death or which has lasted or can be expected to last for a continuous period of not less than 12 months." This definition is so restrictive that more than half of the people who apply for disability benefits are denied by Social Security.

Occupation

Because there are physical and, in some cases, mental hazards associated with some occupations, the occupation of the insured is an important factor. Some policies pay benefits if the insured is unable to perform every duty inherent in his chosen occupation because of illness or accident. Other policies pay benefits if the insured is unable to perform the principal duties of that chosen occupation. Still others pay benefits only if the insured is unable to perform the duties of any gainful employment.

Income Replacement

Some policies ignore the occupational question and base the eligibility for benefits on whether an insured has suffered a loss of income. Insurance to replace income is important because it keeps the family intact, keeps food on the table, and maintains a roof over the family's head. Disability insurance indemnifies the insured for a cessation or reduction of income. The policy ties the benefit payments to a proportion of the actual earnings lost. A full benefit would be paid for total loss of income.

The client's financial position, needs, and feelings will determine which disability plan is best. Some plans, like noncancelable coverage, offer more advantages or benefits, but the insured must be able to afford them. Even if your client has the money to purchase noncancelable coverage, he may not be able to obtain it because of rigid health standards.

WRAP-UP

Health insurance plays an important role in helping people obtain adequate financial protection against heavy medical expenses and lost income due to disability. Despite the necessity for health insurance, most people do not actively seek out and purchase the protection they need. They generally rely on their employer or the government to provide them with adequate medical protection.

As a financial professional, you must be able to assess whether a client's disability income needs are adequately addressed by employer or government programs. If additional coverage is needed, you must be able to honestly and intelligently compare products to show how one policy differs from another in coverage, benefits, and overall treatment of claims.

Demographic studies show that, as it ages, the postwar generation will place unprecedented pressure on the health care system. Employers are already paring down on the staggeringly expensive health care benefits traditionally provided in retirement. The retiree can often end up on his own when it comes to supporting health care costs. This means that a retiree must plan on having extra funds to meet uncovered health care expenses, whether to augment Medicare coverage or to pay for long-term care expenses.

In addition to being knowledgeable about health care, those who advise others on the financial aspect of retirement should also become familiar with the importance of estate planning and wealth distribution. In Unit 13, the final unit of this course, we will take a closer look at how the retirement planner fits into the estate planning team.

UNIT TEST

1. Medicare Part A provides coverage for all of these EXCEPT
   A. inpatient hospitalization
   B. care at a skilled nursing facility
   C. hospice care
   D. required physician services

2. Which of these statements about Medicare benefit periods is CORRECT?
   A. It begins on the day an individual enters a hospital.
   B. It is the period during which no deductible payments apply.
   C. It is limited to one a year for each Medicare recipient.
   D. It ends after 60 days of hospitalization.

3. The deductible under Medicare Part B applies
   A. to each benefit period
   B. annually
   C. only the first time a claim is submitted
   D. for each covered service

4. Medicare Advantage is designed to
   A. standardize how people older than age 65 receive care
   B. replace the need for long-term care insurance
   C. reduce the financial strain on Medicare
   D. encourage more people to enroll in Medicare Part B

5. All of these are covered under a core Medicare supplement plan EXCEPT
   A. Part A coinsurance amounts
   B. Part A deductible
   C. Part B coinsurance amount
   D. 365 additional days after Medicare benefits end

6. Which of these can be used as a benefit trigger in long-term care policies?
   A. Prior hospitalization
   B. Certification of medical necessity
   C. Cognitive impairment
   D. All of these

7. All of the following are common exclusions under a long-term care policy EXCEPT
   A. drug dependency
   B. self-inflicted injuries
   C. alcoholism
   D. Alzheimer's disease

8. Which of these statements is CORRECT?
   A. Prior to age 65, the odds of suffering a long-term disability are greater than death.
   B. Social Security is the most common source of disability income payments.
   C. Income replacement disability policies base eligibility for benefits on the ability of the insured to perform the duties of her job.
   D. Technically, the term disability income policy implies that benefits are tied to the actual amount of income lost.

ANSWERS AND RATIONALES

1. **D.** Medicare Part A, referred to as hospital insurance, does not provide coverage for physician services. Medicare Part B covers that.

2. **A.** The Medicare benefit period begins on the day an individual enters a hospital.

3. **B.** The Medicare Part B deductible applies annually.

4. **C.** Medicare Advantage is designed to reduce the financial strain on Medicare.

5. **B.** The Medicare Part A deductible is not covered under the core Medicare supplement plan.

6. **C.** Severe cognitive impairment that requires substantial supervision and the inability to perform at least two activities of daily living for 90 days are the benefit triggers in long-term care policies.

7. **D.** Alzheimer's disease is not an exclusion under a long-term care policy.

8. **A.** Before retirement, an individual is at greater risk of becoming disabled than of dying.

13

Wealth Distribution

No retirement plan is complete without addressing what everyone must plan for—the distribution of property after one's death. Although most people want to make provisions for those who are financially dependent on them at their death, the prospect of selecting an attorney, formulating an estate plan, and writing a will can be frightening. Thinking about wealth distribution brings a person face to face with her own mortality—something most people prefer not to do. ■

UNIT OBJECTIVES

In this unit, we will discuss how an estate plan can protect the financial future of one's heirs and beneficiaries. We will focus on estate planning and wealth distribution for individuals, business interests, and special situations.

On completion of this unit, you should be able to:

■ describe the process of administering a decedent's estate and distributing assets;

■ list the extra costs that an estate might incur if planning measures are not taken in advance;

■ explain the consequences to a business of the death of an owner and steps that can be taken to ease the transfer of a business at death;

■ discuss issues that can arise for unmarried couples in nontraditional families; and

■ describe measures that can be taken to plan for incapacity.

THE ADMINISTRATION PROCESS

Key Point   The administration process is designed to collect all of a decedent's assets and distribute them to creditors and heirs.

The final chapter in any retirement plan must address how the retiree's property will be transferred or arranged at his death. Planning and saving for a family's financial security may accomplish little if assets and property are ultimately consumed by costs or debts, or are transferred to the wrong individual. Many people, unfamiliar with the theory and practice of estate transfer, think that the passage of their property at death will be a relatively simple and direct procedure and that assets will be transferred intact and without delay to whomever the estate owner desires.

The fact is, property does not automatically pass from one person to another at death, nor is the process smooth or swift—unless a specific plan or arrangement for transfer has been put into effect. Transfer plans can be simple or intricate, but they must be enacted during the estate owner's life to ensure that his property will be disposed of at death according to his wishes. Furthermore, the disposition of property at death is not a right, but a privilege conferred by the state. Each state prescribes the terms and conditions under which property can be transferred, both during life and after death. Consequently, a transfer plan must recognize and conform to these laws.

In order to comply with such laws, most people need some expert advice from certain professionals in developing an estate plan.

There are many ways to affect an estate transfer and many tools are available to create a plan that meets prescribed law and disposes of property in accordance with the estate owner's wishes. While the full range of estate planning techniques is beyond the scope of this text, we will discuss a number of important planning tools, including wills, life insurance, property ownership arrangements, trusts, gifting, and the marital deduction. But first, let's take a brief look at what happens to an estate upon the death of the owner—a process known as estate administration.

Wrapping Up a Decedent's Affairs

Estate administration—or estate settlement, as it is often called—is the legal process of wrapping up a decedent's affairs and disposing of the decedent's property. The process can be smooth or rocky, depending on the plans the estate owner put into effect during life.

The administration of an estate is governed by state statutes and by probate courts. The word *probate* is from the Latin verb *probate*, which means to prove. When people die, the probate court settles any questions about the ownership of property and the payment of debts. The probate court exists only to handle the transfer of the death estate to those entitled to it, whether by virtue of their claims as creditors or as heirs. The entire estate administration is under the court's control until the process has been concluded to the court's satisfaction. Generally speaking, the probate court has three fundamental goals it attempts to achieve during the administration process:

■ Conserve estate assets

■ Protect the rights of the estate's creditors in satisfying their claims

■ Ensure that heirs and beneficiaries receive their inheritance in accordance with the estate owner's wishes or, in the absence of any documents expressing the owner's wishes, in accordance with state statutes

The administrative process will vary for every estate and may be more or less complicated, depending on the size and complexity of the estate. In general, the process consists of six steps that interlock and overlap. Let's briefly look at each of these steps in the estate administration process.

The following types of property arrangements avoid the probate process:

■ Property such as life insurance, annuities, IRAs and qualified plans that are payable to a named beneficiary as well as property that passes through a trust

■ Property that passes via a pay on death or transfer on death account arrangements

■ Property that is owned in joint tenancy or tenancy in the entirety

Property that passes via will does not avoid probate.

ILLUSTRATION 1

The Estate Planning Team

When developing an estate plan, most people need some expert advice from at least four people including their financial advisor, an accountant, an attorney, and a trust officer. These people, working as a team, can analyze a person's affairs and arrange those affairs in a manner that best accomplishes the person's ultimate objectives. Although some overlapping may occur, each individual has a specific job to do.

Financial Advisor

As a financial professional, you are in a unique position to arouse your clients' interest about the problems of effective estate transfer and to motivate them to take action toward a solution. Because you are already a trained salesperson, you are the logical team member to sell the advantages of estate planning. You can point out the many advantages of proper estate planning and urge your clients to put plans into effect.

Accountant

The second member of an estate planning team is an accountant who has specialized knowledge of the estate owner's financial status. The accountant can provide the team with a clear picture of the prospect's finances and needs. In business insurance cases, no one knows a company's financial position better than the accountant who prepares or audits the books. The accountant can reveal bookkeeping or tax problems that may affect the estate plan.

Attorney

Legal questions are involved in most estate planning cases, and legal documents are frequently necessary to make the plans effective and binding. Although all the team members may have some knowledge of the law of wills, trusts, and so on, only an attorney may give legal advice and draft the documents. The attorney should be brought into discussions about estate planning as early as possible to prevent any questions of unauthorized practice of law by other team members.

Trust Officer

Trust officers or trust companies are trained and experienced in the many phases of law, taxes, investments, and business that are necessary to successful trust administration. The trust is essentially an instrument of estate conservation, with certain creative powers and distribution advantages.

Each member of the team operates within the respective guidelines to accomplish the estate owner's objectives—the transfer of property intact to beneficiaries with a minimum tax burden.

Step One—Appointment of the Personal Representative

The first step of the administrative process is the appointment of the personal representative to act on behalf of the estate owner. If the estate owner dies testate (having made a valid will), the personal representative may have been nominated in the will. In this case, the representative is referred to as the executor of the estate.

If the decedent dies intestate (without having executed a will) or if no executor is named in the will, the statutes of his state of domicile normally will require the probate court to appoint someone to act as the personal representative of the estate. In this event, the person appointed is called an administrator.

After the court formally confirms the nomination, the personal representative takes possession of the estate, is responsible for paying debts of, and claims against, the estate, and ultimately distributes the estate assets to the heirs and beneficiaries.

Step Two—Notice to Creditors

The second step in the estate administration process is for the personal representative to give notice of his appointment. By the same action, notice is given to all creditors to make prompt claim for all money due and owing to them. This is accomplished by a published Notice to Creditors, a statement that advises that:

- the estate owner has died;

- the person or institution designated in the notice has been appointed the personal representative on behalf of the estate; and

- creditors should make claim for money due and owing to them.

Step Three—Inventory and Appraisal

The personal representative then assembles the assets of the estate, evaluates them, inventories them, and files that inventory with the court. This inventory represents evidence of the estate assets and includes personal property, real property, life insurance, and any debts and claims on the estate.

In some states, the appraisal or valuation of the property can be made by the personal representative acting independently. In other states, the court must appoint appraisers. In any event, the value as appraised is subject to review by the court and representatives of federal and state tax departments.

Step Four—Interim Administration

After the assets have been valued, the personal representative's real work begins. The fourth step of the administration process involves the sale of estate assets, preservation of assets that are to be passed on, maintenance and operation of a going business, fulfillment of contractual obligations, preparation and filing of tax returns, and accounting tasks.

All of these duties require a keen business sense, a basic understanding of tax laws, a deep sense of the fiduciary relationship involved, and, if possible, a close relationship and knowledge of the decedent's family. In all cases, the personal representative must exercise a high degree of care in actions and decisions affecting the estate.

Step Five—Distribution of the Estate

The next step, distribution of a decedent's estate to heirs and beneficiaries, is generally determined by the decedent's will or, if the decedent died intestate, according to the laws of the state. A court decree ordering distribution will not be made until all debts and other charges have been paid. If the representative makes distribution without first obtaining court approval, he will be personally liable for the payment of any outstanding lawful claims. Thus, the court order of distribution serves to protect the personal representative who makes payment in accordance with its terms. This order and the representative's proof of compliance with its terms entitle the representative to an order discharging him from any further liability arising under the appointment.

Step Six—Discharge of Appointment

As noted previously, after the personal representative makes distribution to the heirs and beneficiaries, he is entitled to an order of discharge. The personal representative files with the court the signed receipts of the various heirs and beneficiaries. At this point, the estate is closed.

Due to the legal requirements the estate administration process (and the estate administrator) must meet, the goals of estate administration (conserving the estate assets and distributing them to creditors, heirs, and beneficiaries) can only be met if proper planning was done before the estate owner's death. If there was not adequate planning, the estate may face:

■ larger than necessary shrinkage factors, including taxes, administration expenses, depreciation, and less liquidity, which will ultimately reduce the estate to be passed on to beneficiaries; and

■ an ultimate distribution that does not conform to the decedent's wishes.

Let's take a closer look at these problems.

PITFALLS FACING EFFICIENT ESTATE ADMINISTRATION

Key Point Assets in a decedent's estate are diminished by taxes, debts, and the need to sell in a hurry.

Key Point Lack of a will and other estate planning measures hinders the administration of an estate and diminishes its value for heirs.

One of the primary problems faced in transferring property from an estate owner to a beneficiary is estate shrinkage. Many estates are subjected to taxes, administration fees, settlement costs, etc. Additional factors—the erosion of the purchasing power of the dollar due to inflation, fluctuating asset value, lack of liquidity to pay individual estate needs within a few months of death, and improper use of settlement options under life insurance contracts—can also cause shrinkage. Lack of provisions for long-term care and costly disability losses due to poor health, can cause expected estate values to shrink dramatically. Additional problems are created if the estate owner fails to make a valid will.

ILLUSTRATION 2

Agent's Perspective

What is a unit on estate planning doing in a course about retirement planning?
It is all a matter of stretching limited resources to do maximum work. Life insurance classically combines estate and retirement planning features. Life annuities, on the other hand, can be used to funnel resources to retirement, excluding the estate.

The objective of your client is the correct mix. Factors to consider are your client's marital status and the number and age of any children. The balance changes as your client gets older. Clients in their 40s, for example, may have a greater concern for life insurance to create an estate to support young children. Clients in their 60s are probably more interested in retirement income, particularly if children are out of school and supporting themselves. Older clients may have a renewed interest in their estates as they see their retirement years passing by.

It pays to have some knowledge of the estate planning process, even if the focus of your work is retirement planning.

Common Estate Shrinkage Factors

As we have seen, the process of transferring a decedent's property to the heirs and beneficiaries must inevitably result in some administration expense that reduces the size of the estate. The extent of this shrinkage depends on the size and complexity of the estate, the nature of the assets, and the actual cash spent for administration costs, debts, and taxes. For the purposes of our discussion, let's look at three shrinkage factors that can affect even small estates:

■ Administration and probate costs

■ Debts and obligations

■ State and federal death taxes

Administration and Probate Costs

The first group of estate shrinkage factors consists of a wide variety of estate obligations or charges that must be met before the estate is closed and the balance is distributed to the heirs and beneficiaries. These liabilities include funeral and administration expenses, including the appraiser's fees for valuing estate property, brokerage fees, attorney's fees, court costs, and various other fees.

Administration costs cannot be dismissed lightly. In small estates, for example, the impact of the administration costs often exceeds that of the death taxes and sometimes constitutes the largest single source of estate shrinkage. Although the costs vary by the size and complexity of the plan of distribution, normal administration costs can cause an average of 4.3% shrinkage in estates more than $5 million to an average 4.6% shrinkage in estates under $50,000.

Debts and Obligations

Generally speaking, any debt or claim that could have been enforced against the decedent during his lifetime is a valid and subsisting claim against his estate. Included in the category of debt are:

■ outstanding bills for recent living expenses;

■ pledges to religious and charitable institutions; and

■ mortgages, leases, installment balances, etc.

Unpaid taxes, income tax payments, and general property taxes are also debts against the estate and are sizable current liabilities that may make deep inroads into estate assets. Although some might argue that debt is not a true shrinkage factor, consider that shrinkage is concerned with the costs and expenses that arise as a result of the estate owner's death. Debts unpaid at the decedent's death would have been paid from current income had the decedent lived. At his death, however, they become immediately payable out of estate assets and are properly considered a major shrinkage factor. In fact, repayment of debt can shrink a $5 million estate by an average of 3.7% and a $50,000 estate by an average of 5.8%. Again, the situation will vary from case to case.

State and Federal Death Taxes

A death tax is a tax on the property transferred or received upon the death of the owner. Death taxes are assessed by both state and federal governments. In many cases, state death taxes will apply even when no federal estate tax is applicable.

State Death Taxes

State taxes charged at death usually include:

- an inheritance tax, which is a levy imposed on the share of the estate going to an individual heir or beneficiary; and

- an estate tax, which is imposed on the estate itself.

The impact of these taxes can be significant and must be given careful attention. Most people fail to understand that the average estate is affected more by state death taxes than by federal taxes.

Federal Estate Tax

The federal estate tax is imposed on the transfer of property owned by the decedent. It is levied without regard to the share received by different beneficiaries or heirs, excepting the property going to a surviving spouse that qualifies for the marital deduction (discussed later in this unit) and property passing to charity. It is a tax on the transfer of property, measured by the value of that property, but it is not a tax on the property itself.

The federal estate tax is calculated in four steps.

1. Determine the gross estate property and its value.

2. Subtract the allowable deductions and the personal exemption.

3. Apply the appropriate tax rates to the result.

4. Deduct any credits to which the estate is entitled.

For current federal estate tax rates and credits, please see the appendix at the end of the book.

In protecting the estate (and ultimately the heirs) against as much shrinkage as possible, the estate owner must provide some liquidity or cash. Sources of liquidity to meet these obligations include current assets, borrowed equity in those assets, or capital created in the form of life insurance. If cash is not available, then further estate shrinkage may occur through the forced liquidation of valuable estate assets to meet the estate's administration costs, debts, and taxes.

No Will or an Invalid Will

In addition to estate shrinkage factors, a second pitfall facing efficient estate administration is the failure of the estate owner to make a valid will. It isn't easy to think about death—so many people avoid the topic and fail to protect their interests and those of their heirs. Almost everyone intends to get organized and make a will someday; yet, an estimated 7 out of 10 adults have never made a will. The most common rationalizations you will hear from your clients for not making a will include the following.

- "I'm not sure what information will be needed."

- "I've never been married so I don't need a will."

- "My husband (or wife) will get everything anyway."

- "My family knows what I want."

- "I'll be dead; why should I care who gets what?"

ILLUSTRATION 3

Federal Estate Tax Under ATRA

The American Taxpayer Relief Act (ATRA), signed into law in 2013, has a major impact on estate, gift, and generation-skipping transfer (GST) taxes. One of ATRA's significant effects is that it prevents a return to the transfer tax laws as they existed in 2001. The federal estate tax system now continues to be similar to what it was in 2012, which is favorable to taxpayers. In 2012, a decedent could pass over $5 million free from estate and gift tax. If ATRA had not been passed, that number would have dropped to $1 million in 2013.

A bit of background will help to appreciate why ATRA is important. Until 2001, a decedent could pass $675,000 exempt from federal estate tax. Anything over that amount was taxed at 55%. Then, the Economic Growth and Tax Relief Reconciliation Act of 2001 (EGTRRA) increased the exemption amount in phases, with the federal estate tax to be repealed completely in 2010—creating a virtually unlimited exemption but only for a brief time. So-called sunset provisions were also written into the law to take effect in 2010, which would have reinstated the federal estate tax to the same rules and rates that applied in 2001, before EGTRRA existed. This would have meant a major tax increase.

However, in 2010, the Tax Relief Act gave some relief—but only briefly—from the tax increase that would have gone into effect after the EGTRRA sunset provisions. The 2010 Tax Relief Act set a large ($5 million) exemption amount, indexed for inflation, and a 35% top rate for 2011 and 2012. However, this law was temporary too because it was set to expire at the end of 2012 when the much-less-favorable pre-EGTRRA rates would return.

ATRA permanently set the exemption amount at $5 million, indexed for inflation. The top tax rate is 40% for decedents dying after 2012. This is an increase from 2012's top rate of 35%, but it is much lower than the 55% rate that would have applied if ATRA had not been passed.

All of this was made moot by the Tax Cuts and Jobs act enacted in late 2017. This legislation significantly increased the exemption at a base amount of $10,000, 000 per person that is indexed to $11,180 per person, $22,360 per married couple for 2018. Under the Tax Cuts and Jobs Act the higher exemption levels will continue to be indexed for inflation through 2025. Unless there are other tax law changes, the exemption will be back at $5,000, indexed for inflation in 2016.

Permanent "Portability"

ATRA also makes "portability" permanent: a decedent's estate can elect to shift the unused exemption amount to the surviving spouse, who can use the exemption either at death or during the surviving spouse's life.

State Death Tax Credit Repealed

ATRA made other significant changes as well, including permanent repeal of the state death tax credit in favor of a deduction. Estate valuation is determined by deducting from the gross estate the amount of any state death taxes paid. This reduces the value of the estate subject to the federal estate tax.

ILLUSTRATION 4

Division of Property Under Intestacy Laws

The division of property varies by state, but the laws generally divide the estate as follows.

- Spouse and one child—each receives one-half of the estate.
- Spouse and two or more children—spouse receives one-third of the estate; all children divide the remaining two-thirds equally.
- Spouse and parents surviving, no children—spouse receives 50%–75% of the estate and parents receive the remainder.
- Parents surviving, no spouse or children—parents receive all of the estate.
- Siblings surviving, no parents, spouse, or children—brothers and sisters receive equal shares of the estate.

Concept of Intestacy

One of the best ways to make sure that the property one owns reaches the designated heirs is by leaving it to them in a will. Should a person die intestate, each state, through statutes and case law, supplies a ready-made will that divides the estate according to each particular state's laws of intestacy. These laws include rigid formulas for dividing property with little or no allowance for a family's special needs.

Although state statutes are designed to be as fair and equitable as possible, intestate distribution, or settling an estate with no valid will, is loaded with problems. The deceased individual's wishes are likely to be ignored and the special needs of survivors and dependents may not be addressed. The consequences of dying without a will include the following.

- **The state will determine who the heirs are and their share of the estate.** In most states, property will be split among the spouse and children, often with a proportionately larger share going to the children than to the surviving spouse.

- **The court will appoint a guardian to care for any minor children.** Failing to provide for a child's care could lead to disaster. The court may choose the least appropriate person to provide for a child's welfare.

- **A court-appointed executor might be costly or insensitive to the estate owner's wishes.** Unless an executor is named in a will to inventory an estate, pay any debts, file income and estate tax returns, and distribute personal assets, a judge will appoint a public administrator to complete these tasks. The process could take much longer than necessary with the costs accruing to the estate.

- **Estate settlement may be more costly.** Without a will to guide the disposition of an estate, the process will take longer and therefore, will be more expensive. Furthermore, a will can direct certain types of transfers that take advantage of specific tax-saving and cost-saving measures, whereas the lack of a will means these measures are lost to the estate.

Fortunately, there are a number of estate planning tools and techniques that can solve or alleviate the problems inherent in intestacy and those associated with estate shrinkage.

ESTATE PLANNING TOOLS AND TECHNIQUES

Key Point A will communicates a decedent's wishes about his estate and may empower an executor to take measures that will save money for the estate.

Key Point Life insurance can create an estate to provide for heirs, and it can create liquidity to prevent forced sales of assets.

Key Point Trusts are property management arrangements that can increase the flexibility of an individual to tailor his estate for maximum benefit to beneficiaries.

Key Point Transfers to spouses and other gift-giving strategies can minimize taxes.

Contrary to widely held beliefs, many of the methods used to transfer property, such as wills and trusts, are not only for the rich. In fact, whatever one's financial position, a variety of techniques can be used to transfer property. Regardless of the tools or techniques selected, the fundamental issues that must be addressed are:

- providing the estate with the liquidity it needs;

- arranging for the proper distribution of property to heirs and creditors;

- minimizing estate taxes; and

- reducing the administrative burden on survivors.

Let's look at the most common methods that can be used to accomplish these goals and effect property transfers.

Wills

While there are many tools available to an estate owner in formulating an estate plan, none is as important as the will. A will is a legal contract that establishes arrangements for property transfer at and after death. Because a will can be declared invalid for a number of reasons, it should be drawn up by an attorney knowledgeable in estate planning. An improperly written or invalid will may be more costly to the beneficiaries than no will at all. For example, a will that ignores a child who is entitled to part of the estate may be contested, and litigation may consume most or all of the estate.

Wills should be reviewed and amended periodically after they are written to reflect changes in a person's financial or personal status. A move to another state, the birth of a child, and the death of a spouse are all reasons to amend a will. Changes are permitted anytime up to the maker's (testator's) death through a codicil, which is usually a one-page document indicating the desired changes in the existing will.

An estate owner may make a specific bequest, leaving a specified item of property to a particular individual. Generally, it is better to leave percentages of the estate rather than a fixed-dollar amount to heirs because the assets may shrink or grow over the years. Some items (property held in joint tenancy, life insurance, U.S. savings bonds, and pension benefits) cannot be disposed of through a will because a co-owner or beneficiary already exists.

A will is more than the conduit for the transfer of property to specific people or organizations. Specific individual needs can be addressed, and the testator may name her own executor. It can continue specific programs the decedent initiated during life, such as gifts to charity and, if properly prepared, can help protect the estate and beneficiaries from shrinkage caused by inefficient transfers, income and estate taxes, and other costs.

Wills, however, become public information through the probate process, so they do not provide the privacy provided by trusts.

Life Insurance

Life insurance can be a valuable estate planning tool. In fact, the primary function of life insurance is to increase the size of an estate—to create, at the insured's death, funds that otherwise would not exist. These funds can be used or arranged as best suits the estate owner—to provide cash or income directly to beneficiaries, to provide liquidity for the estate and prevent liquidation of assets, to fund various trusts employed as tax-saving measures, and so forth. Life insurance can be used as an estate builder, an estate conserver, a funding medium, or a self-maturing investment. Like the will, it serves as the cornerstone of an estate plan, providing maximum flexibility and liquidity at the insured's death.

The proper arrangement of life insurance ownership and beneficiary designations for estate planning purposes is very important. If the objective is to provide liquidity for the estate, the simplest and most direct method is to have the proceeds paid directly to the insured's executor or administrator, who has a fiduciary duty to pay the estate settlement expenses. This arrangement is especially advantageous for modest estates in which shrinkage due to administrative costs and debts can be substantial. If the objective is to benefit one or more individuals and they are specifically named as beneficiaries to the insurance, the proceeds will pass to them outside the estate proper, bypassing the probate process, and will be received income tax free.

ILLUSTRATION 5

Life Insurance and the Gross Estate

If properly arranged, life insurance proceeds paid due to the death of the insured are almost always received by the beneficiary free of income taxes. However, when the issue is the valuation of a decedent's estate for purposes of the estate tax, different rules apply. Life insurance proceeds will be included in the decedent's gross estate if:

■ the proceeds are payable to the decedent's estate, either directly or indirectly;

■ the decedent possessed any incidents of ownership in the policy at death; or

■ the decedent transferred, within three years of death, a policy on his life in which he held incidents of ownership.

Incidents of ownership are the rights to exercise any of the privileges of the policy. They include the right to take out a policy loan; to make beneficiary changes; to receive policy dividends; to withdraw cash values; to assign, surrender, or pledge the policy; and to select or revoke a settlement option.

Property Arrangements

How property ownership is arranged is another way an estate owner can coordinate an effective estate plan and transfer. Property has to be held by a single owner or jointly with others. How a title is held will determine how it passes from one individual to another. Therefore, it is important to know how property is owned in order to know if a particular owner has the right to distribute all or part of it on either a lifetime or postmortem basis. When property is held under a form of ownership called joint tenancy with right of survivorship, it automatically passes to the surviving joint tenant when the first tenant dies, bypassing the probate process. In joint tenancy, each owner has an undivided interest in the property, which means that each has an equal right to make use of and enjoy the property. Any individuals, not just spouses, can be joint tenants.

Joint tenancy does not solve every transfer problem. In some cases, a co-owner can dispose of property without the other co-owner's consent or knowledge. Each co-owner's interest in the property is liable for claims against the other co-owner. And, for estate tax purposes, the IRS has two ways of looking at joint tenancy property. Between spouses only, half the value of the property owned via a joint tenancy with rights of survivorship is included in the estate of the first to die. For nonspousal joint tenancies, all of the value of the property owned via joint tenancy is included in the estate of the first to die unless documentation can be shown that the first tenant to die only established a fractional interest. Then, only that interest will be included in the estate of the first tenant to die.

Joint tenancy should not be confused with other types of multiple ownership such as tenancy in common or community property. Tenancy in common is another form of ownership shared by more than one person, but the arrangements may involve any combination of parties and may be in unequal interests. Furthermore, tenants in common do not have the right of survivorship; the property does not necessarily pass to the other co-tenants at the death. In fact, each separate tenant's interest can be transferred to whomever he wishes through a will, the same as individually owned property.

Some states also permit the concept of community property, an arrangement between spouses only. Property acquired by either spouse during the marriage is considered to be property of the marriage, and each spouse has an equal interest in the property. However, inheritances, gifts, and personal injury awards are not classified as community property. One-half of the property is included in the estate of the first to die. Thus, each spouse controls the ultimate distribution of his half of the community property. Community property arrangements are likely to prevail even when a couple married in a community property state relocates to a noncommunity property state.

Trusts

Depending on the purpose for which they are set up, trusts can be used to safeguard an estate, to manage an individual's money if he becomes ill, to keep survivors out of probate court, and so forth. Trusts are arrangements in which the legal title to property is conveyed by one party, the grantor, to another, the trustee, for the benefit of a third party, the beneficiary. The trustee has a legal obligation to manage the trust in the best interest of the beneficiary.

It has been said that the primary advantage of a trust is to separate the benefits of property ownership from the burdens. The full responsibility for managing trust property is upon the trustee. In addition, trusts can offer:

- support and care of dependent children;

- estate and income tax savings available with irrevocable trusts;

- experienced investment and property management by a trustee;

- protection of assets in the event the grantor becomes incapacitated;

- protection against beneficiaries who might be or later become spend-thrifts; and

- avoidance of probate with respect to the property placed in the trusts.

Trusts can be established to take effect during the grantor's life (an inter vivos, or living trust) or through a will to become operative at the grantor's death (a testamentary trust).

Living Trusts

A living trust is a method of transferring property while an individual is still alive. Property so transferred passes outside the will and avoids the probate process. In many cases, a living trust is preferable to an outright gift of property. With a gift, the grantor or donor has no control over the property after the transaction, whereas a living trust can be arranged so that the grantor retains control, if he desires. Living trusts are also attractive when the grantor's holdings are large and he no longer wants the burden of managing them.

Living trusts can be established as revocable or irrevocable. As you'll recall, with a revocable trust, the grantor retains control over the trust property and reserves the right to revoke, change, or terminate the trust agreement. Though there are no significant tax advantages to these arrangements (the rights retained by the grantor constitute continued ownership), they can offer the grantor a preview of how a contemplated testamentary disposition would work and a way to modify the property arrangement if desired. In this way, revocable trusts are completely flexible.

With an irrevocable trust, the grantor gives up the right to revoke, change, or terminate the trust. Though obviously not as flexible as a revocable trust, an irrevocable trust has the same investment management advantages and can ensure that the property placed in the trust avoids the probate process and its delays. Furthermore, if the grantor completely gives up all control over and rights to the trust property, he can achieve income and estate tax savings.

Testamentary Trusts

When a trust is specified in a will and becomes operative at death, it is a testamentary trust. Because it is part of and dependent on the grantor's will, a testamentary trust has no more effect during the grantor's life than does a will; its existence after the grantor's death is dependent on probate and the enforcement of the will.

A testamentary trust can:

- be used to eliminate the necessity for guardianships in the case of minor beneficiaries;

- create a life income for the older beneficiary such as a spouse, with a gift of the principal to another at the beneficiary's death, therefore avoiding successive transfer taxes;

- provide for discretion and flexibility with regard to the trustee's power to distribute trust income and principal, which would not be possible with a direct will bequest;

- appropriately restrict the use of the trust property by the beneficiary and can incorporate spendthrift provisions that protect the property from dissipation by the beneficiary and from absorption by her creditors; and

- ensure that the decedent controls the disposition of the remainder interest in the trust at the death of the beneficiary.

Life Insurance Trusts

For many estates, life insurance represents the single largest asset held by the estate owner. Frequently, a life insurance trust is established to ensure that the beneficiary—whether an individual or the estate—receives the greatest benefit from the proceeds.

Some life insurance trusts are designed to receive, hold, invest, or administer proceeds of a life insurance policy or policies for the benefit of a policyowner's beneficiary. Typically, these trusts are unfunded, meaning they have no significant principal except the right to receive benefits under a policy at the death of the insured. The right to receive death benefits is normally considered sufficient for establishing a valid trust. At the insured's death, the proceeds are paid to the trustee, who then administers them for the benefit of the beneficiary. One of the benefits of a life insurance trust is that a trustee may have discretionary powers that a life insurance company cannot accept with regard to the payment and administration of proceeds.

Life insurance trusts are often established when the insured has a number of policies, making coordinating an efficient settlement plan difficult. By directing the death proceeds from all the policies to the trust, a single instrument is used to integrate and administer a coordinated plan.

Another type of life insurance trust, an irrevocable life insurance trust (ILIT), is created for the purpose of owning a life insurance policy on the insured. If the insured owns a life insurance policy on herself, the policy death proceeds will be included in the deceased's estate for estate tax purposes. However, if the insurance policy is owned instead by an irrevocable trust, the policy proceeds are not included in the deceased's estate and avoid estate taxation.

Contractual Transfers

In addition to transfers made by ownership and trust arrangements, property may also be transferred by contract. The proceeds of life insurance policies, retirement plans, bank accounts and investment accounts may pass outside a will via beneficiary designations, payable on death bank accounts or transfer on death investment accounts.

It's important to know, however, that contractual transfers avoid probate by removing property from the probate estate, but they do not remove property from the gross estate potentially subject to estate taxes.

The Marital Deduction

The transfer of property between spouses creates an opportunity to use the marital deduction, an estate tax deduction for property that passes from a decedent to his surviving spouse. This deduction is unlimited, meaning that one can give a surviving spouse any amount of property, during life or at death, without incurring gift or estate taxes. Property qualifying for the marital deduction includes, but is not limited to, outright bequests, qualifying life insurance proceeds, the deceased individual's share of joint tenancy with rights of survivorship property, and property in a marital trust when the spouse has a power of appointment over it.

Many estate owners make full use of the marital deduction, passing all of their property to their surviving spouses at death. Prior to the ATRA of 2012, which made the deceased spouse's unused exclusion amount (DSUE) permanent and is also known as the portability rule, this may have created major problems at the death of the second spouse. Prior to the portability rule, the surviving spouse who received all of the property at the first spouse's death could only use her own tax-free unified credit exemption, which often dramatically shrunk the amount or value of the estate at the second spouse's death when the estate was ultimately transferred to children or other beneficiaries.

The portability rule, however, allows estate of the first spouse to die to elect to shift the unused exemption amount to the surviving spouse, who can use the unused exemption in addition to her own. However, the use of the portability rule is not without its costs, namely the preparation and filing of a 706 Federal Estate Tax return, which might not otherwise have to be filed. In general, there is no requirement to file a 706 if the gross estate of the decedent is worth less than the unified credit exemption amount.

Gifting

A gift is any transfer of property for less than its fair market value. Many estate plans consist of a program of carefully planned lifetime gifts. Such a program allows estate owners to distribute property according to their wishes and also provides a means of reducing their current taxes and the taxes on their estate. For the annual amount per recipient that can be excluded without incurring a gift tax, please see the appendix at the end of the book. As a result of this annual exclusion, a large part of many estates may be transferred tax free over a donor's lifetime.

A gifting program makes sense for a number of reasons.

- Taking advantage of the annual exclusion can eliminate some gift or estate taxes.

- Gifts effectively reduce the size of an estate, as well as taxes and administration costs that are generally figured as a percentage of the overall estate.

- Gifts of income-producing property may shift the current tax liability on the income to another party who is in a lower tax bracket.

- Gifts of appreciated investment property can often permanently reduce or eliminate capital gains tax liability.

- Nonfinancial advantages to a gifting program include providing resources to organizations about which the donor cares or having the pleasure of seeing the donee's enjoyment of the gifts while the donor is still living.

Gift Tax Exclusion

To prevent taxpayers from avoiding tax liability by divesting themselves of their property through gifts, a gift tax is imposed on the donor, which is measured by the size of the gift. The annual gift tax exclusion allows an individual to make a nontaxable gift of up to a certain amount every year to each of any number of donees. For the current federal gift tax exclusion amount, please see the appendix at the end of the book. The gift can be made to any party or any number of parties, without regard to the parties' relationship. Gifting property using the gift tax exclusion may present opportunities to lighten an estate without invading the lifetime transfer allowance afforded by the unified credit.

An exclusion of up to two times the individual exclusion amount is allowed for gifts made jointly to third parties by a married couple. This joint method of gifting is known as gift-splitting. A gift tax form should be filed to document split gifts even though a tax is not levied. Only present interests qualify for the annual gift tax exclusion. Unlimited spouse-to-spouse gifts are permitted if the property would normally qualify for the marital deduction.

Charitable Gifts

Gifts may also be made to bona fide charities with favorable tax consequences. Lifetime gifts, within maximum limitations, will be currently deductible on the federal income tax forms of taxpayers who itemize. Lifetime or postmortem transfers to qualifying charities remove the value of the transferred property from a decedent's taxable estate. There is no limit to the amount that may be distributed in a postmortem transfer. Several trust arrangements can be made in which principal and income pertaining to certain property can be allocated among donees, other beneficiaries, and qualifying charities.

TRANSFERRING BUSINESS INTERESTS

Key Point   When an individual owns all or part of a business, a buy-sell agreement is critical to assure continuation of the business after death, to maximize the value of the business for the individual's heirs or both.

When a family business is a major asset of an estate, the value of the business may be impaired substantially by the death of the businessowner, who is frequently the key person in the operation of the enterprise. The importance of planning for business continuation after the death of the estate owner cannot be underestimated. In many cases, life insurance can be used either to maintain the business as a going concern or to retain the values of the business interest for the benefit of the estate following the owner's death. Careful planning, combined with the skillful use of life insurance, may preserve the value of the business until it can be sold or passed to beneficiaries without disrupting business operations.

Buy-Sell Agreements

Every businessowner should have a buy-sell agreement. Many of the problems caused by the death or disability of an owner are resolved by prearranging a sale of the business. A buy-sell agreement is a written arrangement utilizing life insurance policy benefits to provide funds for buying out a deceased owner's or partner's proportional business interest. With a buy-sell agreement, the decedent's family or other designated party receives the economic value of the decedent's share of the business and the business goes on with the remaining owners. The advantages of a buy-sell agreement include:

- identifying a buyer before the owner's death and assuring that the buyer will be able to maintain control of the business;

- setting the price in a normal supply-and-demand environment, thus preserving the value of the business;

- maintaining financial values and economic support for family members; and

- arranging for a smooth transition between owners.

The particular type of buy-sell agreement used will depend on many factors, such as the type of business operation involved and the particular disposition made of the interest.

- A **sole proprietor,** or single owner, may dispose of the business to one or more key employees, or a buy-sell agreement may be used to hand the business over to a family member.

- A **partner** may contract with other partners to sell his partnership interest to them at death through a cross-purchase plan or an entity-purchase agreement (discussed later).

- A **limited liability company (LLC) member** may contract with other members to sell his membership interest to them at death through a cross-purchase plan or an entity-purchase agreement.

- A **close corporation stockholder** may contract with co-shareholders to sell his stock to them at death through a cross-purchase agreement, or to contract with the business to purchase his stock outright at death.

The cash received by the deceased owner's estate on the sale of a business interest may be used to meet the cash demands made against the estate. The balance of the estate owner's assets may then pass substantially intact to the estate owner's family.

Cross-Purchase Plan

Life insurance can be used for full or partial funding of the purchase of the company. For example, a cross-purchase plan is one form of a buy-sell agreement using life insurance to fund the purchase. This plan commits the estate of a deceased owner to sell and a purchaser to buy at a prearranged price. With a cross-purchase plan, each party to the plan owns insurance on the life of the other parties, in an amount equal to his share of the purchase price.

EXAMPLE

To illustrate how a cross-purchase buy-sell agreement operates, assume that a manufacturing business has three equal partners—John, Mike, and Kathy. They agree that in the event of death, the remaining two partners will purchase the deceased owner's share of the business. The business is valued at $5 million. Here's how this cross-purchase arrangement is set up:

Owned by John: $833,000 life insurance on Mike
                   $833,000 life insurance on Kathy
Owned by Mike: $833,000 life insurance on John
                   $833,000 life insurance on Kathy
Owned by Kathy: $833,000 life insurance on John
                   $833,000 life insurance on Mike

If any of the three partners dies, the other partners have sufficient funds provided by the life insurance proceeds to acquire the deceased partner's share. The acquisition compensates the partner's family for the full value of the decedent's interest in the business. Insurance becomes a reliable means of having ready capital for the purchase, which will take place at a time that is virtually impossible to predict.

The Entity-Purchase Plan

In the entity-purchase version of the buy-sell agreement, the business, as a separate entity, owns insurance on the lives of the partners or shareholders, and is itself the beneficiary of the proceeds. At death, the proceeds are paid to the business, which in turn, purchases the deceased's interest from his estate. This price is prearranged or per the terms of a prearranged formula. Because the life insurance is not considered a necessary business expense, the premiums are not tax-deductible. However, death benefits are not taxable and are used to carry on the firm's operations.

Unlike the cross-purchase agreement that obligates each partner to purchase a portion of the deceased partner's interest, an entity-purchase plan allows the partnership as an entity to purchase that interest. The advantages of the entity-purchase plan include equalization of premium payments among partners (regardless of age) and the benefit of cash values while the partners are living. These funds may be used for business expansion or emergencies.

PLANNING FOR ESTATES INVOLVING SIGNIFICANT OTHERS

Key Point   Lifetime relationships not formalized by marriage require special planning measures if the individuals want their partners financially protected.

As lifestyles change, new relationships must be addressed by estate planners. When your client has a significant other or lifetime companion rather than a legal spouse, many estate planning techniques traditionally available to married people may not be appropriate or legal.

For example:

- the marital deduction, as applied to both gift and transfers, cannot be implemented; and

- joint tenancies established with survivorship rights will be subject to the inclusion of 100% of the asset's value in the estate of the first to die unless it can be proven that the property was originally purchased by both parties.

However, the client with a significant other or lifetime companion, whether cohabitating or not, does have a few estate planning opportunities remaining at her disposal.

- **Make a witnessed will.** Without a will, it is very likely the significant other will be entirely disinherited. State intestacy laws make no provision for these relationships.

- **Convert the title to property from sole ownership into a tenancy in common.** This reduces the original sole owner's estate and provides the designated cotenant with property and its corresponding income or appreciation.

- **Name the significant other as the beneficiary of the partner's life insurance and retirement accounts.** As lifestyles change, insurer challenges to beneficiary arrangements are becoming rarer.

PLANNING FOR INCAPACITY

Key Point   An individual should prepare for the possibility that he might become incapacitated and legally and physically incapable of acting on his own behalf.

In addition to concerns about wealth distribution after death, your clients should consider ways to protect their wealth if they become incapable of managing their personal and financial affairs. Although your clients may feel adequately protected by a will, some additional planning is necessary to address loss of mental or physical capacity due to illness or disease.

There are several ways to protect assets and to ensure that their owner's wishes will be carried out. The most common methods used are joint bank accounts, power of attorney, conservatorship, and living wills.

Joint Bank Accounts

A joint bank account permits any account owner to withdraw funds. Such an arrangement is useful for people with poor eyesight or arthritis, which can make writing checks or keeping records difficult. When a bank account is held under joint tenancy, the assets pass directly to the surviving owner. This arrangement usually avoids probate, but some estate taxes may be due on large amounts.

Power of Attorney

A power of attorney is a legal arrangement that allows someone to act on another person's behalf. The provisions of the plan can be limited to paying bills or broadened to cover all finances, including investments. A power of attorney stops being effective when its maker, known as the principal, becomes incapacitated.

To be valid, a power of attorney must be witnessed and notarized as required by state law. Because the exercise of power of attorney is not supervised, mismanagement of a person's assets can and does happen.

Unlike a traditional power of attorney, which becomes invalid if the person granting the right becomes incompetent, a durable power of attorney continues to operate after the incapacity or disability of the principal. Another approach to granting power of attorney is the springing power of attorney that activates only when the principal becomes incapacitated.

Conservatorship

Those families unable or unwilling to enter into joint bank accounts or power of attorney arrangements may petition the court to appoint a conservator or guardian to manage a disabled person's finances and estate. The court determines whether the disabled person is able to make sound decisions and, if not, a conservator is appointed. Once a conservator is appointed, the disabled person has no control over his finances.

Living Wills

Individuals may also have concerns about their wishes regarding medical science's ability to extend life for the terminally ill.

The use of a living will, a legal document that specifies whether extraordinary medical procedures should be used to prolong a person's life, helps to ensure that an individual's desires are respected.

Living wills can specify whether a number of procedures—surgery, pain medication, life support—should be attempted or given when a patient is unable to make decisions about medical care. In states where they are legal, living wills override the wishes of relatives and protect the attending physician against lawsuits.

Although thinking of disability and incapacity is difficult, your clients should be prepared to face the possibility that, at some point, they may be unable to make decisions about their finances and medical care. You can guide them to an attorney who can make the necessary legal arrangements to handle decision-making in the event of incapacity. Your clients then can be assured that their wishes will be respected when important decisions are made on their behalf.

WRAP-UP

Estate planning consists of both financial and nonfinancial decisions that affect the estate owner's beneficiaries. As such, the estate plan should be carefully arranged to accomplish the estate owner's objectives while reducing as many costs as possible.

As a retirement planner, you can aid your clients in planning for their final wealth distribution. How well they accomplish this distribution depends in part on what you can do to help them prepare for it. With your help, your clients can analyze their current financial situation, make decisions about what they must do to transfer their wealth with minimal cost and maximum benefit, and take action to attain those goals.

UNIT TEST

1. When a person fails to prepare a valid will, the division of his property at his death is subject to the laws of

   A. shrinkage
   B. intestacy
   C. estate administration
   D. estate transfer

2. Which of these is NOT an advantage of providing a will for one's surviving family?

   A. Individual needs are addressed.
   B. One can nominate his own executor.
   C. The decedent's spouse and children will not be required to share anything they do not wish to share.
   D. Selected items of property can be distributed to chosen individuals.

3. Which of these is NOT a reason that a buy-sell agreement is beneficial to the estateholder who owns a business?

   A. The surviving owners have less control of the business.
   B. Family members will enjoy continued economic support.
   C. Family members can control the business operations free of interference.
   D. The value of the business is preserved in liquid cash.

4. The federal estate tax is a tax imposed on

   A. the value of all property owned by a decedent
   B. the heirs of a decedent on the value of the property left to them by a will
   C. the transfer of property to a decedent's heirs at death
   D. the percentage share of a decedent's property left to each heir

5. Which of these is NOT a goal of estate administration?

   A. Conserve estate assets
   B. Protect the rights of creditors
   C. Evade estate death taxes
   D. Distribute property to heirs and beneficiaries

ANSWERS AND RATIONALES

1. **B.** Intestacy refers to the condition of dying without a will. If this occurs, an individual's property is divided according to a state's intestacy laws.

2. **C.** Writing a will enables an individual to have a say in dividing his property at death.

3. **A.** A buy-sell agreement can ensure that a businessowner's family will receive full value when the owner dies and ensure that the business will have the wherewithal to continue.

4. **C.** The federal estate tax is a tax on property transferred to a decedent's heirs at the decedent's death.

5. **C.** Estate administration conserves estate assets, protects the rights of creditors, and distributes property to heirs and beneficiaries.

14

Retirement Income Planning

In this unit, we will learn how to structure a retirement income plan. Taking into account a client's objectives and risk tolerance, the primary goal is to ensure that the financial resources the client has earmarked for retirement are used to their fullest but not prematurely depleted. ■

UNIT OBJECTIVES

This is the key issue: making a retiree's assets last for a lifetime. Retirees are no longer adding to their savings by the sweat of their brow. Retirement income needs to be coaxed from the assets already accumulated. Your role as a financial professional is to guide your client through a process that asks a client to do something he has never thought of doing before: budget for 30 years.

On completion of this unit, you should be able to:

- categorize assets by liquidity, risk, and tax status;

- match resources to retirement income needs;

- develop a schedule for liquidation of retirement savings to produce retirement income; and

- recommend solutions that combine Social Security, retirement plan assets, and savings with life insurance and annuities to produce a withdrawal plan that will be sustainable for the client's life.

THE SWITCH FROM RETIREMENT SAVING TO RETIREMENT FUNDING

Key Point   Retirees need a plan to use retirement savings to generate a sustainable income stream for life.

The discipline of retirement planning has traditionally focused on the accumulation phase leading up to retirement and the estate disposition phase, after the retiree's death. Little attention has been given to the critical period that falls between these two points. But as baby boomer retirements approach, longevity rises, and the time between retirement and death grows longer, the need to establish and implement adequate financial plans during retirement is becoming increasingly important.

Financial practitioners would do well to expand their portfolios of product, service, and advisory offerings to address client needs and objectives for the ever-lengthening period between employment and death.

The focus of a retirement plan must switch from the accumulation of funds to the distribution of funds—from retirement saving to retirement funding. At that point, clients need to address a number of issues.

- What kinds of investments should house the client's funds?

- How much income will be needed monthly? Annually?

- To provide income, which investments should be liquidated first? Second?

- What strategies can be used to maximize income?

- How should the retirement funds be accessed to ensure that they last at least as long as the client?

In addition, the income tax treatment given to various investment vehicles plays an important role in the decisions that are made because tax costs can erode not only the accumulated value of an asset but also the income it provides. The client's objectives and risk tolerance are also very important; in fact, they are as significant in the distribution of assets as they are in the accumulation.

As with any kind of financial plan, the creation of a retirement income strategy requires a methodical, systematic approach. The remainder of this unit will focus on such an approach through the following steps.

1. Determine a realistic income need.

2. Quantify and verify annual income draw.

3. Categorize assets; review and adjust asset mix.

4. Create structure for income distribution.

5. Determine asset liquidation sequence; employ appropriate income distribution principles.

6. Use annuities and life insurance to meet client's goals in a retirement income plan.

7. Monitor fund flow.

STEP 1: DETERMINE REALISTIC INCOME NEED

Key Point   Retirees should determine how much they will need to spend during retirement.

At the outset of any retirement income planning session, you should focus on helping your client determine the amount of annual income needed to support the lifestyle he desires. As discussed in Unit 3, the most common sources of retirement income are Social Security benefits, qualified retirement plans, and personal savings and investments. Funds that derive from Social Security and a pension plan are predetermined. Consequently, one of the objectives at this stage of the planning process is to determine the income need above and beyond the base that will be provided by these two sources.

Anticipated retirement income needs should be based on lifestyle. Some clients have a realistic view of what they will need in retirement, others do not. The rule of thumb that bases retirement needs on an estimate of 60%–80% of preretirement income is best reserved for younger clients. For those who are on the brink of retirement, an actual line-by-line estimate of future expenses based on their current expenses (the expense method) will provide a much more precise measure of their income needs. Consequently, this aspect of the planning process is helped by the use of a budget form that outlines and estimates annual expenses. (Refer to the sample expense form in Unit 3.)

Retirement Expenditures

To what extent does spending change during retirement? Based on historical data from the Bureau of Labor Statistics, the following were found to be the average living expenses.

	Ages 55–64	Ages 65–74	Ages 75 and Older
Average Annual Expenditures	$56,267	$48,885	$36,673
Food at home	$4,109	$3,735	$2,958
Food away from home	$2,691	$2,567	$1,397
Alcoholic beverages	$457	$455	$219
Housing	$18,006	$18,838	$13,375
Apparel and services	$1,789	$1,417	$683
Transportation	$9,321	$8,338	$5,091
Health care	$4,958	$5,956	$5,708
Entertainment	$2,852	$2,988	$1,626
Personal care	$674	$692	$499
Reading	$123	$152	$135
Education	$1,044	$318	$102
Tobacco and smoking	$401	$307	$116
Miscellaneous	$802	$807	$745
Cash contributions	$1,941	$2,155	$2,985
Insurance	$520	$372	$240
Pensions and Social Security	$6,578	$2,788	$800

Source: Consumer Expenditure Survey, U.S. Bureau of Labor Statistics, September, 2015

To assist your client with this phase of the planning process, explain that retirement income needs can be grouped into three stages—early retirement, middle retirement, and late retirement. Typically, newly-retired individuals spend more money than those who have been retired for a number of years. In fact, clients in their first few years of retirement may see no difference in their income need compared to the year before retirement. The middle stage is typically the longest and spending tends to decrease somewhat. Late retirement should account for increases in medical expenses, which can be quite large.

The advisor should also point out the potential change in cash flow that retirement may bring. If, for example, the client's income will be less, fewer taxes will be owed and withholding could be adjusted. Additional deductions may be available. At the same time, clients should know that they may have to estimate and pay taxes quarterly if they no longer have income withheld.

At this point in the planning process, your role is to guide your clients in setting realistic income needs and expectations.

Does the Income Need Match Available Assets?

Once the annual income need is determined, the next step is to assess the income sources the client will have at his disposal. Social Security will cover some portion of the income need, as will pension benefits. If the client is younger than full retirement age, he will have to decide whether to take early benefits from Social Security, even though the benefits will be less.

Many advisors now recommend that their clients take Social Security as soon as possible. If the money is not needed, it can be invested. No one can predict with certainty the future of the Social Security program and the client could come out ahead by taking early benefits, given the client's longevity.

If you offer this recommendation to your clients, make sure they understand that the level of benefits they will receive will be permanently reduced, even after they reach their full Social Security retirement age.

Other advisors, however, recommend waiting as long as possible, up to age 70, to take advantage of the 8% year increase in Social Security retirement benefits.

For many individuals, benefits from Social Security and a pension plan will provide only a portion of the income they will need in retirement. Hopefully your clients did not underestimate the importance of personal savings to their retirement plans. The difference between what a client needs and what a client will receive from Social Security and a pension is what must be generated from personal savings. And often, this difference determines the standard of living the client will enjoy during retirement.

The following table illustrates the approximate capital needed to generate various annual incomes for 25 years, assuming a 3% inflation rate and a 7% investment return. Also assumed is an annual Social Security benefit that begins at $17,000 and a $10,000 annual fixed pension.

Annual Income Need	Amount Provided by Social Security and a Pension	Difference	Capital Needed to Generate Difference for 25 Years
$50,000	$27,000	$23,000	$ 500,000
$75,000	$27,000	$48,000	$1,100,000
$100,000	$27,000	$73,000	$1,700,000
$150,000	$27,000	$123,000	$2,800,000

Knowing these numbers will enable you to help your clients assess whether their annual retirement income needs are realistic or supportable.

EXAMPLE

If a 62-year-old client says his annual income need in retirement is $100,000, even with Social Security and a pension providing about ¼ of that income, the client is still going to need a capital base of about $1.7 million when he retires. Is that realistic? Does he have $1.7 million? If not, the client will have to either postpone retirement or scale back on his income requirement.

Some clients have unrealistic expectations about the behavior of the market and what it may bring them in the future. Rather than adjust their income expectations to match their retirement assets, they'll assume market results that will enable them to support their desired lifestyles. An individual who expects a 14% annual rate of return throughout his retirement period will have to take on excessive risk and still will not likely achieve that result.

You should also be alert to the client who ignores the effect of inflation. For example, if your client tells you that the nest egg she's accumulated will generate an annual income of $75,000, which she plans to consume while leaving the principal to her children, you need to explain the effects of inflation. Even if it creeps along at only 3% per year, the purchasing power of her annual income will be three-quarters of what it originally was in only 10 years. In 20 years, her purchasing power will be cut almost in half.

To keep from getting caught short, this client would have to continue to build her assets during her early post-retirement years. She could continue to work, work part-time, aim her investment strategy toward generating greater growth, or plot a revised retirement income strategy.

STEP 2: QUANTIFY AND VERIFY ANNUAL INCOME DRAW

Key Point A retiree should determine the amount needed from savings to meet expected expenses.

Once you have determined a realistic initial income goal, it should be quantified as a percentage of the client's assets that he can look to withdraw each year. Using a percentage of assets measure is more flexible than an annual fixed-dollar measure. Fixed-dollar withdrawal plans increase the possibility of taking too much or too little, given varying market and economic conditions.

EXAMPLE

If a client's annual income need above and beyond his pension and Social Security is $73,000 and his asset base is $1.7 million, then his initial annual draw from his retirement savings would be 4.3%.

But even a percentage measure should be assessed. In other words, given a specific rate of withdrawal, how secure is the client's income stream? How long will those savings last? These are questions that advisors should be prepared to discuss with all of their retiring clients. The concerns are that too large a withdrawal rate will deplete retirement assets too early and that too small of a withdrawal rate will create an unnecessarily lower standard of living.

The Impact of Risk

Three finance professors at Trinity University in Texas conducted a series of studies to determine how long investment portfolios would last, based on various rates of withdrawals and historical market data. The study looked at five portfolios consisting of different allocations of stocks and bonds. The researchers applied various withdrawal rates (measured as a percentage of initial portfolio value) in order to answer the question posed by every retiree: "What is the likelihood of my portfolio lasting as long as I will?"

The success rate is the rate at which the portfolio succeeded in sustaining the withdrawal amounts annually for the payout period indicated. As you can see, withdrawals of 3% virtually ensure that a portfolio, no matter what its allocation mix, will last at least 30 years. Withdrawals of 4%–5% are also highly successful, but you can see how asset allocations within the portfolio begin to play a role. At 6% withdrawals, the success rates begin to drop, and at 7% and higher withdrawal rates, there is significant risk that the portfolios will not be sustained.

This study was conducted using historical data that reflects the ups and downs of the economy and the markets over a 69-year period (1926 through 1995). According to Ibbotson, the inflation rate for this period was 3.1%, the return on large cap stocks was 10.5%, and the return on long-term corporate bonds was 5.7%. The premise of the study is that if a withdrawal rate proves sustainable based on historical year-to-year returns, then it seems likely that the rate will be sustainable during future periods. The danger of relying on historical data is that it is no guarantee of future market conditions or performance.

Further Studies

Using the Trinity study as a foundation, others have conducted their own research, adding different dimensions to this issue. Using random Monte Carlo simulations and powerful spreadsheet applications, these probability studies not only confirm the Trinity research, but they also draw clear links between the degree of risk a portfolio carries and its ability to survive and sustain withdrawals over the retirement period.

For instance, one might assume that each of three different retirement portfolios, all averaging a 10% return, could support the same withdrawal rate. This is not necessarily so. The more risk a portfolio carries, the greater the chance it will fail to sustain the same withdrawal rate over the same period of time as one that carries lower risk.

EXAMPLE

An investment advisory firm compared how different portfolios—each averaging an annual return of 10% but reflecting standard deviation (risk) of 10%, 15%, and 20%—sustained a 6% withdrawal rate over a 30-year period. Out of 1,000 trials, the study found that only 1% of the portfolios failed to sustain 5% withdrawals at 10% risk, but 23% failed at a risk rate of 20%. As the study noted, not all 10% returns are equal.

Advisors should ensure that clients understand the difference between average rates of return and actual rates of return. Whereas a portfolio might provide an average rate of return of 10% over a period of 20 or 30 years, it is not likely—in fact, it is nearly impossible—that this rate will be earned each and every year. A withdrawal plan must account for risk and inevitable market downturns.

ILLUSTRATION 1

Sources of Retirement Income

Portfolio Allocation	Payout Period	Success Rate at Annual Withdrawals of . . .									
		3%	4%	5%	6%	7%	8%	9%	10%	11%	12%
Stocks 100%	15 years	100	100	100	91	79	70	63	55	43	34
	20 years	100	100	88	75	63	53	43	33	29	24
	25 years	100	100	87	70	59	46	36	30	26	20
	30 years	100	95	85	68	59	41	34	34	27	15
Stocks 75% **Bonds 25%**	15 years	100	100	100	95	82	68	64	46	36	27
	20 years	100	100	90	75	61	51	37	27	20	12
	25 years	100	100	85	65	50	37	30	22	7	2
	30 years	100	98	83	68	49	34	22	7	2	0
Stocks 50% **Bonds 50%**	15 years	100	100	100	93	79	64	50	32	23	13
	20 years	100	100	90	75	55	33	22	10	0	0
	25 years	100	100	80	57	37	20	7	0	0	0
	30 years	100	95	76	51	17	5	0	0	0	0
Stocks 25% **Bonds 75%**	15 years	100	100	100	89	70	50	32	18	13	7
	20 years	100	100	82	47	63	16	8	4	0	0
	25 years	100	93	48	24	59	4	2	0	0	0
	30 years	100	71	27	20	59	0	0	0	0	0
Bonds 100%	15 years	100	100	100	71	39	21	18	16	14	9
	20 years	100	90	47	20	14	12	10	2	0	0
	25 years	100	46	17	15	11	2	0	0	0	0
	30 years	80	20	17	12	0	0	0	0	0	0

Source: Cooley, Hubbard, and Walz, "Retirement Savings: Choosing a Withdrawal Rate That Is Sustainable" (*AAII Journal*, February 1998, Vol. XX, No.2). Inflation-adjusted portfolio success rates: 1926 to 1995. Stocks are represented by the S&P 500 index. Bonds are represented by long-term corporates. Inflation rates are based on the CPI.

Model Portfolios for Retirees

The issue of risk emphasizes the importance of portfolio allocation. Allocations should be an integral part of the retiree's planning process, upon retirement and throughout its duration. One of the most common questions that retirees ask is, "How should I position my portfolio?" Although details on this subject are beyond the scope of this text, a brief sampling of model retirement portfolio allocations, based on broad risk tolerance considerations, is appropriate.

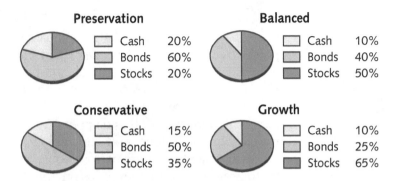

Preservation		
Cash	20%
Bonds	60%
Stocks	20%

Balanced		
Cash	10%
Bonds	40%
Stocks	50%

Conservative		
Cash	15%
Bonds	50%
Stocks	35%

Growth		
Cash	10%
Bonds	25%
Stocks	65%

Note that every portfolio in this illustration—even the preservation portfolio—consists of some equity investments. Planning for 25 or 30 years of retirement requires positioning for continued growth. As the authors of the Trinity study determined, the presence of common stocks in a retiree's portfolio provides upside potential and creates the opportunity for higher sustainable withdrawal rates.

The inclusion of bonds in a retirement portfolio increases the sustainability of low- to mid-level withdrawal rates and adds certainty. So, too, does cash. Note that every sample portfolio—even the growth portfolio—consists of some cash. Portfolios that consist of all stocks or all bonds are too risky to support long-term withdrawals, so they should be balanced with low-risk cash (or near-cash) investments. This serves two purposes.

- The low-risk investments decrease the overall risk that the portfolio would carry.

- Cash or near-cash can be used to fund withdrawals during market downturns.

Many planners advocate that retirees maintain enough money in money markets, CDs, or very short-term bond funds to cover two to three years of living expenses. In addition to cutting overall risk, a safety net of cash that could support a retiree's needs for this duration will avoid having to sell off equity investments during market downs.

The result is a retirement portfolio that is balanced to the unique needs of the retiree: a combination of equity, bonds, and cash investments that will safely support moderate, yet realistic, withdrawal rates over many years. A client on the verge of retirement who still has assets in a company's 401(k) plan or profit-sharing plan should consider a rollover to an IRA and select investment options for that vehicle that support or enhance his allocation plan. This will also serve to put the client more firmly in control of the future distribution of these assets.

Rule of Thumb for Withdrawal Rates

As a rule of thumb, many planners advocate annual withdrawal rates of 4%–5%. If history is any guide to the future, an annual withdrawal of 4%–5% of one's retirement assets would easily enable the funding of an income stream for 25 to 30 years. It is also likely to ensure that much of the retiree's assets will be available to pass on to survivors and heirs.

Of course, the 4%–5% withdrawal rate should be adjusted, depending on the client and the situation. An individual who retires early and anticipates a long payout period should plan on lower withdrawal rates. A retiree whose portfolio endures weak or bad market performance early in retirement may find it necessary to make some critical adjustments—perhaps to the withdrawal rate or the portfolio's allocation, or both. These kinds of adjustments would probably not be required of a retiree whose early retirement years saw good market performance. The compounded returns that such a retiree earned would help his portfolio grow enough to sustain later downturns.

Warn clients to refrain from equating their annual withdrawal rates to the rate of return they earn on their investments or increasing their withdrawals in years when they experience better-than-anticipated returns. These practices ignore the consequences of inflation and leave no cushion to cover periods when returns are low or negative.

STEP 3: CATEGORIZE ASSETS

Key Point   In setting up a plan for liquidating retirement savings, it is important to know the tax status of each asset.

Once you've determined a realistic retirement income withdrawal rate, the next question is, "Where will the money come from?" A client's retirement assets can be housed in a variety of vehicles: nonqualified investment and savings accounts, nonqualified annuities, company stock, IRAs, 401(k)s, life insurance, and so forth. For purposes of creating a retirement income flow, what assets should be tapped first?

Making an asset liquidation decision is helped by first sorting the client's assets by their tax treatment—taxable, tax-deferred, or tax-free. For example, a basic sorting might follow these lines:

Currently Taxable	Tax-Deferred	Tax-Free
Savings accounts (pass-book, CDs, etc.)	Stocks and stock mutual funds	Roth IRAs
Money market accounts	Nonqualified annuities	Municipal bonds and municipal bond funds
Corporate bonds and corporate bond funds	Life insurance cash values	
Dividends	Qualified plans, traditional IRAs, 403(b) plans, etc.	

Next, note the kind of tax that each asset currently generates or will generate when distributed—ordinary or capital gains. The difference between taxation at ordinary income rates versus capital gains rates can be significant. For federal individual income tax and capital gains rates, please see the appendix at the end of the book. These rates are subject to change, but in general, capital gains rates are lower than ordinary income rates.

Currently Taxable	Rate	Tax-Deferred	Rate	Tax-Free	Rate
Savings accounts (passbook, CDs, etc.)	Ordinary	Stocks and stock mutual funds	Capital gains	Roth IRAs	Zero
Money market accounts	Ordinary	Nonqualified annuities	Ordinary	Interest on municipal bonds and municipal bond funds	Zero
Interest on corporate bonds and corporate bond funds	Ordinary	Life insurance cash values	Ordinary		
Dividends	Capital gains	Qualified plans, traditional IRAs, 403(b) plans, etc.	Ordinary		

Some assets may fall into more than one group. Dividend-paying stock, for example, generates current qualified dividend income but growth is not taxed until the stock is sold (and capital gains rates would apply). The rate at which an asset is taxed is one of the criteria in determining when it will be put to use in an asset liquidation sequence.

Define Portfolio Mix

As this cataloging of assets takes place, a picture of the client's asset mix should become apparent, and the advisor can help analyze how the portfolio is allocated. At the most basic level, this analysis should identify cash holdings, equity holdings, and bond or fixed-income holdings, as illustrated earlier. This exercise spotlights important issues and will raise a number of questions.

■ Is the mix in line with the client's income needs and anticipated withdrawal rates?

■ Should some assets be reallocated to support what is now a goal of income and preservation as well as growth?

■ Should mutual fund assets be repositioned or reallocated to minimize the number of trades (and taxable transactions) that normally take place during the course of a year?

■ Can high turnover funds or investments be redistributed to traditional or Roth IRA accounts?

■ Should tax-free bonds be purchased to support the risk-free portion of the portfolio?

An appropriate liquidation strategy will be based on—and highly dependent on—a number of objectives that a portfolio should strive to encompass: liquidity, safety, diversity, stability, and flexibility. Depending on the client's needs for any specific income period, these factors and the goals they support within the client's portfolio will also determine how, when, and which funds will be liquidated. Now is the time to help the client position his portfolio to support the goals that have been established for retirement.

STEP 4: CREATE A STRUCTURE FOR INCOME FLOW

Key Point   Low-risk liquid investments are used for cash needs now and in the immediate future; riskier higher return investments are earmarked for needs that are farther in the future.

Once you have classified the client's assets and adjusted the portfolio mix to match the retirement income need, you are ready to address the question, "In what order should the assets be used?"

To create a foundation for the flow and use of retirement income, many planners advocate the "bucket" approach. This requires segmenting the retirement portfolio and taking withdrawals from the various segments, depending on market conditions and financial results. As experts point out, one of the limits to the Trinity University study is that it uses average portfolio returns and assumes that annual withdrawals are made equally from all holdings. The bucket approach is more realistic.

The retirement portfolio is divided into three investment segments, each of which supports the income needs of a specific time frame or market condition. Rather than taking withdrawals from the portfolio as a whole, withdrawals are taken from individual segments or buckets.

The first bucket is earmarked for living expenses and consists of enough cash in savings, money market, and checking accounts to cover day-to-day expenses for about one or two years. Clients who have extremely low-risk tolerance levels may want to keep up to three or four years' expenses in extremely liquid reserves.

The second and third buckets are the longer-term investment support vehicles that will take turns funding the cash bucket as it is depleted. They are comprised of equity investments and less risky investments, such as short-term bonds and fixed annuities. Depending on the condition of the market in any given year, withdrawals are taken from the appropriate bucket. During years when the market is performing well, withdrawals are taken from the sales of stocks and stock funds. During poor performing years, withdrawals are funded by bonds and fixed-income assets. This prevents having to sell equity investments during market downturns.

Using a balanced portfolio model as a guideline, the fixed investment portion of the portfolio should support eight to nine years of living expenses. If a client planned to draw down 5% of his assets each year to fund his retirement, his portfolio might be constructed as follows:

- Cash: 5% (representing one year of income needs)

- Fixed investments: 40%–45% (representing eight to nine years of income needs)

- Equity investments: 50%–55% (positioned for continued growth)

Investment Options

It is beyond the scope of this course to detail how each portion of the portfolio should be constructed, but we can say that the equity portion should be designed to support the highest possible return per unit of risk. This will require diversification among large, intermediate, and small cap stocks as well as international stocks.

For the fixed investment portion of the portfolio, a laddered approach may be appropriate. This requires the use of a series of secure, high-quality corporate bonds or Treasury bills with staggered maturities. For example, this might consist of 2-, 4-, and 6-year treasury notes. When the 2-year note matures, those funds are directed into the cash account, the 4-year note replaces the 2-year note, and the 6-year note replaces the 4-year note. This strategy creates a continual flow of income; Treasury notes and bonds can be purchased for almost any maturity.

Another option for the fixed portion of the portfolio is an immediate annuity, term certain or life.

STEP 5: DETERMINE ASSET LIQUIDATION SEQUENCE

Key Point Retirees should generally hold on to tax-favored assets as long as possible, but there are exceptions due to the required minimum distribution rules that apply to IRAs and retirement plans.

As to the sequence in which assets should be used and withdrawn from their individual buckets, there are many schools of thought, almost all of which are driven by tax considerations. Still, there is little consensus. Outlined in the following is a traditional liquidation sequence that has been recommended and used by many practitioners. However, like so many aspects of the retirement planning process, the determination of an asset liquidation sequence must be based on each client's unique needs and situation. One size does not fit all. Chances are, some kind of blended strategy that is flexible to adapt to changing circumstances will be the best plan.

Taxable Assets First

Generally, traditional thinking is that retirees should tap their taxable assets first, preserving their tax-deferred and tax-free money for as long as possible, thus enabling these funds to accumulate even more. This may be critical if the retiring client is younger than 59½. Withdrawing funds from qualified plans and IRAs before this point will likely incur a 10% penalty charge in addition to income tax. (An important exception is noted in the following.) Obviously, one objective of retirement income planning is to avoid any penalty.

Another reason to look first to one's taxable assets is that while most qualified plan funds are taxed at ordinary income rates, capital gains treatment may be available to certain nonqualified investments. The gain on the sale of stock, for example, is taxable as capital gain. The savings derived from being taxed at the capital gains rate compared to the generally higher ordinary income rate can be significant. For the retired client, these savings represent income that can be consumed or funds that can be invested.

Based on this traditional approach of drawing initially from taxable assets, here are some ideas.

■ Look first to use liquid and near-cash assets—money markets and CDs. The interest they generate is taxable anyway. As funds are withdrawn, these accounts can be replenished periodically with the proceeds from the sale of stocks. Keep in mind that most retirees should maintain some portion of their assets in low-risk, highly liquid accounts. As noted earlier, this portion should equate to about one to three years' worth of expenses.

■ Many planners recommend that much of the cash or bond portion of a retiree's portfolio be invested in a series of secure, short-term investments with staggered maturities. For example, a retiree who wants a fairly liquid account that covers four years of expenses could use a money market account to cover one year, with the balance covered by 1-, 2-, and 3-year Treasury notes. Day-to-day expenses are funded by the money market account. When the 1-year bill matures, those funds are directed into the money market account, the 2-year bill replaces the 1-year bill, and the 3-year bill replaces the 2-year bill.

■ From the cash portion of the client's portfolio, we turn to his stock investments. Clients have some control over when stock gains (and losses) are taken and recognized for income tax purposes. Gains on (nonqualified) stock investments held longer than one year will be taxed at the capital gains rate rather than at the ordinary income rate. During years when clients' returns are particularly good, this portion of their portfolios should be the source of income. This preserves the client's cash and near-cash, for when the market is depressed and the sale of stock would result in little gain or loss.

■ When stock is sold for a gain, clients could consider offsetting the tax on gain by selling some of their portfolio losers for a tax-deductible loss. The fact that the sale of a stock creates a tax loss does not negate the fact that the transaction generates cash. In fact, if the tax loss can be used to reduce taxable gains, the combined gain and loss transactions become nontaxed.

■ If the client receives a windfall from the sale of stock and the proceeds are more than necessary to cover expenses or replenish liquid accounts, the excess can be invested in tax-favored municipal bonds or T-bills.

Special IRA Considerations

Avoiding the use of qualified accounts to fund the early years of retirement may not be the appropriate approach if the client has a lot of money in an IRA or qualified account or is likely to accumulate a great deal in such an account before the age of 72. The reason is due to the minimum distribution requirement.

The more money an IRA or qualified account houses, the larger the required distribution is when the client reaches age 72. And the larger the required distribution is, the greater the tax liability is. Minimum withdrawal requirements could actually force some clients to receive more money (including principal) than they need. Thus, it may be more appropriate for the client who has substantial assets in an IRA or qualified plan to tap this money first, in order to draw down the account balance, lessen the amount that will have to be withdrawn after age 72, and therefore minimize the tax hit that would otherwise be payable.

Drawing down IRA assets can begin before age 59½ without the 10% penalty, if the withdrawal is taken as substantially equal periodic payments (annuitized or amortized) over life. If this strategy is employed, make sure the client understands that the payments must be taken (and taxed) for at least five years or until he turns 59½, whichever is later. Any change to a substantially equal periodic payment plan before this time could lead to severe, retroactive penalties.

Estate Planning Considerations

Drawing down IRA assets first may also make sense from an estate planning perspective. IRA assets are included in the owner's estate at death for estate tax purposes, and an IRA beneficiary must pay income tax on his withdrawals from the account after it is inherited. By contrast, shares of stock receive a stepped up basis when they pass from a decedent to his beneficiary. This means that a beneficiary's basis in the stock is its value when it was received from the decedent. If the beneficiary subsequently sells the stock, the tax is limited to the gain that was derived while owned by the beneficiary.

EXAMPLE

Julie is the sole beneficiary of her late father's $500,000 IRA. Claude is the sole beneficiary of his mother's estate, which includes $500,000 worth of stock. Julie can cash out the IRA, or she can leave the funds in her father's IRA and draw required distributions annually over her lifetime. In either event, taxes will be due on the amount distributed. If Claude sells his stock for $500,000 after inheriting it, no taxes will be owed because the tax basis in the stock is adjusted at his mother's death.

Qualified Assets Next

After taxable accounts, the next items in a traditional asset liquidation sequence are traditional IRAs, qualified plans, and deferred annuities. By holding off utilizing these accounts, they have been able to accumulate more, due to the powerful combination of tax deferral and compounding. As mentioned earlier, clients who have funds remaining in a qualified employer plan should consider rolling over to an IRA so that they have control over how and when to take withdrawals.

Distributions from traditional IRAs cannot be delayed beyond age 72. Distributions from qualified employer plans must begin the later of age 72 or when the client retires.

Conflicting Considerations

For some clients, taking qualified assets after nonqualified assets may not be the best approach. Following are issues you should discuss with your clients.

■ Funds withdrawn from IRA accounts are fully taxed at ordinary rates. By reserving IRA accounts for later liquidation, the client may be building assets that will be heavily taxed. What will the client's income tax bracket be 7 or 10 years into retirement compared to what it is at retirement?

■ At the same time, the required minimum distribution rules now in place force less money out of qualified accounts than in the past. Consequently, having to draw down IRA assets before age 72 due to fear of being forced into a higher tax bracket may not be as big of a concern now as it was only a few years ago. Likewise, because IRA beneficiaries can now stretch required distributions—and the consequent taxes— over their lives (after the owner's death), the burden of inheriting a large IRA account is significantly eased.

■ Withdrawals from IRA accounts allow other funds invested in stocks to continue growing. If stock is left intact for later liquidation (as long as it is not traded heavily), the client effectively enjoys continued tax deferral. When payable, the tax on liquidated stock is at capital gains rates. Here the advisor can help clients leverage capital gains versus ordinary income situations.

Other Qualified Plan Issues

Strategies for asset distribution from qualified plans must address many issues. Probably the most important is avoiding penalties, whether for taking qualified distributions before age 59½ or failing to take required distributions after age 72. If clients must take qualified money before age 59½, the best approach to avoid the penalty is to use a substantially equal periodic payment strategy.

For those who want to avoid the ongoing minimum distribution requirement, a rollover or conversion to a Roth IRA may be an option. Although taxes would be due on the taxable portion of the conversion when it is affected, the funds placed in a Roth IRA will grow tax-free and will not be subject to required distributions. The account may be left intact to pass on to heirs or it may be accessed by the owner for any amount. As long as the account is held for five years or longer and as long as the owner is age 59½ or older when money is taken, withdrawals from a Roth are tax free.

Another decision facing many retirees is what to do with the company stock that was held in their company retirement plans. One choice is to roll the stock over into an IRA for continued tax deferral and growth, but doing so will subject the assets to required distribution rules and taxation at ordinary rates. Another option is for the retiree to take out the shares and pay tax on the basis (the amount the company paid to acquire the shares). If and when the retiree subsequently sells the stock, the gain over basis will be taxed at long-term capital gains rates. It is important to note that this strategy could have negative effects for the estate and beneficiary if the stock is not sold. Unlike other stock, these shares do not receive a step-up in value at the retiree's death. The beneficiary inherits the original cost basis (based on what the employer paid) and will have a larger capital gains tax liability if and when he sells the shares.

Tax-Free Assets Last

The last items in an asset liquidation sequence are generally those that generate tax-free returns. These would include Roth IRAs and municipal bonds. Tapping Roth IRAs last will enable these accounts to continue to grow and accumulate during retirement. As noted previously, a Roth IRA must be held for at least five years before distributions can begin if taxes are to be avoided. When accessed, as long as the client is older than age 59½ and the account has been held for five years, the funds are entirely tax-free.

STEP 6: USING ANNUITIES AND LIFE INSURANCE IN A RETIREMENT INCOME PLAN

Key Point   Life insurance and annuities have important roles, both in structuring lifetime income, and in providing liquidity and flexibility for retirees.

Once you have addressed how much, how long, and from where, you are in a better position to recommend specific asset distribution methodologies. More than likely, a combination of methods will be used because no single method can fully support a comprehensive retirement income plan. We have already discussed a number of these methodologies. Here, we will take a look at how annuities and life insurance can be used in a retirement income plan. Both are specifically designed to address financial needs late in life.

Annuitization

Using a strategy of annuitizing assets calls for the client to allocate some portion of his accumulated assets to purchase an immediate annuity. The annuity is structured to pay a benefit for the client's lifetime or for the joint lifetimes of the client and a designated beneficiary. Depending upon the client's risk tolerance, the immediate annuity may be a fixed annuity or a variable annuity.

Advantages of Annuitization
The principal advantage to annuitization is its guarantee of an income that will last for the client's entire lifetime.
Additionally, the favorable income tax treatment afforded by the annuity rules returns the cost basis ratably to the payee, tax-free, over his life expectancy, thereby resulting in a somewhat reduced income tax liability.

Disadvantages of Annuitization
The principal disadvantage clients find in annuitization is the resulting lack of liquidity. Specifically, the funds allocated to the immediate annuity are generally unavailable to the annuitant except as periodic payments once annuity payments begin. However, some newer immediate annuities permit the annuitant to commute the contract—that is, trade future periodic payments for their present value, in effect trading not-yet-received annuity payments for a discounted lump sum.
If a fixed immediate annuity is selected, the fixed-level periodic payments will tend to lose buying power over time due to inflation.
If a variable immediate annuity is selected, it will tend to keep pace with inflation in times of generally increasing markets, but the periodic payment may reduce in periods of declining markets.

Systematic Annuity Withdrawals

Implementing a strategy of systematic annuity withdrawals calls for the client to allocate accumulated assets to a deferred annuity. Once the deferred annuity has been funded, withdrawals are taken as needed to provide the client's retirement income. The annuity may be a fixed annuity or a variable annuity.

Advantages of Systematic Withdrawals
One of the important advantages relates to the tax treatment of the funds not withdrawn. Under this strategy, only the funds withdrawn by the client each year are taxable. All other funds in the annuity continue to enjoy income tax deferral.
With age, many people become more conservative in their investment philosophy. That increased conservatism is often evidenced by a change of asset allocation from equity to debt investments, requiring the sale of stocks and the purchase of bonds. If the change in the allocation of assets is done outside of an annuity or life insurance contract, it will result in the recognition of income to the extent of any gain on the stock sale and may incur sales commission costs. If the asset allocation change is done inside the deferred annuity (assuming, of course, that the client owns a variable annuity), there is no income tax liability and no sales commissions to be paid.
Allocating funds to a deferred annuity may also help avoid taxation. Funds that otherwise would have been allocated to the cash portion of the client's portfolio can be invested in a deferred annuity. The client's income tax liability will be reduced accordingly.
Another advantage of implementing a systematic annuity withdrawal strategy rather than annuitization is the continuing liquidity of the funds. Subject to any surrender charges, the client may withdraw as much of the funds remaining in the contract as he chooses.

Disadvantages of Systematic Withdrawals
One of the important benefits of purchasing an immediate annuity is the guarantee of an income that the client cannot outlive. The same guarantee does not apply to an annuity withdrawal strategy. Because the funds in the deferred annuity under this strategy are not annuitized but are, instead, simply withdrawn, the client may outlive his funds.
Another disadvantage is the tax treatment of the funds withdrawn. Withdrawals from an annuity receive LIFO (last-in, first-out) tax treatment, meaning that the earnings on the cash value are deemed to be withdrawn first. As a result, annuity withdrawals are taxable as ordinary income (rather than capital gains) to the extent that any gain remains under the contract.
In addition to the LIFO ordinary income tax treatment of withdrawals, they may also be subject to contract surrender charges. Although many deferred annuities permit annual withdrawals without surrender charge up to some percentage are (typically 10%) of the cash value, a withdrawal in excess of the surrender charge-free amount may result in the imposition of substantial charges, especially in the early years of the contract.
A word of caution about deferred annuities and older clients: deferred annuities can be ideal retirement funding vehicles and ideal retirement income distribution vehicles, but they may not be appropriate as late-life investment purchases. The fact is, almost all deferred annuities carry surrender charges that can extend seven or eight years into the contract. Unless the client has a sufficiently long investment horizon, the purchase of a deferred annuity during retirement may not be suitable.

Accessing Life Insurance

Life insurance, principally because of its family-protection function, enjoys a uniquely favorable tax treatment. Withdrawals and surrenders from life insurance policies are afforded first-in, first-out (FIFO) tax treatment under which all premiums are deemed to be withdrawn before any gain is withdrawn. This means that no tax is imposed upon cash value withdrawals unless and until withdrawals exceed premiums paid. In addition, policy loans are not considered withdrawals and are generally received tax-free, and death benefits are received income tax free. (Different and less favorable tax treatment applies if the policy is a modified endowment contract.)

These three advantages—FIFO withdrawal treatment, tax-free loans, and income tax-free death benefits—may enable policyowners (notably universal life owners) to access cash values far in excess of basis without incurring any income tax. Under this distribution strategy, a policyowner at retirement will cease life insurance premium payments. He will then take withdrawals, either in a lump sum or periodically, from the policy's cash value until the total amount of the withdrawals is equal to the policy's cost basis, which is usually the total premium paid. Because of the FIFO treatment, these withdrawals are received tax free.

When withdrawals have been taken to basis, cash value continues to be accessed through policy loans. Unless the life insurance policy is subsequently surrendered, the loans are also received tax free. When the life insurance policy matures as a death benefit, remaining death benefits (which may have been reduced substantially due to the withdrawals and loans) are generally received income tax-free by the beneficiary.

Advantage of Drawing Funds From Life Insurance
The principal advantage of this strategy is the potentially complete absence of income taxation of the funds received through withdrawals and policy loans.

Disadvantages of Drawing Funds From Life Insurance
The most significant disadvantage of this withdrawal/policy loan strategy is the substantial erosion of the death benefit. Unless the client's need for life insurance has greatly diminished or can be met with the reduced death benefit, this strategy may not be appropriate.
Another disadvantage of this strategy is the absolute need to keep the life insurance policy in force to avoid the recognition of taxable income equal to the policy loan amount (which had previously been received tax free). Because the policy loan amount could be substantial, surrender of the policy could result in a large income tax liability without any remaining surrender proceeds to pay the taxes due.
Implementing this policy withdrawal/loan strategy also results in an additional cost that tends to offset some of the client gains resulting from tax free access. Because the tax treatment afforded life insurance requires that there be a death benefit, there are costs to support that death benefit. As the client ages, those costs may be quite significant.

Combining Annuitization and Withdrawal

Sometimes the most appropriate strategy calls for combining two or more techniques. A combination strategy that has several advantages uses a fixed annuity, a variable annuity, and a mutual fund. Employing an asset-harvesting strategy of annuitization and asset withdrawal requires that assets be divided into separate pools. In this case, these funds are allocated to an immediate fixed annuity, an immediate variable annuity, and a mutual fund that mirrors a broad-based financial index, such as the S&P 500. The immediate annuities provide an income for the client's lifetime, and withdrawals are made from the mutual fund and are equal to the IRS minimum required distributions. This latter amount, by approximating required minimum distributions, enables the mutual fund to last for the duration of the client's life expectancy. Of course, nonqualified annuities are not subject to required distribution rules and any amount can be taken under a withdrawal plan.

Advantages of the Combination Strategy
Combining these three products results in tax advantages, some income guarantees, and a certain amount of liquidity. The life income received from the annuities is partially tax-free, ordinary income until the client's cost basis has been recovered. The redemption of mutual fund shares is also received partly as a return of basis and partly as a capital gain or loss and thereby provides some additional tax benefit.
Both of the immediate life annuities guarantee an income that the client cannot outlive. The income from the immediate variable annuity, however, may increase or decrease. In addition, liquidity is maintained in the mutual fund to the extent that all of the funds have not been withdrawn.

Disadvantages of the Combination Strategy
Under this strategy, the client can avoid many of the disadvantages of noncombination strategies. However, the client may outlive a part of his income. Specifically, the assets in the mutual fund could be exhausted.
The annuity income that the client receives in excess of basis is taxed at less favorable ordinary income rates rather than capital gains rates.

STEP 7: MONITOR THE FLOW OF FUNDS

Key Point   Review the client's situation yearly and make changes that reflect changing needs and circumstances.

If there is a time to remain close to clients and their financial situations, it is during their retirement years. Not only is there a need to periodically liquidate retirement assets and move funds into the liquid account, but both practitioner and clients need to periodically re-evaluate the chosen strategy. No strategy is perfect for every client in every circumstance. As time goes on, the strategy must be assessed in light of the client's changed needs and the fluctuating value of the assets resulting from market movements.

The client's spouse may have died or been moved to a nursing home. As a result, the client's need for funds may have either diminished or increased. Furthermore, a long-lasting bear market may have reduced the client's assets to levels that could be considered dangerously low at the current withdrawal rate and require a temporary or permanent income reduction. As we noted early in this course, change is one of the few things that is certain, and the advisor needs to ensure that his recommendations continue to accommodate those changes. At the very least, plan for a review with your client once a year.

WRAP-UP

Much of this course considers ideas for stretching retirement savings dollars. Whether your clients make use of the tax-deferral power of qualified retirement plans, or purchase whole life insurance to protect their families against an untimely death and build a cash reserve for retirement, the whole idea is economy—structuring an individual's savings to maximize the resources that will be available for living during retirement.

This unit took the mix of assets to be determined during preretirement years. Once the retirement years are reached, it is no longer material what measures were taken or not taken before retirement. At that moment, new strategies come into play. At that moment, it is a new game—planning the order for liquidating assets so that nothing is squandered.

UNIT TEST

1. Which of these is considered to be an advantage of annuitization?

    A. It guarantees income that will last for the client's lifetime.
    B. Once annuitized, the client's draw from the annuity is limited to the annuity payment.
    C. A fixed, level periodic payment tends to lose buying power over time due to inflation.
    D. Payments under a variable annuity could be reduced if there is a declining market.

2. Which of these is NOT a phase of retirement planning?

    A. Estate disposition
    B. Tax minimization
    C. Accumulation
    D. Distribution

3. Which of these asset types are considered tax deferred?

    A. Money market accounts
    B. Municipal bond interest
    C. Stock gains
    D. Corporate bond interest

4. Non-annuity withdrawals from an annuity are taxed on _____ basis.

    A. a FIFO
    B. an exclusion ratio
    C. a tax-free
    D. a LIFO

5. Which of these is NOT an advantage of using life insurance withdrawals as a source of retirement income?

    A. FIFO withdrawals
    B. Loans are tax free
    C. The need to prevent a policy lapse
    D. Tax-free death benefit

ANSWERS AND RATIONALES

1. **A.** Annuities offer a guarantee of income that will last for a client's lifetime. The other statements, while true, represent disadvantages of annuitization. Annuitization does limit liquidity and flexibility.

2. **B.** Tax minimization is not a specific phase of retirement planning. It is part of all phases of retirement planning from accumulation to distribution to estate disposition.

3. **C.** Appreciation in the value of a stock is not subject to tax until the stock is sold. This constitutes tax deferral.

4. **D.** Non-annuity withdrawals from an annuity are taxed under the unfavorable LIFO basis. That is, withdrawals are treated first as taxable earnings and later as tax-free returns of capital.

5. **C.** If the policy lapses, policy loans will be retroactively taxed as withdrawals.

Review Test

Important Information Regarding This Review Test

This exam was designed for review purposes and may be used to fulfill your training and firm element requirements. This exam has not been approved for insurance continuing education and cannot be used for this purpose. If you need insurance continuing education credit for this course, a different exam is required.

Contact Kaplan Financial Education at 1-800-423-4723.

1. Which of the following statements regarding senior consumers is FALSE?

    A. They tend to want to reduce the number of investments they hold.
    B. They lean toward conservative investments.
    C. Their primary investment objective is accumulation.
    D. They are drawn to more liquid investments.

2. A client is setting up a trust and wants to make sure she is able to change the terms of the trust should the situation change. Which of the following types of trusts would provide this option to the client?

    A. Revocable trust
    B. Testamentary trust
    C. Rabbi trust
    D. Irrevocable trust

3. An individual is filing to begin receiving Social Security benefits and has decided to enroll in Medicare Part B. The individual is told that part of the premium will have to be paid to enroll in the program. The individual will be responsible for approximately what percentage of the premium?

    A. 25%
    B. 50%
    C. 75%
    D. 100%

4. A premature distribution from an IRA would be exempt from the premature distribution penalty under all of the following circumstances EXCEPT

    A. to pay for qualifying medical expenses
    B. upon the death of the IRA owner
    C. to correct an excessive contribution to the IRA
    D. as a result of hardship

5. The administration of an estate is governed by state statutes and probate courts. There are many steps involved in the process. The first step in the process is

    A. to appoint the personal representative
    B. to give notice to creditors
    C. inventory and appraisal
    D. interim administration

6. Ted and Ariel, both age 25, are looking to purchase life insurance. They are concerned about having the maximum available coverage but do not have a lot of money at the current time to pay in premiums. Which of the following types of life insurance policies would be most suitable for them to purchase at this time?

    A. Variable life insurance
    B. Term insurance
    C. Whole life insurance
    D. Universal variable life insurance

7. An individual who wants to maintain a level standard of living after retirement should expect to cover what percentage of retirement income with personal savings and investments?

    A. 15%
    B. 35%
    C. 45%
    D. 75%

8. With respect to qualified long-term care insurance plans, which of the following statements is FALSE?

    A. Most long-term care policies pay on a reimbursement basis.
    B. All plans must require prior hospitalization before benefits begin.
    C. Premiums are tax deductible under IRC Section 213.
    D. The coverage provided is in excess of Medicare and Medicare supplement plans.

9. Jill celebrated her 72nd birthday in March of this year. By what date must she take her first distribution from her traditional IRA?

    A. April 1 of this year
    B. December 31 of this year
    C. April 1 of next year
    D. December 31 of next year

10. Which of the following statements regarding retiring under Social Security is FALSE?

    A. Benefits do not begin automatically; they must be applied for.
    B. Social Security retirement benefits are subject to income taxation.
    C. An individual needs to have worked and contributed to the Social Security system for approximately 10 years to qualify for retirement benefits.
    D. In order to collect full Social Security retirement benefits, an individual must cease working.

11. A customer is thinking about purchasing a corporate bond, and her investment objective is current income. The customer is concerned about taking a high degree of risk and had heard that some bonds issued by corporations are backed by collateral. Which of the following corporate bonds would be backed by collateral?

    A. Income bond
    B. Mortgage bond
    C. Subordinated debenture
    D. Debenture

12. Ten years ago, Merle invested $25,000 in a single-premium fixed deferred annuity. Today, the value of the annuity account is $40,000. If this year, at age 52, Merle withdraws $10,000, how will that withdrawal be taxed?

    A. The $10,000 will be fully subject to ordinary income tax and a premature distribution penalty of 10%.
    B. The $10,000 will be penalized by a 10% premature distribution penalty but will not be subject to income tax.
    C. A portion of the $10,000 will be subject to ordinary income tax, and the same portion will be subject to a premature distribution penalty of 10%.
    D. The $10,000 will be received tax and penalty free.

13. Joe, age 72, must take $5,000 as a required distribution from his IRA this year. What is the penalty if he takes a $7,000 distribution instead?

    A. $0
    B. $200
    C. $500
    D. $1,000

14. All of the following are covered by Medicare Part A EXCEPT

    A. hospitalization
    B. skilled nursing care facility
    C. surgeon's fees
    D. hospice care

15. All of the following would bypass the probate process at an individual's death EXCEPT

    A. proceeds paid to a named beneficiary under a life insurance policy
    B. payment of trust assets to a named beneficiary under a trust arrangement
    C. property passing to a survivor under a joint tenancy
    D. property passing to named heirs under the terms of a decedent's will

16. Which of the following types of retirement plans does NOT require mandatory distributions?

    A. Roth IRA
    B. Traditional IRA
    C. 401(k)
    D. SIMPLE plan

17. All of the following statements regarding Medicare are true EXCEPT

    A. application for Medicare Part A is automatic when one applies for Social Security retirement benefits
    B. application for Medicare Part A can be made at age 65 even if one plans to delay Social Security retirement benefits
    C. enrollment in Medicare Part B is optional
    D. Medicare Part D covers hospital expenses

18. A highly compensated employee is looking to defer receipt of some salary until retirement. An advantage of this is that the employee will
   A. be taxed on the benefits when the benefits become nonforfeitable
   B. be taxed on the benefits at death
   C. be taxed on the benefits when the benefits are paid out
   D. never be taxed on the benefits, as the benefits are not subject to taxation

19. An employer is looking to set up a retirement plan for employees that will tell them the exact amount of money that they will be receiving each month when they retire. What type of retirement plan is the employer looking to establish?
   A. 401(k)
   B. Defined benefit
   C. Defined contribution
   D. SIMPLE

20. A customer wants to start an investment portfolio and is looking for an investment that will provide diversification. Which of the following investment products would an investment representative recommend to the client?
   A. Individual stocks
   B. Mutual funds
   C. Individual corporate bonds
   D. Commodities

21. Which of the following defines the renewability provision for long-term care policies?
   A. The insurer must renew the policy each year for the first five years but may require evidence of insurability after that.
   B. The insurer may renew the policy at its discretion but may not raise premiums.
   C. The insurer must renew the policy each year but may raise premiums after the first claim.
   D. The insurer must renew the policy each year but may raise premiums for entire classes of insureds.

22. Which of the following types of retirement plans can include a provision for the distribution of funds due to hardship?
   A. Traditional IRAs
   B. Roth IRAs
   C. 401(k)s
   D. TSAs

23. A small business is looking to establish a retirement plan for its employees. They have found that there is a type of retirement plan the business can establish that is suited for companies with 100 or fewer employees. What type of retirement plan have they found?
   A. 403(b)
   B. SIMPLE
   C. Profit sharing
   D. 401(k)

24. Under which plan can an employer pick and choose which employees will participate?
   A. Simplified employee pension plan
   B. Deferred compensation plan
   C. SIMPLE 401(k) plan
   D. Profit-sharing plan

25. Which of the following would be considered a fundamental and necessary tool for planning any and all dispositions?
   A. Will
   B. Testamentary trust
   C. Marital deduction
   D. Charitable gifting program

ANSWERS TO REVIEW TEST

1.	**C.**	14.	**C.**
2.	**A.**	15.	**D.**
3.	**A.**	16.	**A.**
4.	**D.**	17.	**D.**
5.	**A.**	18.	**C.**
6.	**B.**	19.	**B.**
7.	**C.**	20.	**B.**
8.	**B.**	21.	**D.**
9.	**C.**	22.	**C.**
10.	**D.**	23.	**B.**
11.	**B.**	24.	**B.**
12.	**A.**	25.	**A.**
13.	**A.**		

Appendix

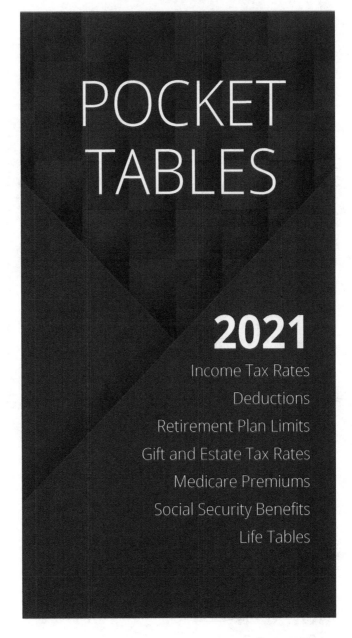

POCKET
TABLES

2021
Income Tax Rates
Deductions
Retirement Plan Limits
Gift and Estate Tax Rates
Medicare Premiums
Social Security Benefits
Life Tables

2021 Pocket Tables

These 2021 Pocket Tables include both the 2021 numbers and the corresponding numbers for 2020.

During 2020 the Coronavirus Aid, Relief, and Economic Security Act (CARES Act) was enacted to provide financial relief during the global pandemic. The CARES Act included a number of temporary changes. The CARES Act short-term changes are not included in these 2021 Pocket Tables.

CONTENTS

POCKET TABLES 2021 ©2021 by Kaplan, Inc. All rights reserved. No part of this publication may be reproduced without written consent from the publisher. The information in Pocket Tables is summary in nature and is current only as of January 1, 2021. Users of this publication are advised to refer to the relevant legislation or other applicable materials to ensure accuracy and comprehensive coverage of the applicable material. Further, changes to legislation or applicable administrative actions that become effective after that date may make the information provided in this publication no longer current. For information, contact:

332 Front St. S., Suite 501 I La Crosse, WI 54601
1-800-824-8742

ISBN: 978-1-07-881031-9

2021 Federal
Individual Income Tax Rates

Single Individuals

| Taxable Income | | | % on | Of the |
Over	But Not Over	Tax	+ Excess	Amount Over
$0	$9,950	$0.00	10%	$0
9,950	40,525	995	12%	9,950
40,525	86,375	4,664	22%	40,525
86,375	164,925	14,751	24%	86,375
164,925	209,425	33,603	32%	164,925
209,425	523,600	47,843	35%	209,425
523,600	. . . . .	157,804.25	37%	523,600

Joint Returns and Surviving Spouses

| Taxable Income | | | % on | Of the |
Over	But Not Over	Tax	+ Excess	Amount Over
$0	$19,900	$0.00	10%	$0
19,900	81,050	1,990	12%	19,900
81,050	172,750	9,328	22%	81,050
172,750	329,850	29,502	24%	172,750
329,850	418,850	67,206	32%	329,850
418,850	628,300	95,686	35%	418,850
628,300	. . . . .	168,993.50	37%	628,300

Heads of Households

| Taxable Income | | | % on | Of the |
Over	But Not Over	Tax	+ Excess	Amount Over
$0	$14,200	$0.00	10%	$0
14,200	54,200	1,420	12%	14,200
54,200	86,350	6,220	22%	54,200
86,350	164,900	13,293	24%	86,350
164,900	209,400	32,145	32%	164,900
209,400	523,600	46,385	35%	209,400
523,600	. . . . .	156,355	37%	523,600

Married Filing Separate Returns

| Taxable Income | | | % on | Of the |
Over	But Not Over	Tax	+ Excess	Amount Over
$0	$9,950	$0.00	10%	$0
9,950	40,525	995	12%	9,950
40,525	86,375	4,664	22%	40,525
86,375	164,925	14,751	24%	86,375
164,925	209,425	33,603	32%	164,925
209,425	314,150	47,843	35%	209,425
314,150	. . . . .	84,496.75	37%	314,150

Estates and Trusts

| Taxable Income | | | % on | Of the |
Over	But Not Over	Tax	+ Excess	Amount Over
$0	$2,650	$0.00	10%	$0
2,650	9,550	265	24%	2,650
9,550	13,050	1,921	35%	9,550
13,050	. . . . .	3,146	37%	13,050

1

2020 Federal
Individual Income Tax Rates
Single Individuals

Taxable Income		Tax	+	% on Excess	Of the Amount Over
Over	But Not Over				
$0	$9,875	$0.00		10%	$0
9,875	40,125	987.50		12%	9,875
40,125	85,525	4,617.50		22%	40,125
85,525	163,300	14,605.50		24%	85,525
163,300	207,350	33,271.50		32%	163,300
207,350	518,400	47,367.50		35%	207,350
518,400	.....	156,235.00		37%	518,400

Joint Returns and Surviving Spouses

Taxable Income		Tax	+	% on Excess	Of the Amount Over
Over	But Not Over				
$0	$19,750	$0.00		10%	$0
19,750	80,250	1,975.00		12%	19,750
80,250	171,050	9,234.00		22%	80,250
171,050	326,600	29,211.00		24%	171,050
326,600	414,700	66,543.00		32%	326,600
414,700	622,050	94,735.00		35%	414,700
622,050	.....	167,307.50		37%	622,050

Heads of Households

Taxable Income		Tax	+	% on Excess	Of the Amount Over
Over	But Not Over				
$0	$14,100	$0.00		10%	$0
14,100	53,700	1,410.00		12%	14,100
53,700	85,500	6,162.00		22%	53,700
85,500	163,300	13,158.00		24%	85,500
163,300	207,350	31,830.00		32%	163,300
207,350	518,400	45,926.00		35%	207,350
518,400	.....	154,793.50		37%	518,400

Married Filing Separate Returns

Taxable Income		Tax	+	% on Excess	Of the Amount Over
Over	But Not Over				
$0	$9,875	$0.00		10%	$0
9,875	40,125	987.50		12%	9,875
40,125	85,525	4,617.50		22%	40,125
85,525	163,300	14,605.50		24%	85,525
163,300	207,350	33,271.50		32%	163,300
207,350	311,025	47,367.50		35%	207,350
311,025	.....	83,653.75		37%	311,025

Estates and Trusts

Taxable Income		Tax	+	% on Excess	Of the Amount Over
Over	But Not Over				
$0	$2,600	$0		10%	$0
2,600	9,450	260		24%	2,600
9,450	12,950	1,904		35%	9,450
12,950	.....	3,129		37%	12,950

2

Standard Deductions

	2021	2020
Standard deduction for single individuals	$12,550	$12,400
Standard deduction for joint returns or surviving spouses	25,100	24,800
Standard deduction for heads of households	18,800	18,650
Standard deduction for married individuals filing separate returns	12,550	12,400
Additional standard deduction for married taxpayers age 65 or older or blind*	1,350	1,300
Additional standard deduction for single taxpayers age 65 or older or blind*	1,700	1,650
Maximum standard deduction for individual claimed as a dependent on another taxpayer's return (not to exceed amounts listed above)	1,100 (or 350 plus earned income if greater)	1,100 (or 350 plus earned income if greater)
Personal and dependency exemptions	0	0
Phaseout of itemized deductions and personal exemptions begins at . . .	Suspended for tax years through 2025	Suspended for tax years through 2025

J=joint; H=head of household; S=single; MS=married filing separately
* Taxpayers who are both age 65 or older and blind may claim twice the amount indicated as their additional standard deduction.

Federal Alternative Minimum Tax

Individuals: An alternative minimum tax (AMT) is imposed on items of income that would otherwise receive advantageous tax treatment. Taxpayers must pay the greater of (1) the AMT or (2) the regular income tax. Income subject to the AMT is the sum of AGI, modified to take into account adjustments and preference items, minus AMT itemized deductions and minus an exemption amount based on filing status.

	2021	2020
Income threshold for 28% rate (AMT is 26% up to this amount)	$199,900 (J, S, H, ET) $99,950 (MS)	$197,900 (J, S, H, ET) $98,950 (MS)
Exemption amounts	$114,600 (J) $73,600 (S, H) $57,300 (MS) $25,700 (ET)	$113,400 (J) $72,900 (S, H) $56,700 (MS) $25,400 (ET)
Phaseout of AMT exemption amount begins at . . .	$1,047,200 (J) $523,600 (S, H, MS) $85,650 (ET)	$1,036,800 (J) $518,400 (S, H, MS) $84,800 (ET)
Kiddie tax exemption amount (child's earned income plus)*	$7,950	$7,900

J=joint; S=single; H=head of household; MS=married filing separately; ET=estates and trusts
* The kiddie tax exemption amount shall not exceed the exemption amount for a single taxpayer.

Corporations: The corporate AMT was repealed under the Tax Cuts and Jobs Act.

3

Education Exclusions, Deductions, Credits

The following are education tax benefits available for students and their parents and the phaseout of these tax benefits for upper income taxpayers based on adjusted gross income (AGI) or modified AGI (MAGI).

Tax Benefit	Basic Rule	Phaseout Range 2021	Phaseout Range 2020
Savings bond income exclusion	Excluded if used to pay qualified higher education (Phaseout based on MAGI)	J: $124,800–$154,800 O: $83,200–$98,200	J: $123,550–$153,550 O: $82,350–$97,350
Coverdell Education Savings Accounts	$2,000 maximum annual contribution (Phaseout based on MAGI)	J: $190,000–$220,000* O: $95,000–$110,000*	J: $190,000–$220,000* O: $95,000–$110,000*
Deduction for qualified higher education expenses	Deductible "above the line" up to: $4,000 below phaseout range; $2,000 within phaseout range; and $0 above phaseout range (Phaseout based on AGI)	Expired	Expired
Educational loan interest deduction	Deductible up to $2,500 (Phaseout based on MAGI)	J: $140,000–$170,000 O: $70,000–$85,000	J: $140,000–$170,000 O: $70,000–$85,000
American Opportunity Tax Credit (formerly Hope Scholarship Credit; per student if no credit claimed for student for 2 prior years)	Credit on 100% of first $2,000 plus 25% of next $2,000 (Phaseout based on MAGI)	J: $160,000–$180,000* O: $80,000–$90,000*	J: $160,000–$180,000* O: $80,000–$90,000*
Lifetime Learning Credit (per taxpayer regardless of the number of students)	Credit on 20% of first $10,000 (Phaseout based on MAGI)	J: $119,000–$139,000 O: $59,000–$69,000	J: $118,000–$138,000 O: $59,000–$69,000

J=joint; O=filers other than joint filers; H=head of household; MS=married filing separately; S=single
* This phaseout does not adjust annually for inflation.

Child Tax Credit

Tax Benefit	Reduction Rule	Income Limit
$2,000 credit for each qualifying child; up to $1,400 is refundable	Reduction of credit by $50 for every $1,000 that modified adjusted gross income exceeds income limit	$400,000 (J) $200,000 (S, H, MS)

H=head of household; J=joint; MS=married filing separately; S=single

Kiddie Tax

For 2021, unearned income of a child who is age 18 or younger and certain dependent children ages 18 through 23 is not taxed for the first $1,100, taxed at the dependent's rate for the next $1,100, and taxed at the higher of the parents' top marginal rate or the child's tax rate for unearned income over $2,200.

Adoption Credit

Individuals may take a nonrefundable credit of up to $14,400 in 2021 per child for qualified adoption expenses ($14,300 in 2020). The credit amount is phased out for modified adjusted gross income between $216,660–$256,660 in 2021 ($214,520–$254,520 in 2020).

Federal Tax on Capital Gains and Qualified Dividends

Rates for Individuals

Short-term capital gains have a holding period of 12 months or less. Short-term capital gains are taxed at the ordinary income rate. The following chart applies to qualified dividends with a holding period of 60 days or more and long-term capital gains.

Long-Term Capital Gains Rate	Single Taxpayer	Married Filing Jointly	Head of Household	Married Filing Separately
0%	Up to $40,400	Up to $80,800	Up to $54,100	Up to $40,400
15%	$40,401–$445,850	$80,801–$501,600	$54,101–$473,750	$40,401–$250,800
20%	Over $445,850	Over $501,600	Over $473,750	Over $250,800

Federal Net Investment Income Tax

A 3.8% Net Investment Income tax is imposed on certain unearned investment income. The tax applies to the lesser of a person's net investment income or modified adjusted gross income that exceeds certain threshold amounts ($200,000 for single or head of household; $250,000 for married filing jointly or surviving spouse; and $125,000 for married filing separately). The tax also applies to the lesser of an estate's or trust's undistributed net investment income for the tax year or any excess of its adjusted gross income over the dollar amount at which the highest tax bracket for estates or trusts begins for the tax year ($13,050 for 2021 and $12,950 for 2020). Investment income includes dividends, taxable interest, annuities, rents and royalties, capital gains, and passive income from partnerships and S corporations. It excludes distributions from IRAs and qualified plans, tax-exempt interest, and nontaxable veterans benefits.

Federal Tax on Corporate Income

The Tax Cuts and Jobs Act changed the corporate tax rate to 21% of taxable income. The deduction for a portion of a corporation's income that is attributable to qualified U.S. production activities has been repealed.

Health Savings Accounts

	2021		2020	
	Individual	Family	Individual	Family
Minimum required health plan deductible	$1,400	$2,800	$1,400	$2,800
Maximum allowed health plan deductible	7,000	14,000	6,900	13,800
Maximum allowed out-of-pocket limit	7,000	14,000	6,900	13,800
Contribution limit*	3,600	7,200	3,550	7,100

*Individuals age 55 or older are eligible to make an additional HSA contribution of $1,000.

Business Deductions, Credits, and Fringe Benefits

		2021	2020
Bonus depreciation	Applies to qualifying new MACRS property	100%	100%
Section 179 expense election	First-year expense election up to limit	$1,050,000	$1,040,000
Section 179 expense phaseout	Limit reduced by cost of property placed in service in excess of amount	$2,620,000	$2,590,000
Business mileage rate	Deduction per mile driven for business use	$0.56	$0.575
Charitable mileage rate	Deduction (charitable) per mile driven for charitable purposes	$0.14	$0.14
Moving mileage rate	Deduction per mile driven on a deductible move	$0.16	$0.17
Medical mileage rate	Deduction (medical) per mile driven for medical purposes	$0.16	$0.17
Qualified transportation—transit passes or commuter vehicle	Maximum employee pretax contribution per month	$270	$270
Qualified transportation—parking	Maximum employee pretax contribution per month	$270	$270
Foreign earned income exclusion	Employees may exclude income for services in a foreign country up to indicated amount	$108,700	$107,600
Section 1244 stock loss deduction	Loss on small business stock (1244 stock) as ordinary loss up to limit	$100,000* (joint return) $50,000* (others)	$100,000* (joint return) $50,000* (others)
Rental real estate exception to passive activity loss rules	Up to $25,000 of passive losses attributable to real estate may be taken against non-passive income, phased out above indicated level of AGI	$100,000*	$100,000*

* Not adjusted for inflation.

Benefit, Contribution, and Compensation Limits for Qualified Plans

The Internal Revenue Code (the Code) provides dollar limitations on benefits and contributions under qualified plans. The Code also limits the amount of compensation that can be taken into account when computing benefits and contributions. The 2021 and 2020 limits appear as follows. Limits on employee elective contributions are provided in a separate table.

Type of Limit	2021	2020
Annual benefit for defined benefit plans [I.R.C. §415(b)(1)(A)]	$230,000	$230,000
Annual limit on annual additions* to defined contribution plans [I.R.C. §415(c)(1)(A)]	58,000	57,000
Maximum annual compensation for each employee that can be taken into account for any plan year [I.R.C. §401(a)(17) and §408(k)(3)(C)]	290,000	285,000
Minimum compensation amount for SEP plan participation [I.R.C. §408(k)(2)(C)]	650	600
Compensation level for highly compensated employees (HCEs) other than 5% owners (for nondiscrimination rules) [I.R.C. §414(q)(1)(B)]	130,000	130,000
Compensation level for key employees other than 5% owners (top-heavy rules for vesting and minimum benefits [I.R.C. §416(i)])	185,000 (officers) 150,000 (1% owners)	185,000 (officers) 150,000 (1% owners)

*Annual additions to an employee's account, which are defined as the total of employer contributions, employee contributions, and forfeitures, are limited to the lesser of the dollar amount indicated or 100% of compensation. This limit must be coordinated with a rule applicable to profit-sharing plans, SEPs, and stock bonus plans that limit contributions to 25% of compensation. This lower limitation does not apply to employee elective contributions or forfeitures, so annual additions may exceed 25% of compensation as long as employer contributions meet the 25% limit.

IRA and Employee Contribution Limits

The following are limits for IRA contributions and employee elective contributions to the indicated types of employer-sponsored retirement plans.

Year	IRAs	401(k), 403(b), and 457 Plans*	SIMPLE Plans
2021	$6,000	$19,500	$13,500
2020	6,000	19,500	13,500

*Existing salary reduction SEPs (SARSEPs) are also covered by this limit.

Catch-Up Contribution Limits

Individuals who are age 50 or older may increase their contributions over the regular limits shown in the IRA and Employee Contribution Limits table by the following catch-up amounts.

Year	IRAs	401(k), 403(b), and 457 Plans	SIMPLE Plans
2021	$1,000	$6,500	$3,000
2020	1,000	6,500	3,000

IRA Phaseouts

	2021	**2020**
IRA deduction is phased out (for active participants in an employer plan) for modified adjusted gross incomes between . . .	$66,000–$76,000 (S, H) $105,000–$125,000 (J) $0–$10,000 (M, S)	$65,000–$75,000 (S, H) $104,000–$124,000 (J) $0–$10,000 (MS)
IRA deduction is phased out (spouse is active participant in an employer plan but individual is not) for modified adjusted gross incomes between . . .	$198,000–$208,000	$196,000–$206,000
Roth IRA contribution limit is phased out for modified adjusted gross incomes between . . .	$125,000–$140,000 (S, H) $198,000–$208,000 (J) $0–$10,000 (MS)	$124,000–$139,000 (S, H) $196,000–$206,000 (J) $0–$10,000 (MS)
Conversion from traditional to Roth IRA is allowed if modified AGI does not exceed . . .	No income limit	No income limit

H=head of household; J=joint; MS=married filing separately; S=single

Required Minimum Distributions

In most cases, the required minimum distribution that must be made from most retirement plans and IRA accounts after age 70½, and for those reaching 70½ after 2019, age 72, is determined by dividing the account value at the end of the previous year by the divisor found for the account owner's age on the Uniform Distribution Table. An account owner with a beneficiary-spouse more than 10 years younger may use an IRS joint-life table to find the divisor, which in all cases is larger than the divisor shown here, resulting in smaller required distributions.

Age	Divisor	Age	Divisor
70	27.4	93	9.6
71	26.5	94	9.1
72	25.6	95	8.6
73	24.7	96	8.1
74	23.8	97	7.6
75	22.9	98	7.1
76	22.0	99	6.7
77	21.2	100	6.3
78	20.3	101	5.9
79	19.5	102	5.5
80	18.7	103	5.2
81	17.9	104	4.9
82	17.1	105	4.5
83	16.3	106	4.2
84	15.5	107	3.9
85	14.8	108	3.7
86	14.1	109	3.4
87	13.4	110	3.1
88	12.7	111	2.9
89	12.0	112	2.6
90	11.4	113	2.4
91	10.8	114	2.1
92	10.2	115 and after	1.9

Comparing IRA Options

Question	Traditional IRA	Roth IRA
Are there income limits on the ability to make nondeductible contributions?	No.	Yes. Phaseouts for single filers: $125,000–$140,000 ($124,000–$139,000 for 2020); for joint filers: $198,000–$208,000 ($196,000–$206,000 for 2020); married filing separately: $0–$10,000 (same as 2020).
Is there an annual contribution limit?	Yes, $6,000* per person to all IRAs for 2021.	Yes, $6,000* per person to all IRAs for 2021.
Are contributions deductible?	Yes, for nonparticipants in an employer plan. For others, contributions may be deductible depending on income level (see IRA Phaseouts on page 8).	No. All contributions are nondeductible, after-tax contributions.
How are withdrawals taxed after age 59½?	Withdrawals are subject to tax. Exception: pro rata share of nondeductible contributions.	Withdrawals are tax free if account is held 5 years. Contributions are withdrawn tax free at any time.
How are withdrawals taxed before age 59½?	Withdrawals are subject to tax. A 10% penalty is added except in the case of: • death; • disability; • substantially equal periodic payments; • "first" home purchase (up to $10,000); • qualified higher education expenses; • unreimbursed medical expenses; • health insurance for unemployed; • qualified reservist distributions; • pro rata share of nondeductible contributions; or • birth or adoption of a child (up to $5,000).	Contributions are withdrawn tax free. Withdrawals of earnings from accounts held 5 years are tax free in the case of: • death; • disability; or • "first" home purchase (up to $10,000). Withdrawals of earnings are subject to tax but no penalty in the case of: • substantially equal periodic payments; • qualified higher education expenses; • unreimbursed medical expenses; • health insurance for unemployed; • qualified reservist distributions; or • childbirth or adoption expenses. All other withdrawals of earnings are subject to tax plus 10% penalty.

*May be increased by $1,000 for individuals age 50 or over.

Affordable Care Act Penalties and Credits

Individuals: The Tax Cuts and Jobs Act effectively eliminated the Federal ACA penalty for individuals. Some states have their own mandates and penalties. The SECURE Act repealed the excise tax on high-cost employer-sponsored plans (the Cadillac tax) and the medical device excise tax.

Businesses: In 2021, employers with 50 or more full-time employees may have to pay a penalty if they do not offer qualifying health insurance to at least 95% of full-time employees and their dependents. An employer with fewer than 25 employees who average less than $50,000 in annual compensation may get a tax credit of up to 50% of its premium costs (35% for tax-exempt employers) if it pays at least half the premium for qualifying health insurance coverage.

10

Qualified Long-Term Care
Insurance Premiums

Premiums paid for qualified long-term care insurance are deductible as medical expenses in 2021, subject to the in-excess-of-10%-of-AGI limitation that applies to medical expenses. The AGI limit was 7.5% in 2020. Deductions for qualified long-term care insurance premiums are subject to additional dollar amount limitations that vary depending on the insured's age. The maximum deductible amounts for 2021 and 2020 appear as follows.

Age	2021 Maximum	2020 Maximum
40 or less	$450	$430
more than 40 through 50	850	810
more than 50 through 60	1,690	1,630
more than 60 through 70	4,520	4,350
older than 70	5,640	5,430

Federal Estate Tax Formula 2021 and 2020

A. Gross Estate $ _____

B. Subtract:
- Claims Against Estate
- Administration Expenses
- Funeral Expenses
- Marital Deduction
- Charitable Deductions
- State Death Tax Deduction
- Total Deductions −

C. Taxable Estate $ _____

D. Add: All Post-1976 Adjusted Taxable Gifts   + $ _____

E. Adjusted Taxable Estate $ _____

F. Calculate Tentative Tax on "E"[1] $ _____

G. Subtract: Total Gift Taxes Payable[2] on Post-1976 Gifts   − _____

H. Gross Estate Tax Payable Before Credits $ _____

I. Subtract:
- Estate Tax Credit for 2021 ($4,577,800 in 2020) $4,625,800
- Credit for Foreign Death Taxes
- Credit for Tax on Prior Transfers
- Total Credits −

J. Net Estate Tax $ _____

K. Add: Generation-Skipping Transfer Tax   + _____

L. Federal Transfer (Estate and Generation-Skipping) Tax Payable $ _____

[1] Calculate tentative tax using the Federal Gift and Estate Tax table on the next panel.
[2] Enter amount that would have been payable if changes made by the 2010 tax legislation had been in effect at the time of the gift.

Federal Gift Tax Formula 2021 and 2020

A. Aggregate of all prior and present *taxable gifts* $ _____

B. Tentative gift tax on "A" (from current tax table) $ _____

C. Aggregate of all prior (only) *taxable gifts*   _____

D. Tentative gift tax on "C" (from current tax table)   − _____

E. Tentative gift tax on present gift ("B" less "D") $ _____

F. Gift tax credit for 2021 ($4,577,800 in 2020) $4,625,800

G. Aggregate gift tax credit taken for prior post-1976 gifts (but not more than "C")   − _____

H. Gift tax credit available for current gift ("F" less "G" but not more than "E")   − _____

I. Gift tax payable for current gift ("E" less "H") $ _____

11

Federal Gift and Estate Tax Amounts

Rule	2021	2020
Annual gift tax exclusion per recipient	$15,000	$15,000
Annual gift tax exclusion for gifts to noncitizen spouse	159,000	157,000
Estate tax installment election: Amount subject to 2% interest on tax due to closely held business; above that 45% of applicable federal rate	1,590,000	1,570,000
Special use valuation: Limit on estate reduction using this technique (value of actual use of real estate rather than highest and best use)	1,190,000	1,180,000

Federal Gift and Estate Tax 2021 and 2020*

Taxable Gift or Estate		Tentative Tax	
From	To	Tax	Rate on Excess
$0	$10,000	$0	18%
10,001	20,000	1,800	20%
20,001	40,000	3,800	22%
40,001	60,000	8,200	24%
60,001	80,000	13,000	26%
80,001	100,000	18,200	28%
100,001	150,000	23,800	30%
150,001	250,000	38,800	32%
250,001	500,000	70,800	34%
500,001	750,000	155,800	37%
750,001	1,000,000	248,300	39%
1,000,001	. . . . .	345,800	40%

Gift and Estate Exclusion Amount/Credit

	Credit	Exclusion Amount
2020	$4,577,800	$11,580,000
2021	$4,625,800	$11,700,000

* In addition to the federal estate and gift taxes, these rates apply to the federal generation-skipping transfer tax (GSTT) in 2021 and 2020.

Medicare Premium and Cost-Sharing Amounts

		2021	2020
Part A	Premium per month (if not eligible through payroll tax)	$471	$458
	Hospital and mental health inpatient deductible per benefit period	$1,484	$1,408
	Hospital inpatient coinsurance per day (Days 61–90)	$371	$352
	Hospital inpatient coinsurance per lifetime reserve day (Days 91 and after; up to 60 days over lifetime)	$742	$704
	Skilled nursing facility coinsurance per day (Days 21–100)	$185.50	$176
	Hospice prescription drug co-pay	$5	$5
	Hospice respite care coinsurance	5%	5%
Part B	Base premium per month	$148.50*	$144.60*
	Income threshold for additional premium	$88,000 (S, MS) $176,000 (J)	$87,000 (S, MS) $174,000 (J)
	Deductible per year	$203	$198
	Coinsurance	20%	20%
	Home health care coinsurance for durable medical equipment	20%	20%
Part D	Base premium (actual premiums vary by plan)	$41.00	$32.74
	Income threshold for additional premium	$88,000 (S, MS) $176,000 (J)	$87,000 (S, MS) $174,000 (J)
	Deductible	$445	$435
	Cost threshold for coverage gap (combined total spent by enrollee and plan)	$4,130	$4,020
	Enrollee's cost per prescription during coverage gap after discounts are applied	25% (brand name) 25% (generic)	25% (brand name) 25% (generic)
	Out-of-pocket expense limit for catastrophic coverage	$6,550	$6,350
	Minimum cost-sharing during catastrophic coverage (enrollee pays 5% coinsurance if greater than co-pay shown)	$9.20 (brand name) $3.70 (generic)	$8.95 (brand name) $3.60 (generic)

S=single; MS=married filing separately; J=joint
* Most people who receive Social Security benefits pay less than this amount. High-income enrollees will pay the base premium or a higher amount.

12

Social Security Tax

The tax supporting Old-Age, Survivors, and Disability Insurance (OASDI) and Medicare (Hospital Insurance – HI) is collected for employees under the Federal Insurance Contributions Act (FICA) and for self-employed individuals under the Self-Employment Contributions Act (SECA). The total amount is the same, but under FICA the tax is split between employer and employee. The tax for OASDI applies only to earned income up to the wage base. No limit applies in the case of the tax for HI. An additional 0.9% HI tax applies to earned income in excess of certain income thresholds in 2021 and 2020.*

	OASDI		HI		Combined Tax Rate
	Tax Rate	Wage Base	Tax Rate	Wage Base	
Employee	Employee: 6.2% (2020 and 2021) Employer: 6.2% (2020 and 2021)	$142,800 (2021) $137,700 (2020)	1.45%* (employee) 1.45% (employer)	No limit	15.3% (2021 and 2020)
Self-employed	12.4% (2020 and 2021)	$142,800 (2021) $137,700 (2020)	2.9%*	No limit	15.3% (2021 and 2020)

* The threshold levels for the additional 0.9% HI tax are $250,000 for married taxpayers filing jointly, $125,000 for married taxpayers filing separately, and $200,000 for single taxpayers and heads of household.

Social Security Eligibility Figures

		2021	2020
Quarters of coverage	An individual gets a quarter of coverage (out of 40 required to be fully insured) after earning . . .	$1,470	$1,410
Reduction of retirement benefits before FRA*	One dollar of benefits is withheld for $2 in earnings above . . .	$18,960/yr. ($1,580/mo.)	$18,240/yr. ($1,520/mo.)
Reduction of retirement benefits in year FRA attained	One dollar of benefits is withheld for $3 in earnings above . . .	$50,520/yr. ($4,210/mo.)	$48,600/yr. ($4,050/mo.)
SSI** federal payment standard	Individual	$794/mo.	$783/mo.
	Couple	$1,191/mo.	$1,175/mo.
SSI resources limits	Individual	$2,000	$2,000
	Couple	$3,000	$3,000
SSI student exclusion limits	Monthly	$1,930	$1,900
	Yearly	$7,770	$7,670
Disability thresholds	Substantial gainful activity (non-blind)	$1,310/mo.	$1,260/mo.
	Substantial gainful activity (blind)	$2,190/mo.	$2,110/mo.
	Trial work period	$940/mo.	$910/mo.

* FRA (full retirement age) is age 66 for retirements occurring in 2021 for birth years 1943–1954 and age 66 years and 2 months for birth year 1955.
** SSI (Supplemental Security Income) is benefits for disabled adults and children with limited income and resources, and for people age 65 and older without disabilities who meet the financial limits.

Social Security OASDI Benefits

		2021	2020
Maximum benefit (per month)	Worker retiring at FRA	$3,148	$3,011
Estimated average retirement benefit (per month)*	Retired worker	$1,523	$1,479
	Retired worker, spouse	$2,563	$2,491
Estimated average survivor benefit (per month)*	Surviving spouse, two children	$2,962	$2,888
	Aged surviving spouse	$1,434	$1,400
Estimated average disability benefit (per month)*	Disabled worker	$1,261	$1,238
	Disabled worker, spouse, child/ren	$2,195	$2,141
Cost-of-living adjustment (COLA)		1.3%	1.6%

* Amounts are shown before that year's COLA is applied.

13

Results of $1,000 Invested Annually
at Various Annual Interest Rates
Over Various Periods of Time
(Investment Made at Beginning of Each Year)

Years	4%	6%	8%	10%
1	$1,040	$1,060	$1,080	$1,100
2	2,122	2,184	2,246	2,310
3	3,246	3,375	3,506	3,641
4	4,416	4,637	4,867	5,105
5	5,633	5,975	6,336	6,716
6	6,898	7,394	7,923	8,487
7	8,214	8,897	9,637	10,436
8	9,583	10,491	11,488	12,579
9	11,006	12,181	13,487	14,937
10	12,486	13,972	15,645	17,531
11	14,026	15,870	17,977	20,384
12	15,627	17,882	20,495	23,523
13	17,292	20,015	23,215	26,975
14	19,024	22,276	28,152	30,772
15	20,825	24,673	29,324	34,950
16	22,698	27,213	32,750	39,545
17	24,645	29,906	36,450	44,599
18	26,671	32,760	40,446	50,159
19	28,778	35,786	44,762	56,275
20	30,969	38,993	49,423	63,002
21	33,248	42,392	54,457	70,403
22	35,618	45,996	59,893	78,543
23	38,083	49,816	65,765	87,497
24	40,646	53,865	72,106	97,347
25	43,312	58,156	78,954	108,182
26	46,084	62,706	86,351	120,100
27	48,968	67,528	94,339	133,210
28	51,966	72,640	102,966	147,631
29	55,085	78,058	112,283	163,494
30	58,328	83,802	122,346	180,943
35	76,598	118,121	186,102	298,127
40	98,827	164,048	279,781	486,852
45	125,871	225,508	417,726	790,795
50	158,774	307,756	619,672	1,280,299

United States Life Tables 2017

Age	Male	Female	Age	Male	Female	Age	Male	Female	Age	Male	Female
0–1	76.13	80.98	28–29	49.60	53.90	56–57	24.57	27.85	84–85	6.24	7.41
1–2	75.65	80.43	29–30	48.66	52.93	57–58	23.77	26.98	85–86	5.81	6.90
2–3	74.68	79.46	30–31	47.73	51.97	58–59	22.99	26.12	86–87	5.40	6.42
3–4	73.70	78.48	31–32	46.80	51.00	59–60	22.21	25.27	87–88	5.03	5.97
4–5	72.72	77.49	32–33	45.87	50.04	60–61	21.44	24.42	88–89	4.67	5.54
5–6	71.73	76.51	33–34	44.93	49.07	61–62	20.68	23.58	89–90	4.35	5.14
6–7	70.75	75.52	34–35	44.00	48.11	62–63	19.92	22.75	90–91	4.04	4.77
7–8	69.76	74.52	35–36	43.07	47.15	63–64	19.17	21.93	91–92	3.76	4.42
8–9	68.77	73.53	36–37	42.14	46.19	64–65	18.42	21.11	92–93	3.49	4.09
9–10	67.77	72.54	37–38	41.21	45.23	65–66	17.69	20.30	93–94	3.25	3.79
10–11	66.78	71.55	38–39	40.28	44.28	66–67	16.96	19.51	94–95	3.03	3.52
11–12	65.78	70.55	39–40	39.36	43.33	67–68	16.25	18.72	95–96	2.83	3.26
12–13	64.79	69.56	40–41	38.43	42.38	68–69	15.55	17.94	96–97	2.64	3.03
13–14	63.80	68.57	41–42	37.51	41.43	69–70	14.86	17.18	97–98	2.47	2.82
14–15	62.81	67.58	42–43	36.60	40.49	70–71	14.18	16.43	98–99	2.32	2.62
15–16	61.83	66.59	43–44	35.69	39.55	71–72	13.52	15.69	99–100	2.18	2.45
16–17	60.86	65.60	44–45	34.79	38.62	72–73	12.86	14.96	100–101	2.05	2.29
17–18	59.90	64.62	45–46	33.89	37.70	73–74	12.22	14.24	101–102	1.94	2.15
18–19	58.94	63.64	46–47	33.00	36.77	74–75	11.60	13.54	102–103	1.84	2.02
19–20	57.98	62.66	47–48	32.12	35.86	75–76	10.98	12.85	103–104	1.74	1.90
20–21	57.04	61.68	48–49	31.25	34.94	76–77	10.39	12.18	104–105	1.66	1.80
21–22	56.10	60.70	49–50	30.38	34.04	77–78	9.80	11.52	105–106	1.59	1.71
22–23	55.17	59.73	50–51	29.52	33.14	78–79	9.24	10.88	106–107	1.52	1.62
23–24	54.24	58.76	51–52	28.67	32.24	79–80	8.69	10.25	107–108	1.46	1.55
24–25	53.32	57.78	52–53	27.84	31.36	80–81	8.16	9.65	108–109	1.41	1.48
25–26	52.39	56.81	53–54	27.01	30.47	81–82	7.65	9.06	109–110	1.36	1.43
26–27	51.46	55.84	54–55	26.18	29.60	82–83	7.16	8.49			
27–28	50.53	54.87	55–56	25.37	28.72	83–84	6.69	7.94			

Source: National Vital Statistics Reports, Vol. 69, No. 8, Centers for Disease Control and Prevention (August 7, 2020, revised October 1, 2020).

14

Inflation Rate History
(Based on the Consumer Price Index)*

Year	Annual Inflation Rate (%)	Year	Annual Inflation Rate (%)	Year	Annual Inflation Rate (%)	Period Ending	Total Inflation for Period (%)	Average Annual Inflation for Period (%)
1961	1.4	1981	11.0	2001	2.6	(10-year period)		
1962	1.3	1982	5.0	2002	1.5	1970	32.4	2.8
1963	1.0	1983	2.9	2003	2.3	1980	114.3	7.9
1964	1.3	1984	4.3	2004	2.5	1990	58.0	4.7
1965	1.6	1985	3.1	2005	4.7	2000	30.9	2.7
1966	3.5	1986	1.8	2006	2.1	2010	25.8	2.3
1967	2.8	1987	4.4	2007	2.8	2020	19.0	1.8
1968	4.5	1988	4.2	2008	4.9	(20-year period)		
1969	5.7	1989	4.3	2009	-1.3	1980	183.8	5.4
1970	5.7	1990	6.2	2010	1.1	1990	238.5	6.3
1971	4.1	1991	3.4	2011	3.9	2000	106.8	3.7
1972	3.2	1992	3.0	2012	2.0	2010	64.6	2.5
1973	7.4	1993	2.7	2013	1.2	2020	50.1	2.1
1974	11.9	1994	3.0	2014	1.7	(30-year period)		
1975	7.9	1995	2.5	2015	0.0	1990	348.3	5.1
1976	5.5	1996	3.0	2016	1.5	2000	343.1	5.1
1977	6.6	1997	2.2	2017	2.2	2010	160.0	3.2
1978	8.3	1998	1.5	2018	2.5	2020	95.2	2.3
1979	12.2	1999	2.6	2019	1.8	(40-year period)		
1980	12.6	2000	3.5	2020	1.2	2000	486.8	4.5
						2010	457.2	4.4
						2020	207.4	2.9

* The consumer price index used is the CPI-U for all urban consumers as reported by the National Bureau Labor Statistics. The figure for the most recent year includes the period October 2019 to October 2020.

IRS Table 2001:
One-Year Term Premiums for $1,000
of Life Insurance Protection

The IRS currently uses Table 2001 to value the economic benefit provided to an employee when life insurance is provided by an employer. The premium listed represents the assumed cost of $1,000 of term insurance.

Age	Premium	Age	Premium	Age	Premium
31	$.90	51	$2.52	71	$22.72
32	.93	52	2.81	72	25.07
33	.96	53	3.20	73	27.57
34	.98	54	3.65	74	30.18
35	.99	55	4.15	75	33.05
36	1.01	56	4.68	76	36.33
37	1.04	57	5.20	77	40.17
38	1.06	58	5.66	78	44.33
39	1.07	59	6.06	79	49.23
40	1.10	60	6.51	80	54.56
41	1.13	61	7.11	81	60.51
42	1.20	62	7.96	82	66.74
43	1.29	63	9.08	83	73.07
44	1.40	64	10.41	84	80.35
45	1.53	65	11.90	85	88.76
46	1.67	66	13.51	86	99.16
47	1.83	67	15.20	87	110.40
48	1.98	68	16.92	88	121.85
49	2.13	69	18.70	89	133.40
50	2.30	70	20.62	90	144.30